STUDIES IN WELSH HISTORY

Editors

RALPH A. GRIFFITHS   KENNETH O. MORGAN
GLANMOR WILLIAMS

—

8

WALES IN AMERICA

SCRANTON AND THE WELSH, 1860–1920

WALES IN AMERICA

SCRANTON AND THE WELSH

1860–1920

by

WILLIAM D. JONES

*Published on behalf of the
History and Law Committee
of the Board of Celtic Studies
of the University of Wales*

UNIVERSITY OF WALES PRESS
UNIVERSITY OF SCRANTON PRESS
1993

©William D. Jones, 1993

The right of William D. Jones to be identified as author of this work has been asserted by him in accordance with the Copyright, Design and Patents Act 1988.

All rights reserved. No part of this book may be reproduced, stored in a retrieval system, or transmitted, in any form or by any means, electronic, mechanical, photocopying, recording or otherwise, without clearance from the University of Wales Press, 6 Gwennyth Street, Cardiff CF2 4YD.

Published in the United States of America by the University of Scranton Press
Editorial Office: University of Scranton, Scranton, PA 18510

British Library Cataloguing-in-Publication Data

A catalogue record of this book is available from the British Library.

ISBN 0–7083–1202–0

Library of Congress Cataloging-in-Publications Data

A catalogue of this book is available from the Library of Congress.

Library of Congress Catalog Number 93–060155

ISBN 0–940866–20–X

Typeset in Wales by Megaron, Cardiff
Printed in England by Hartnolls Limited, Bodmin, Cornwall

EDITORS' FOREWORD

Since the Second World War, Welsh history has attracted considerable scholarly attention and enjoyed a vigorous popularity. Not only have the approaches, both traditional and new, to the study of history in general been successfully applied to Wales's past, but the number of scholars engaged in this enterprise has multiplied during these years. These advances have been especially marked in the University of Wales.

In order to make more widely available the conclusions of recent research, much of it of limited accessibility in post-graduate dissertations and theses, in 1977 the History and Law Committee of the Board of Celtic Studies inaugurated this new series of monographs, *Studies in Welsh History*. It was anticipated that many of the volumes would originate in research conducted in the University of Wales or under the auspices of the Board of Celtic Studies. But the series does not exclude significant contributions made by researchers in other universities and elsewhere. Its primary aim is to serve historical scholarship and to encourage the study of Welsh history. Each volume so far published has fulfilled that aim in ample measure, and it is a pleasure to welcome the most recent addition to the list.

PREFACE

Had my great-uncle, Samuel Jones, not emigrated to the United States in 1895, I doubt if this book – or the University of Wales Ph.D. thesis of which it is a revised version – would ever have been written. When I was a young boy I assumed that the United States had acquired the name 'Uncle Sam' because my Uncle Sammy had gone to live there. I was also convinced he had been a cowboy – a Welsh John Wayne who tamed the wild and lawless West. The truth is more mundane though not necessarily less romantic. He was, in fact, an Ammanford tinplate worker who eventually joined the ranks of the American steel industry in Aliquippa, Pennsylvania. Given my early interest, it was perhaps inevitable that later, when I was fortunate enough to have the opportunity to do full-time postgraduate research, I chose to focus on the Welsh in America. As I read, it struck me that my blurring of the two 'Uncle Sam' identities was not completely the wayward fantasy of a younger, innocent imagination. The history of emigration is a rich, human epic; it is the story of families: their hopes, their fears, their disappointments, their achievements – and their break-up. For those who left, the ties of family and friends were immensely influential factors in the emigration process. For those who stayed at home, the existence of America was inseparable from the fact that relatives or friends were living there. However small the actual number of Welsh who settled in the United States, it seems that few families in Wales are without an American dimension in some form or another.

In 1981, whilst pursuing my studies in the United States, I retraced my great-uncle's footsteps to Aliquippa, but on that occasion I failed to discover any recollection of his family. I followed him, too, to the American city where he lived and worked briefly before settling permanently in Aliquippa, and where my own research had inexorably drawn me: Scranton, Pennsylvania. More than any other town or city in the New World, Scranton was a household word in late nineteenth–early twentieth century Wales because of the unparalleled size of its

Welsh community and its resulting connections with the homeland. I arrived in Scranton late one Sunday evening and was immediately whisked off to a Welsh church service. To this day I can recall vividly my initial impressions, although they are ones that are as difficult to articulate as they are to forget. Perhaps it was a sense of *déjà vu*; certainly it was the impact of finally being in a place whose past I had studied for some considerable time, but which was still, until then, little more than a name. During my ensuing stay at Scranton it was exhilarating to discover the richness of the available source materials on the history of the Welsh in the city, and indeed the richness of the fascinating story that was emerging from them. In the following pages I have tried to convey some of the excitement of the various historical experiences of the Welsh in Scranton and of the voyage of discovery on which, thanks to them, I was privileged to sail. It has been a voyage which could not have been possible without the help, advice and encouragement of many people.

The list of those I would like to acknowledge and thank is so long that it seems it might stretch across the Atlantic; certainly my debt of gratitude to them is fathoms deep. I am greatly indebted to Emeritus Professor Glanmor Williams for encouraging me to prepare this work for publication in the first place, for his helpful comments and advice, and, not least, his patience. The other two editors of the 'Studies in Welsh History Series', Professor Ralph Griffiths and Professor Kenneth O. Morgan, also read the manuscript and I have benefited enormously from their corrections and comments. The text has been much improved as a result of their thoroughness. I alone, of course, am responsible for the failings and errors which remain.

Whilst carrying out my research I was very fortunate to receive the willing assistance of many individuals, libraries, archives and other such institutions on both sides of the Atlantic. I am especially grateful to Professor Rowland Berthoff for his invaluable help in locating sources and references and to Professor Charlotte Erickson and Professor Edward Hartmann for their advice and suggestions. Dr John Harris, too, was kind enough to respond readily to my pleas for information. For their help and guidance I should also like to thank the staff at Cardiff Central Library, the National Library of Wales, Aberystwyth,

PREFACE

the Lackawanna Historical Society, Scranton, Scranton Public Library, the BALCH Institute and the National Records Service Branch Library, both in Philadelphia, and the Pennsylvania Anthracite Heritage Museum. I am greatly indebted, too, to the late Revd William R. Lewis, former Director of the Lackawanna Historical Society; he provided me with much information on the Welsh in Scranton which cannot be found in the written record.

Ms Liz Powell of University of Wales Press guided the work through to publication expertly and with much tolerance in the face of my sometimes idiosyncratic patterns of work. I am also grateful to Arwel Hughes and the Photography Department of the National Museum of Wales for their help with the maps and illustrations. Mrs Anne Knowles gave invaluable assistance in deciphering the intricacies and perplexities of the United States censuses, and without the help of Dr Douglas Bassett and Dr Chris Williams, preparing the text would have been a far more difficult task.

On a personal level I should like to extend warm thanks to Mrs Ceinwen Hughes of Scranton for her hospitality and her real Welsh welcome during my visits to the city. Over the years I have also had much help and encouragement from friends and colleagues, especially in Llafur (the Welsh Labour History Society) and the National Museum of Wales. They are too numerous to mention but the debt of gratitude I owe to them all is great. Some of them have often wondered why this book has taken so long to reach the light of day; to them, and to those who know where the time goes, my sincere thanks for their faith and support.

Above all I should like to thank Professor David Smith, who supervised my Ph.D. thesis, for his friendship and scholarship. He has been a constant source of inspiration, knowledge and wisdom and it is a great privilege to have had the opportunity of working with him.

Finally, my greatest debt is to my late parents, Samuel Gwynfor and Eira Mona Jones. This book is dedicated to them.

W.D.J.
Cardiff, 1993

CONTENTS

LIST OF ILLUSTRATIONS		xiii
TABLE OF APPENDICES		xiv
INTRODUCTION		**xv**
I	THE PUBLIC FACE OF WELSH SCRANTON	1
II	THE WELSH AND SCRANTON'S ANTHRACITE INDUSTRY	28
III	WELSH CULTURAL LIFE IN SCRANTON	87
IV	GILDING THE DRAGON: FAIRS, BARDS AND EMPIRE LOYALISTS	146
V	THE CRACKED MIRROR	202
CONCLUSION		**243**
APPENDICES		249
BIBLIOGRAPHY		259
INDEX		271

ILLUSTRATIONS

1. The D.L. & W's Hyde Park Mine.
2. Breaker boys at work in the north-east Pennsylvania anthracite coalfield.
3. The first Welsh Baptist Church in Scranton.
4. The Welsh Philosophical Society's second 'National Eisteddfod' at Scranton, 1980.
5. The 1921 Welsh Day at Rocky Glen, Scranton.
6. 'Voices from the "other side" ' (cartoon).
7. Railway advertisement for the 1893 World's Fair Eisteddfod.
8. The American Gorsedd's membership certificate.
9. The Scranton Choral Union.
10. Robert H. Davies (Gomerian) of Pittsburgh.
11. Judge H. M. Edwards of Scranton.
12. Revd T. Cynonfardd Edwards.
13. John F. Davies of Scranton.

TABLE OF APPENDICES

Appendix 1	British Emigration to the United States, 1820–1950.	249
Appendix 2	Population of the United States Born in Wales, 1850–1970.	249
Appendix 3	Distribution of Population of the United States Born in Wales, 1900, by States.	250
Appendix 4	Distribution of Population of the United States Born in Wales, 1900, by Counties (with Chief Centre).	252
Appendix 5	Distribution of Population of the United States, Born in Wales, 1900.	253
Appendix 6	Map of the North-East Pennsylvania Coalfield.	254
Appendix 7	Scranton: Population, 1860–1980.	255
Appendix 8	Scranton: Foreign-Born Population, 1870–1920.	255
Appendix 9	Map of Scranton in 1914 showing Major Mines.	256
Appendix 10	Distribution of Foreign-Born Population of Scranton, 1910, by Wards.	257

I
INTRODUCTION

In October 1872 a Welsh-American newspaper, the *Drych*, reprinted an article from Wales's *Herald Cymraeg* which dealt with the character of the Welsh trans-Atlantic immigrants:

> The question 'What of our nationality across the Atlantic?' should be asked more often . . . There are scores of thousands of them there and though scattered . . . they succeed in preserving their national characteristics . . . with the same ceaseless enthusiasm as we in the old country . . . It is true that nearly all of them, after arriving in the West, rush to study the institutions and form of government in America . . . They quickly earn the reputation for being the best citizens their adopted country possesses . . . Yet though they rush to make themselves notable American citizens, they do not allow this to interfere with their Welsh Nationality: . . . It is the maintenance of their nationality which makes the Welsh the most respectable citizens, the bravest soldiers and the best Christians in the United States. Before politics, the Welshman thinks of his chapel, his bible and his eisteddfod. It has been presumed that the secret of the magic which enables us to keep our distinction lay in Wales . . . but the Welsh-Americans prove that these everlasting elements are in the Welsh nature itself.[1]

It is hardly surprising that the *Drych* reprinted this article. Although the passage quoted undoubtedly says as much about the *Herald Cymraeg*'s perception of the nature of Welshness in Wales as it does about that in America, in the latter context it reported a remarkable success story. Despite living in the United States, the Welsh immigrants were still utterly Welsh. They were able to maintain their Welshness because of certain inherited characteristics such as a sense of nationality, a distinctive culture and identifiable standards of respectable behaviour. Yet as well as being Welsh, these characteristics also enabled them to be the best of American citizens.

But how did the Welsh immigrants themselves regard their Welshness and its relationship with new cultures, outlooks and,

---

[1] *Drych*, 24 Oct. 1872. Quotations from sources in the Welsh language have been translated by the author.

more crucially perhaps, the pressures that living in a new country brought to bear on their nationality? Equally, gazing in the opposite direction to the *Herald Cymraeg*, what images of their former homeland did they treasure? This book examines these aspects of the Welsh experience in the United States during the late nineteenth and early twentieth centuries. It does so mainly by focusing on the Welsh in Scranton, Pennsylvania, the largest single concentration of Welsh people in the world outside Wales and England during the period that was, in many respects, the golden age of Welsh-American history.

The Welsh immigrants who flocked to Scranton were contributors to a unique chapter in the history of the Welsh people and continuators of a tradition that is centuries old. The involvement of the Welsh in the history of what became the United States of America may or may not have begun with the maritime adventures of Prince Madoc ab Owain Gwynedd in AD 1170 but it still encompasses centuries, vast acres of settlement and a wide variety of motives and occupations.[2] It stretches from the early seventeenth century, when a smattering of indentured servants crossed the Atlantic to settle in the Colonies, right through to the present day, and the process obviously still continues. Over the centuries the emigration of the Welsh has been inspired and stimulated by a wide variety of motives – religious (such as the Quakers who fled from religious persecution in the late seventeenth century), economic, political, cultural and even what might be termed nationalistic, those attempts to establish a new Wales on American soil (such as the setting up of the Brynffynnon colony in Tennessee by Samuel Roberts in the 1850s). Welsh people have settled to a greater or lesser extent in most areas of the United States, and

---

[2] There are a number of surveys of the history of the Welsh in America. See Rowland T. Berthoff, 'The Welsh', in Stephan Thernstorm (ed.), *Harvard Encyclopaedia of American Ethnic Groups* (Cambridge, Mass., 1980), pp. 1011–17; Alan Conway (ed.), *The Welsh in America* (Cardiff, 1961), and 'Welsh emigration to the United States', in D. Fleming and B. Bailyn (eds.), *Dislocation and Emigration: The Social Background of American Immigration*, Perspectives in American History, vol. VII (Cambridge, Mass., 1974); E. G. Hartmann, *Americans from Wales* (Boston, 1967); Maldwyn A. Jones, 'From the old country to the new: the Welsh in nineteenth century America', *Flintshire Historical Society Publications*, XXVII (1975–6), pp. 85–100; David Williams, *Cymru ac America: Wales and America* (Cardiff, 1946); Glanmor Williams, 'A prospect of paradise? Wales and the United States, 1776–1914', in *idem*, *Religion, Language and Nationality in Wales* (Cardiff, 1979), pp. 217–36. For the Madoc myth see Gwyn A. Williams, *Madoc: The Making of a Myth* (London, 1980).

INTRODUCTION   xvii

during the last four hundred years these settlers have represented a diversity of occupations – agricultural and industrial workers, domestic servants and housewives and a coterie of professionals from preachers and teachers to opera singers and popular entertainers.

Yet despite the diversity of the tradition, despite centuries, vast acres and different motives and occupations, the overwhelming presence of the Welsh in the United States was chronologically, geographically and occupationally concentrated. It was largely a late nineteenth–early twentieth century phenomenon, for it was during these years that Wales came closest to experiencing a mass migration to the United States and the Welsh immigrant presence was at its greatest strength.[3]

From the middle of the last century onwards, the nature of the emigration from Wales to the United States changed dramatically in two ways. First, there was a marked increase in the number of emigrants. According to the United States Commissioner General of Immigration, 89,603 Welsh settled in the United States between 1820 and 1950; all but 5,500 did so between 1850 and 1930. The U.S. Census returns paint a similar picture. In 1850 there were just under 30,000 foreign-born Welsh in the United States. By 1890 the figure had more than trebled to reach a peak of 100,079.[4] Unfortunately our statistical knowledge of the emigration is fragmented and woefully inconclusive because records were often not compiled at all, and those that were are inaccurate and unreliable. Not only do we lack valuable quantitative data on the occupations of the emigrants, their areas of origin and the number who re-emigrated to Wales; we cannot even be sure of the exact number of emigrants.[5] It is probable that the actual figures were rather

---

[3] The following survey of Welsh industrial emigration to, and settlement in, the United States, c. 1850–1920, is far too brief to do justice to the subject. It is intended as an introduction only in order to establish the context for what follows. For a fuller treatment see my original Ph.D. thesis, 'Wales in America: Scranton and the Welsh c. 1860–1920' (University of Wales, 1987), pp. 6–24. See also Rowland T. Berthoff, *British Immigrants in Industrial America* (Cambridge, Mass., 1953).

[4] See appendices 1 and 2.

[5] For a discussion of the nature of the statistical record of Welsh emigration see Berthoff, *British Immigrants*, pp. 4–11; Maldwyn Jones, 'The background to American emigration from Britain in the nineteenth century', in Bailyn and Fleming, op. cit., pp. 3–92, (especially 22–9); David Williams, 'Some figures relating to emigration from Wales', *Bulletin of the Board of Celtic Studies*, VII (1935), pp. 396–415.

higher – perhaps double those officially compiled. Even then, however, it must be recognized that the number of Welsh who emigrated and settled in the United States was still very small, both in total size and in relation to Wales's population, compared to other British immigrants, let alone those from other European countries. The Welsh in America represented, in the words of Alan Conway, 'little more than a corporal's guard'.[6] The reasons why the Welsh were less keen to emigrate than other nationalities are still a matter of debate.[7]

The second major change in the character of the emigration was in the type of emigrant. Whereas before the mid-nineteenth century the emigrants came mainly from the rural areas of Wales, from then on they came predominantly from the industrial areas, the vast majority of them from south Wales. As a whole the late nineteenth–early twentieth century emigration was diverse, and the emigrants represented a wide variety of occupations: farmers, professional and commercial males, skilled trades, labourers, female domestic servants, female dressmakers and trades, and female clerks and professionals.[8] Yet the emigrants who were largely responsible for the striking growth in the Welsh presence in the United States during the second half of the nineteenth century were Welsh miners, iron and steel workers and tinplate workers, together with slate quarrymen from north Wales, and their families.

The emigration of Welsh industrial workers seems to have been overwhelmingly motivated by economic considerations; simply, they moved in search of a better life. The reasons for a phenomenon as complex and personal as emigration, however, can never be totally explained, because we cannot know what passed through the minds of potential emigrants. Historians

---

[6] Conway, 'Welsh emigration', p. 178. During the early years of the twentieth century the average annual influx to the United States from Italy was more than double the number of Welsh who arrived between 1820 and 1950. Between 1815 and 1914, 35 million Europeans emigrated to the United States. Maldwyn Jones, *American Immigration* (Chicago, 1960), p. 200.

[7] See Brinley Thomas, 'Wales and the Atlantic economy', in *idem* (ed.), *The Welsh Economy, Studies in Expansion* (Cardiff, 1962), pp. 1–29; Dudley Baines, *Migration in a Mature Economy: Emigration and Internal Migration in England and Wales, 1861–1900* (Cambridge, 1985); Conway, 'Welsh emigration', pp. 269–71; Maldwyn Jones, 'The background to American emigration', pp. 78–9.

[8] The classifications are taken from figures compiled by the British Board of Trade in 1913. For a study of Welsh emigrants in the year 1851 see William E. Van Vugt, 'Welsh emigration to the U.S.A. in the mid-nineteenth century', *Welsh History Review*, 15, No. 4 (Dec. 1991), pp. 545–61.

have pointed to the existence of certain 'push' and 'pull' factors which could stimulate industrial workers to settle in the United States. Social and working conditions in the industrial areas were harsh, wages were low, and the boom and slump nature of the economy made life precarious and insecure. Adverse economic conditions at home, especially during times of industrial disputes, wage cuts and depression, may have influenced many to emigrate. In turn, the United States presented attractions which were on offer even during times of relative prosperity in Wales. Welsh industrial workers possessed a trump card which greatly increased their chances of a better life across the Atlantic: industrial skills. Industrialization in Wales had half a century of a head start over that in the United States. Consequently, Welsh expertise in puddling iron, cutting coal or rolling tin-plate was highly prized and in great demand in industrializing America, and it commanded higher wages and privileged positions.[9] Emigrant letters that have survived tend to confirm that it was the prospect of higher wages that attracted Welsh industrial workers and their families to America.[10]

It is likely that the vast majority of emigrants were influenced by these factors. Yet, as Dudley Baines has recently pointed out, we must be careful about any explanations which depend on the characteristics of the environment from which the emigrants came or to which they were going. Emigration was the result of individual choice in which personal motives played a large part. It could depend on the age and gender of the emigrants as well as on their social and economic conditions.[11] Late nineteenth-century newspaper reports suggest that some Welsh were fleeing debts and the consequences of misdeeds, though these were perhaps unlikely to be more than a very small minority. Some emigrant families may even have been swept along by the emigration fever that occasionally gripped certain industrial districts.[12] In many respects, because of the lack of evidence, the causes and processes of Welsh emigration are still something of

---

[9] See Berthoff, *British Immigrants*, pp. 21–79; Conway, 'Welsh emigration', pp. 226–65.
[10] See Conway, *The Welsh in America*, pp. 164–282.
[11] Dudley Baines, *Emigration from Europe, 1815–1930* (London, 1991), pp. 13–19.
[12] *Tarian y Gweithiwr* 26 Sept. 1879, 18 June 1880, 5 May 1881, 18 Aug. 1882.

an enigma. Unfortunately there is much that we shall probably never know.

On arrival in the United States most Welsh industrial workers continued their calling, in effect making the Atlantic one long craft corridor. This central feature of the emigration decisively influenced the geographic settlement of the Welsh and the location of the Welsh presence in the 'New Country' during the second half of the nineteenth century.[13] The vast majority of Welsh industrial families headed for the industrial areas, and there was a great deal of mobility as many moved westwards with the industrial frontier and as new coalfields were opened up. By the end of the nineteenth century Welsh gold miners could be found in California, lead miners in the Rockies, copper miners in Montana and coalminers in Pennsylvania, Ohio, California, Utah, Illinois, Indiana, West Virginia and Tennessee. Indeed, some Welsh miners seemed determined to prove that as well as a Cornishman there ought to be a Welshman at the bottom of every hole in the ground.[14]

But the singular feature of Welsh settlement in the United States during these years is the remarkable concentration of the Welsh in one state, Pennsylvania. Here, in 1900, lived nearly 38 per cent of the 93,586 first-generation Welsh in the United States. Twenty-three per cent of that 93,586 lived in just three counties in Pennsylvania. There were 5,245 in Pittsburgh, and Allegheny County in general, but even that figure was dwarfed by the 16,286 foreign-born Welsh who lived in the two adjoining counties of Lackawanna (with Scranton as its centre) and Luzerne (centre Wilkes-Barre, a mere eighteen miles from Scranton) in north-east Pennsylvania.[15] Despite the millions of acres in which the Welsh could have chosen to settle in the United States, in 1900 over 17 per cent of them were living together in an area about twice the size of the Rhondda Valley in the south Wales most of them had left.

The emigration of the Welsh to the United States and their subsequent settlement there have spawned a historiography and

---

[13] See appendices 3, 4 and 5.
[14] See Conway, *The Welsh in America*, pp. 64–5, 231–2; Berthoff, *British Immigrants*, pp. 21–79, *passim*.
[15] See appendices 3, 4 and 5. For an account of the Welsh in Wilkes-Barre, see E. G. Hartmann, *Cymry yn y Cwm. The Welsh of Wilkes-Barre and the Wyoming Valley* (Wilkes-Barre, 1985).

a tradition of writing. In the nineteenth and early twentieth centuries those Welsh-Americans who wrote about their history and contemporary profile adopted an antiquarian and genealogical approach. They concentrated on celebrating their nationality's contribution to their adopted country, either as individual Welshmen (almost universally) or as a group, and on lauding their religious and national affiliations.[16] In one of the first articles on the Welsh in America which appeared in a national American journal, in the *Atlantic Monthly* in March 1876, Revd Erasmus W. Jones acknowledged this when he confessed that 'I am aware that this subject in the hands of native Welshmen is in danger of suffering injustice, owing to the natural tendency we have of overestimating the excellences of our own nation, and of cherishing undue zeal for its peculiarities.'[17]

Of course, the tendency of immigrant or ethnic writing to be parochial and filio-pietistic is not confined to the Welsh; all immigrant groups in America have suffered from what Glanmor Williams has described as 'the besetting sin of the historiography of American emigration: excessive praise of the feats and merits of one particular group or nation'.[18] In the case of the Welsh, the nature of such writing has prevented an understanding of the complexities of the experiences of the Welsh immigrants during the period when their presence was at its greatest strength. Fundamentally, it is a problem of the historical sources of evidence. Our most obvious evidence for examining the nature of Welsh-American communities and life and the thoughts and attitudes of Welsh-Americans are their own words – in speeches at cultural events, articles, essays and editorials – which have survived in the columns of the Welsh-American press. There was a flourishing press in both Welsh and English,

---

[16] See, for example, Revd R. D. Thomas, *Hanes Cymry America* (Utica, 1872); Ebenezer Edwards (William Penn, pseud.), *Facts about Welsh Factors, Welshmen as Factors in the Foundation and Development of the U.S. Republic* (Utica, 1899); F. J. Harries, *Welshmen and the United States* (Pontypridd, 1927); Thomas L. James, 'The Welsh in the United States', *Cambrian*, XII (1892), pp. 4–7, 74–7; Erasmus W. Jones, 'The Welsh in America', *Atlantic Monthly* XXXVII (Mar. 1876), pp. 305–13.

[17] Erasmus Jones, loc. cit., p. 305.

[18] Glanmor Williams, 'A prospect of paradise', p. 233. The literature on American immigration and ethnicity generally and on certain specific groups is massive. For introductions see the various entries in Thernstorm, op. cit.; Maldwyn Jones, *American Immigration*; John Bodnar, '*The Transplanted*'. *A History of Immigrants in Industrial America* (Bloomington, 1985).

involving numerous short-lived newspapers and periodicals and a few, like the *Drych*, which were published throughout the period.[19] The nature of the Welshness of the Welsh-Americans was also expressed in cultural activity, for their idea of Wales was an active force not a passive reflection. It led to the holding of cultural events and the organizing of institutions and societies.

The type of evidence that we find in the late nineteenth–early twentieth century Welsh-American press largely consists of the opinions of those who set the norms of Welsh-American life and who were most actively concerned with interpreting their Welshness and nurturing a consciousness of it. As such, the evidence reflects the preoccupations of what might be described as Welsh-American literary opinion, and it may not necessarily represent the views of other Welsh immigrants. In fact, it did not; those who wrote on the subject tended to exclude facets of Welsh immigrant life that were distasteful, and their writings contain large assumptions which have effectively removed an integral part of the Welsh immigrant experience from our written history.

It is only by examining the Welsh in America in microcosm that we can analyse these issues. The 'bias' inherent in Welsh-American sources necessitates the use of other evidence and the most effective way of finding this is by focusing on a particular community. A local study enables the Welsh to be located in the context of a total culture, and by so doing we can measure and evaluate their relations with other ethnic groups. It also facilitates a close examination of the Welsh ethnic group itself, in order to identify the dynamics of immigrant life, the cultural diversity of the group, the structure of the community and the processes of adjustment and acculturation. And if there is one particular locality that almost demands this type of study, it is Scranton, Pennsylvania, the epicentre of Welsh-America during its golden era.

---

[19] For a discussion of the Welsh-American press see D. R. Hopkin, 'Welsh immigrants to the U.S. and their press, 1840–1930', in Christiane Harzig and Dick Hoerder (eds.), *The Press of Labor Migrants in Europe and North America, 1880s–1930s* (Bremen, 1985), pp. 349–67.

I
THE PUBLIC FACE OF WELSH SCRANTON

Modern-day Scranton, Pennsylvania, bears relatively few traces of its rich Welsh heritage. The clapboard houses many of the Welsh built for themselves on the hill on the West Side of the city during the second half of the nineteenth century are still there, and some still house descendants of the original immigrants. Here and there, businesses and stores carry Welsh names, but they are a mockery of the vibrant Welsh commercial district that once flourished along Main Avenue. The Welsh churches stand proud but forgotten; for years they have ceased to be either exclusively Welsh or even places of worship at all. On specific dates the dying embers of a once flourishing cultural life splutter into the open – the St David's Day banquet, the annual Cymanfa Ganu and the occasional Welsh service. The fall of Scranton's Welshness in many ways symbolizes the decline of the wider city. Scranton's mines and breakers, with their cacophony of sound and double fugue of steam and whistle, were musical proof of its industrial symphony. During the past half-century their departure has directed a gradual but now total decrescendo, leaving the eerie silence that most coal towns have in common when they live on after the mines. And like many of those former coal towns throughout the world, Scranton now looks to the heritage industry for its future, with its Anthracite Museum and, more recently, as 'Steamtown USA'. But compared to its past, today the city as a whole is as tranquil as the Washburn Street or 'Welsh' cemetery in Hyde Park, where the bulk of its late-nineteenth-century Welsh lie buried, among them the sixty victims of the Avondale mine disaster of 1869 and the two Welsh miners shot by the militia during the 1871 strike. But if its Welshness is now almost minimal, the modern face of Scranton ultimately emphasizes the extent and intensity of its Victorian Welsh experience.

A Welsh immigrant arriving in Scranton for the first time a century ago would have found himself or herself in the largest Welsh community in America. Then, the city's Hyde Park district was the vortex of Welsh-America, with its steep hillside covered no longer with trees but with Welsh people. Perched half-way up the slope were two whole blocks of Welsh stores, businesses, saloons, banks, funeral homes, churches and legal and medical establishments. If the 'greenhorn' was an immigrant from industrial south Wales, as would be most likely, then the resemblances between the two areas must have been startling, because in most of the key areas of life Hyde Park could easily have been mistaken for one of the colliery towns that were rapidly growing up almost simultaneously in the valleys of south Wales. Indeed, as one of Scranton's leading Welsh citizens, Judge H. M. Edwards, remembered in 1909:

> Is it any wonder that the Welsh emigrants coming to Hyde Park felt themselves at home at once? The Welsh church, the Welsh Sunday School, the Welsh Eisteddfod, the Welsh societies, relatives, friends and acquaintances were all here waiting for them... Hyde Park, to thousands of incoming Welshmen, was another Wales.[1]

And across the sooted Lackawanna River, past the shanties and the vast railway depots and breakers, lay Scranton itself, with 'its newness and roughness – its helter-skelter way of doing things – its push and enterprise – its rapid growth and busy hum – its work-a-day dress – its grime and smut and business air'.[2] Scranton's rapid industrialization and urban growth created an environment that both influenced the Welsh immigrants' perception of themselves and moulded their existence. The late nineteenth- to early twentieth-century Welsh experience in Scranton was inextricably entwined with the booming metropolis that was as vibrant in its economic rhythms as it was diverse in its ethnic counterpoint.

The city of Scranton – the 'Friendly City' – is situated on the Lackawanna River in north-east Pennsylvania, some six miles above its confluence with the Susquehanna River.[3] Originally

---

[1] *Druid*, 21 Oct. 1909.
[2] Scranton *Daily Times*, 14 July 1873, quoted in Rowland T. Berthoff, 'The social order of the anthracite region', *Pennsylvania Magazine of History and Biography*, LXXXIX (July 1965), pp. 261–91.
[3] Philip V. Mattes, 'Condensed history of the city of Scranton', in idem, *Tales of Scranton* (Scranton, n.d.), p. 107. For histories of Scranton see also David Craft et al., *History of Scranton, Pennsylvania* (Dayton, 1891); F. L. Hitchcock, *History of Scranton and its*

densely forested Indian hunting ground, the area is first believed to have been visited by Europeans in the late seventeenth century. Around 1743 a tribe of Capoose Indians settled there and named it after themselves (Capoose was in fact the first of many names by which the locality would be known). White settlers penetrated the area in the mid-eighteenth century, although during the War of Independence their presence was obliterated by pro-British forces and Iroquois Indians at the Battle of Wyoming in 1778. When Luzerne County was first established in 1788, the site of the Capoose settlement was included in the nearby township of Providence. In the same year, Philip Abbot set up a grist mill in the Deep Hollow, the site of modern-day Scranton. In 1798 this enterprise was purchased by the Slocum Brothers, who also constructed a forge, a distillery and a saw mill. By 1822, however, these operations had ceased and there were few indications to suggest that this agricultural frontier would become the industrial metropolis of Scranton. In 1840 the total population was only 1,169. The chief occupations of the inhabitants of the three minuscule villages which made up Providence township – Providence or Razorville itself, Hyde Park and Dunmore – were farming and lumbering; none was engaged in mining.[4]

The fifth decade of the nineteenth century saw the beginnings of an irrevocable change in the character of the area. Industry came to Slocum Hollow, as the site of Scranton was then known, as inexorably as the locomotive which disturbed Nathaniel Hawthorne's peace in that other Sleepy Hollow on 22 July 1844.[5] In the 1840s the area became, in Burton Folsom's words, 'the battleground where American independence from English iron would be fought and won'.[6] The early industrial history of Scranton lies firmly in the pioneering phase of the American iron industry and particularly in the use of anthracite coal as a smelting fuel. All the raw materials necessary for the manufacture of pig iron – iron ore, sulphur, lime and coal – were

People (2 vols., New York, 1914); Thomas Murphy, *History of Lackawanna County* (Scranton, 1928) (hereafter *Hist. Lack. Co.*). See also appendix 6.
[4] A. B. Galatin, 'History of Scranton', in *Scranton City Directory, 1867–1868*, pp. 5–11; Mattes, loc. cit., pp. 107–12.
[5] Leo Marx, *The Machine in the Garden. Technology and the Pastoral Idea in America* (New York, 1964), pp. 11–16.
[6] Burton W. Folsom Jr., *Urban Capitalists: Entrepreneurs and City Growth in Pennsylvania's Lackawanna and Lehigh Regions, 1800–1920* (Baltimore, 1981), p. 25.

available in abundance, hidden beneath the rural tranquility of
the lower Lackawanna Valley. In 1840, attracted by the
potential of the area, Selden T. Scranton and his brother
George, operator of the Oxford Iron Furnace in New Jersey,
bought up the Slocum property and built a blast furnace and a
nail works.[7]

By the middle of the decade, however, the project had failed
miserably. The remoteness of the area and the lack of adequate
transportation facilities would have imposed severe restrictions
had their product been of a high standard. Unfortunately for
them it was not. Ironically, in the light of the city's eventual
success story, the local ores proved to be of a low grade and
resulted in poor-quality nails. With bankruptcy imminent, the
Scrantons gambled boldly. They redirected their efforts towards
mass-producing heavy iron rails and secured a large order from
the New York and Erie Railroad. In many ways the budding
entrepreneurs were in the right place at the right time. During
the mid-1840s the British iron companies which usually satisfied
the bulk of American demand were increasingly preoccupied
with the domestic railway construction boom. Consequently,
prices in America rose drastically, creating an excellent opportunity for American capitalists, and especially those in eastern
Pennsylvania who were developing an iron industry which
utilized anthracite. Although it was by no means inevitable, the
Scrantons succeeded in fulfilling their contract by 1848. This
not only put them among the first Americans to mass-produce
rails; it also secured Scranton's future as an ironmaking centre
and launched the city on its rapid industrial revolution.[8]

Following their success, the Scrantons began to build the
infrastructure of a major industrial city around their now
flourishing ironworks. Between 1850 and 1853 two railroads
were built, giving access to markets both in upstate New York
and in New York City itself. These were incorporated into the
Delaware, Lackawanna and Western Railroad Company,
which was to dominate the industrial life of Scranton for the
remainder of the century. The ironworks were also incorporated

---

[7] Ibid., p. 25; W. David Lewis, 'The early history of the Lackawanna Iron and Coal
Co.: a study in technological adaptation', *Pennsylvania Magazine of History and Biography*,
XCVI (Oct. 1972), pp. 424–68, (at 428–38); B. H. Throop, *A Half Century in Scranton*
(Scranton, 1895), pp. 296–7

[8] Lewis, loc. cit., pp. 440–65; Folsom, op. cit., pp. 25–8.

when the Lackawanna Iron and Coal Company was formed in 1853.⁹ Churches and houses had already begun to be built soon after the arrival of the Scrantons, but now, flush with industrial success, the pace of urban development was accelerated. Streets were laid out, lots sold, company houses built and a company store was established.¹⁰ Capital flowed in as newcomers such as Mattes, Merrifield and Throop began to invest in the new metropolis and join the ranks of the city's ruling industrial and business élite. But it was still the Scranton family which dominated, with George as President of the D.L. & W. and Selden at the head of the L.I. & C. Their magnificent new houses on Quality Hill proclaimed their status as founders and builders of the growing settlement. Inevitably, after a brief spell as Harrison, the town which they had nurtured became known first as Scrantonia and then, permanently, as Scranton.¹¹

Yet if it was the iron industry which placed Scranton on the industrial map of America, its future lay in anthracite. As ironmaking was the primary purpose of the Scranton family, their coalmining operations were geared completely towards the needs of the blast furnaces. But coal would not be subsidiary to iron for long. In the 1850s the Scrantons began to mine coal for export out of the region.¹² Their transformation into coalowners as well as ironmasters inaugurated a new phase in Scranton's industrialization, one which led to the emergence of the city as the premier settlement in the Lackawanna Valley and ultimately to its being christened the 'Anthracite Capital of the World'.¹³

If the Scrantons were doomed to disappointment over the quality of the iron ores in their mineral property, they could hardly complain about the richness of its coal reserves. The great north-east Pennsylvania anthracite coalfield consists of three major regions – the Wyoming–Lackawanna or Northern, the Middle or Lehigh and the Southern or Schuylkill. Scranton is located in the heart of the Northern coalfield and is underlain

---

⁹ Folsom, op. cit., p. 33; Lewis, loc. cit., p. 466; J. C. Platt, *Reminiscences of the Early History of 'Dark Hollow', 'Slocum Hollow', 'Harrison', 'Lackawanna Iron Works', Scrantonia and Scranton Pa.* (Scranton, 1896), p. 15.
¹⁰ J. C. Platt, op. cit., pp. 21–4; Throop, op. cit., pp. 263–76.
¹¹ Folsom, op. cit., p. 33; Galatin, op. cit., pp. 47–51, 62–4.
¹² Lewis, loc. cit., pp. 465–6; Folsom, op. cit., pp. 32–4.
¹³ Folsom, op. cit., pp. 38–9.

by around twelve seams of good-quality anthracite. Moreover these seams contain less refuse and are subject to less folding than those in other parts of the coalfield.[14] Yet coalmining as a primary industry came to Scranton relatively late. Entrepreneurs had begun to speculate in coal during the war of 1812, encouraged by the rapid rise in wood prices caused by the shortage of timber. After the ending of hostilities, anthracite continued to be used as it was readily available and, provided efficient transportation was at hand, cheap. However, communications were poor and expensive, and this hindered a more systematic exploitation of the reserves, a universal experience in developing coal regions during the nineteenth century. Initially canals provided the breakthrough in each of the three coalfields. In the north the key development was the building in the early 1820s of the Delaware and Hudson Canal from the Hudson River to Honesdale and the completion of a gravity railroad from there to Carbondale at the top of the Lackawanna Valley. Prime movers in the project were the Wurtz brothers of Philadelphia, who as early as 1814 began to develop the anthracite reserves in the Carbondale area. The following year they sent a shipload of coal by raft to Philadelphia, but they were unable to find a market for it. The building of the canal reflected their switch to cater for the growing domestic market in New York City. Its completion led to a fall in the price of coal and a growth in demand. In 1829 a total of 7,000 tons were shipped along the canal; within four years shipments had risen to 110,000 tons.[15]

Under the stimulus of the canal, Carbondale emerged as the first major centre of anthracite mining in the Lackawanna Valley. With its locational advantage, the Delaware and Hudson Canal Company continued to develop it and turned it into a company town. As it grew it attracted migrants from the surrounding farms and villages and immigrants from Europe. Yet despite predictions to the contrary in the 1830s and 1840s,

[14] P. H. Moore, 'The anthracite industry' in Murphy, *Hist. Lack. Co.*, pp. 131–60 (especially 133). For discussions of the industrial and social history of the north-east Pennsylvania anthracite coalfield see Robert D. Billinger, *Pennsylvania's Coal Industry* (Gettysburg, 1964); Peter Roberts, *The Anthracite Coal Industry* (New York, 1901); Donald L. Miller and Richard E. Sharpless, *The Kingdom of Coal. Work, Enterprise, and Ethnic Communities in the Mine Fields* (Philadelphia, 1985).

[15] Miller and Sharpless, op. cit., pp. 1–50; Roberts, op. cit., pp. 62–5; Billinger, op. cit., pp. 9–12; Moore, loc. cit., pp. 134–5, 137.

Carbondale never became 'the grand emporium of north-east Pennsylvania'.[16] It lost its premier position in the Lackawanna Valley to Scranton in the 1850s. The crucial development which enabled the latter to succeed was the D.L. & W.'s decision to export coal. It was undoubtedly a shrewd move by the company.[17] To an extent, perhaps, it had no choice because the lack of good-quality ores and limes threatened to cripple the iron industry, and already ores from other areas were being brought to the works in large quantities. Nevertheless the prospects of entering the coal trade no doubt appeared tempting in their own right. To begin with, the demand for anthracite, both as a domestic heating fuel and as a coking material, was growing steadily. Equally important, and a factor with major implications for the structure of the local anthracite industry and its labour relations, the D.L. & W. had mining privileges written into its charter. Consequently, it was able to market its own coal along its own railway and succeeded in capturing a market for it in upstate New York. (The Pennsylvania Coal Co. and the Delaware & Hudson Railroad Co., the other two coalmining railroad companies which dominated the Northern coalfield, had already cornered the New York City trade.) The opening of the Diamond Mine at the foot of Hyde Park hill by the D.L. & W. in 1852 and its buying-up of smaller coal companies throughout the late 1850s and early 1860s transformed Scranton into a coal metropolis. Between 1841 and 1872 Scranton's coal companies produced over 22 million tons of anthracite.[18] By the first decade of the twentieth century there were around sixty mines and collieries in the city and total annual production was around 6 million tons.[19]

During the second half of the nineteenth century both the city and its economy grew in size, status and importance. In 1866 Scranton was given a city charter, and the two nearby older boroughs of Hyde Park and Providence were incorporated within it.[20] Another major victory was achieved in 1878 when,

[16] Folsom, op. cit., pp. 18–24.
[17] Ibid., pp. 38–9.
[18] Moore, loc. cit., pp. 137, 149.
[19] Hitchcock, vol. 1, pp. 79, 81. In 1912 it was estimated that if all the coal mined in one month in Scranton were loaded into one single train of coal trucks, it would stretch from Scranton to New York City (around 180 miles). Ibid., p. 181.
[20] Mattes, loc. cit., p. 113.

despite fierce opposition from Wilkes-Barre, the new county of Lackawanna was created. This severed Scranton from the hold of Luzerne County and made it the administrative as well as the economic centre of the Lackawanna Valley.[21] A modern urban centre began to replace the crude frontier mining patch. Parks were laid out, a hospital and a library were built, and streets were improved. On the economic side, the Scranton family encouraged businesses and commerce to move into the city. Slowly but surely the city sapped the capital and entrepreneurial potential of the rest of the valley and became the centre of an urban network, dominating all the coal towns around it – Pittston, Jermyn, Dickson City, Archbald, Olyphant, and Carbondale. Although Scranton dominated here, however, in turn it became subordinate to New York City capital as the nineteenth century wore on, particularly in the coal, iron and railroad industries. Faced with the choice between refusing to expand, which would result in the collapse of the staple industries, and seeking outside capital to help with the heavy investment needed to keep its industries competitive, Scranton's industrial leaders chose the latter. As the industries grew in size, their ownership usually shifted to wealthier corporate investors in New York City.[22]

Nevertheless, Scranton was no mere industrial fiefdom. A Board of Trade was set up, and Scranton attracted a wide variety of smaller industries and services, businesses far too small to interest the big financial operators of New York. Manufacturers came to exploit the city's coal and iron base, producing goods both for export and for the local heavy industries. In the 1870s a textile industry was established, and throughout the late nineteenth century banking, shopping, public utility and entertainment enterprises were set up. Communications were also expanded, and by 1880 Scranton was the junction of four railroads. Not only did these open up new markets; they also brought secondary repair shop industries.[23] In all, Scranton's economy underwent a marked degree of diversification during the second half of the century. In 1890, apart from the coal

[21] Ibid., p. 115; Throop, op. cit., pp. 149–53. One of Scranton's leading Welshmen, Lewis Pughe, was largely responsible for the drawing-up and passing of the new constitution.
[22] Folsom, op. cit., pp. 41, 84–5; Murphy, *Hist. Lack. Co.*, p. 421.
[23] Folsom, op. cit., pp. 96–9.

operations and the ironworks, the city could boast the Providence Stone Foundry, the Green Ridge Iron Works, the Sauquoit Silk Manufacturing Co., Harvey's Silk Mill, Gallands Underwear Manufactory, the Lackawanna Carriage Works, the Scranton Glass Co., the Scranton Wood Working Co. and the Scranton Gas Works.[24] Indeed, such was Scranton's urban and economic vibrancy that it not only possessed one of the world's first electric street cable-car systems, giving it the nickname 'Electric City', it was also the home of the first Woolworth's department store and the International Corresponding Schools.[25]

Despite its economic diversification, however, Scranton was still dependent on its heavy industrial base. (As late as 1920, over 30,000 workers were connected with the coal industry.) Nor were these foundations as secure as they seemed. Although the last two decades of the nineteenth century saw unparalleled economic expansion and urban redevelopment, the onset of the new century brought developments which undermined Scranton's boom-town atmosphere and signalled the beginning of its decline. In 1901 the Lackawanna Steel Works were dismantled and moved to the new steel town of Lackawanna, near the Great Lake port of Buffalo, in order to gain easier access to the ores of the Mesabi Range in Minnesota.[26] The greatest setback, however, occurred during the 1920s, when, after reaching its peak in 1917, the anthracite industry sank into a depression as disastrous in its implications as that experienced in the south Wales coalfield during the same period. The increasing costs of mining and a series of strikes allowed oil and gas producers to capture the domestic fuel market. As demand fell, the coal companies ceased operations, creating widespread unemployment. The decline of the industry reverberated through the city's economy, seriously affecting the subsidiary industries dependent on it. The introduction of synthetic clothing after the First World War also led to the collapse of the local textile industry.[27] All these developments occurred before

[24] *Williams' Scranton Directory*, 1890.
[25] Ibid.; Mattes, loc. cit., p. 116; Murphy, *Hist. Lack. Co.*, p. 409; Folsom, op. cit., pp. 99–100.
[26] Folsom, op. cit., p. 100; Murphy, *Hist. Lack. Co.*, p. 409.
[27] Folsom, op. cit., p. 100.

the onset of the Great Depression of the 1930s, which even further accelerated the city's economic decline.

The collapse of Scranton's economy in the 1920s and 1930s brought an abrupt end to the industrial and urban prosperity which the city had experienced during the late nineteenth and early twentieth centuries. It also led to a reversal of the trend which had reflected and complemented the city's economic growth during the same period: population expansion. In the 1930s, for the first time in its history, Scranton's population began to fall. Out-migration and population decline were the last cruel blow to the city's fortunes for, during its rise and heyday, what Scranton had attracted above all was people. Far outnumbering the entrepreneurs who flocked to the city were those who came to supply the most essential commodity of all: labour. It was they who charged and tapped the furnaces, cut the coal and manned the railways, and it was they who set the city firmly on a course of relentless population expansion. Barely 7,000 in 1850, the population had jumped to 35,000 by 1870, 75,000 by 1890 and to well over 100,000 by 1900, when Scranton was easily the third largest city in Pennsylvania and the thirty-eighth largest in the United States.[28] Although it drew its fair share of uprooted farmers from the surrounding districts, the bulk of its population was the result of immigration. Throughout the late nineteenth and early twentieth centuries, Scranton was not only a vibrant industrial metropolis; it was also, to a marked degree, a city of immigrants.

If the capital for Scranton's growth was a judicious mix of Scranton family enterprise and New York City speculation, its labour was European. In this respect it differed little from the wider anthracite region or, indeed, from Pennsylvania as a whole, which absorbed more immigrants than any other state except New York. Yet the striking feature of Scranton's immigration experience is its intensity. In 1870 nearly half of its population was foreign-born.[29] A decade later, Scranton was recorded as the city with the twenty-eighth largest foreign-born element in the United States, but a more telling statistic was the number of foreign-born in relation to total population. Here

---

[28] U.S. Census Office, *Twelfth Census of the United States: 1900* (Washington, D.C., 1904), vol. I, p. 432. See also appendix 7.
[29] See appendix 8.

THE PUBLIC FACE OF WELSH SCRANTON 11

Scranton ranked twelfth; the corresponding figures for Pittsburgh and Philadelphia were twenty-fourth and thirty-fourth respectively.[30] By 1910 Scranton's foreign-born element had reached over 35,000, mainly through a large influx of immigrants from Italy, Germany and the Austrian empire during the previous two decades. If the foreign-stock figures are examined, then Scranton's immigrant heritage becomes even more startling. During its heyday, around 75 per cent of Scranton's inhabitants were either themselves born abroad or had parents who were born in another country.[31]

These immigrants were a diverse mixture, and Scranton's cosmopolitanism became even more marked with the eastern European and Italian influx at the end of the century. For most of the nineteenth century, however, ethnic Scranton was dominated by the so-called 'older' immigrant groups, particularly the Irish, the Germans, the Scots, the English and the Welsh. Representatives of each of these nationalities had begun to arrive in the 1840s, and they grew in number as the city's industrial and urban development intensified.

Throughout the second half of the nineteenth century, the largest immigrant group in Scranton was the Irish. There were already 1,795 Irish in the city by 1854, and at its peak in 1890 the foreign-born Irish element numbered nearly 8,500. There were three major areas of Irish settlement in the city: the shanty towns to the north-west (wards 3 and, later, 21); the south-east (wards 12, 19 and 20) and the tenements crowded between the Lackawanna River and the D.L. & W. railroads (wards 6, 7 and 8). The Irish were overwhelmingly Catholic in religion and Democratic in politics, and they controlled that party's machine. Apart from some notable exceptions they were at the bottom of the economic ladder, being mostly employed as unskilled labour, particularly in the mines. As well as being poorly paid, Irish immigrants invariably suffered from bad housing conditions, and they were frequently the target of anti-Catholic and anti-Irish prejudice. Their often robust style of life did little to disprove the prevailing stereotypes or prevent the close attention of law-enforcement agencies, despite the fact that

---

[30] U.S. Census Office, *Tenth Census of the United States: 1880* (Washington, D.C., 1883), vol. I, p. 471.
[31] See appendix 8.

many Irish served in the police force. Like that of the Welsh, much Irish cultural activity centred on their religion, although the tavern was perhaps their most important social institution. The chief Irish organizations were the Ancient Order of Hibernians and the fraternal organizations, which provided both group identity and outlets for the talents of the more ambitious members of the community.[32]

The second largest immigrant group in Scranton at the end of the nineteenth century was the Germans. Over 15,000 people of German stock lived in the city in 1910, and throughout the latter part of the nineteenth century there was a constant foreign-born element of around 4,000. Despite their numbers, however, the Germans lacked the cohesion of other immigrant groups in the city. Although there were clearly identifiable German 'blocks', the immigrants were scattered throughout the city. Moreover, unlike the Welsh and the Irish, religion could not be a unifying social and cultural force, as the German community was itself divided along Catholic and Protestant lines. Finally, although many of the Germans found employment as labourers in the mines, they were economically far more diverse than the other major immigrant groups, and were represented in a wide variety of skilled trades. Nevertheless, in common with the other groups, the German community in Scranton had its own organizations, insurance companies and social and cultural institutions, particularly musical ones.[33]

Immigrants from mainland Britain were also well represented in Scranton's ethnic mix. Although the Scottish element was small (at its peak the number of foreign-born Scots was 576), large numbers of English people were attracted to the city. In 1870 there were 1,444 foreign-born English, and at its peak in 1900, the figure stood at 3,692. Despite their numbers, they were rather an obscure ethnic group and the dynamics of English

---

[32] U.S. Bureau of the Census, *Thirteenth Census of the United States: 1910* (Washington, D.C., 1913), vol. I, pp. 610–11; Phoebe Gibbons, 'The miners of Scranton', *Harpers New Monthly Magazine*, 55 (1877), pp. 916–27, *passim*; J. C. Platt, op. cit., p. 26; James Rodechko, 'Irish–American society in the Pennsylvania anthracite region, 1870–1880', in John E. Bodnar (ed.), *The Ethnic Experience in Pennsylvania* (Lewisburg, 1973), pp. 19–38 (at 21–2, 28–9, 33); Samuel Emlen Walker, 'Terence V. Powderly – labor mayor. Workingmen's politics in Scranton, 1870–1884' (unpublished Ohio State University Ph.D. Dissertation, 1973), pp. 43–5. See also appendices 8 and 10.

[33] Walker, op. cit., pp. 45–6; Gibbons, loc. cit., *passim*; *Williams' Scranton Directory*, 1890; David E. Jones, 'Music in Lackawanna County' in Murphy, *Hist. Lack. Co.*, pp. 338–47 (especially 340). See also appendices 8 and 10.

immigrant life in Scranton are difficult to evaluate. They did form patriotic and benefit societies, notably the Sons of St George, but they did not have a strong group identity or cohesion.[34] Lacking a distinctive culture or a different language, there was little to distinguish them from native-Americans. Whatever the nature of their own experience, however, in Scranton the English were overshadowed both culturally and numerically by those who had emigrated from the western side of Offa's Dyke, the Welsh.

The Welsh were a powerful force in Scrantonian life. Until the last decade of the nineteenth century they were the second largest immigrant group in the city, and they continued to be a sizeable proportion of the population for much of the first half of the twentieth.[35] Nor was their impact on Scranton merely numerical. They were intimately involved in most phases of its growth and economic development, and in many ways the fortunes of the Welsh immigrant group mirrored those of the city itself. The Welsh could even claim that their nationality had guided Scranton's destiny from the very beginning of its modern history, for it had been a Welshman who had triggered off its industrial expansion.

The genesis of the Welsh involvement in Scranton's history was undoubtedly dramatic. The Scranton family's success with their new blast furnace in the early 1840s had not been an easy one. Two attempts were made in the autumn of 1841 to blow the furnace; both were failures. Another effort was made on 3 January 1842, but again in vain. By now matters were very serious, as the young entrepreneurs' capital, financial credibility and even their very futures looked doomed. In desperation Selden Scranton went to Danville, Pennsylvania, in search of someone with experience of using anthracite to make iron. He returned in mid-January with a certain John F. Davis, a native of Tredegar. Davis was well versed in the hot-blast process of smelting iron ore, a technique that had originated in south Wales and was by that time being used to good effect by Welsh ironworkers in towns such as Danville and Catausaqua. His

---

[34] *Williams' Scranton Directory*, 1890; Craft, op. cit., p. 544. See also appendices 8 and 10.
[35] See appendix 8.

ironmaking magic succeeded where Yankee exuberance had failed, and his supervision and improvements finally enabled the furnace to be put in blast. The episode well illustrates the important role Welsh industrial workers so often played in pioneering America's industrialization, and equally it demonstrates why Welsh skill was such a sought-after commodity.[36]

John F. Davis's crucial intervention not only helped to change the course of Scranton's history by triggering industrial expansion; it also opened up the area as a centre for Welsh immigration. Davis remained in employment at the ironworks, and by 1844 mine foreman Evan Williams had arrived. The first in a line of Welsh immigrant 'padrones' in Scranton, Williams was apparently responsible for a significant Welsh influx into the town. Within a decade there were eighty-one Welsh families, a total of 413 individuals, in Scranton.[37] Their presence signalled that by the mid-1850s the pattern of earlier Welsh settlement in the Lackawanna Valley had been decisively transformed. For although John F. Davis had been one of the first Welshmen in Scranton, he was by no means the first of that nationality in the valley as a whole.

The first Welsh immigrants in the Lackawanna Valley were in fact farmers, not industrial workers. The same gravity railroad which the D. & H. built to ship out Carbondale coal also enabled Welsh farmers to penetrate the upper part of the valley. In 1829 a small group arrived at Neath, Bradford County. Another reached Springbrook in 1832 and proceeded, in true Welsh immigrant pioneer fashion, to name it New Wales. Two years later, a third settlement was established at Clifford Township, Susquehanna County. Here, apparently, the new immigrants were so struck by the similarities between their new surroundings and the ones they had left that they named it Welsh Hill.[38] They were by no means the first nor the last Welsh immigrants to see parts of America as a Welsh landscape reincarnate. For decades, these three settlements remained as a

---

[36] J. C. Platt, op. cit., pp. 8–9; Hitchcock, vol. 1, p. 18. For biographical details of John F. Davis (1809–82) see *Scranton Republican*, 1 April 1882. The hot-blast process had been pioneered in the Ynyscedwyn Ironworks in the Swansea Valley and had been introduced at Catausauqua, Pa., by David Thomas. It enabled the development of the eastern Pennsylvanian iron industry. Williams, *Wales and America*, p. 81.
[37] J. C. Platt, op. cit., p. 26.
[38] Daniel J. Williams, *One Hundred Years of Welsh Calvinistic Methodism in America* (Philadelphia, 1937), pp. 160–1; R. D. Thomas, op. cit., pp. 63–5.

small but vivid contrast to the character of Welsh immigration to the lower part of the valley.

The first major concentration of Welsh people in the Lackawanna Valley was at Carbondale. Fittingly, it was the opening up of the anthracite mines by the D. & H. which brought them there, thus setting a precedent for future Welsh immigrants for the remainder of the century. Welsh mining skill was not slow to follow the D. & H.'s initiative. In 1830, after a nerve-racking six-week voyage across the Atlantic, a party of seventy miners who, with their families, numbered almost two hundred, arrived in Philadelphia. They had been brought from Wales for their coalmining experience, and were met at the port by Maurice Wurtz of the D. & H. He sent them along the canal and the railroad to Carbondale. The fact that the journey took two weeks is an indication of how isolated the newly opened up area was at that time.[39] Thereafter more Welsh miners and their families followed, and by 1833 three separate denominational churches had been formed.[40] Carbondale had a sizeable Welsh community before Scranton was even on the map. Indeed, in the same year as the Scrantons arrived in Slocum Hollow, the Carbondale Welsh were present in sufficient numbers to occasion comments on their drinking habits in the local press.[41]

Carbondale remained the largest Welsh settlement in the valley until the 1850s, when it was outstripped by the rapidly growing Welsh element in Scranton. With the increase in the tempo of industrial emigration from Wales to the United States in the 1850s and 1860s, Scranton's Welsh population increased spectacularly. By 1870 there were 4,177 Welsh foreign-born in the city, almost 12 per cent of its total population and a quarter of its foreign-born.[42] Within fifteen years, therefore, the largest Welsh community in the United States had exploded into existence in Scranton. Although the 1880 Census recorded a decrease in the number of foreign-born Welsh in the city,[43] by

---

[39] *Druid*, 24 July 1907, 30 Apr. 1908; R. D. Thomas, op. cit., p. 63; Moore, loc. cit., p. 150.
[40] David Jones *Memorial Volume of the Welsh Congregationalists in Pennsylvania* (Utica, 1934), pp. 23–30; D. J. Williams, op. cit., pp. 89–92.
[41] *Carbondale Journal*, 11 June 1840. See also below, ch. 5, p. 210.
[42] See appendix 8.
[43] Many Welsh left Scranton to seek work elsewhere during the depression and long industrial disputes that occurred during the 1870s, and probably fewer came to the city because of the adverse state of the local economy.

1890 they had reached nearly 5,000. As in the United States as a whole, this was the peak year. Thereafter the figure declined slowly until 1910 (when there were only 700 fewer first-generation Welsh in the city than there had been twenty years previously) and then fell sharply to only 2,500 or so. The foreign-born figure alone, however, is not a true indication of the numerical strength of the Welsh in Scranton. In 1890, for example, there were also in the city nearly 5,000 people who were born in the United States but one or both of whose parents had been born in Wales.[44]

During the second half of the nineteenth century Scranton's thriving iron and, especially, coal industries made the city an irresistible magnet and an obvious destination for industrial families from south Wales. But it is difficult to ascertain why it was so much more popular than other Welsh settlements in industrial America. It is highly likely that the Welsh came to Scranton through the process of chain migration. The gospel of its attractions was spread through letters, family connections and positive recruiting efforts, particularly, apparently, on the part of the proselytizing Benjamin Hughes, the General Inside Superintendent of the largest coal company in the area, the D.L. & W.[45] Apart from miners and iron and steel workers and their families, the commercial and business potential of a large new settlement also attracted a coterie of Welsh craftsmen, tradesmen, professionals, dressmakers and domestic servants. Indeed, if the Scranton family and the city's financial élite were relentless in their efforts to create a modern, urbanized industrial centre, the Welsh were only too eager to help them build it.

The settlement pattern of the Welsh in Scranton resembled that of other towns where the Welsh settled in significant numbers. Until the 1860s there were two general areas of settlement, both largely determined by the main occupation of the immigrant workers. Some of the early Welsh ironworkers who moved to Scranton in the 1840s to help fulfil the Erie Railroad's rail contract settled near the ironworks in South

[44] U.S. Census Office, *Eleventh Census of the United States: 1890* (Washington, D.C., 1893), vol. I, pp. 708–28.
[45] For biographical details of Benjamin Hughes see Ebenezer Edwards, op. cit., pp. 406–7; *Portrait and Biographical Record of Lackawanna County, Pennsylvania* (New York, 1897), pp. 185–6. See also below, ch. 2, pp. 34–5.

Scranton. In fact it was the Welsh who first settled the Shanty Hill district, which later became predominantly Irish.[46] The second area of settlement was in West and North Scranton, in the old boroughs of Hyde Park and Providence, where the majority were coal miners and their families.[47] It was in Hyde Park, situated on a hill across the Lackawanna River from the main part of Scranton, that the influx of miners in the 1850s and 1860s mainly settled, and anthracite coal was the foundation of the new community in more ways than the purely geological. It is generally believed that the first mine in Hyde Park was sunk in 1850, when the Park Coal Co. drove a slope (drift) to the School Fund seam.[48] Initially mining operations took place along the river between Hyde Park and Scranton, in what was later to become ward 14. Here, in 1852, the Mount Pleasant Shaft was opened, as was the Diamond, whose complex included the first steam-operated coal breaker in the valley. More mines were opened in the late 1850s and 1860s. Most were located either along the river or in the back valley behind Hyde Park, so that the growing Welsh community was surrounded by mines and breakers within twenty years. No section of Scranton was to furnish more coal than Hyde Park, underlain as it is in places by sixty feet of the purest anthracite.[49]

The voracious appetite for Hyde Park's 'black diamonds' decisively shifted the balance of the Welsh settlement pattern. Many of those who had originally settled in Shanty Hill moved to the West Side in the mid- and late 1850s to be nearer their place of work. The shift can be illustrated by the fortunes of the early Welsh churches in Scranton, in much the same way as the later formation of daughter churches would indicate a decline in the use of the Welsh language. The Welsh Congregationalist denomination first began meeting in a schoolroom near the blast furnace in 1853; by 1855 they had built a church on Mifflin Avenue in the centre of Scranton.[50] In 1853, however, Judson

---

[46] J. C. Platt, op. cit., p. 26; 'It was the Welsh not the Irish who first settled in Shanty Hill Section', undated *Scrantonian* article in 'The Welsh' file in Lackawanna Historical Society, Scranton.
[47] Thomas Murphy, *Old Home Week Souvenir and History of Hyde Park* (Scranton, 1924), p. 55 (hereafter *Hist. Hyde Park*).
[48] Ibid.
[49] Ibid., p. 33; Moore, loc. cit., p. 139. See also appendix 9.
[50] *Sixtieth Anniversary of Church Charter, First Welsh Congregational Church, Scranton, Pennsylvania, 1864–1924* (Scranton, 1924) (no pagination); Davy Edgar Jones (ed.), *One*

Clark of Carbondale opened coal mines in the Notch, or Market Street, area of Providence, and one of the congregation, Rhys Price, was appointed to oversee them. As was so often the case, skilled Welshmen followed the foreman, and a number of the congregation moved from Shanty Hill to Hyde Park and Providence, where a Welsh Congregational Church was founded in 1855. Meanwhile those living in Hyde Park eventually established their own church in 1858. By 1870 the Mifflin Avenue Church had transferred to its Hyde Park counterpart and the building was sold.[51] A similar fate befell the Baptists. They had also first held services in Shanty Hill, before building a church on Mifflin Avenue. Nevertheless the inexorable drain of brawn and brain to Hyde Park severely depleted the congregation, and the church moved there permanently in the 1860s.[52]

Elsewhere in the Lackawanna Valley, too, early Welsh settlement had led to a sizeable Welsh presence in the mining towns to the east and west of Scranton. These towns had sprung up in the wake of industrial developments in the city and in Carbondale. Again the establishing of Welsh churches is a useful indicator. In the case of Jermyn, a Welsh Congregational Church was founded in 1865. It was the Welsh who first settled Olyphant in 1858, and a Baptist church appeared the following year. Soon after mining operations began in Taylor in 1854, Welsh miners began to arrive, whilst it was a Welshman, Edward Jones, who controlled mining operations in Archbald for most of its formative years.[53] In all, nearly 8,000 people of Welsh stock lived in Lackawanna County (excluding Scranton) in 1910.[54]

It was Hyde Park, however, which was the premier Welsh settlement in the valley. The Welsh communities in Olyphant, Jermyn and Taylor were largely satellite communities, mirroring the status of those towns in the wider Scrantonian

Half Century of Work. History of the Providence Welsh Congregational Church of Scranton (Scranton, 1905), p. 18.

[51] Davy Edgar Jones, op. cit., pp. 29–30; *Sixtieth Anniversary*, op. cit.

[52] *Seventy-Fifth Anniversary of the First Welsh Baptist Church, Scranton, Pennsylvania, 1850–1925* (Scranton, 1925), pp. 8–10.

[53] R. D. Thomas, op. cit., pp. 56, 60, 61. For biographical details of Edward Jones see Dwight J. Stoddard, *Prominent Men of Scranton and Vicinity* (Scranton, 1906), p. xi.

[54] U.S. Bureau of the Census. *Thirteenth Census of the United States: 1910* (Washington, D.C., 1913), vol. I, p. 578.

economy. Hyde Park's predominance, both within Scranton and in the rest of the valley, was clearly demonstrated by the 1910 census. In that year, for the first time, the census recorded the number and nationality of the foreign-born in each of the city's wards. Although the returns indicate that all had at least some Welsh representation, they also show that over half the foreign-born Welsh in the city – 2,613 out of a total of 4,137 – lived in four adjoining wards in the central district of Hyde Park (wards 4, 5, 6 and 15). Moreover, in three of these (wards 4, 5 and 15) the Welsh were easily the largest immigrant group. In 1910, 672 foreign-born Welsh lived in ward 4, almost twice as many as the next largest immigrant groups, the Russians and the English. In the far more heavily populated ward 5, the Welsh were also numerically superior, although it also contained large numbers of Russians, Italians and Irish. It was in ward 15, however, that the Welsh dominated the most. Here there were 300 more Welsh than Irish and 400 more than each of the roughly equal English, German and Russian groups.[55]

Hyde Park, then, was Scranton's 'Welsh town', but it was never exclusively Welsh. It was one of the most cosmopolitan and densely populated areas of Scranton, and its steep slopes housed representatives of most countries from which emigrants flocked to the United States. Nevertheless the West Side did bear an undeniable Welsh stamp, for beyond the bare statistics of the census return there was ample visible proof of Hyde Park's Welsh character and of the public impact of its unparalleled Welsh presence.

The 'Welshness' of Hyde Park's outward appearance was apparent to all observers even apart from the unmistakeable 'll', 'ch' and 'rh' consonantal contortions of countless coal-lined lips. Hyde Park has its Welsh street names: Price Street, Jones Street, Evans Court, Roberts Court and Edwards Court. Eynon Street in ward 15 was actually named after one of the founding fathers of the Welsh immigrant community, Thomas Eynon; his merchandise store was one of the first Welsh businesses in Hyde Park, and his son Albert was one of the best-known Welshmen in Scranton because of his position as the cashier at the West Side Bank.[56] There was even an area of Hyde Park known as

---

[55] Ibid. See also appendix 10.
[56] Murphy, *Hist. Hyde Park*, p. 41. For biographical details of Thomas Eynon see

Patagonia (it is still referred to as such by older residents of the city). Legend has it that the name was coined because some Welsh families migrated from there to the Welsh colony in Argentina during the early 1870s.[57] On the streets themselves, all manner of buildings, shop-fronts and billboards publicized the character of Hyde Park's major constituency. Along the main thoroughfare itself, Welsh churches reached for heaven, proud of their role as late nineteenth-century social centres and glorying in their symbolism as the stone-and-mortar proof of the much proclaimed Welsh religiosity. Moreover, the two blocks squared by North and South Main Avenues, Hyde Park Avenue and Jackson, Luzerne and Washburn Streets were crammed full of Welsh business establishments, offering a wide variety of services of a more secular nature. Throughout the late nineteenth and early twentieth centuries, Hyde Park possessed a flourishing Welsh commercial centre, which not only provided the community with many of its 'natural' leaders but was also responsible for much of the continuity of an identifiable Welsh presence on the West Side.

A substantial Welsh business section had come into existence in Hyde Park by 1870. *Webb's Scranton Directory* of that year recorded a wide range of shops and services run by Welsh people.[58] Apart from the fresh foodstuffs which farmers from the surrounding district sold from barrels most weekday mornings, Welsh families had no shortage of choice if they preferred to buy provisions from those of their own nationality.[59] There was the co-operative store, for instance, on North Main Avenue, which Welsh and English miners had established in 1864 and chartered in 1867. Initially William B. Daniels, later clerk of the courts in the city, was its manager, although in 1870 that role was filled by George B. Evans. The 'co-op' sold groceries, dry goods, hardware, boots and shoes, and was a successful venture until the cumulative effects of strikes and depression put it out of business in the late 1870s.[60] As part of the same building, Richard J. Hughes ran a stove and tinware shop; in 1871 one of

Portrait and Biographical Record, pp. 516–17.
[57] *Drych*, 1 Feb., 26 Aug. 1875; ex inf. the late W. R. Lewis, Scranton.
[58] Most of the following paragraph is based on the entries in *Webb's Scranton Directory*, 1870–1.
[59] Scranton *Morning Republican*, 12 Jan. 1871.
[60] Murphy, *Hist. Hyde Park*, p. 69.

his employees, William Lewis, amused himself by making a tin squirrel house which eventually found a home in T. Galligan's liquor store.[61] A few doors down along Main Avenue, at the corner of Jackson Street, was the substantial establishment of Henry D. Jones. Not only could customers purchase groceries, tea and coffee, ham, shoulders, butter, lard and eggs here; the proprietor could also provide passage tickets and drafts to England, Ireland, Wales and to and from all parts of the world when he had his emigration agent cap on. No doubt many a Welsh immigrant came to Hyde Park with money and tickets sent by means of his good offices. The corner of Jackson and Main had a plethora of Welsh businesses of all kinds. Here B. G. Morgan, Druggists, sold burning and lubricating oils, window glass, paints, schoolbooks and stationery; Thomas Jones gave Welsh haircuts; Mrs John P. Williams dealt in fancy goods and millinery, and behind the Hyde Park Hotel David J. Davies was the proprietor of a 'First Class Livery Stable'. In the same area, Lewis C. Davis was prepared to be 'constantly on hand' to make 'to order in the most superior and workmanlike manner' the clothes, cassimeres and vestings of every description which made him a 'fashionable Merchant Tailor'. Virtually next door, E. M. Thomas, boot dealer, kept a watchful eye on his nearby rival in trade, J. S. Williams, but no doubt took as much pride in the variety of his own wares as in his knowledge of the commodities his Welsh customers would most need. He sold 'Everything, From a Light Fancy Boot or Shoe to a Heavy Miner's Boot'. Across the road, Esdras Howell and D. T. Richards kept a dry goods and groceries store. Like their co-operative counterparts, they lost heavily during the strike years of 1869 and 1871.[62]

Perhaps the most diverse commercial enterprise on the 'corners', as this central area of Hyde Park was known, was William M. Reese's 'New York Market', situated on Main Avenue, next door to Thomas the Boots and opposite Odd Fellows Hall. The proprietor was a dealer in 'vegetables, fresh fish, oysters, clams, smoked and dried meats, foreign and domestic fruits, nuts, etc.'.[63] In 1871-2 Reese also branched out into the liquor trade,[64] perhaps to keep up with the

[61] Scranton *Morning Republican*, 13 Mar. 1871.
[62] Murphy, *Hist. Hyde Park*, p. 41.
[63] *Webb's Scranton Directory*, 1870-1.
[64] *Boyd's Wilkes-Barre City Directory*, 1871-2.

competition. Within a bottle's throw of his door were the saloons of John J. Edwards, Mary E. Evans, David F. Jones and Thomas Thomas. Thirsty Welsh miners, then, need not have stayed parched – and as we shall see later it seems they did not.[65] For those of them who wished to drink in a more 'Welsh' environment there was always the Cambria Hotel. Elsewhere in Hyde Park in 1870 were a number of other Welsh businesses which provided similar services to those in the centre, as well as blacksmiths, painting firms, a horseshoe nail maker, a slate dealer, a toy dealer, a private educationalist and lastly, but surely not the least, Mrs William M. Thomas's Welsh Boarding House.[66]

Most of the Welsh commercial enterprises in existence in Hyde Park in 1870 survived until the turn of the century. A familiar landmark on South Main Avenue to generations of Hyde Parkian eyes was William Price and Son's Funeral Parlour and Furniture Warehouse, first established in 1859.[67] Moreover, by 1890 many new businesses had also been established in Hyde Park by Welsh immigrants and their children. In 1889 the *Scranton Republican* commented on the building boom on the West Side which was apparently keeping all contractors busy, among them Daniel Williams and W. R. Williams.[68] One project under construction was two stores for D. D. Evans and Co. of South Main Avenue, one for dry goods and the other for general merchandise. (Perhaps the strain of running two new stores was too much for D. D. Evans himself – he died the following year.)[69] In 1890 *Williams' City Directory* recorded an almost endless list of Welsh grocery stores and meat and dry goods traders, four milk depots and a baker, whilst Henry Jones kept a restaurant on Washburn Street. There was, therefore, no shortage of facilities for Welsh families to purchase the 'Welsh cookies' and 'faggots' for their *te-bach*, three aspects of Welsh immigrant culture which became permanently stamped on the Scrantonian imagination. Also listed in 1890 were Welsh barbers, booksellers, boot and shoe repairers, bottlers, carpenters, builders, dressmakers, druggists, cigar and tobacco

[65] See below, ch. 5, pp. 204–12.
[66] *Webb's Scranton Directory*, 1870–1.
[67] Murphy, *Hist. Hyde Park*, p. 99.
[68] *Scranton Republican*, 27 July, 8, 26 Aug. 1889.
[69] Ibid., 27 July 1889, 20 Dec. 1890.

shops, a plumber, a carpet weaver, a photographer, and an elocutionist, Sarah J. Jones. There were at least seven Welsh confectioner's shops in Hyde Park alone, and J. D. Williams and Brothers, Ice-Cream and Confection Manufacturers and Retailers, had two shops in Hyde Park and one in Scranton itself. The company had been set up by Joshua Williams senior when he moved to Scranton in 1864, having formerly been a mining superintendent in Jermyn. For the musically minded, Benjamin W. Phillips kept sheet music and musical goods in his store on Jackson Avenue, whilst those of them seeking tuition had a choice of four Welsh music teachers in Hyde Park, among them Daniel Protheroe, one of the chief characters in the drama surrounding Scranton's choral entries in 1893 World's Fair Eisteddfod at Chicago.[70]

The Hyde Park Welsh business community maintained a remarkable degree of continuity through its flourishing years, and in so doing undoubtedly contributed greatly to the stability of the Welsh settlement. Continuity was achieved in three ways: sons often took over the family business; in some cases former employees set up on their own; and thirdly, former Welsh business premises were taken over by new Welsh enterprises. Future County Commissioner Morgan Thomas set up his own business on Jackson Street, Hyde Park, in 1890 after serving for years as foreman and salesman with J. D. Williams and Co., South Main Avenue.[71] When B. G. Morgan, the druggist, erected the West Side Bank building and opened his store there, John Davies, another Welsh druggist, took over his former premises on South Main Avenue. In the 1880s George W. Jenkins, at one time an employee of Morgan, took over his former boss's store; his son, Harry, was still running the business in the 1920s.[72]

For much of the late nineteenth century, Welsh-speaking postmen delivered the mail in Hyde Park. This symbolizes both the Welshness of that section and the degree to which the Welsh were represented in all aspects of the city's public life. From 1873 to 1883 the Hyde Park postmaster was Thomas D.

[70] *Williams' Scranton Directory*, 1890; Murphy, *Hist. Hyde Park*, pp. 37–8.
[71] *Scranton Republican*, 23 Aug. 1889; *Steinke's Story of Scranton with Who's Who and Why in Cartoons* (Scranton, 1914), p. 128.
[72] Murphy, *Hist. Hyde Park*, p. 77.

Thomas, born in Blaina, Monmouthshire, and a former mine foreman who had been crippled in an accident in the Mount Pleasant mine in 1867.[73] When the free delivery system was introduced after 1883 and the Hyde Park office was abolished, the tradition of Welsh involvement in the postal service continued. A *Postal Guide* issued by the letter carriers in 1897 contained a number of Welsh names. They ranged from assistant postmaster, D. W. Powell, through to clerks, carriers and officers of branch No. 17 of the National Association of Letter Carriers, including the president, John H. Phillips, and the secretary, John R. Thomas. Phillips himself was responsible for ensuring that all the correspondence to properties along North and South Main Avenue – many of them Welsh – was delivered correctly, whilst his colleagues Thomas O. Williams and Eliezer S. Evans served the remainder of the Hyde Park district.[74] That consistent Welsh office-holder David M. Jones was also postmaster between 1889 and 1893,[75] just one example of the marked involvement of the Welsh in Scranton's political history. Many Welshmen served as Republican office holders, though despite a few attempts, that of D. M. Jones among them, none succeeded in being elected mayor. Welshmen dominated the Republican caucuses in Hyde Park, whilst usually the Welsh were the pillars of that party's vote.[76]

Welshmen also patrolled the city in the name of law and order. Throughout the late nineteenth and early twentieth centuries there were a number of Welsh policemen, whilst at the turn of the century R. J. Edwards of Providence was police captain and John Davies of Hyde Park his deputy.[77] In education, too, the Welsh were well represented. George Phillips, George Howell and Rhys Powell all served as superintendents of schools in the city, whilst in 1878 William R. Williams was elected as school controller in ward 15.[78] During the 1880s the school controller for ward 5 was John Courier Morris, a leading figure in Scranton's political and newspaper

---

[73] Ibid., p. 47; Hitchcock, op. cit., vol. I, p. 445.
[74] Letter Carriers of Scranton, Pennsylvania, *Postal Guide* (Scranton, 1897), *passim*.
[75] Murphy, *Hist. Hyde Park*, p. 47. For biographical details of David M. Jones (1839–96), who was originally from Rhymney, see Hitchcock, op. cit., vol. I, pp. 222–3.
[76] See below, ch. 2, pp. 73–9.
[77] *Taylor's Scranton City Directory*, 1900.
[78] Murphy, *Hist. Hyde Park*, p. 61.

circles as well as in the cultural activities of the Welsh. Apparently Morris was responsible for the appointment not only of George Phillips and other Welsh headmasters but also of many a Welsh janitor, schoolmistress and music teacher. According to the *Drych*, his efforts were a tribute to his 'influence and patriotism'.[79] One Welsh headteacher at least gained quite a reputation for his disciplinary methods. In 1893 the *Scranton Republican* reported that complaints had been issued against Principal J. T. Jones of ward 4; it was alleged that he had a tendency for inflicting corporal punishment far too severely.[80]

Throughout the late nineteenth and early twentieth centuries, the Welsh in Scranton provided legal, medical and insurance services for both their own nationality and the wider population of the city. Among the many Welsh doctors who practised in Hyde Park were Revd E. B. Evans, for many years a practitioner in spiritual as well as more conventional medicine, John M. Williams and, at the turn of the century, Dr William Rowland Davies, founder of the Lackawanna County Medical Society's *Journal*, the first such publication in east Pennsylvania.[81] The Welsh were also strongly represented in the legal profession. There were a number of prominent lawyers in their ranks, the most important being H. M. Edwards, William T. Lewis and George Maxey, each of whom served as district attorney for Lackawanna County.[82] There were also a number of Welsh insurance agents, both in Hyde Park and in the city itself, notably Daniel J. Evans and James D. Evans. Before entering the legal profession in 1871, H. M. Edwards had been an insurance agent in the firm of Edwards and Davies, general agents for the National Life Insurance Co. of New York with offices in the Co-operative Building. Many Welsh lawyers also functioned as public notaries and real-estate brokers, probably the most prominent being Thomas R. Hughes, a leading member of the Hyde Park community, whose office was in the same building as the Welsh Philosophical Society Library.[83]

---

[79] *Drych*, 14, 21 Jan. 1886.
[80] *Scranton Republican*, 17 Feb. 1893.
[81] Murphy, *Hist. Hyde Park*, pp. 705–7; *Steinke's Story*, op. cit., p. 75.
[82] Murphy, *Hist. Hyde Park*, pp. 49, 73; idem, *Hist. Lack. Co.*, pp. 567–8; *Steinke's Story*, op. cit., pp. 45, 180.
[83] *Webb's Scranton Directory*, 1870–1; *Taylor's Scranton City Directory*, 1900.

The Welsh community was also served by financial organizations which had been set up specifically to cater for its needs. During the second half of the nineteenth century there were three such institutions, although they were in existence for varying lengths of time. The Pioneer Building and Loan Association was established before 1870, but seems to have collapsed shortly afterwards.[84] A more successful venture was the Cambrian Mutual Fire and Insurance Co., set up in 1871 with the purpose of insuring the property of Welsh people in Lackawanna and adjoining counties. It was eventually merged with a New York State company in the 1890s.[85] The pride of the West Side's financial sector, however, was the West Side Bank, originally chartered in 1874. For most of its existence, the bank was exclusively Welsh in its management. Indeed, in 1898 there were four Welshmen with the surname Williams on its board of trustees, three of whom became president and none of whom was related to the others. As the official history of the bank noted, 'this could only have occurred in Scranton, where the Welsh-Americans dominated.'[86] All three of these institutions were established and controlled by a small group of individuals, notably Benjamin Hughes, D. M. Jones, Thomas D. Davies and H. M. Edwards, and their involvement was in many ways a creation and a reflection of their high profile in the community. The Welsh also worked in, and in some cases became directors of, the main city banks, whilst in the early years of this century, three new banks were set up on the West Side, all by Welshmen. In 1904 Colonel Reese A. Phillips was the prime mover in founding the Keystone Bank; in 1910 Walter H. Jones set up the Electric City Bank, and finally, in the early 1920s, Gomer C. Davis became the first president of the Hyde Park Deposit Bank.[87]

During the second half of the nineteenth century, therefore, there came into existence in Scranton a Welsh presence whose strength was unmatched elsewhere in the United States. From

---

[84] *Webb's Scranton Directory*, 1870–1.
[85] Craft, op. cit., pp. 318–19; Murphy, *Hist. Hyde Park*, p. 43.
[86] Thomas Murphy, *History of the West Side Bank of Scranton, Pennsylvania, 1874–1949* (Scranton, 1949), pp. 3–4, 28.
[87] *Idem, Hist. Hyde Park*, p. 81.

John F. Davis's vital intervention onwards, the Welsh involvement had expanded and matured along with the city the Welsh had helped to build, and they had flourished as it prospered. One of the most obvious manifestations of their presence and its impact was Hyde Park's vibrant Welsh commercial and professional centre, and the equally intense participation of the Welsh in the city's public sector services and political life. As well as providing employment and an outlet for business ambitions, Hyde Park's Welsh commercial sector was a useful vehicle for attaining prominence and standing in the community itself. Almost universally, such advancement was matched by involvement in Welsh social and cultural activities; the Welsh shopocracy in Hyde Park was an integral element of the community's 'natural' leadership.

Above all, however, the Welsh businesses, professionals and public servants created an environment in which it was possible to be Welsh. They stamped an unmistakable Welsh identity on Hyde Park and, to a certain extent, they were strong enough to maintain it. During the late nineteenth and early twentieth centuries, in its outward appearances at least, Hyde Park was a mini-Wales. Here Welsh postmen walked along Welsh-named streets to deliver letters from Wales to Welsh homes; on their rounds they passed and served Welsh stores, Welsh saloons, Welsh funeral homes, Welsh banks, Welsh churches and that veritable boiler-room of Welshness, the *Baner America* block, with its myriad of Welsh businesses and the Welsh Philosophical Society Library. Had these Welsh postmen stopped to buy the *Scranton Republican*, they could have read news of Wales.[88] Moreover, in the course of their duties they rubbed shoulders with Welsh ministers, insurance agents, dressmakers, policemen, domestic servants, iron and steel workers, housewives, doctors, male and female clerks and teachers – and, of course, Welsh miners. If Hyde Park was the daily proof of the dynamic public face of Welsh Scranton, then it was also a face which was indelibly scarred with anthracite.

---

[88] During the 1880s and 1890s, the *Scranton Republican* regularly included 'Welsh notes' in its 'West Side' column. See, for example, ibid., 21 Oct. 1891.

II
THE WELSH AND SCRANTON'S ANTHRACITE INDUSTRY

'When I first attended a Welsh church at Scranton,' wrote Phoebe Gibbons in an article entitled 'The Miners of Scranton' in *Harpers New Monthly Magazine* in 1877,

> I was surprised at the nice appearance of the congregation and I afterward [*sic*] inquired whether there were any miners there. But on my late visit I learned an almost invariable means of discovering who have [*sic*] worked in the coal mines. On the back of my host's hands were many blue spots, looking like faint tattooing. These were the marks where he had been cut by the coal. Miners frequently have one or more of these blue scars upon the face. The coal dust doubtless remains in the wounded place, like Indian ink in tattooing; and by these marks you can perceive that men have been miners, though their occupation now be quite different.[1]

Phoebe Gibbons's innocence regarding the presence of Welsh miners in the church she attended is more than compensated for by her later, and accurate, realization that working in the mines often had inescapable consequences. At the time of her writing, the bulk of the Welsh living in Scranton were mineworkers and their families, and this alone highlights the importance of the anthracite industry to the Welsh immigrant experience in the city. Its significance goes deeper. Their involvement in the industry was complex and it had a number of direct, yet ambiguous, implications which extended far beyond the workplace. Like the blue scars which made miners instantly recognizable, the Welsh community itself bore the stamp of the industry which, to a large extent, had both created it and helped determine its nature. But the history of the Welsh in Scranton's anthracite industry is not only one of an intense involvement; it is also one of dramatic desertion. By the end of the century the store and the office, not the coalface, had become the primary Welsh male occupational experience. Anthracite may have lingered in the faces of some Welshmen, but the sense of identity

---

[1] Gibbons, loc. cit., p. 921.

and the communal cement which their relationship with anthracite had provided were lost, and with equally inescapable consequences.

I INDUSTRY AND SOCIETY

The Welsh community which had come into existence in Scranton by the early 1870s was then overwhelmingly a mining community. Although, in general, Welshmen, and to a much more limited extent unmarried Welsh women, worked in a wide range of occupations in the city, at this time the majority of Welsh males were mineworkers. The mines were an exclusively male preserve – as far as is known, unlike the coalfields of Wales, female labour was not at all employed in the north-east Pennsylvania anthracite industry. A high percentage of Welsh mineworkers were miners. The city directories of the 1870s reveal the striking frequency with which male heads of households with Welsh names were listed as miners, a large percentage of whom lived in Hyde Park. *Webb's Scranton Directory* of 1870–1, for example, illustrates this pattern with an almost thunderous monotony. Out of the 163 of those listed under Davis, fifty-two were miners living in Hyde Park, and most of the remainder were either miners or mine labourers.[2] The impression that a large number of Welsh males in Scranton at this time were miners is more than confirmed by the returns of the 1870 Manuscript Census and by qualitative evidence culled from newspaper reports and obituaries. A recent study of Welsh and Irish immigrant families in Scranton found that in 1880 nearly 45 per cent of the heads of Welsh households in the city were contract miners.[3]

As well as being miners or labourers, Welshmen occupied a wide variety of other jobs in the industry, both above and below ground. The pay rolls of the largest coal operator in the area, the D.L. & W., show that the company employed Welsh engineers, draughtsmen, foremen, carpenters, bricklayers, platemen, door boys, mule drivers, slate pickers and general helpers. Among the

[2] *Webb's Scranton Directory*, 1870–1.
[3] John E. Bodnar, 'Socialization and adaptation: immigrant families in Scranton, 1880–1890', *Pennsylvania History*, XVIII, No. 2 (April 1976), pp. 147–62 (especially 150).

twenty-six on its sundry pay roll in January 1870 were four Welsh machinists, two Welsh weighmasters and a Welsh chainman. In the company's Boston mine that same month, apart from a number of miners, there were Welsh runners, headmen, rockmen and platemen, whilst David Thomas and John Davis, helped by a James Thomas, were building a ventilation furnace underground. On the surface, slate boss Charles R. Edwards had at least seven Welsh slate-pickers under his command.[4]

The Boston mine's Welsh slate-pickers illustrate that the anthracite industry also provided employment for Welsh boys as well as men. Although it was illegal for boys under the age of twelve to work underground, there was no prohibition regarding the age of the 'breaker boys' who were employed to remove any slate in the mined coal.[5] Many Welsh families sought extra income by sending sons and, as we shall see later, daughters, out to work at an early age, in some cases as early as six years old, and ages were often falsified for this purpose.[6] John Bodnar has calculated that 17 per cent of Welsh males in Scranton during the late nineteenth century started work before they were ten years old, and, remarkably, 100 per cent of them did so when they were in the eleven–fifteen age group.[7] Initially employed on the surface, Welsh boys would later take on jobs underground, either as door boys or mule drivers, until eventually they become labourers and then miners in their own right.[8] The tendency of Welsh sons to follow their fathers' calling was almost universal and it is one of the most striking aspects of the picture of Scranton's Welsh families which emerges from the 1870 Manuscript Census. The familial nature of the Welsh mining connection in the city is symbolized by the family of Thomas Powell, a Welsh miner in ward 1. Both his sons were also employed in the mines: eighteen-year-old Joseph was a miner, whilst Robert, aged twelve, was a door boy.[9]

[4] Pay roll, Jan. 1870, Delaware, Lackawanna and Western Railroad Co. (Coal Department) Papers, Lackawanna Historical Society, Scranton (hereafter D.L. & W. Papers).
[5] Berthoff, 'Social order', p. 278. See also Francis H. Nichols, 'The children of the coal shadow', *McLure's*, XIX (February 1902–3), pp. 435–44, and Miller and Sharpless, op. cit., pp. 121–5.
[6] Gibbons, loc. cit., p. 921; Bodnar, loc. cit., pp. 159–61. See also below, pp. 46–7.
[7] Bodnar, loc. cit., p. 160.
[8] Roberts, op. cit., p. 166.
[9] U.S. Manuscript Census, Scranton, 1870.

Mining, therefore, was a family tradition among the Welsh in Scranton, a fact which emphasizes their marked degree of occupational homogeneity, the extent of their concentration in the anthracite industry and the scale of their dependence on that industry as a source of employment. But the nature of their involvement was more complex because, paradoxically, it revolved around the theme of domination as well as subservience. If a large number of Welsh workers in Scranton relied on the mining industry for a livelihood, so too did it, in turn, rely on them. This enabled them to exercise a marked degree of control within it and to occupy a privileged position amongst its overwhelmingly immigrant workforce. The contribution that Welsh skilled labour at the coalface made to Scranton's growth as 'Anthracite Capital of the World' is inestimable. The necessity of that skill for the smooth running of the local industry influenced the actions of employers even on those occasions – as during the 1871 strike – when their large army of Welsh miners appeared to be a mixed blessing.[10] The industry also offered wider opportunities for economic and social advancement, influence and status, for, beyond their labour, the coal companies in Scranton also leaned heavily on the Welsh for managerial and supervisory personnel. In fact, Welshmen enjoyed a near-monopoly of such positions of power and responsibility. This was a marked feature of the Welsh involvement in the industry from the beginning, and it was the most influential factor which determined Welsh domination. It also had a decisive impact on other aspects of Welsh immigrant life and on relations between the Welsh and other ethnic groups.

In Scranton the Welsh were strongly represented in all ranks of supervisory or managerial positions in the mines: as superintendents, inside and outside foremen, and fire-bosses.[11] *Webb's Scranton Directory* of 1870–1 lists three Welsh superintendents, at least ten Welsh inside foremen and many more Welsh fire bosses. Nearly all of these officials lived in Hyde

---

[10] See below, pp. 51–73.
[11] The chain of command in a mine began with the superintendent, who had overall responsibility for running it day to day. Below him were the inside and outside foremen, who were in charge of underground and surface operations respectively. The inside foreman was usually in charge of around two hundred men, among them a number of assistants known as fire-bosses, depending on the size of the mine. Roberts, op. cit., pp. 88–9. For a full account of the duties of these officials see ibid., ch. 5, *passim*.

Park. Moreover, if a mine had a Welsh superintendent or inside foreman, then invariably some of the fire bosses were of the same nationality. At the D.L. & W.'s Oxford mine in 1870, for example, the inside foreman was a John L. Lewis, and among his fire bosses was an Edward Lewis.[12]

A high Welsh representation at supervisory level was a feature common to the whole of the anthracite region and, indeed, to most of the coalfields in the United States.[13] In Scranton, however, the Welsh penetration into important positions in the industry went beyond the mines themselves; Welshmen also occupied some of the key positions in the most powerful coal company in the area, the D.L. & W. Throughout the late nineteenth century, the D.L. & W.'s central office had a distinctly 'Welsh' flavour. During that time the company's general inside superintendent was Benjamin F. Hughes, and between 1872 and 1889 his assistant was Thomas D. Davies. The company's chief engineer, Henry D. Phillips, was also Welsh, and a quartet of influential Hyde Park Welshmen was completed by Phillips's assistant, Richard Evans.[14]

The prominent Welsh presence in the higher echelons of the D.L. & W. was forcefully demonstrated during the events which followed Thomas D. Davies's resignation in 1889. Before his appointment as Hughes's assistant, Davies had been the inside foreman at the Bellevue mine, and in 1889 he left the company in order to take charge of the New York and Scranton Coal Co.'s interests in Forest City and Peckville to the north-east of Scranton, and to supervise the opening of new mines in the Schuylkill coalfield by a syndicate from Baltimore and Philadelphia.[15] His departure led to a great deal of speculation in Scranton as a whole, and particularly in Hyde Park, as to who would be his replacement. It was rumoured in the press that his successor would be John T. Williams, at the time a joint partner in Williams and Co. General Stores on Main Avenue, Hyde Park. Although no longer in the mines, Williams had for many years been an inside foreman with the company and had also represented the county in Harrisburg and been responsible for

[12] *Webb's Scranton Directory*, 1870–1; pay roll, 1870, D.L. & W. Papers.
[13] *Drych*, 27 Apr. 1871; Berthoff, *British Immigrants*, p. 54.
[14] Pay roll, 1870, 1880, D.L. & W. Papers; *Scranton Republican*, 5 Dec. 1889.
[15] *Scranton Republican*, 5 Dec. 1889.

the passing of the Free Props Act. However, it was Thomas H. Phillips, then foreman at the Storrs mine and an ex-superintendent of mines with the Jermyn Coal Co., who eventually assumed Davies's mantle.[16] Nor was he the last addition to the D.L. & W.'s 'Welsh' dynasty. By 1898 Colonel Reese A. Phillips, the inside foreman at the Oxford mine, had become Hughes's assistant and he, in turn, became general inside superintendent on Hughes's death in 1900. The Colonel's success marked the culmination of a breathtaking rise through the ranks, which had begun with his employment as a door boy.[17]

In his study of the anthracite miners during the late nineteenth century, Harold Aurand suggests that the miners' opportunities for gaining promotion in the industry were limited because of the relatively small number of supervisory and managerial positions which were available.[18] In this context the success rate of the Welsh in the Scranton area becomes even more remarkable, and it immediately poses the question of why the Welsh were able to secure a high representation in such positions. Undoubtedly, the mining skill of the Welsh was an important asset. Knowledge of mining and its practices, in most cases acquired in the south Wales coal industry, ensured that many Welshmen were among the foremost authorities on coal in the north-east Pennsylvania coalfield. Thomas D. Davies, for example, was once described by the *Scranton Republican* as a man 'whose equal as a mining expert can hardly be found in the anthracite regions'.[19] There is evidence to suggest, however, that the almost apostolic succession of the Welsh to important positions in the mines, and particularly in the D.L. & W., was not only the result of their expertise but also of a factor which permeated the whole Welsh involvement: favouritism.

If the Welsh occupied a privileged position in the industry, they equally took advantage of it to further the interests of their own nationality and to perpetuate their own dominance. The

[16] Ibid., 23 Dec. 1889, 8 Oct. 1890.
[17] *Druid*, 6 June 1907. For biographical details of Col. Reese A. Phillips (1863–1922), see ibid., 6 June 1907, 22 Aug. 1922.
[18] Harold W. Aurand, *From the Molly Maguires to the United Mine Workers: The Social Ecology of an Industrial Union, 1869–1897* (Philadelphia, 1971), pp. 55–8.
[19] *Scranton Republican*, 5 Dec. 1889.

general agent of the D.L. & W. in Scranton, W. R. Storrs, told his New York superior, Sam Sloan, that the Welsh 'are clannish and the best places at their disposal are given to their friends'.[20] In general, their discrimination was condoned and the impression is that the Welsh were given a free hand in the day-to-day running of the industry's underground operations. Mine labourers of other nationalities often voiced accusations that the coal companies actually colluded with Welsh foremen and Welsh miners to prevent them from securing jobs as miners.[21] The tendency towards favouritism among the Welsh manifested itself at all levels in the industry, and it began at the very top of the Welsh mining fraternity's hierarchy with the man who was responsible for all the D.L. & W.'s underground appointments, Benjamin Hughes, the doyen of Scranton's Welsh mine supervisory 'élite'.

Benjamin Hughes (1824–1900) was one of the most important men in late-nineteenth-century Scranton, and undoubtedly the most important Welshman. A leading figure in Hyde Park's political, cultural and commercial life, his influence was ultimately a consequence of the powerful position he occupied in the D.L. & W. Hughes was born in Brynmawr, Breconshire, in 1824, the son of a foreman at the Nantyglo Ironworks. He emigrated to the United States in 1848. In 1855, after working as a miner in Pottsville for seven years, he became superintendent of the D.L. & W.'s Diamond mine in Hyde Park, and ten years later he was appointed as that company's general inside superintendent, the second most important position in the industry throughout the Lackawanna Valley. As such, he was in charge of underground operations in all the D.L. & W.'s mines, which by 1890 included responsibility for around 7,000 men. Hughes's mining credentials were impeccable: widely regarded as the foremost expert on mining in the north-east Pennsylvania coalfield, he was a member of the American Institute of Mining Engineers and served on the Pennsylvania Board of Examiners for mine inspectors.[22]

Throughout his life Hughes dedicated himself to furthering the interests of his countrymen, particularly in the mining

[20] W. R. Storrs to Sam Sloan, 21 Aug. 1871, D.L. & W. Papers.
[21] Scranton *Morning Republican*, 11 May 1871.
[22] Ebenezer Edwards, op. cit., pp. 406–7; *Portrait and Biographical Record*, op. cit., pp. 185–6; Bob Owen, *Bywgraffiadau Cymry Americanaidd* (n.p., 1960), p. 55.

industry. He was in many ways the father of the Welsh community in Scranton since he actively recruited Welsh miners to the city and provided them with jobs.[23] He was also largely responsible for setting up the Welsh Philosophical Society, which was a training ground for Welsh mining supervisors.[24] There seems to be little doubt that Hughes was personally responsible for the large number of Welsh officials in the D.L. & W. (particularly in its key positions), who were more often than not close friends who mirrored his involvement in all aspects of the life of the wider community.[25] Such was his devotion to ensuring that the Welsh maintained their predominant position in the company's hierarchy that he often wrote to his subordinates in the Welsh language, especially regarding misdemeanours on their part which he did not wish the company and his superior, W. R. Storrs, to know about. In November 1897, for example, he wrote to S. D. Phillips, a superintendent at one of the D.L. & W.'s mines:

> A word in Welsh to you and in the utmost secrecy. In short, I heard one of the officers talking about you in this way: He might be a good man, but he seems a little too lenient. He does not see that his orders are carried out strictly ... I am telling you this so that you can be more careful in future ... Take this as brotherly advice and do not make a fuss about it, then perhaps you will be here after I have left this position.[26]

The Welsh also practised favouritism in the mines themselves. Welsh inside foremen were notorious for granting the best places in the mine to their friends and to miners of their own nationality in general. These practices created widespread resentment among mineworkers of other nationalities, which was perhaps only to be expected. The significance of the activities of Welsh mine bosses, however, is more complex, since their discrimination was inextricably related to a much wider demonology: their general reputation for being of low character and for running tyrannical regimes in the mines and oppressing

---

[23] Berthoff, 'The Welsh', p. 1012.
[24] See below, ch. 3, pp. 95–6.
[25] Reese A. Phillips may well have been one D.L. & W. official who benefited from Hughes's preferences. Apparently, when he was a member of the company's Surveyors' Corps in the mid-1880s, he was personally hand-picked for promotion by Hughes. *Druid*, 6 June 1907.
[26] B. Hughes to S. D. Phillips, 30 Nov. 1897, D.L. & W. Papers.

the workers. This not only affected relations with other ethnic groups; it also created tensions among the Welsh themselves.

The duties of the inside foreman gave him power which could be either abused or respected. He was responsible for adjusting prices for extra work done in the mine, recording its progress, ordering supplies and working out aggregate expenses. His task was largely that of keeping production costs as low as possible, and this was done mainly by clamping down on the various allowances paid to the men for 'dead' work such as timbering and opening new headings. The zeal with which he pursued these duties and the manner he adopted whilst carrying them out depended on his own character and the pressure exerted on him by his superiors. In addition, the prevailing wage system which operated in the industry, whereby the prices paid for cutting coal varied according to the seam, further increased the foreman's power. This offered him the opportunity of exercising unfair choice when allocating the most lucrative stalls (known as chambers) in the mine.[27]

The evidence regarding the conduct and practices of Welsh mine bosses in Scranton – and indeed throughout the northeast Pennsylvania coalfield – is often inconclusive, contradictory and difficult to assess. In part this is because their activities were clandestine, and indications of malpractice usually emerge in personal testimonies (especially as in those of other nationalities) which naturally may have been biased or exaggerated. Also, the variable factor which ultimately governed the conduct of each Welsh inside foreman was the personality of the individual who actually held the position. Moreover, as E. J. Annwyl pointedly reminded the *Drych*'s readers in 1874, even if an angel from heaven came down to act as a boss, he would not be able to please everybody.[28]

There is, indeed, evidence to suggest that some Welsh foremen did treat their workmen fairly and, in turn, were liked and respected. There are numerous reports of workmen in Scranton giving gifts and tributes to Welsh bosses.[29] One example is what the *Scranton Republican* called the 'caning' of Howell Harris of Hyde Park on 11 April 1890. This occurred

[27] Roberts, op. cit., pp. 89, 116–18; Moore, loc. cit., p. 150.
[28] *Drych*, 19 Feb. 1874.
[29] See, for example, ibid., 1 Sept. 1871, 6 Jan. 1876.

when the miners and employees at the D.L. & W.'s Diamond mine presented him with a gold cane, following his resignation as assistant foreman in order to become the inside superintendent at Connell and Co.'s new Lackawanna mine. Apparently every workman had contributed to the fund and the whole affair was 'splendid proof of Mr. Harris' popularity as a foreman'.[30]

Yet individual exceptions notwithstanding, the weight of the evidence suggests that the unenviable popular reputation of Welsh mine foremen was deserved. Many of them did adopt an overbearing manner and discriminated widely against other nationalities in favour of their own. During the latter part of the 1871 strike in the city, Welsh foremen were singled out as special targets of hostility on the part of non-Welsh mineworkers, far more than the coal companies themselves. Resolutions condemning their activities were duly passed.[31] Irish labourers, especially, complained that even though a number of them had worked in the industry for many years, Welsh foremen had not granted them their own stalls, although newly arrived Welsh immigrant miners received stalls almost immediately. Apparently, Welsh foremen also adopted other 'tricks' to cheat labourers. These included holding a stall under another name and getting a labourer to work it. The foreman then pocketed the wages himself and paid the labourer only the customary one-third, despite the fact that the latter had done all the work.[32]

These practices prevailed throughout the anthracite region, and the discontent they engendered sometimes led to violent reprisals. Two of the victims of the Molly Maguires, and many more targets of their threats, were Welsh mine foremen. One, J. P. Jones, a foreman at the Lansford mine, was murdered in 1875 for blacklisting an Irishman.[33] Most of the Mollies' activities were confined to the Schuylkill coalfield. Nevertheless sufficient incidents took place in Scranton to suggest that the

[30] *Scranton Republican*, 11 Apr. 1890.
[31] See below, pp. 65–6.
[32] Scranton *Morning Republican*, 12, 13 May 1871.
[33] *Drych*, 12 Mar. 1885; Wayne G. Broehl Jr., *The Molly Maguires* (London, 1964), pp. 332, 333, 340, 342. The other Welsh mine foreman murdered by the Mollies was Morgan Powell of Summit Hill and formerly of Tredegar. The actual reason for his assassination in 1871 is not known, though in all probability it was as a direct result of his position. *Drych*, 21 Dec. 1871.

antagonisms created by the possible tyranny and discrimination of some Welsh mine officials could lead to retaliation against them. In 1872 a David Thomas was attacked and beaten up near Dickson's Works. It was a case of mistaken identity because the assailants' intended victim was Morgan Bowen, a mine superintendent and one of the pillars of the Hyde Park Welsh community.[34] In 1891 W. D. Thomas, the Greenwood mine's superintendent, was assaulted by a Michael King. Apparently, King had been sacked by Howell Brooks, the Welsh inside foreman, and Thomas had refused to give him his job back.[35]

The activities of Welsh mine foremen also created tensions among workers of their own nationality. In this respect the behaviour of mine bosses in terms of their own sense of ethnicity is ambiguous because, although many of them did favour their countrymen, they could be just as domineering in their attitudes towards Welsh miners as they were towards other nationalities. The character of Welsh mine bosses in the anthracite industry, and the attitudes of Welsh miners towards them, were often commented on in the press and elsewhere by Welsh observers from both within and outside the industry. These contributions generally acknowledged that emnity between Welsh supervisors and their subordinates did exist, although they expressed diverse opinions as to its causes.

In 1871 a correspondent to the *Drych* complained about the bitterness which Welshmen directed at those of their own nationality who had risen to managerial positions in the mines, even though they were, by and large, hard-working and respectable.[36] In an eisteddfodic essay on the defects of the Welsh in America published the following year, H. M. Edwards maintained that one of the greatest of those defects was the lack of unity and co-operation between Welsh bosses and Welsh workers in the mining industry. He believed that envy drove many Welsh miners to disparage the achievement of their supervisors. Nevertheless he also acknowledged that Welsh bosses often forgot 'the rock from which they had been hewn' and took advantage of their positions to settle old scores.[37]

---

[34] Scranton *Morning Republican*, 13 Aug. 1872.
[35] *Drych*, 26 Feb. 1891.
[36] Ibid., 27 Apr. 1871.
[37] H. M. Edwards, 'Diffygion y genedl Gymreig yn America', *Y Glorian* (1872),

These sentiments were echoed by others. The Welsh-American bard 'Cuhelyn' informed the *Drych* in 1870 that he hoped the four Welshmen who had recently bought a mine in Schuylkill County would not forget that they too had been workers once.[38] Perhaps the most savage indictment of Welsh mine bosses was a long article entitled 'Oppressing the workers' by 'Hen Golier' of Ashland, Pennsylvania, which appeared in the *Drych* in 1885.[39]

In his article, 'Hen Golier' retold the events of the Molly Maguire murders. Though strongly condemnatory of the actions of the Irish, he was nevertheless of the opinion that they were to a certain extent understandable reactions to the almost feudal conduct of 'upstart bosses'. He maintained that some mine bosses – and he was clearly referring to Welsh ones – regarded men as being more expendable than mules, and treated them as such. The miners and labourers knew this and felt it to the core. Bosses behaved in a low-handed manner and were derisive of their former workmates, many of whom were more intelligent, more knowledgeable and of a higher character than themselves. On the whole, 'Hen Golier' thought it was not the most suitable men who became bosses; rather, it was those who were cheeky, rotten, and willing to oppress their fellow workers in order to please and make money for their masters. Many Welsh bosses belonged to chapels, yet they operated the most corrupt regimes and used the vilest possible language in the mines. They were full of their own self-importance:

> . . . they must be in the forefront in the chapel, in every committee, in every donation, in every festival and the better of every minister; and they are, of course, so knowledgeable, and so capable in their criticism that they can discuss, measure and weigh them all up. They do this at work, surrounded by a lot of men who must smile in appreciation, even though they are poking fun at their [i.e. the bosses'] behaviour in their hearts. I have had to listen to a boss in this way but there was no point in my saying anything derogatory, otherwise I would surely feel his displeasure in my work . . . Good people, are they not important men! While they are in command, bosses are often flattered by those who try and get a little something for themselves and their families . . . [but] no men are so disrespectful as those bosses who have lost their places.

pp. 15–20, 44–6, 85–7, 108–10, 118–19.
[38] *Drych*, 6 Jan. 1870.
[39] Ibid., 12 Mar. 1885.

Bosses, concluded 'Hen Golier', should remember that it was their duty to be respectful and gentlemanly towards the workers, who after all were the source of the wealth and success of the mining companies and who deserved as much consideration as the investors.[40]

As well as its graphic description of the management style of at least some Welsh mine bosses, perhaps the most significant aspect of the diatribe of 'Hen Golier' is its revelation that the power and the character of the bosses had wider implications. Their ability to either favour or to victimize those under their command, of whatever nationality, enabled them to demand – and receive – both deference and status not only in the mines themselves but in other aspects of the lives of mineworkers. Equally, although Welsh miners could undoubtedly benefit from the bosses' favouritism towards those of their own nationality, there was a price to be paid, and this could create tensions over and above those which could normally exist between boss and workman. Ultimately, the observations of 'Hen Golier' highlight one of the most important repercussions of the Welsh involvement in the anthracite industry in Scranton: the impact of the Welsh permeation of managerial and supervisory positions on the structure and daily life of the Welsh community as a whole.

In a community as dependent on the mining industry as Hyde Park was, those who achieved prominence in the industry inevitably secured the status and power to take a leading role in the commercial, political and cultural life of the Welsh immigrants and become the community's natural leaders. 'Many of the big men of the section in the last sixty-five years', declared Thomas Murphy in 1924, 'have been men of the mines'; and he singled out above all Benjamin Hughes and Col. Reese A. Phillips.[41] There is even evidence to suggest that the manner in which Welsh mine bosses ran Hyde Park was even more sinister and pervasive. In an article in the *Drych* in 1874 a Hyde Park Welshman, writing under the pseudonym 'Mwnwr', examined the nature of the relationship between bosses and workers as far as religion, cultural activities and commerce were concerned,

---

[40] Ibid.
[41] Murphy, *Hist. Hyde Park*, p. 24.

and concluded that Hyde Park was 'Slave Athens in Free America'.[42]

'Mwnwr' wondered whether the nature of daily life in Hyde Park was any less oppressive than that in south Wales, despite the fact that they were living in America, the land of freedom. Far more bosses patronized the Welsh Baptist Church than any other, and it was easier for a Baptist worker to get work with a Baptist boss than with a boss who belonged to another denomination. Congregationalist or Calvinistic Methodist bosses also preferred workers of their own denomination, the result being that mines often had a majority of workers who were members of one particular denomination. Every boss was also a mason, a clear message to those who wished to become bosses themselves. Nor were the cultural activities of the Welsh immigrants without a role in the 'system'. According to the author, the 1872 eisteddfod had failed miserably because it had become known as the eisteddfod of the bosses. The Welsh Philosophical Society was merely a meeting place where Welsh bosses commended and honoured each other. Those who were not bosses applauded all that was said, whatever the quality, an example of the servile attitude workers – Mwnwr himself included – adopted towards 'bossism'. As far as commerce was concerned, some bosses also ran, or were partners in, stores, and he cited examples. They had a guaranteed patronage:

> ... we are so slavish in our spirit and so very careful to keep the boss happy, and our wives, who get what the family needs from the store, are more careful than we are to keep him and his wife happy; the boss knows this as well as we do ... a worker [will] change the store he shops in because ... 'That's where the boss trades now' ... This is the freedom of America, or the freedom of the Welsh Athens of America! ... freedom for the boss to rule over us in work and in the town, and freedom for us to make him rich ... This is not fair, legal, and just ... for the workers ... I prefer the Company Store which is open to the world in its dealings, like our shop in Scranton, than the screws and the underhand, secret, cunning oppression we get in Hyde Park.[43]

It is difficult to come to any firm conclusions as to whether Mwnwr's accusations regarding the existence and extent of bossism in Hyde Park were justified. His is a personal testimony,

[42] *Drych*, 19 Mar. 1874.
[43] Ibid.

although he did insist in his article that workers and their families were all aware of the situation and it was a major talking-point. Certainly some of his assertions were accurate. The involvement of Welsh mine bosses in masonic orders and in the churches and cultural institutions of the Welsh in Hyde Park was very marked, and some were involved in commercial enterprises.[44] His condemnation of the bosses' oppression, and equally the workers' servility, is much harder to evaluate. His article did not evoke any responses in the *Drych*, but on other occasions allegations regarding Welsh 'bossism' in Scranton were discussed in its columns. Again, however, these controversies expressed diverging opinions and offered conflicting evidence. In August 1870, 'Gwaneglais', a miner at the Diamond mine in Hyde Park, alleged that many of the Welsh workers in the mine had been forced by the mine boss, Reese T. Evans, to take out subscriptions to *Baner America* 'through the instrument of the screw'. Evans was apparently a shareholder in the paper.[45] These accusations were vehemently denied by other correspondents. One, 'Llais y Lluaws' ('The Voice of the Majority' – the name may or may not be significant), declared: 'Is it that alien concept "screwing" if a supervisor goes round with someone else to collect money or names for a chapel, or a poor widow, or a college or a paper?'[46] Another, 'Undebwr', asserted that Welsh workers had far too independent a spirit to take notice of any attempt at a 'screw', if indeed one existed.[47] In yet another response, a David Crouk maintained that one of the reasons for the large number of Welsh saloons in Scranton was that those who had been victimized by the bosses had little hope of alternative employment beyond opening taverns.[48]

Ultimately, perhaps, what one person saw as reasonable could be interpreted by another as oppression. Yet these controversies do demonstrate that Welsh mine bosses held

---

[44] In a letter to Sam Sloan in 1871 W. R. Storrs acknowledged the importance of the Welsh churches as a breeding ground for mine officials. See below, pp. 55–6. In his study of the anthracite industry written at the turn of the century, Peter Roberts stated that foremen or their relatives sometimes opened their own 'company' stores. This system was generally frowned upon, and complaints usually resulted in the foreman being transferred elsewhere. Roberts, op. cit., pp. 136–7.
[45] *Drych*, 11, 18 Aug. 1870.
[46] Ibid., 1 Sept. 1870.
[47] Ibid., 10 Nov. 1870.
[48] Ibid., 18 Aug. 1870.

powerful positions in Welsh society in Scranton, and this alone could create tensions among their own nationality. Welsh bosses may actively have tried – successfully or unsuccessfully – to abuse their power and exploit men and women of their own nationality. Certainly, given the tendencies towards favouritism that did exist, Welsh miners were aware of the possibilities that the friendship of, and deference to, their Welsh mine superiors could open up – whether they chose to act upon it or not.

The existence of a Welsh supervisory élite in Scranton, and its wider implications, is but one major area where the complex nature of the Welsh involvement in the anthracite industry directly affected the wider community. To the rank and file Welsh miners, their wives and children, who formed the majority of Scranton's Welsh population, other features of their involvement equally influenced their daily lives and the character of their community. Their citizenship of the 'Kingdom of Coal' determined that their existence was insecure and precarious, and in many ways the fortunes of the whole Welsh community fluctuated with those of the industry.[49] Welsh mining families had to accommodate to the constant threat of death or injury at work and the possibility of hardship because of slumps, irregular wages and intermittent working days. These were a universal experience in all mining families, regardless of nationality, and they also contributed greatly to the Welsh community's societal cohesion and reinforced its sense of shared ethnicity.

Nevertheless, the complexities and ambiguities of the Welsh involvement at a higher level in the industry were also echoed in the daily experience of the rank and file Welsh miner. Whilst the Welsh shared with other nationalities a susceptibility to the vagaries of mining, they occupied a privileged position and took advantage of it. This had profound implications for inter-ethnic group relations, since the job classification underground was also drawn along ethnic lines. The resentment created by Welsh

[49] The phrase is derived from Miller and Sharpless, op. cit. For a study of a mining community in the Southern anthracite coalfield and its relationship with the industry see Anthony F. C. Wallace, *St. Clair: A Nineteenth-Century Coal Town's Experience with a Disaster-Prone Industry* (New York, 1987). See also the various essays in David L. Salay (ed.), *Hard Coal, Hard Times: Ethnicity and Labor in the Anthracite Region* (Scranton, 1984).

dominance of the industry conflicted with the common bond which existed between all mineworkers and, paradoxically, it further strengthened the ethnic dimension which underpinned the relationship between the Welsh and anthracite. As well as uniting the workforce, the prevailing practices and conditions of work within the industry could also divide.

Mining was a dangerous occupation and many a Welsh immigrant's hopes for a better life came to an abrupt and premature end in the mines. The Welsh community suffered greatly from the real price of coal, especially during those years when its involvement was at its most intense. For all mineworkers, Welsh and non-Welsh alike, the constant threat of death or injury at work was a strong unifying force which countered ethnic barriers, the demarcation of skill, and even the division between boss and workman. The fear that a mineworker who left for work in the morning might not return in the evening was a daily experience, collectively endured and collectively shared. This scenario was in fact the subject of one of the most popular ballads among the Welsh in north-east Pennsylvania: 'The Miner's Doom', sung to the tune of 'Adieu to Cambria'. The ballad describes the death of a miner in a shaft accident and contrasts the happiness of his family home as he goes to work with its sorrow in the aftermath of the tragedy.[50] Episodes such as the one described by the ballad were common, and they add a macabre ring to the advertisement which Charles Laramy, a furniture seller and coffin maker in the Schuylkill coalfield, placed in the *Drych* in the early 1870s. He announced that he would be pleased to see his fellow-Welsh call on him, and he thanked them for the support he had already received.[51] There were three Welsh funeral directors in Hyde Park during the late nineteenth century;[52] many of their fellow-Welsh were forced to call on their services in September 1869, following the Avondale mine disaster.

Although the mine was situated in Plymouth, near Wilkes-Barre, Avondale was as much a tragedy for Scranton as it was

[50] George Korson, *Minstrels of the Mine Patch: Songs and Stories of the Anthracite Industry* (Philadelphia, 1938), pp. 108, 203.
[51] *Drych*, 6 Jan. 1870.
[52] *Webb's Scranton Directory*, 1870–1; *Williams' Scranton Directory*, 1890.

for the immediate area. It was also, as Ellis Roberts has correctly described it, a 'Welsh' tragedy.[53] Nearly all of the 108 victims were Welsh, many of them newly arrived. Around sixty of them lived in Scranton, and their bodies were buried in the Washburn Street Cemetery in Hyde Park, watched by a stunned community. Many of the gravestones – some of granite specially imported from Pembrokeshire – are inscribed in the Welsh language. The appalling loss of life occurred when a fire in the shaft set the breaker immediately above it alight. Like all mines at that time, Avondale had no second exit, and those below ground suffered an agonizing death from gas and suffocation. On that fateful day, at least, there was no delineation between foreman, miner or labourer, for Evan Hughes, the inside foreman and Benjamin Hughes's brother, died along with his subordinates.[54] So, too, did the 'two Welshmen brave', who

> ... without dismay
> And courage without fail
> Went down the shaft, without delay
> In the mines of Avondale.[55]

In a selfless action, which well illustrates both the courage of the miners and their solidarity in the face of common danger and adversity in the mines, Thomas W. Williams and David Jones had gone down the shaft to see if anyone was still alive. They did not return.[56]

The Avondale disaster stands as the most obvious reminder – if one were ever needed – of how dangerous was the industry on which the community relied, and how high the price of that dependence could be. Even so, despite its horror, it gives only a partial impression, for the anthracite seams of north-east Pennsylvania claimed their revenge far more in single, daily incidents than in the headline-grabbing cataclysms which contemporary newspapers reported with an almost lavish glee.

---

[53] Ellis W. Roberts, *When the Breaker Whistle Blows: Mining Disasters and Labor Leaders in the Anthracite Region* (Scranton, 1984), p. 7. As a result of the disaster, the Welsh Baptist Church in Edwardsville lost all but three of its male members and there were as many widows in Wales as in the U.S.A. For an account of the Avondale disaster see ibid., pp. 7–15.
[54] Scranton *Morning Republican*, 11 Sept. 1869.
[55] Stanza from the anthracite mining ballad 'The Avondale Mine Disaster', in Korson, op. cit., p. 190. For a full discussion of anthracite ballads relating to Avondale see ibid., pp. 180–2, 188–91.
[56] Scranton *Morning Republican*, 11 Sept. 1869.

Deaths from roof falls, especially, dotted the newspaper columns and inspectors' reports – miners who were victims of the dreaded Wyoming carbonaceous shale, the 'man-killer' in local mining parlance.[57] Examples such as those of the Revd William B. Williams, who died as a result of a roof fall in Hyde Park's Continental mine on 10 October 1879, or of John Parry, formerly of Blaenafon, who suffered the same fate in another mine in Hyde Park a fortnight later, are almost without number.[58]

The possibility of injury or death because of mining was not confined to the mines themselves. Faulty early mining methods and the rapaciousness of the coalowners made Hyde Park highly susceptible to cave-ins caused by the collapse of old workings. Often these led to the destruction of houses and sometimes to the loss of life.[59] In November 1871 the *Miners' Journal* reported that the frequency of such occurrences was not making Hyde Park a very comfortable place to live in at that time.[60] The Welsh miner's wife, therefore, had not only to contend each working day with the possibility of widowhood or the loss of a son. There was also the chance that she herself and her younger children could suffer injury because most of her time was spent in the home.

Because of the scarcity of the evidence immediately available, little is known about the daily lives of Welsh miners' wives and daughters in Scranton, and even less about their thoughts and priorities. In 1880 only 4 per cent of Welsh wives in Scranton were in paid work outside the home. Although job opportunities for women were limited in comparison to those for men, some were available in Scranton's textile industry.[61] Daughters, like sons, were sent out to work at a young age. In 1880, 15 per cent of Welsh girls aged between six and ten were in employment, though unfortunately we have no evidence regarding the place

[57] Roberts, op. cit., p. 163. See also Perry K. Blatz, 'Ever-shifting ground: work and labor relations in the anthracite coal industry, 1868–1903' (unpublished Princeton University Ph.D. Thesis, 1987), pp. 275–318.
[58] *Tarian y Gweithiwr*, 29 Oct., 28 Nov. 1879.
[59] Murphy, *Hist. Hyde Park*, pp. 423–7. Ironically, cave-ins also provided jobs for Welshmen. A number of Welsh craftsmen worked in the 'cave gangs' which coal companies employed to repair damage caused by subsidence. Ex inf. Mrs Ceinwen Hughes, Hyde Park, whose husband worked in one of the cave gangs.
[60] Pottsville *Miners' Journal*, 18 Nov. 1871.
[61] Bodnar loc. cit., p. 161. See also Pamela Kneller, 'Welsh immigrant women as wage earners in Utica, New York', *Llafur*, 5, No. 4 (1991), pp. 71–8.

or nature of their work. In the same year 30 per cent of girls between eleven and fifteen and 80 per cent of those between sixteen and twenty were in employment, presumably in the textile mills and domestic service.[62] To mining families, income earned by daughters was as essential as that from sons. Paid work, however, was the preserve of single women before marriage; once married, they looked after the house.

The impression from the evidence that does exist is that the experience of Welsh miners' wives in Scranton was very similar to that of their countrywomen in the coalfields of Wales.[63] Phoebe Gibbons recorded in 1877 that miners' wives 'generally hold the purse. As soon as he gets his pay and his fill of beer, the miner hands his wages over to his wife who acts as treasurer with much discretion, making all the purchases of the house and transacting the business of the family.'[64] She quoted the testimony of one miner's wife who told her:

> My husband is a good workman. He never lost any time by drinking or anything like that. I nearly supported the family by my own sewing and taking boarders. Ever since I have been married I tried to keep our own table, and could generally do it unless I was sick. I most always had a good deal of my own way, but I always consulted him. He always gives me his wages. I think when a man gives his wife his wages she feels more interest. I'd kick up a big fuss if he did not give me his wages.[65]

Gibbons also reported that it was the women who prepared the mineworkers' baths and was of the opinion that 'the Welsh woman is ambitious for her husband's shoes to shine . . . and she blacks the shoes of all the family . . . until the girls are old enough to relieve her.' Shining shoes was apparently something that American-born girls refused to do.[66]

It seems, then, that the Welsh miner's wife in Scranton managed the family economy, cleaned the house and clothing, prepared food, kept the family intact and bore more wage earners: Welsh women in Scranton often bore up to eight or nine

---

[62] Bodnar, loc. cit., pp. 158–9, 161.
[63] Angela V. John, 'A miner struggle? Women's protests in Welsh mining history', *Llafur*, 4, No. 1 (1984), pp. 72–90; Dot Jones 'Counting the cost of coal: women's lives in the Rhondda 1881–1911', and Deirdre Beddoe, 'Munitionettes, maids and mams: women in Wales, 1914–1939', in Angela V. John (ed.), *Our Mothers' Land: Chapters in Welsh Women's History 1830–1939* (Cardiff, 1991), pp. 109–33, 189–209.
[64] Gibbons, loc. cit., p. 920.
[65] Ibid.
[66] Ibid.; Berthoff, 'The Welsh', p. 1014.

children.⁶⁷ As recent studies of women in the south Wales mining valleys have emphasized,⁶⁸ she was confined to the home and segregated from the workplace and productive process. The domestic sphere was the sole province where she had influence or authority. But that authority was limited. Even though Welsh miners' wives in Scranton held the traditional responsibility for managing the family budget, they did not have real control. As Angela John has pointed out, not only was the miner's wife dependent on her husband declaring most of his earnings, but both miner and wife, and the whole family, were also bound by external forces which were determined by the mining industry.⁶⁹ Welsh mining families in Scranton suffered hardship not only because of death, injury or cave-ins, but there were also other aspects of employment in the anthracite industry which brought about the same result.

The anthracite industry was susceptible to slumps, and during the late 1860s and 1870s it experienced a prolonged depression which created much hardship throughout the anthracite region.⁷⁰ In February 1875 *Tarian y Gweithiwr* reported that times were very hard for many Welsh families in Hyde Park, and in some cases families of seven or more had no bread in the house.⁷¹ By June of the following year the 'terrible' poverty in Hyde Park was causing anxiety because apparently all were now in the same circumstances. Meetings were being held to organize appeals for help.⁷² Even during times of relative prosperity regular employment and wages were by no means guaranteed because of two inherent characteristics of the industry: short-time working and the chaotic wages system.

Intermittent working in the anthracite industry was largely caused by the seasonal nature of demand. In this respect, winter was a far more consistent period of employment than the summer months.⁷³ During the summer of 1889, for example, the Hyde Park, Continental and Archbald mines were on a four-day week.⁷⁴ Between 1875 and 1899, around 36 per cent of the

---

⁶⁷ Gibbons, loc. cit., p. 920; Bodnar, loc. cit., p. 161.
⁶⁸ Angela John, loc. cit.; Beddoe, loc. cit..
⁶⁹ Angela John, loc cit., p. 75.
⁷⁰ Aurand, op. cit., pp. 67–8.
⁷¹ *Tarian y Gweithiwr*, 26 Feb. 1875.
⁷² *Drych*, 22 June 1876.
⁷³ Blatz, op. cit., pp. 194–274; Roberts, op. cit., pp. 120–2.
⁷⁴ *Scranton Republican*, 11 July 1889.

maximum possible working days in the industry were lost through short-time working, effectively causing a wage loss of similar percentage to the mineworkers. The Welsh miners' wages were often irregular because of the system of payment which prevailed in the industry. Welsh contract miners – the bulk of the Welsh workforce – were employed on a piece-rate system, and their wages fluctuated with the amount of coal cut. This in turn varied according to the seam and even the chambers in which they worked (their relationship with the foreman was often of some importance here), and their own individual skill. Moreover deductions from the miners' wages for tools, oil and powder and the allowances paid to them for dead work varied considerably.[75]

Nevertheless, the working conditions of Welsh miners, like all miners in the industry, were better than those of other, less skilled workers underground. As contract miners, they were the highest-paid and they could often exercise a great deal of independence in the way they organized their work.[76] Besides, they worked fewer hours in the mine. Each miner had a labourer to load the cut coal, for which the latter received one-third of the former's wages. This 'villainous system of labour', as one Welshman described it in the 1870s, bred great inequalities. Whereas the miner normally went home after about six hours in the mine, having cut enough coal during that time, the labourer had to remain behind to fill the trams and could work up to twelve or fifteen hours each day.[77] The large amount of leisure time which Welsh miners had at their disposal enabled many to pursue educational courses in order to gain better positions. A Scranton Welsh newspaper editor – probably W. S. Jones of *Baner America* – told Phoebe Gibbons that when he worked in a Carbondale mine, he had usually finished his day's work by noon. He used his afternoons to write essays for eisteddfod competitions.[78]

The inequality between the workload, the duration of working hours and the wages of miners and labourers alone created great resentment on the part of the latter. The

[75] Roberts, op. cit., pp. 102–8, 121.
[76] Aurand, op. cit., p. 33.
[77] *Gwladgarwr*, 16 Dec. 1873, quoted and translated in Conway, *The Welsh in America*, p. 193; *Drych*, 3 Mar. 1870.
[78] Gibbons, loc. cit., p. 922.

antagonisms between the two groups of workers were exacerbated by the ethnic division of the workforce, which coincided with the demarcation of skill. The miners in Scranton were largely Welsh, English and Scottish; the labourers were predominantly Irish and, to a lesser extent, German. To the Irish labourers especially, the relatively privileged status of the Welsh miner, coupled with the possibility of his gaining preferential treatment, reinforced the perception of Welsh domination and oppression in Scranton's anthracite industry. During the 1871 strike an Irish labourer in Hyde Park described the experiences which led him to conclude that the Welsh miners of that section were tyrannical:

> When I worked in Hyde Park, I was not only obliged to do my own work but the greater part of that miner that hired me. It was John or Pat or Jacob or Hans 'give me the drill, the scraper, the needle, the wedge; go get some tamping and then help me tamp the hole'. This I was expected to do after drilling four out of five feet of hole, while he was sitting down talking to some of his neighbouring miners, while we poor devils innocently believed him to be preparing a cartridge to be put in the hole that we had to drill, and when there was enough coal cut, no matter how hard or how long the labourer had to work, Mr. Welshman put on his coat and went home to enjoy himself in the bosom of his family, cultivate his mind if he felt so disposed or engage in any other amusement. And we get a nominal one-third of the sum total, whilst we performed nine-tenths of the sum total of work.[79]

It was not only the actual conditions of work which galled the labourers. Being unskilled, they were in a far more vulnerable position and susceptible to the will of Welsh miners as well as of foremen. Like the latter, Welsh miners sometimes discriminated against Irish labourers in favour of their own nationality. Usually, a newly arrived Welsh immigrant miner would first labour for a friend or a relation before getting a stall of his own. To accommodate newcomers, Welsh miners occasionally ejected their Irish helpers. In April 1874, for example, Reese T. Williams, a Scranton Welsh miner, was arrested for assault and battery on Austin Keating, his Irish labourer, with intent to kill. Williams had apparently told Keating that he was no longer required, as Williams wanted the job for a friend of his. The

---

[79] Scranton *Morning Republican*, 11 May 1871.

Irishman refused, whereupon Williams set off a charge in his face, sending him into fits. Williams and some of his fellow Welsh miners then proceeded to pelt him with coal. He narrowly escaped. When he later returned to the mine, he was again assaulted by Williams and his friends, and would probably have been killed had not a German intervened.[80]

The Scrantonian anthracite industry, therefore, was a vortex of conflicting forces and tensions which could both unite and divide mineworkers along lines of skill and ethnicity. Because of the concentration of the Welsh in the industry, with its contradictory interplay of privilege and subservience, these ambiguities extended into their community in general. The powerful yet ambiguous implications of the nature of their involvement prevailed at all times to help determine the attitudes of the Welsh in the city. Yet it is only in the revelation of episodes or 'moments' that we can fully understand all the complexities of their experience. There was one key event in the history of the Welsh mining community in Scranton which, in action, laid bare this confusion of factors and forces: the 'Welsh strike' of 1871.

II THE 'WELSH STRIKE' OF 1871

In December 1870 the miners in the Northern anthracite coalfield went on strike in protest against a 30 per cent wage cut. This was the latest in a series of reductions they had suffered during the previous five years as a result of the severe crisis in the anthracite industry at that time. During the Civil War between 1861 and 1865, wages had quadrupled because of the increased demand for coal and the labour shortage caused by miners enlisting in the Union armies (among them Company G., 77th Regiment, composed of Welsh miners from Scranton). After the war, however, demand dropped, and demobilization, immigration and cuts in production created a labour surplus. The end of the boom plunged the industry into a prolonged depression, which exacerbated its inherent defects of over-production and over-investment and forced the coal companies to cut back costs. The crisis was further worsened by a polarization of relations between capital and labour due to the

[80] Pottsville *Miners' Journal*, 17 Apr. 1874.

growth of corporate control of ownership and of unionism to counter it.[81]

The striking miners in the Northern coalfield succeeded in persuading the leadership of the anthracite mineworkers' union, the Workingmen's Benevolent Association, to call a general strike throughout the north-east Pennsylvania coalfield. The miners in the other two regions failed to come out in support, and the focal point of the strike quickly became the Scranton area, where the strikers faced the united opposition of the three so-called 'Scranton' companies, the D.L. & W., the D. & H. and the Pennsylvania Coal Co. Here the miners held out until the end of May in an attempt to maintain their wage-rates and to secure the 'basis', a system whereby wages rose or fell according to the price of coal (similar to the 'sliding scale' which operated in the coal industry in south Wales during the late nineteenth century). Repeated attempts at arbitration foundered, and the miners were forced to accept the lower rate of wages and return to work without the basis.[82]

Initially, the Welsh miners in Scranton were apparently reluctant to go on strike. Once they decided to do so, however, they were unanimously behind it and determined to stay out until a favourable settlement had been secured. Writing in 1877, Phoebe Gibbons was of the opinion that the 'leading Welshmen' would have preferred compromise, but were outvoted by 'the more reckless of their own nation'. Nevertheless, she also acknowledged that 'once engaged the Welsh were the most determined, being unwilling to yield until they had effected something,' and she went on to quote the recollections of some Welsh miners culled from the interviews she had conducted in the mid-1870s. One apparently told her: 'I believe they would have held out to this day,' whilst another stated, 'they would have emigrated: they had strong talk of going out West in squads.'[83] Many Welsh miners and their families did leave

[81] *Workingmen's Advocate* (Chicago), 10 Dec. 1870; Aurand, op. cit., pp. 9–19; George Ule Virtue, 'The anthracite coal combination', *Quarterly Journal of Economics*, X (Oct. 1895–July 1896), pp. 296–323; 'The true history of the coal trouble', *Nation*, XII (1871), pp. 152–4, 254–6.

[82] Aurand, op. cit., pp. 78–80. For accounts of the W.B.A. and of early unionism among the anthracite mineworkers see ibid., pp. 65–78; Roberts, op. cit., pp. 192–3; Marvin W. Schlegel, 'The Workingmen's Benevolent Association', *Pennsylvania History*, X (1943), pp. 243–67.

[83] Gibbons, loc. cit., pp. 925–6.

Scranton during the course of the strike. Most moved to the Schuylkill anthracite coalfield, where the miners remained in work, although some migrated to the West or even returned to Wales. Indeed, so large was the number of Welsh who left the area during the first three months of the strike alone that the *Scranton Republican* felt compelled to suggest that if the mines ever actually worked again, the amount of Welsh labour at hand would be greatly diminished.[84]

The determination and the solidarity of the Welsh miners who stayed in the city to fight it out with their employers were the principal reasons for the lengthy duration of the conflict. In their struggle they were aided by a number of factors, each of which reflected fundamental characteristics both of the Welsh miners themselves and of the wider Welsh community. To begin with, the Welsh miners had greater economic reserves to draw on than other mineworkers. They earned relatively higher incomes, and many had savings which they could use to sustain themselves in the event of a long stoppage. Moreover, as Phoebe Gibbons noted, the small gardens which characterized Welsh households also supplemented incomes, and these served as a cushion against hard times and during industrial disputes.[85]

Their role in the 1871 strike also demonstrated the strength of the Welsh miners' commitment to unionism. They dominated the local branch of the W.B.A. both at leadership and rank and file level, and during the dispute both the president and the secretary of the miners' strike committee in the city were Welshmen, John P. Lewis and Watkin H. Williams respectively.[86] The address of Thomas Watkins, one of the W.B.A's Welsh leaders, at a meeting of Hyde Park miners during a dispute two years earlier reflected the prominent part the Welsh played in the organization and their widespread support for it. He stated that it was always the Welsh who stood up to speak, and wished all nationalities to be heard.[87] Equally, the determination of the Welsh to stay out until a favourable settlement had been reached revealed the extent of their desire for the 'basis'. In this respect, their solidarity during 1871 was

[84] Scranton *Morning Republican*, 10 Mar. 1871; Berthoff, *British Immigrants*, p. 55.
[85] Gibbons, loc. cit., p. 926.
[86] Scranton *Morning Republican*, 10, 24 Mar., 18, 20 May 1871.
[87] Wilkes-Barre *Record of the Times*, 1 Sept. 1869.

not a new phenomenon. Two years earlier, W. R. Storrs of the D.L. & W. informed his company's New York office: 'Our Hyde Park miners, particularly the Welshmen, are very firm for the basis. They say the companies must yield.'[88] The prominent role the Welsh played in the W.B.A. and in the 1871 strike did lead to charges that they were 'a class notorious for their striking propensities'.[89] (This accusation was hardly justified perhaps, considering their reluctance to go on strike in 1871, as in 1869, and their refusal to do so in 1870.) The lack of evidence makes it difficult to determine whether any Welsh miners had been involved in strike activity in Wales before emigrating, although it is known that one Welsh miner living in Scranton in 1871, Ebeneser Rees, had been victimized for advocating unionism in the upper Swansea Valley during the late 1860s.[90]

Beyond their own determination, their economic resources and their commitment to unionism, the fundamental factor which enabled the Welsh miners to stay out on strike for so long was that their own solidarity was reinforced by a marked degree of ethnic solidarity. During the dispute the Welsh miners gained widespread, though not total, support from their wider community. In the words of Samuel Walker, the Welsh community was able 'to mobilize its ethnic, religious, civic and linguistic cohesiveness to exercise a style of group discipline unmatched by any other group in the city'.[91]

The striking Welsh miners received a great deal of support from merchants of their own nationality. An E. Jones of Taylorville informed *Baner ac Amserau Cymru* that all the Welsh merchants in Scranton, Hyde Park, Providence and Taylorville had the utmost sympathy for the workmen and 'never before had such unity been seen.' In particular, he singled out John Levi, a Hyde Park general merchant and a leading member of the Welsh community.[92] In some respects perhaps, Welsh commercial interests, mindful as they were of the importance of the patronage of Welsh miners and their families, had very little

---

[88] W. R. Storrs to Sam Sloan, 2 Aug. 1869, D.L. & W. Papers.
[89] Scranton *Daily Democrat*, quoted in Walker, op. cit., p. 68.
[90] *South Wales Voice*, 12 Aug. 1965. Rees later returned to Ystalyfera where he set up a printing works and began publishing *Llais Llafur*.
[91] Walker, op. cit., p. 43.
[92] *Baner ac Amserau Cymru*, 27 May 1871, quoted and translated in Conway, *The Welsh in America*, pp. 190–1.

option but to support the strikers. Nevertheless, their positive attitude contrasts with that of non-Welsh businessmen, who found themselves trapped between the two sides of the conflict and who maintained an ambivalent stance until it became clear that the strike was breaking.[93]

As well as securing aid from the Welsh commercial sector, the striking Welsh miners could draw on the support of other sections of the community. Many Welsh ministers publicly championed the strikers' cause from their pulpits and actively campaigned on their behalf. One in particular, Revd William Roberts of the First Welsh Baptist Church, was later remembered as 'the strongest pillar of the men' during the dispute.[94] Yet perhaps the strongest testimony to the depth of the support for the Welsh miners was that some Welsh mine foremen clearly felt that their loyalty to their countrymen was greater than that due to their employers. One, Enoch Davis, immediately informed the W.B.A. when he found out that some German labourers were planning to return to work. Forewarned, a crowd of miners was able to assemble at the mine and prevent the strikebreakers from entering. Although no doubt applauded in Hyde Park, Davis's conduct incurred the wrath of the *Scranton Republican*, which accused him of demonstrating a gross betrayal of the trust placed in him by his employer.[95] Episodes such as these undoubtedly contributed to the coal companies' reappraisal of the value of Welsh mining skill during the strike. Three weeks after the end of the dispute, W. R. Storrs informed his superior in New York that 'our intentions are to make all foremen from some time to come out of other material than Welshmen if we can find them, cutting both the Welsh Baptist and Methodist Churches.'[96] Both Enoch Davis's actions and Storrs's intended change of policy demonstrated the complexity of the relationship between the involvement of the Welsh in the anthracite industry and their sense of ethnicity. Likewise, Storrs's admission of the possibility that non-Welsh supervisors

---

[93] Walker, op. cit., p. 68. In general, Scrantonian business interests were opposed to the W.B.A. and also antipathetic to the large corporations because they were controlled by capital from outside the region. The latter were deemed to have no concern for the well-being of the area beyond a profitable return on their investment.
[94] Berthoff, 'The Welsh', pp. 1014–15.
[95] Scranton *Morning Republican*, 21 Apr. 1871.
[96] W. R. Storrs to Sam Sloan, 12 June 1871, D.L. & W. Papers.

might not be found and his confirmation that the Welsh churches were training grounds for such officials re-emphasize the privileged position the Welsh mining fraternity enjoyed and the role some Welsh cultural institutions played in perpetuating it.

Yet widespread as it was, the Welsh community's support for its striking miners was not unanimous. Some Welshmen adopted an ambivalent stance during the dispute, none more so than one prominent member of the Baptist Church which W. R. Storrs would later attempt to ostracize, Benjamin Hughes. Hughes found himself trapped in a no-win situation, torn between his loyalty to the D.L. & W. and the need to maintain his standing in the Welsh community, which, in general, was strongly behind the strikers. He could not overtly condemn the strike for fear of losing face among the Welsh, nor could he openly support it and risk losing his influence with the company. As far as can be detected, he maintained a discreet silence throughout the dispute. Equally, the strike brought out the ambivalent feelings with which both sides regarded him. He was distrusted by the city's ruling industrial and business élite simply because he was Welsh. He was distrusted by the Welsh miners because of his position with the company, and possibly justifiably so, if W. R. Storrs's interpretation of Hughes's attitude towards the strike was accurate. In July, after the end of the strike, Storrs told Sam Sloan: 'Hughes no doubt to some extent sympathizes with the Welshmen, but is ashamed of their late conduct during the last strike and, I believe, is working for our interest.'[97] Some of the Welsh in Hyde Park may have realized where Hughes's loyalties ultimately lay rather earlier, for in March there was an abortive attempt to oust him from his seat on the Scranton Select Council.[98] From the outset the strike was a source of embarrassment to Hughes, and probably to other higher-ranking Welsh officials in the industry, but it was even more so after April. During that month the Welsh began to adopt violent tactics to maintain the strike, and the full force of the community's support became only too apparent.

Until April the strike held firm. There were growing demands among the labourers for some of the mines to be reopened, but

[97] Ibid., 12 July 1871, D.L. & W. Papers.
[98] Scranton *Morning Republican*, 26 Mar. 1871.

the employers refused in order to minimize the risk of violent reprisals or of alienating the Welsh miners.[99] Their policy highlights the degree of leverage which the latter possessed. Welsh skill was essential to the smooth running of the local anthracite industry, whilst the Welsh vote was crucial to the fortunes of the Republican Party, which represented Scranton's business interests. Early in that month, however, the employers changed their strategy and made concerted efforts to break the strike. A number of Welsh miners were sacked, and Irish and German labourers were employed in their places. With these the coal companies attempted to reopen the mines.[100]

In response, the Welsh miners adopted their most effective weapon in enforcing the strike: mass intimidation. Such tactics often resulted in violence, and during the first week of April a number of serious distrubances took place. One incident occurred when a number of mine labourers from Bellevue, Patagonia and Hyde Park held a meeting to discuss the possibility of returning to work. They were attacked by 'a crowd of frenzied Welsh females' and some twenty or thirty men, who threw stones and called them blacklegs and 'every opprobrious epithet their filthy tongues could muster'.[101] Those present at the meeting were driven away by the women, who continued to throw stones, whilst the men who accompanied them applauded and urged them on. Eventually the men also joined in the violence, and in the general mêlée which ensued numerous shots were fired and several were injured. Apparently a number of boys also joined the fray. When the labourers attempted to reconvene their meeting nearby, they were intercepted by a crowd of W.B.A. members. Outnumbered by about ten to one, they were badly beaten up. Many of the injured were Irish. On the same day, some two hundred people armed with clubs and weapons stopped the Church mine working by enticing out the strike-breakers and allowing them to go home peacefully on the assurance that they would not return to the mine. Other incidents during 4–8 April involved the activities of roving

---

[99] Walker, op. cit., p. 67.
[100] Pottsville *Miners' Journal*, 17 May 1871; *Drych*, 15 June 1871.
[101] Scranton *Morning Republican*, 7 Apr. 1871. The women's attack, and the *Republican*'s vocabulary, are strikingly reminiscent of similar actions by women in resisting strike-breakers in the Welsh coalfields and the manner they were reported in the press. See Angela John, loc. cit., pp. 77–9; Rosemary A. N. Jones, 'Women, community and collective action: the *Ceffyl Pren* tradition', in Angela John, op. cit., pp. 17–41, 34–7.

bands of W.B.A. men, who smashed up strike-breakers' homes, attacked mine foremen and burned down a coal breaker. Two labourers were killed in these clashes.[102]

The disturbances demonstrated the strength of the communal support which the striking Welsh miners enjoyed. All sections of the community participated, regardless of age or sex, whilst in some cases crowds numbering up to a thousand harassed the strike-breakers.[103] Equally, their actions, though violent, met with strong approval among Welsh immigrants in the city. After disturbances at Tripp's Slope on 7 April, W. R. Storrs informed Sam Sloan that 'the rioters were Welsh and Irish and as far as we can judge, all their classes [are] in full sympathy with . . . [the] outrageous proceedings . . . The representative Welshmen do not join the crowd but lay back and would do nothing to stop the movement.'[104]

The strikers' tactics were successful and in general the mines remained closed. However, their actions inaugurated a new phase in the struggle. In the wake of the violence, the mayor appealed to Governor Geary for assistance. The latter dispatched a detachment of the Pennsylvania National Guard, under the command of Major General Edwin S. Osborne, and martial law was declared in the city.[105] The arrival of the state militia was a blow to the strikers' ability to maintain the strike, because the soldiers would henceforth be used to protect parties of strike-breakers. Moreover, the April disturbances had other repercussions which influenced the future course of the strike. The prominent role of the Welsh in those events led to their being identified – correctly – as the principal force behind the strike, and employers and business interests began to stir up anti-Welsh feeling in order to manipulate the ethnic divisions in the workforce and speed up a general return to work. In this respect, a hostile reaction on their part was perhaps to be expected. At a deeper level, however, their response was influenced by the crisis the events of the first week of April had created in the prevailing image of the Welsh immigrant community.

[102] Scranton *Morning Republican*, 7, 8, 10 Apr. 1871; Craft, op. cit., pp. 220–6; Walker, op. cit., p. 70.
[103] Scranton *Morning Republican*, 8 Apr. 1871.
[104] W. R. Storrs to Sam Sloan, 8 Apr. 1871, D.L. & W. Papers.
[105] Craft, op. cit., p. 220.

The actions of the Welsh miners and their families contradicted widely accepted assumptions regarding the behaviour and character of the Welsh. Generally, the city's ruling élite held them in high regard. The central tenets of this complimentary image were articulated by the Pottsville *Miners' Journal*'s Scranton correspondent in October 1870:

> Hyde Park is one of the finest mining towns in the state. It is almost entirely settled by miners, three quarters of whom are Welsh. They have a number of beautiful churches which will do credit to any town in the state, fine public buildings and many of the houses are very fine residencies and everything presents an air of comfort. They are nearly free of such nuisances known as grog shops which so terribly demoralize communities and those that do exist, we were informed, are not kept by Welshmen. They are an orderly, thrifty and religious community . . . So quiet and orderly is this Welsh town.[106]

Given the existence of this prevailing image of the Welsh immigrant community, it is hardly surprising perhaps that their prominent role in the April disturbances occasioned amazement. Referring to Welsh behaviour in particular, the *Record of the Times* declared: 'that Hyde Park, of all places, so praised for the intelligence and thrift of its miners should have been the scene of the first riot bred of the suspension, is astonishing.'[107] The shock felt by the élite and Yankee Americans in general in Scranton was quickly followed by retaliation, and from the first week of April onwards, manifestations of increasing native-American (or nativist) hostility towards the Welsh became a marked feature of the dispute.

There had been some flickerings of anti-Welsh feeling on the part of native-Americans even before the April disturbances. In March, American Republicans in ward 5 in Hyde Park rebelled against the nomination of Watkin H. Williams as that ward's representative on the city's Common Council. Although a regular Republican, Williams was also the secretary of the miners' strike council, but the defectors' dissatisfaction seems to have been equally influenced by the fact that he was Welsh. They voted with the Democrats to defeat his election, an action which the *Scranton Republican* interpreted as a return to 'know-

---

[106] Pottsville *Miners' Journal*, 8 Oct. 1870.
[107] Wilkes-Barre *Record of the Times*, 12 Apr. 1871.

nothingism'.[108] After the April disturbances, however, native-American hostility towards the Welsh intensified and became far more overt. One Welsh miner who was refused credit at the store of General Bushnell, a Yankee and a prominent Republican, was dismissed with the words 'You are nothing but my enemy anyhow.'[109] A local volunteer group, the Thomas Zouaves, was disbanded by General Osborne because of its Welsh membership and its pro-Welsh sympathies, which had been demonstrated in friendly baseball matches between its members and teams of striking Welsh miners.[110] Some Welsh alleged that either Osborne or the mayor had deliberately given arms to some of the labourers. The Welsh were increasingly stigmatized as un-American,[111] sentiments echoed by the *Daily Democrat* when it declared that 'of all the people that touch these shores, the Welsh [sic] are the hardest to Americanize.'[112]

The *Daily Democrat*, representing as it did the Democratic, and largely Irish and German, factions in the city, could hardly be expected to be pro-Welsh. A more significant development was the change in the attitude of the *Scranton Republican*, which represented the middle-class, Anglo-Saxon Republican element in Scranton.[113] In normal times the newspaper was liberal in its praise for the Welsh immigrants and particularly for those in Hyde Park. The latter's reputation for hard work, thrift and home ownership was a subject of frequent comment in the *Republican*'s editorials. 'Such a class of men,' it declared in 1873, the tumult of two years earlier long forgotten, 'are a benefit to any community,' and it urged other workers to follow their example.[114] Yet if the *Republican*'s benevolence was influenced by its perception of the determinedly 'middle-class' ethos of the

---

[108] Scranton *Morning Republican*, 24, 25, 27 Mar. 1871.
[109] Undated newspaper report from *Hyde Park Courier* in Terence Vincent Powderly Papers, Series G, Scrapbooks, 1873–1904, Yale University. In 1882 Bushnell stood as the Republican candidate in the mayoral election, when he again seems to have given vent to his anti-Welsh feelings. In the hearing of a Welshman he maintained that 'The Welsh and Irish miners should like swine be driven into the sea' whilst during his campaign he accused the Welsh of lacking intelligence and being no better than cattle. Ibid.
[110] Scranton *Morning Republican*, 15 Mar., 4 Apr. 1871; *Drych*, 6 July 1871.
[111] *Drych*, 25 May, 6 July 1871.
[112] Scranton *Daily Democrat*, 3 May 1871, quoted in Walker, op. cit., pp. 68–9.
[113] Samuel Emlen Walker, 'Varieties of workingclass experience: the workingmen of Scranton, Pennsylvania, 1855–1885', in Milton Cantor (ed.), *American Workingclass Culture: Explorations in American Labor and Social History* (Westport, Conn., 1979), pp. 361–76 (especially 371).
[114] Scranton *Morning Republican*, 25 Apr. 1873.

Welsh, it was also underpinned by an awareness of political and economic realities. As the voice of both Scrantonian business interests and the Republican Party, the newspaper needed to be mindful of the importance of Welsh mining skill and the Welsh Republican vote.

During the strike, therefore, the *Republican* had to adopt an anti-strike attitude, but it could not do so too overtly for fear of alienating the Welsh. Initially, it tempered its approach. It frequently expressed sympathy with the miners, and instead attacked the leaders of the W.B.A., although its efforts to divide the rank-and-file Welsh miners and their leadership made little impact.[115] But when it became clear that the Welsh miners were the principal force in sustaining the strike and that they were receiving widespread support from their own ethnic group, the *Republican* abandoned both its ambivalence and its pro-Welsh attitude. From the first week of April onwards, it began to launch increasingly venomous attacks not only on the Welsh miners but on that nationality in general. It accused the Welsh of being the 'Ku Klux Klan' branch of the W.B.A. and did its utmost to stir up animosities between them and other immigrant groups, particularly by inflaming anti-Welsh feeling among Irish and German labourers. 'It is strange', the newspaper observed on 12 April, 'that the little dependency of Wales should have a patent for the exclusive manufacture of mining bosses.'[116] Its tone grew even more disparaging as the strike wore on. On 12 May it reported that Welsh miners were begging in the street and commented:

> It is an interesting though not a new phase of Welsh character to see men who pretend to have feelings of honor enough to attach themselves to an organisation which is bringing them to the verge of starvation, and yet are mean enough to adopt the calling of the lowest beggar, rather than betake themselves to honorable labor.[117]

The *Scranton Republican*'s vendetta created widespread resentment amongst the Welsh. B. G. Morgan, the prominent Hyde Park druggist, refused to sell the newspaper in his store.[118] *Baner America*, the Scranton Welsh newspaper, devoted the bulk

---
[115] Ibid., 14, 21 Apr., 8 May 1871.
[116] Ibid., 12 Apr. 1871.
[117] Ibid., 12 May 1871.
[118] Scranton *Morning Republican*, 17 Apr. 1871.

of its columns to both a spirited defence of the Welsh and an equally vehement verbal assault on the *Republican* and the city's other nationalities.[119] Indignation among the Welsh seems to have been matched by their bewilderment at the *Republican's* volte-face and the unenviable attention it showered on them. In the *Drych* a month after the end of the strike, a letter-writer who styled himself 'Cymro' maintained that the Welsh had withstood all the opprobrium like martyrs, but the response of the majority had been amazement at the turn of events.[120] The main purpose of his letter, however, was to offer reasons for what had occurred.

'Cymro' began by pointing out that, in general, Americans, and especially the *Scranton Republican*, were generous in their praise of the Welsh. Yet by the end of the strike, they had become deadly enemies. He maintained this was partly caused by the behaviour of the Welsh as a people in the strike. During the first disturbances in April, William Scranton had apparently been confronted by armed Welsh strikers as he attempted to reopen a mine. He threatened to shoot them but was forced to withdraw, as a number of rifles were pointed in his direction. After the disturbances both he and the *Scranton Republican's* editor had succeeded in getting a number of Irish and Germans to restart work but were unable to find any Welsh who were willing to do so. Consequently, '. . . from this time on the persecution was directed completely at the Welsh. The persecution was the result of this one fact, that there were no traitors among them as there were in the midst of other nationalities.' 'Cymro' also had a further explanation for the open vilification of the Welsh. This was the Americans' low opinion of all immigrant groups, including the Welsh, which occasionally surfaced in various circumstances but was seen at its most intense during the strike. According to the writer, many Americans regarded immigrants as unsuitable for citizenship unless they were prepared to cast their votes to elect the former into office. Immigrants were merely 'white niggers':

> We are regarded as good 'citizens' while we work quietly, without interfering in matters that are our concern just as much as they are the concern of those who were born here. Oh, everything is all-right as long as

[119] Ibid., 8 June 1871. Unfortunately copies of *Baner America* are not extant.
[120] *Drych*, 15 June 1871.

we accept American roguery quietly at all times, and then during elections we will receive their earnest recommendations to remember to vote this or that ticket. They wish us to believe we are so respectable; yet lift the veil, and it can be seen that most Americans' benevolence is a Judas Kiss.[121]

'Cymro' painted a more complex, and ultimately perhaps a more realistic, picture of native-American attitudes towards the Welsh. His explanations suggest that the strike had brought to the surface the more sinister undercurrents beneath native-Americans' outward benevolence. The Welsh had been castigated not only because of their conduct but also because they had dared to step out of line. Although it is difficult to detect a particular set of circumstances which brought it to the fore as in 1871, there is evidence to suggest that native-Americans looked upon the Welsh with a deep-rooted distrust, and it may well be that Welshmen were tolerated only as long as they remained docile and content to cut coal and vote Republican. To William Scranton, one of the prime *bêtes noires* of the Welsh, they were 'apt to be a little tricky and to lie a little more or less gently as it suited their purposes'.[122] It is also possible, however, that 'Cymro' underestimated the part that apprehension at the communal strength of the Welsh played not only in native-American hostility but also in that of other immigrants. The Welsh reputation for sticking together was disliked by all sections of the non-Welsh in Scranton. Phoebe Gibbons noted that 'they have been accused of bearing malice, and of being clannish, or of "keeping together". "I think", says a Scotsman, "that this is why they keep up the Welsh language".'[123] Undoubtedly, suspicion of the Welsh was influenced by the tightly knit community which they had established in Hyde Park. This potent mixture of occupational, linguistic and cultural cohesion could attract open praise for its communal virtues. Yet at a profounder level perhaps, it also served to draw attention to its excluding and exclusive strength, particularly on those occasions when, as during the 1871 strike, the full force and potential of that strength became evident.

[121] Ibid.
[122] William W. Scranton to E. H. Hatfield, 9 June 1880, Joseph H. and William W. Scranton Papers, Lackawanna Historical Society, Scranton, quoted in Berthoff, 'Social order', p. 216.
[123] Gibbons, loc. cit., p. 916.

The exceptional circumstances of the latter part of the strike also seriously affected relations between the Welsh and other immigrant groups in the city. Normally these groups coexisted relatively amicably, though latent antagonisms were always present.[124] The continuation of the strike and the prominent role of the Welsh in sustaining it created tensions which ignited deep-rooted ethnic resentments and further isolated the Welsh. This polarization was in many ways a direct result of the widening rift between the miners and labourers on strike, but it was exacerbated by the fact that the divisions in the workforce were reinforced along ethnic lines. The ethnic dimension to the job classification in the mines ultimately enabled the employers to inflame further the passions against the Welsh and to break the strike, since it led to the mass defection of the labourers from the W.B.A. during the last two weeks of the dispute.

Demands from the labourers for a return to work grew steadily throughout the strike. The Welsh dismissed their calls as being either an attempt to take Welsh miners' places or an indication of their cowardice – the 'spineless Irish' as John Powell called them.[125] The former accusation may hold some truth. There was also an economic reason for the labourers' desire for an end to the dispute. Being lower-paid, they had smaller reserves than the Welsh to draw on. It seems also that the commitment of the Irish and German labourers to unionism was less marked than that of the Welsh.[126]

On 22 April a mass meeting of German labourers voted overwhelmingly for a return to work, despite continued Welsh threats of violent retaliation against those who did so. To protect themselves they organized a vigilance committee, whose members were prepared to turn out at any time, day or night. Three days later, around sixty of the L.I. & C.'s German and Irish employees restarted work at that company's No. 4 mine.[127] By the beginning of May more and more Irish and German labourers wanted a resumption. However, the W.B.A. refused to call off the strike, even though it was clearly breaking and a

[124] Berthoff, 'Social order', pp. 266–7.
[125] *Gwladgarwr*, 15 July 1871, quoted and translated in Conway, *The Welsh in America*, pp. 191–2.
[126] Walker, op. cit., p. 42. German mineworkers in Scranton were usually emigrants from the rural areas of the home country.
[127] Craft, op. cit., pp. 223, 224.

split in the union became inevitable. This eventually occurred during a series of meetings among Irish, German, English and Scottish mineworkers on 11 May. They resolved to accept the wage rates offered by the employers and a number agreed to restart work at Briggs' Shaft, which William Scranton intended to reopen on 15 May.[128]

The split in the W.B.A. reflected both the extent of the Welsh miners' domination of it and the labourers' antipathy towards them and, increasingly, towards Welsh people in general. The labourers felt that the union represented merely the rights of the miner, and especially the Welsh miner, and whatever their own interests, they had to acquiesce in its decisions. Father Richard Hennessey, a local priest, urged the labourers 'to stand together as Catholics, with Irish and Germans, and forever ignore the Welsh miners' union'.[129] At a deeper level, however, both the antagonism against the Welsh and the split itself were ultimately fuelled by resentment at Welsh domination, not only of the union but of the whole industry in the Scranton area. Speeches at the labourers' meetings and letters in the local press articulated long-term grievances regarding the conduct and practices of Welsh miners, and Welsh foremen in particular.[130] Again, as in the case of ruling groups' change of attitude towards the Welsh, the immediate circumstances of the strike brought to the surface the scale of that nationality's control of the anthracite industry and highlighted the resentment which their efforts to exploit it engendered among other nationalities. This resentment could widen into general hatred of the Welsh, particularly on the part of the Irish. The labourers' leader, John Mckugh, told a meeting that Welshmen oppressed the rights of the Irish.[131] In a scathing letter to the *Scranton Republican* during the second week of May, 'A Doomed Laborer' not only criticized the Welsh in Scranton but even extended his condemnation to the way the Irish were treated in Wales:

> The Welsh say that the mines are theirs by inheritance ... that they were as rich as the companies to sustain the suspension and that they should

---
[128] Scranton *Morning Republican*, 12 May 1871; Craft, op. cit., p. 225.
[129] Scranton *Morning Republican*, 12 May 1871; *Irish World*, 27 May 1871, quoted in Walker, op. cit., p. 72.
[130] Scranton *Morning Republican*, 12, 13 May 1871.
[131] Ibid., 12 May 1871.

force the companies into compliance with their terms, starve the Irish, English and Scotch out of the coalfields and that then the coast was clear for them to do as they have done in Wales – to hunt down Irishmen as they have done from Aberdare to Mountain Ash . . . They grow rich on other men's toil . . . get more pianos, more harmoniums, and hundreds of other things that we hard toiling Irish cannot enjoy. We cannot afford to dress our wives in silks and satins. Now is the time for the English, Irish, Dutch and Scotch who have never got anything but drudgery from the Welsh foremen.[132]

Such acrimonious feelings against the Welsh were widespread during the last weeks of the strike. Their 'tyranny' was often alluded to, whilst they were repeatedly called 'petty tyrants' and 'Welsh banditti' who were 'full of bombast'.[133] These passions actually led to efforts to boycott any relations with the Welsh ethnic group as a whole, particularly as during the first week of May Welsh miners, wives and children readopted violent, if increasingly desperate, measures to prevent a mass return to work and the break-up of the W.B.A.[134] A meeting of labourers passed resolutions which stated that 'the cowardly and dastardly assaults . . . [are] nothing short of premeditated assassination of Irishmen' and that 'we Irishmen, laborers and miners throughout this district dissever and stand aloof from having any connection respecting union and fraternity with Welshmen in the future.'[135] Other resolutions went even further. A joint meeting of English, German and Irish mineworkers declared that they had agreed never to associate themselves with Welsh miners because 'in their late murderous outrages they have shown us they are a class of beings who should never be allowed to associate with peaceable and law abiding citizens.'[136]

By the middle of May, then, the strike had become far more than an industrial dispute. As a *New York Times* reporter suggested apprehensively, it had 'resolved itself into a war of races'.[137] The determination of the Welsh to maintain the strike had led to their increasing isolation as they found themselves ranged against not only native groups but also the Irish and Germans and even the Scots and English. In many ways the

[132] Ibid., 9 May 1871.
[133] Ibid., 9, 11 May 1871.
[134] Ibid., 11, 12 May 1871.
[135] Ibid., 10 May 1871.
[136] Pottsville *Miners' Journal*, 17 May 1871.
[137] *New York Times*, 11 May 1871, quoted in Walker, op. cit., p. 72.

stage was set for the final act which would see the prevailing passions raised to fever pitch. That moment occurred on 17 May, when the latest phase of violence culminated in the shooting of two Welsh miners by the state militia. It was an incident which had both immediate and far-reaching consequences, and its memory, perhaps even more than that of the strike itself, lived on to haunt a generation of Welsh immigrants in Scranton.

The incident occurred when a group of mainly Irish strike-breakers at the Briggs' Shaft mine were being escorted home by the state militia, led by William Scranton, and a party of labourers bearing Remington rifles. As they proceeded along Luzerne Street, Hyde Park, they were jeered at, threatened and spat upon by a crowd of Welsh men, women and boys. Near Oddfellows Corner, the junction of Luzerne Street and South Main Avenue, the party was confronted by another crowd of around two hundred Welsh who blocked the road. These were armed with stones and, according to one report, had revolvers. They began to hurl abuse at the strike-breakers. For some reason one of the labourers, Michael Cairns, otherwise known as 'Fenian', raised his rifle and fired, killing two men in the crowd.[138] Seeing that members of the militia were also preparing to fire, William Scranton knocked up their rifles, and in so doing undoubtedly prevented further bloodshed.[139] The crowd fled, amid great howling and screaming, and the party continued on its way. For a while, according to the *Scranton Republican*, 'there was not a soul to be seen but the two victims lying by the fence'. Soon, however, an even larger crowd congregated at the scene, 'the Welsh women giving full vent to the force of their lungs in the most terrific howls'. The bodies were later taken to Co-operative Hall, escorted by a large crowd drawn from all sections of the Welsh.[140]

Both men killed, Benjamin Davis and Daniel Jones, were miners, members of the W.B.A., natives of Wales and respected

---

[138] *Scranton Morning Republican*, 18 May 1871. At his trial Cairns said he had fired because one of the victims had thrown a stone which hit him on the leg while the other had used threatening language. The Welsh, however, maintained that Cairns had fired without provocation; no stone had been thrown and the two victims were innocent. Ibid., 18, 20, 22 May 1871; Murphy, *Hist. Lack. Co.*, p. 387; Gibbons, loc. cit., p. 926.
[139] Murphy, *Hist. Lack. Co.*, p. 387.
[140] Scranton *Morning Republican*, 18 May 1871.

members of the Hyde Park community. Jones was a member of the Hyde Park Welsh Calvinistic Methodist Church and was popularly known as 'Spurgeon' because of his habit of indulging in a little local preaching. He also occasionally wrote for the *Drych* under the pseudonym 'Dewi Gwyllt'.[141] The Welsh community was incensed by their deaths which it regarded as an outrage not only against Hyde Park but against the Welsh nationality in general. In response, the Welsh embarked on a number of retaliatory actions which were 'national' in character and signified that an even greater tightening of the ethnic group's ranks had taken place.

Immediately after the shooting Hyde Park was full of rumours that the labourers had been responsible, and there were widespread calls for reprisals against them, and in some cases against the whole, predominantly Irish, population of Bellevue. Alderman D. M. Jones, one of Hyde Park's most prominent figures, issued a warrant for Cairns's arrest. It seems his action was dictated as much by his indignation as a Welshman as by his sense of public duty. Cairns could not be found, so instead the officer in charge arrested William Garrety, president of the newly-formed Laborers' Association. Some 2,000 Welsh witnessed the arrest, calling for blood, and Garrety only narrowly escaped a lynching.[142] Welsh pressure also led to the arrest of William Scranton, much to the disgust of the *Scranton Republican*. Although the charges against him dealt only with his part in the April violence, there is little doubt that his arrest was the result of his presence at the shooting, which further inflamed his demonology among the Welsh. Some thought that Scranton had played a more overt role in the deaths of Jones and Davis. One Welsh witness testified that on encountering the Welsh crowd on 17 May, Scranton had shouted 'We'll give them the price of labor.'[143]

D. M. Jones's actions in demanding justice for his nationality were matched by the efforts of other prominent Hyde Park Welshmen, many of whom were not directly connected with the mining industry. Barely had the alderman signed the arresting papers when a dispatch, entitled 'Blood', was sent to Governor

---

[141] Ibid.; *Drych*, 25 May 1871; Gibbons, loc. cit., p. 926.
[142] Scranton *Morning Republican*, 18 May 1871.
[143] Ibid., 22 May 1871.

Geary in order to give 'a truthful and strictly correct statement' of the shooting. It maintained that 'two of our most peaceful and estimable citizens' had been killed without provocation. Among its signatories were Watkin H. Williams, secretary of the miners' strike council, B. G. Morgan (the druggist who had refused to sell the *Scranton Republican* since April), and Capt. Thomas D. Lewis of the Thomas Zouaves (the local volunteer group which had been disbanded by General Osborne because of its Welsh sympathies).[144] At Cairns's trial two days later, other prominent leaders of the Welsh community, such as Revd M. A. Ellis and H. M. Edwards, appeared as witnesses for the prosecution. At least one Welsh mine fire-boss also testified, echoing Enoch Davis's actions earlier in the dispute.[145]

Perhaps the most potent indication of the indignation of the Welsh community and its 'national' response was the burial ceremony of the two victims. This also demonstrated how isolated the Welsh were during the closing days of the strike. The stores in Hyde Park were closed and the Welsh were the only ethnic group present at the proceedings. After separate services in the deceased's homes, a long cortège formed for the procession to the Washburn Street Cemetery. Three hundred W.B.A. men marched in front of the coffins, forty carriages and members of the Hyde Park and Providence Ivorite Lodges followed behind, whilst women marched on the pavements alongside the carriages. A large crowd, eventually numbering around three thousand brought up the rear. The *Drych*'s reporter estimated that in all there were between eight and ten thousand people present, excluding the members of the state militia who ringed the cemetery. Throughout, the services and the hymn singing at the cemetery were in the Welsh language, and despite the potentially inflammatory presence of the militia there were no incidents. The impression from newspaper reports is that it was an extremely poignant occasion, although the *Scranton Republican*, which had almost welcomed the shooting and regarded it as a justifiable act of retaliation, declared it to be one 'of great pomp and circumstance'. 'Surely,' it insisted, 'some distinction should be made at public funerals between the honor deserved by those who fall at the post of duty . . . and those

[144] Ibid., 20 May 1871.
[145] Ibid., 22 May 1871.

individuals struck down in the act of creating violence and bloodshed.'[146]

Despite the intensity of the Welsh reaction to the shooting, the death of two of their number finally broke the spirit of the Welsh miners and the strike quickly came to an end. Although there were isolated incidents in which the Welsh attempted to prevent labourers working, in general their intimidatory tactics and their picketing of most of the mines ceased after the tragedy.[147] Perhaps the *Scranton Republican* was correct when it asserted that the Welsh had been taught a severe lesson; certainly the episode must have come as a shock, particularly as throughout the latter part of the strike many of the Welsh in Hyde Park believed that the militia would not in any circumstances open fire on them.[148] The Welsh miners' decision to return to work was surely also influenced by the futility of staying out. Long before the shooting it was clear that their cause was lost. Although the mines had remained closed for nearly five months, the supply of coal on the market had not been effectively reduced, and demand was beginning to fall as summer approached. Within a week of the death of the two Welsh miners, virtually all the mines in Scranton were working again.[149]

The prominent part played by the Welsh miners in the strike led to some reprisals against them on the part of the employers. Many were victimized, although, contrary to threats in the *Scranton Republican*, the majority were returned to their old positions (yet another indication of the importance of Welsh mining skill and the leverage it enjoyed).[150] In this respect the Irish labourers' hopes of supplanting Welsh miners by returning to work early were frustrated. Furthermore, W. R. Storrs's intention of not promoting the Welsh to supervisory positions seems to have been only temporary, if put into practice at all. If the tight control the Welsh exercised in the industry was relatively unaffected by their conduct, the W.B.A. in the area was decimated and it virtually disappeared. A year later, barely

---

[146] Ibid., 20 May 1871; *Drych*, 25 May, 6 July 1871.
[147] Scranton *Morning Republican*, 22 May 1871.
[148] Ibid., 18 May 1871.
[149] Walker, op. cit., pp. 72, 74.
[150] Scranton *Morning Republican*, 23 May 1871; Aurand, op. cit., p. 84.

two hundred could be mustered to attend a union rally in the city.[151]

The termination of the dispute did not defuse the passions it had created; in fact, Welsh feelings, further inflamed by the shooting, remained at fever pitch. They embarked on their own retribution and ostracized those who had either voiced opposition to the strike or had been ambivalent towards it. The Revd W. G. Cullis made the fatal mistake of citing the actions of William Scranton as an example during a sermon on 'Individualism'; members of his congregation protested immediately and two local merchants, fearful of being boycotted if they were associated with such views, resigned their membership. Sporadic boycotts of merchants did take place, and at least two other ministers were physically barred from their churches because of their anti-strike stance.[152] Since the shooting, the Welsh had begun to hold general meetings, partly in order to raise money to try to convict William Scranton and Cairns.[153] These caused consternation among non-Welsh groups. On 23 May Storrs informed Sam Sloan: 'Our Welch [sic] friends are holding exclusive meetings which excite Irish jealousy and some fear may lead to trouble,' especially as the main purpose of these gatherings was 'to prevent trade or intercourse with any but Welshmen'.[154]

The Welsh also maintained their agitation against the *Scranton Republican*. Two days after the shooting its Welsh night editor, Ellis R. Williams, was assaulted by half a dozen Welshmen for refusing to comply with requests among the Welsh that he resign in protest against the newspaper's anti-Welsh statements.[155] The Welsh also embarked on an active campaign to prevent people of their nationality buying the newspaper, and meetings to drum up support for their efforts continued well into the summer. Apparently Welsh ministers and community leaders played a prominent part in these gatherings, during which all sorts of insults were directed at the *Republican*. In

---

[151] Aurand, op. cit., p. 86.
[152] Scranton *Daily Democrat*, 27 May, 3 June 1871, quoted in Walker, op. cit., pp. 74–5.
[153] *Drych*, 25 May, 6 July 1871.
[154] W. R. Storrs to Sam Sloan, 23 May 1871, D.L. & W. Papers.
[155] Scranton *Morning Republican*, 20 May 1871. Williams did in fact resign, though it is not recorded whether he was influenced by his experience. In a move which symbolized the imminent defection of the Welsh mining vote to the Democrats, Williams joined the Scranton *Daily Democrat*. Ibid., 27 June 1871.

response, the newspaper sarcastically derided its enemies' efforts:

> For over a month, these chosen people of God have canvassed Luzerne... erasing and threatening as occasion suited in order to lessen our subscription lists. When these highly moral and temperate bands of missionaries complete their job we will hope they will publish the results of their labors. By all means Taffys, paint a list of the reclaimed and show what you have done.[156]

In the coming months the 'Taffys' would show that their campaign against the newspaper would take on an unexpected political dimension which would do far more than damage the *Republican*'s subscription lists.

The 1871 strike has been examined in detail because of its own importance and also for what it tells us about the complex nature and implications of the Welsh involvement in the anthracite industry. The strike was an event which dominates the history of the Welsh in Scranton. In some respects it was a unique episode: never again did the Welsh miners, or indeed the Welsh ethnic group, find themselves in such an isolated position. The strike also revealed, in action, fundamental characteristics of the Welsh miners and their wider community, and the complexities of their relations with other, non-Welsh groups. In particular, it highlighted the inextricable relationship between the concentration of the Welsh in the industry and their community's sense of ethnicity. The Welsh miners' solidarity during the strike and the lengthy duration of their struggle were possible only because of the strength they derived from the fusion of their consciousness of ethnic and occupational identities and the support they received from their ethnic group. Indeed, it is an indication of the powerful ties of ethnic identity among at least some Welsh community leaders that they supported the miners, perhaps because in the latter stages of the dispute it became an ethnic conflict. As Samuel Walker has pointed out, in going on strike the Welsh miners also demonstrated that they had developed an incipient, if weak, class-consciousness, and this spilled over into their campaign for

[156] Ibid., 8, 19 June 1871.

independent political action in the aftermath of the dispute. Perceiving that their economic and social status was declining in the face of the growth of impersonal, monopolistic corporations, the miners were increasingly willing to see themselves as a separate class and to take collective action.[157]

The subsequent history of the Welsh in Scranton's anthracite industry after 1871 shows that their sense of ethnicity and occupational identity would continue to be important determinants of their attitudes and actions in the industry itself, and in the spheres of politics and unionism. In the years after 1871, too, a consciousness of class identity flickered in exceptional circumstances.[158] As long as the Welsh remained concentrated in the industry, that industry continued to influence greatly the daily lives of the Welsh in the city and their responses to their situation. But by the time the nineteenth century drew to a close, great changes had taken place which effectively ended the mutual and intimate relationship between the Welsh and the industry they had dominated, and depended on, for so long.

III AFTERMATH: THE LONG RETREAT FROM THE COAL FACE

One of the most important repercussions of the 1871 strike for the Welsh miners in Scranton was that it led to a temporary reappraisal of their political allegiances. Normally, Welsh miners in the city, and indeed Welshmen generally, were staunchly Republican because of 'traditional' loyalties and the control which the Irish and German factions exercised over the Democratic Party. Ethnic motivation was the dominant feature of the political life of Scranton during the late nineteenth century; to some extent, both the Republicans and the Democrats were ethnic groups, and political campaigns in the city were often based on ethnic antagonisms.[159] The Welsh miners' experience during the strike, however, initiated a mass defection from the Republican Party and an involvement in independent political action. Accustomed political loyalties were also

---

[157] Walker, loc. cit., pp. 365–9.
[158] I have discussed Welsh miners' attitudes towards politics and unionism after 1871 in my Ph.D. Thesis. See Jones, 'Wales in America', pp. 97–109.
[159] For a discussion of the importance of ethnic considerations in late nineteenth-century Scrantonian politics see Walker, op. cit., pp. 8, 36–107.

ignored on other occasions in the years after 1871, notably in 1877–8, following a period of bitter industrial unrest in Scranton. It must be stressed that these breaks from the normal voting pattern were exceptions. Nevertheless, though brief, their occurrence demonstrates that again, during recurrent crises in the anthracite industry, the involvement of Welsh miners in the industry could not only reinforce their sense of ethnicity; it could also lead to a willingness to transcend traditional ethnic rivalries and even to a redefining of a central tenet of their ethnic identity.

The failure of the 1871 strike led many Welsh miners to embrace independent political, as opposed to industrial, action to defend their interests. During the summer of 1871 an independent party began to take shape, and in August it was organized as the Labor Reform Union of Luzerne County.[160] It grew rapidly in popularity, not only among Welsh miners but also, it seems, among other enfranchised Welshmen not connected with the industry. It was clear that Welsh voters were determined to defect *en masse* from the Republican Party. Some wrote letters to the *Daily Times* – any dealing with the *Scranton Republican* had been effectively boycotted – to publicize their intentions.[161] Seeing the real threat that Welsh allegiance to the new party posed for the Republicans, the *Republican* went on the attack against the new party's Welsh leadership in an effort to divide it from rank-and-file Welsh voters. The foremost target was *Baner America* and the Jones brothers, W. S. and David M., who had also joined the workingmen's party and had urged the Welsh to vote for it in that newspaper. On at least two occasions the *Republican* directed acerbic editorials against W. S. Jones, and in one it maintained that *Baner America's* shareholders and Hyde Park's 'representative' Welshmen in general disapproved of the editor's new position.[162] This may well have been so. The Hyde Park community's accepted political leaders, notably Benjamin Hughes and Henry D. Davies, were Republican diehards. It is possible that, because of their ambiguous positions during the strike, their influence was not as pervasive as it would normally

[160] Walker, op. cit., p. 76.
[161] Scranton *Morning Republican*, 8 June 1871.
[162] Ibid., 24, 31 July 1871.

have been. If the *Scranton Republican's* claims were accurate, then the Welsh defectors were not only prepared to change their voting behaviour; they did so in the full knowledge that they were going against their own political leadership.

All the predictions of a massive Welsh electoral shift were confirmed in the Luzerne County elections of October 1871. No L.R.U. candidates stood during these elections, but there were major Welsh defections to the Democrats. The Irish Democratic vote held, so that almost all that party's candidates were elected.[163] It was during the Scranton mayoral election in the spring of 1872, however, that the full force of the Welsh miners' alienation from the Republican Party and the extent of their support for independent political action became apparent. The L.R.U. candidate, Ebeneser Leach, narrowly lost to the Democrat and secured 75 per cent of his votes in Hyde Park and Providence (wards 1, 2, 4 and 5), the heartlands of the Welsh miners. The Welsh shift in favour of the L.R.U. was all the more decisive because the Republican candidate was himself a Welshman. In an effort to woo back the Welsh vote, the party had nominated Lewis Pughe, a prominent local merchant. Despite being Welsh, however, Pughe failed to gain any significant support among his own nationality during his campaign. Even efforts to tout him as a friend of the workmen, to stir up anti-Irish feeling and to discredit the Welsh leaders of the L.R.U. evoked little response. Pughe came an embarrassing third with only half the number of votes cast for Leach; his fate demonstrated, in a negative way, how important the Welsh vote was to the fortunes of the Republicans.[164]

Despite the intensity of their support for the independent political party and their disaffection from the Republicans during the 1872 mayoral election, the remainder of the year saw a return to 'normal' political behaviour on the part of the Welsh miners. Once a protest had been made, interest in the L.R.U. waned, and its demise was sealed by a healing of the rift between

---

[163] Scranton *Weekly Republican*, 19 Oct. 1871; Walker, op. cit., p. 76.
[164] Scranton *Weekly Republican*, 8 May 1872; Walker, op. cit., pp. 77–80. Lewis Pughe (1820–92) was one of the most successful businessmen in Scranton and a prominent figure in the city's banking and commercial circles. Originally from Montgomeryshire, he had emigrated first to Carbondale in 1842, where he set up a successful tailoring business. For biographical details see Throop, op. cit., pp. 149–52; Stoddard, op. cit., p. iv.

the Welsh and the Republican Party, possibly aided by a fading of the antagonisms which the previous year's strike had created. The errant Welsh votes that had stifled Lewis Pughe's ambitions returned to enable the Republican gubernatorial candidate to be elected late in 1872, and although some Welsh in Hyde Park campaigned for Horace Greeley, the Welsh in Scranton were almost unanimous in their support for General Grant in that autumn's presidential election. Even *Baner America* came out in favour of the Republican candidate despite its recent stance in local elections.[165]

The electoral behaviour of the Welsh during 1871 and 1872 ultimately emphasizes the depth of their commitment to the Republican Party. At the same time their actions demonstrate that, given certain exceptional circumstances, they were quite capable of diverging from the traditional pattern. Their voting behaviour in those years was as complex in its motivation as was their own confused response to the movement from being 'Welsh' to becoming 'American'. It was influenced by both anti-Republican sentiment and by a positive support for independent political representation. These factors blunted traditional antagonisms towards the Irish in particular. Yet, paradoxically, the Welsh defections of 1871–2 were still in many ways an ethnic response, although one aimed not at traditional targets but rather at the Republican Party and its supporters who had vilified the Welsh during the strike, and perhaps even at Welsh Republican political leaders themselves. Even if, in general, affiliation to the Republican Party was a determining characteristic of Welsh ethnic identity, 'Welshness' did not necessarily always express itself in this direction.

In 1877–8, following a period of violent and intense industrial unrest in Scranton during the summer of 1877, Welsh miners again defected from the Republican Party and became involved in independent political action. This coincided with the formation and growth of a local Greenback-Labor Party and the successful mayoral election which its candidate, Terence V. Powderly, fought in 1878.[166] In many ways the defections of

---

[165] *Drych*, 24 Oct. 1872; Pottsville *Miner's Journal*, 7 Sept. 1872; *Scranton Wochensblatt*, 15 Aug. 1872; Walker, op. cit., p. 80.
[166] Powderly, an Irish machinist, was re-elected as mayor in 1880 and 1882 (though not on an independent labour party ticket) and was also involved in organizing the

1877-8 mirrored the political behaviour of the Welsh miners six years earlier, although on the latter occasion their attitudes towards politics were coloured by parallel developments in unionism, especially the formation and growth of the Knights of Labor. Despite initial involvement, ethnic considerations and, above all, anti-Irish feeling ultimately triumphed among the Welsh to dictate their withdrawal from both organizations.

During its formative years in Scranton there was extensive Welsh involvement in both the rank and file and leadership of the Knights of Labor. The first Knights of Labor assembly in the city was set up in 1875 by locomotive engineers. In 1876 a number of miners' assemblies were organized, largely by those who had been involved in the W.B.A. They included John F. Williams and John H. Powell, who became chairman of the miners' central committee during the 1877 miners' strike.[167] That dispute began in July 1877 when, in response to a depression in the anthracite industry and a series of wage cuts between 1875 and 1877, the D.L. & W.'s mineworkers demanded a 25 per cent increase. When this was refused, they went on strike.[168] Their action coincided with the national railroad strike of that year which brought all rail operations, as well as coal production, to a halt in the city during the last week of July.[169] The railworkers capitulated shortly afterwards but the mineworkers held out until October, when they were forced to return to work without an increase. The early stages of the dispute were punctuated by a number of disturbances which culminated in a violent episode on 1 August. Incensed by a rumour that William Scranton had stated he would soon have the miners working for thirty-five cents a day, a large crowd

Knights of Labor in Scranton. He later became its national leader. For an account of his activities in Scranton and biographical details see Vincent J. Falzone, 'Terence V. Powderly: politician and progressive mayor of Scranton, 1878–1884', *Pennsylvania History*, XLI, No. 3 (July 1974), pp. 289–309.

[167] Craft, op. cit., pp. 542–3; *Druid*, 1 Jan. 1923. John H. Powell (1839–1922) was originally a miner from Aberdare who emigrated to America in 1866. A strong trade unionist, he became a prominent miners' leader in the Scranton area. He was also a respected bard and an active member of the Welsh Philosophical Society.

[168] *Labor Standard*, 12, 26 Aug., 2 Sept., 1876, 11 Aug. 1877; Aurand, op. cit., p. 110. For accounts of the industrial disputes in Scranton during 1877 see Samuel C. Logan, *A City's Danger and its Defense, or Issues and Results of the Strike of 1877 containing the Origin and History of the Scranton City Guard* (Scranton, 1887); Murphy, *Hist. Lack. Co.*, pp. 388–92; Throop, op. cit., pp. 316–25; Walker, op. cit., pp. 89–97.

[169] For the 1877 railroad strike see Philip. S. Foner, *The Great Labor Uprising of 1877* (New York, 1977).

gathered in the city and went on a destructive rampage. Some attempted to lynch Mayor Mckune. In response the Scranton City Guard fired into the crowd, killing four (all of them Irish) and wounding twenty-five. Following the killings, the Pennsylvania National Guard patrolled the city for three months.[170]

After the 1877 disturbances, many Welsh miners renewed their interest in independent political action and shifted their support to the Greenback-Labor Party which Powderly had formed in the city the previous year.[171] Some acted as committee members for the party, and in October 1877 it began to publish its own newspaper, the *Industrial Advocate*. The editor was John H. Powell, and it also contained a 'Welsh Department'.[172] In the 1877 autumn county elections the Welsh defected *en masse* from the Republican Party; in wards 4 and 5 in Hyde Park the margin was six to one and three to one, respectively, in favour of the Greenback-Labor Party. There was also a similar defection of Irish votes from the Democrats, and as a result the Greenback-Labor candidates swept the board.[173]

During the autumn of 1877, then, both Welsh and Irish mineworkers put their faith in collective action and transcended traditional occupational and political antipathies. In December 1877, however, a series of events within both the Knights of Labor and the Greenback-Labor Party seriously undermined continued Welsh involvement. At the party's nominating convention open hostility broke out between the Welsh and the Irish because it failed to nominate any Welsh candidates. Worse, as far as the Welsh were concerned, Powderly defeated Powell in the election for the party's mayoral candidate.[174] Later that month Powell announced that he would not support the Greenback-Labor ticket and resigned as editor of the *Industrial Advocate*. Some newspaper reports suggested that Powell had been sacked, and it is highly probable that the reason for his departure, either voluntary or forced, was a coup by the Irish faction on the newspaper's board of managers which disfranchised nearly all its Welsh members and replaced them with

---

[170] *Labor Standard*, 11 Aug., 16, 23 Sept. 1877; Throop, op. cit., pp. 18–19; Ellis Roberts, op. cit., p. 23.
[171] Walker, op. cit., p. 89; Falzone, loc. cit., pp. 291–2.
[172] *Scranton Republican*, 3 Oct. 1877; *Druid*, 1 Jan. 1923; Craft, op. cit., p. 366.
[173] Scranton *Weekly Republican*, 14 Nov. 1877; Walker, op. cit., pp. 86–7, 97.
[174] *Scranton Republican*, 28 Jan. 1878; *Drych*, 14 Feb. 1878.

Irishmen.¹⁷⁵ The growing Irish dominance of the Knights and the Greenback-Labor Party led Welsh miners to be increasingly ambivalent towards both organizations.

The uncertainty of the Welsh position as the 1878 mayoral election approached was further confused by the decision of the Republicans and Democrats to fuse in the face of the labour threat and field D. M. Jones as a Citizen Party candidate. Although Jones's nomination was perhaps rather ironical, considering his involvement in the 1871–2 workingmen's party, it was nevertheless a shrewd choice and undoubtedly one intended to lure the Welsh vote away from the Greenbacks. Jones was well respected among the Welsh – he was once described as Hyde Park's 'favourite' – and had a long record of public office.¹⁷⁶ The key to the hopes of both candidates was the Welsh vote, and their campaigns were dominated by efforts to cultivate it. The Citizen Party raised the old bogey of an Irish police force to frighten the Welsh, whilst Powderly appealed to the latter to remember the 1871 strike (again rather ironically, considering his opponent's overt defence of his own ethnic group that year). The outcome of the contest showed how divided Welsh allegiances were. Powderly succeeded in capturing enough of the Welsh votes to be elected, but Jones carried the predominantly Welsh wards 4 and 5 in Hyde Park which had voted overwhelmingly Greenback-Labor the previous autumn.¹⁷⁷ For the second time in six years, a Welshman failed to become mayor of Scranton.

The Welsh miners reverted to the Republican Party in 1878 because of the appeal of D. M. Jones and the growing Irish influence in the Greenback-Labor Party. A similar fate befell their involvement in the Knights of Labor. The overwhelming Irish control of that organization in Scranton meant that the Welsh miners kept their distance, and towards the end of the 1870s they became involved in unions which were set up as an alternative to the Knights.¹⁷⁸ The latter continued to attempt to

---

¹⁷⁵ *Scranton Republican*, 25 Feb. 1878.
¹⁷⁶ Scranton *Weekly Republican*, 13 Feb. 1878; Scranton *Morning Republican*, 13 Mar. 1871.
¹⁷⁷ *Drych*, 14 Feb. 1878; Walker, op. cit., pp. 105–7.
¹⁷⁸ Most of these were short-lived. The most important was the Miners and Laborers' Amalgamated Association, which gained much support from Welsh, English and German miners in the anthracite region after 1885. It collapsed after the failure of the

recruit Welsh miners, but with little response.[179] Eventually, the local anthracite unions affiliated to the United Mine Workers of America, which had organized most of the anthracite region by the turn of the century.[180] In the Scranton area there was some Welsh involvement in the leadership of the U.M.W., and Welsh names appear on the various grievance committees set up by the union.[181] In general, however, it seems that Welsh miners were not as active as they were in the bituminous coalfields of western Pennsylvania or Ohio. In part, as Rowland Berthoff has pointed out, this was because the Welsh had difficulty in gaining credibility at union leadership level when so many of their countrymen were increasingly occupying managerial positions in the industry.[182] Fundamentally, however, the decline in active Welsh participation in union affairs undoubtedly reflected the fact that by the beginning of the twentieth century they were no longer a powerful and influential element in the workforce.

During the last years of the nineteenth century the Welsh community in Scranton experienced a profound and irrevocable occupational transformation. This transformation was so complete that by the turn of the century it was no longer the almost monolithic mining community it had been a generation earlier. Its mining character was lost because Welshmen had left the mines and, of equal importance, others were not entering them in the first place. The extent of their withdrawal from the mining industry can be detected in the city directories and the returns of the Manuscript Census. Whereas *Webb's Scranton Directory* of 1870–1 revealed an almost stereotypical pattern of a Welsh name listed as a miner, thirty years later Taylor's *Scranton City Directory* painted a markedly different picture. The latter lists a wide variety of occupations alongside Welsh names as well

---

1887 strike. The Knights in Scranton refused to support this strike, causing acrimony between the two organizations. Aurand, op. cit., pp. 118–21.

[179] In January 1887 W. R. Storrs told Sam Sloan: 'Some effort is being made to get the miners to join the Knights. So far our Welshmen keep out of it.' W. R. Storrs to Sam Sloan, 30 Jan. 1887, D.L. & W. Papers.

[180] The U.M.W. was successful in transcending ethnic rivalries even though it remained an uneasy alliance between 'old' and 'new' immigrant groups in the anthracite workforce. Aurand, op. cit., pp. 130–44.

[181] *Scranton Republican*, 15 Aug. 1899; *United Mine Workers Journal*, 13 Sept. 1900.

[182] Berthoff, 'The Welsh', p. 1015.

as a significant number of widows, presumably of Welsh miners. The description 'miner' is relatively sparse in comparison to 'clerk' or 'laborer' (that is, general labourers, and not necessarily mine labourers). The trend continued. Out of the ninety-two heads of families listed under the surname Evans in the 1910 directory, a mere nine were miners, and only eleven of the seventy-seven listed under Jones were similarly recorded. In the 1920 directory there was only one miner with the surname Thomas and two named Williams living in Scranton.[183]

The returns of the 1900 Manuscript Census for Scranton reveal a further dimension to the changing character of the community. Mining was no longer a family tradition and Welsh sons were not following their fathers' occupation, in sharp contrast to the norm during the early years of the community. The sons of Welsh families who were still living at home were now engaged in commerce and the professions as clerks, bank tellers, shop assistants and even doctors, lawyers and insurance agents.[184] First-generation Welsh miners and, to an even greater extent, their sons were remarkably successful in achieving upward mobility. John Bodnar has calculated that between 1880 and 1890, 39 per cent of the sons of Welsh families who remained in the city were upwardly mobile, and 45 per cent of those in nuclear families.[185] Many of Scranton's Welsh breaker boys and door boys left the industry to establish their own concerns, like Thomas D. Davies's son, T. Ellsworth Davies, or, like those who came of age at the turn of the century, to enter the professions.[186] John Bodnar actually attributes the high rate of Welsh upward mobility to the fact that Welsh sons were given greater exposure to adult occupations at an early age. This allowed them to learn valuable industrial skills which improved their chances of attaining occupational advancement.[187]

The Welsh in Scranton were able to secure jobs outside the mines and attain upward mobility because opportunities for alternative employment were increasingly available in the city

---

[183] Taylor's *Scranton City Directory*, 1900; *Scranton City Directory*, 1910; *Scranton City Directory*, 1920.

[184] U.S. Manuscript Census, Scranton, 1900.

[185] Bodnar, loc. cit., pp. 156–7.

[186] T. Ellsworth Davies established the Collins and Davies Merchant Store in Hyde Park in 1892 after beginning his career as a door boy in the mines at the age of fourteen. *Scranton Republican*, 5 Dec. 1889, 4 Sept. 1891, 27 Feb. 1892.

[187] Bodnar, loc. cit., p. 161.

as its economy diversified during the late nineteenth century. In the smaller mining towns in the area the defection of the Welsh from the mining industry necessitated migration. In Scranton, however, the Welsh were able to stay in the city, and as it matured into a major urban centre, with a widening industrial base and a growing commercial, administrative and public services sector, the Welsh community, in occupational terms, diversified with it.[188]

The drive for upward mobility among both first-generation Welshmen and their American-born children was in part a response to, and equally a reflection of, a deep change of attitude towards mining. The Welsh no longer regarded it as the premier and most obvious avenue for employment, as it had formerly been. This reappraisal was simultaneously prevalent in Welsh communities in most of the coalfields in the United States. In 1913 a commentator on the Welsh settlements in the Pennsylvania bituminous coalfield noted: 'Sons of Welshmen never work in the mines, unless it is a case of failure everywhere else.' This, he continued, 'is a healthy state of affairs compared to the days when almost every Welshman sought work in the mines'.[189]

The success rate in gaining upward mobility among first-generation Welsh miners and their American-born children, the wider change in attitudes towards mining, and the availability of alternative employment in the Scrantonian economy would themselves have led to a gradual decrease in the number of Welsh mineworkers in the city. However, the impact of these long-term developments was accelerated by a decisive intervention which sealed the end of Welsh involvement: the influx of labour into the industry from southern and eastern Europe. The concentration of Slavic and Italian immigrants in the mines lessened the industry's appeal to the Welsh, and consequently strengthened the impetus to seek out alternative employment, and drove them out of mining.

By the end of the nineteenth century a drastic recomposition of the workforce in the industry had taken place.[190] It affected

---

[188] Ibid., p. 149. See above, ch. 1, pp. 7–9.
[189] *Druid*, 24 Apr. 1913.
[190] For accounts of the recomposition of the workforce and its impact see Frank J. Warne, *The Slav Invasion and the Mine Workers: A Study in Immigration* (Philadelphia, 1904); Henry Rood, 'The mine laborers in Pennsylvania', *Forum*, XIV (1892–3), pp. 110–22; Miller and Sharpless, op. cit., pp. 172–81; Berthoff, *British Immigrants*,

the whole of the anthracite coalfield – and indeed most of the coalfields in the United States – but if first became apparent in the Schuylkill coalfield during the late 1880s. By the early 1890s the change had spread to the northern region and the Scranton area.[191] In the conditions which prevailed in the industry at the end of the century, the labour provided by the new influx was far more attractive to the employers than that of the Welsh and the other 'older' immigrant groups which had formerly made up the bulk of the workforce. The Poles, Hungarians and Italians were prepared to accept lower wages, being content with a minimum level, whilst in contrast the Welsh, English, Scots, Irish and Germans demanded wages which would permit them to maintain a reasonable standard of living. Mining was also becoming less and less of a skilled occupation. Although there were no major advances in mechanization in the anthracite industry until well into the twentieth century, there were improvements in blasting techniques which minimized the need for hand-cutting the coal. Furthermore, by the end of the century most of the richer seams had been worked out and production was concentrated in the thinner, more dangerous seams. Here, strength was more useful than skill, whilst the new immigrants were prepared to accept the riskier conditions and to work longer hours in the mines. This was in marked contrast to the Welsh miners, whose relatively short working days had always been a central feature of their work practices. Ultimately, the old Welsh trump card – mining skill – was rapidly becoming irrelevant as far as the rank-and-file Welsh miner was concerned.[192]

The crisis created by the new influx did not end the career potential which the anthracite industry could offer some ambitious Welshmen. The changing composition of the workforce enabled even more Welshmen to achieve managerial and supervisory positions in Scranton's mines. *Taylor's Scranton City Directory* of 1900 listed almost as many Welsh mine bosses as miners in the city.[193] A visitor to the mines in the area in 1910

pp. 55–8.
[191] Warne, op. cit., pp. 48–56. Between 1880 and 1900, the number of East European employees in the anthracite industry rose from 5 to 50 per cent.
[192] Warne, op. cit., pp. 76–83; Miller and Sharpless, op. cit., pp. 172–81; Billinger, op. cit., pp. 16–20.
[193] Berthoff, *British Immigrants*, pp. 55–6; *Taylor's Scranton City Directory*, 1900.

recorded that the managers and superintendents were Welsh, the foremen and bosses Irish, and the contract miners Poles and Lithuanians.[194] Moreover, with the growth of the Pennsylvania Mines Inspectorate, a small minority made their presence felt at this level. The Hyde Park Welsh community bred a succession of mine inspectors at the turn of the century, notably David T. Williams and Llewellyn M. Evans.[195]

If the Welsh domination of managerial and supervisory positions in Scranton was perpetuated or even increased as a result of the dramatic changes in the industry, it was a hierarchy without a base. The vast majority of Welsh miners who were unable to gain promotion were faced with a bitter dilemma: either to stay in the mines and work for lower wages or to withdraw from the competition and seek work elsewhere. Most chose the latter. Vain attempts were made to prevent the new influx into the mines, through lobbying for immigration laws and introducing English-language qualifications into miners' certificate examinations.[196] In an article on Pennsylvania's mineworkers in *Forum* in 1892, Henry Rood painted a vivid picture of how 'day after day unschooled Americans, Irish and Welshmen discuss the immigration question and either curse Congress or pray that it may realize what will happen to the nation if these swarms are allowed to fester and breed misery in the land.'[197]

But the tide could not be stopped, and throughout the anthracite region the Welsh retreated from the mines. Most Welsh ex-miners in Scranton stayed in the city, although some did try their luck in other coalfields in the United States. In 1891, for example, fifty-seven Welsh miners left for Indian Territory, where new coal mines were being opened up.[198] Others went home to Wales. In Rowland Berthoff's memorable description: 'Down to the Scranton Depot on their way home trooped scores of Welshmen in 1890, their American citizenship forgotten.'[199]

---

[194] Quoted in Berthoff, *British Immigrants*, p. 56.
[195] Murphy, *Hist. Hyde Park*, p. 24. For the growth of the Pennsylvania mine inspectorate see Roberts, op. cit., pp. 96–7.
[196] Warne, op. cit., pp. 78–9, 87–8.
[197] Rood, loc. cit., p. 115.
[198] *Scranton Republican*, 15 Mar. 1891.
[199] Berthoff, *British Immigrants*, p. 55.

The nature and the implications of the recomposition of the workforce in the anthracite industry were encapsulated by a John R. Williams of Algoma, West Virginia, formerly of Wilkes-Barre and originally from Aberdare, in 1895:

> Pennsylvania is swarming with foreigners – Poles, Hungarians, Slavish, Swedes, and Italians etc. – who are fast driving the English, Welsh, and Scotch miners out of competition. Noticeably, the Poles and Hungarians are a harder-working people and physically stronger men than the English and Welsh. They live much harder and at about half the cost and can stand more and harder work than our countrymen.
>
> Before the influx of the foreigners I have named into this country, the Welsh had the best show of the mines here . . . but . . . whole cargoes of foreigners I have named now practically monopolize the business, and no longer will America hold out a friendly hand to the British miner who must stay at home and do the best he can there or come here and starve.[200]

In Scranton – indeed throughout the north-east Pennsylvania coalfield – the departure of the Welsh from the mines during the last years of the nineteenth century signalled the end of an era, as John Williams's epitaph correctly suggested. No longer did they have the 'best show' of the mines, and no longer were they reliant on coal for a livelihood. By the turn of the century Welshmen in Scranton had migrated into commercial and professional – perhaps even 'middle-class' – America and the blue scars on many of the faces were now reflected by starched white collars.

Yet a price had to be paid for this break-out from the open prison of the anthracite industry, and the exodus *en masse* from the mines was far more than an occupational shift. Fundamentally, it took away one of the strongest bonds which had kept the Welsh community together and given it a distinctive identity. Their complex roles as, at the same time, the serfs and the aristocracy of Scranton's 'Kingdom of Coal' bolstered, and drew on, their sense of ethnicity to make the Welsh response during 1871–2 possible. The strike and its political aftermath had seen a flicker of an alternative definition of Welshness, and it was one which on occasion flared briefly during the remainder of the decade. In 1871 a consciousness of ethnic, occupational and even class identity had fused and the Welsh had acted both as

---

[200] John R. Williams to William Thomas, 10 Nov. 1895, National Library of Wales MS 3293 E, also quoted in Conway, *The Welsh in America*, pp. 204–10 (especially 205).

Welsh people and as a working class. But as the later history of political and union activity showed, permanent class consciousness was incompatible with traditional ethnic and occupational identities, and it was the latter which reigned supreme. The potential for uniting all these interests was always there as long as the Welsh maintained their intense involvement in the industry and that industry continued to create periodic crises. Their departure from the mines finally aborted the underdeveloped embryo of an alternative tradition which had been conceived in 1871.

Paradoxically, however, during the last years of the nineteenth century that sense of ethnicity was itself in crisis. The fatal blow which East European and Italian immigration dealt to the involvement of Welsh people in the industry had even deeper repercussions for their own perception of themselves. The new 'alien' immigrants – John R. Williams's 'foreigners' – as the Welsh saw them, blurred the distinctions between the Welsh and native-Americans at the same time as Welsh families diversified occupationally and merged socially into the wider Scrantonian economy. The loss of the powerful cohesive force and distinct identity which their concentration in the anthracite industry provided was one crucial instigator of the crisis in which the Welsh community found itself at the turn of the century. That crisis was made all the more traumatic by the realization that not only had a monolithic mining community been dissolved; the same generation had experienced the rise and fall of the epicentre of Welsh-language culture in America.

III
WELSH CULTURAL LIFE IN SCRANTON

In the *Druid* in October 1909, Judge Henry M. Edwards, the *éminence grise* behind most Welsh cultural initiatives in Scranton during the late nineteenth and early twentieth centuries, compared the Hyde Park of his earlier years with that of the time at which he was writing. Between 1864 and 1875, he declared,

> it was undoubtedly the greatest Welsh center in the United States. The services in the Welsh churches then were altogether in the Welsh language. The Welsh people were better church-goers then than they are now... The Eisteddfods then were conducted almost altogether in Welsh ... In the last fifteen or twenty years, there has been a great change. The use of the Welsh language is less and less every year and it is safe to say that fifteen years hence there will be very little Welsh spoken. The Welsh churches will be altogether English, instead of half English, as they are now. Nevertheless the Welsh spirit will remain.[1]

Judge Edwards's reminiscences accurately encapsulated some of the major cultural changes experienced by the community he had lived in for over forty years.[2] In its early years, Welsh culture flourished with an intensity unmatched elsewhere in the United States. Indeed by the late 1860s Hyde Park had been christened the 'Welsh Athens of America'.[3] By the first decade of the twentieth century, however, the cultural life of the Welsh had been decisively and irrevocably transformed. Welshness had waned, but its legacy still lingered to infuse the expression of that Welsh spirit to which the learned judge referred: Welsh-Americanism.

I THE WELSH ATHENS OF AMERICA

The Welsh immigrants who flocked to Scranton during the

---

[1] *Druid*, 21 Oct. 1909.
[2] For biographical details of H. M. Edwards (1844–1925), see ibid., 15 Dec. 1925; Stoddard, op. cit., pp. xvi–xvii.
[3] *Drych*, 20 Apr. 1871.

middle decades of the nineteenth century brought with them the culture and language of the homeland. They transplanted and nurtured that culture in the city to such an extent that Welshness was written large in an effervescence of literary, musical, religious and eisteddfodic activity. Hyde Park possessed in abundance all the ingredients for brewing a 'Welsh' cultural life of unparalleled quality and vitality.

Hyde Park could boast a rich seam of active literary talent which alone justified its reputation as the 'Welsh Athens of America'. Over fifty recognized Welsh bards lived in the city. Many of them had made their names in eisteddfodau in Wales and were among the foremost Welsh-American men of letters. They included Revd Joseph E. Davies ('Ieuan Ddu'), John Hughes ('Irlwyn'), Isaac Benjamin ('Bardd Coch'), Samuel Williams ('Gwentyddfardd') and, during his stay in the city in the late 1860s, Revd Fred Evans ('Ednyfed'). Some were chaired bards – the highest possible bardic achievement – notably T. B. Morris ('Gwyneddfardd') and H. M. Edwards ('Harri Ddu').[4] Known universally to readers of the *Drych* as 'y bois', they frequently met at the house of another of Welsh-America's most prominent *literati*, David C. Powell ('Dewi Cwmtwrch'), who was the doyen of eisteddfodic essay competition winners, both in Wales and in the United States, and a Scranton correspondent of the *Drych* for over half a century.[5]

Hyde Park's seemingly bottomless purse of literary resources was directly responsible for a further indication of its pre-eminence as the 'Welsh Athens of America'. In the 1860s and 1870s, Scranton was a major centre of the Welsh-American press, and a number of Welsh-language newspapers and periodicals were published there. Until it was taken over by the *Drych* in 1877, the weekly *Baner America* had an eventful nine-year existence, well illustrated by its role in the 1871 strike and its embroilment in local politics.[6] The genesis of the paper dated back to April 1868, when a meeting of potential shareholders of 'a new weekly Welsh newspaper on a broad

---

[4] R. D. Thomas, op. cit., Dosran C., p. 58.
[5] *Drych*, 14 Apr. 1892, 17 Nov. 1910.
[6] Murphy, *Hist. Lack. Co.*, p. 357; Bob Owen, 'Welsh American newspapers and periodicals', *National Library of Wales Journal*, VI (1950), pp. 373-84 (especially 374).

national basis' felt that such a medium was needed because of 'the influence of the Welsh element on the American continent, their attachment to their language and their love of literature'.[7] Many of those who contributed either as editors, managers or shareholders during the succeeding decade were among the most prominent Welshmen in Scranton. Initially, the newspaper was heavily dependent on local ministers of religion for editorial and literacy posts. Revd Morgan A. Ellis and Ednyfed played a key role in the late 1860s, whilst *Baner America's* first political editor was H. M. Edwards, who was making his début in the world of the Welsh-American press. Although national in scope, much of the newspaper's content was of a local character.[8]

Two other Welsh-language newspaper initiatives came out of the Scranton Welsh community in the late 1870s, although both were short-lived. The first issue of *Tarian y Bobl* appeared in 1877, and it was owned and edited by one who was destined to be Scranton's leading Welsh newspaperman, John Courier Morris. The newspaper was Republican in politics, and its collapse later in the same year may have been caused by the defection of many Welsh votes to the Greenback-Labor Party.[9] In 1879 D. J. Evans, the last owner of *Baner America*, began *Baner y Gweithiwr*. This also failed within a matter of months, signalling the end of Scranton's reign as a centre of the Welsh-language American press.[10]

Apart from newspapers, several short-lived Welsh-language periodicals were established in Scranton during the late 1860s and 1870s. Most of these focused specifically on Welsh literature. Notable here was *Y Ford Gron* which existed briefly during 1868, and the far more successful *Yr Ymwelydd* which first appeared in 1871.[11] The latter was owned and edited by H. M. Edwards and according to the *Scranton Republican*, was 'replete with wit and humor'.[12] It published the editor's own literary

---

[7] *Carbondale Advance*, 2 May 1868.
[8] R. D. Thomas,, op. cit., Dosran C., pp. 63–4; Bob Owen, 'Welsh American newspapers', p. 374.
[9] Murphy, *Hist. Hyde Park*, p. 81. See above, ch. 2, pp. 77–9.
[10] Ibid., pp. 81, 84. Bob Owen cites *Baner y Gweithiwr* as *Baner y Bobl*, perhaps confusing it with Courier's *Tarian y Bobl*. Bob Owen, 'Welsh American newspapers', p. 383.
[11] *Ford Gron*, 1 (Jan. 1867), title page; R. D. Thomas, op. cit., Dosran C., p. 65; Bob Owen, 'Welsh American newspapers', pp. 380, 384.
[12] Scranton *Morning Republican*, 10 Mar. 1871. An English-language version of this

and poetic compositions as well as those of other local *literati*, such as Dewi Cwmtwrch and Ednyfed. Another Welsh-language periodical published in Scranton in these years was John Courier Morris's *Y Pwnsh Cymraeg*. This was satirical in nature and was based on the English *Punch* and the Liverpool *Y Pwnsh Cymraeg*. It seems to have created quite a stir during its brief life in the mid-1870s. According to one local historian, 'the people did not warm up to the brand of humor it contained and it died quickly.'[13] The American national periodical of the Welsh Calvinistic Methodists, *Y Cyfaill O'r Hen Wlad*, was also published in the city during the 1860s and 1870s. Its editors were the prominent local ministers and men of letters, Revd Morgan Ellis of Hyde Park and Revd William Roberts of Bellevue.[14]

Welsh-language publications did much both to establish and to enhance Hyde Park's prestige as the 'Welsh Athens of America'. They also reflected the fact that at this time the Welsh community was overwhelmingly Welsh-speaking. Apparently a great many of the Welsh could also speak English, or at least had some knowledge of it,[15] but it was the Welsh language that was the main medium of conversation, and it pervaded all aspects of immigrant life. Businessmen used it in their advertisements, and one of the first acts of the new Welsh management of the West Side Bank in 1874 was to print a thousand leaflets in the Welsh language outlining the organization's aims and terms.[16] Even the Welsh drunkards along Main Avenue were reputed to sing and swear in Welsh.[17]

The Welsh language had its widest public usage in the activities of the cultural institutions and societies which the Welsh immigrants established in Scranton. It was the strength and vibrancy of these organizations which sealed the reputation of Hyde Park and the city in general as a hive of Welsh culture. As such, they were not only expressions of a distinctive Welsh cultural identity; they were also the most powerful forces which

periodical, *The Visitor*, was also published.
[13] Murphy, *Hist, Hyde Park*, p. 85: Bob Owen, 'Welsh American newspapers', p. 382.
[14] *Cyfaill o'r Hen Wlad*, XXXIII (Jan. 1870), title page; R. D. Thomas, op. cit., p. 64.
[15] Scranton *Morning Republican*, 10 June 1875. Evidence of the number of Welsh-speakers in Scranton is of necessity impressionistic because no statistical record has survived.
[16] Murphy, *History of the West Side Bank*, p. 8.
[17] *Drych*, 28 July 1870.

nurtured and maintained it. The most important of these institutions and societies were undoubtedly the Welsh churches, whose presence and activities literally towered over community life.

Welsh religious Nonconformity put down strong roots in Scranton during the nineteenth century. For many of the Welsh it was not only a particular religious belief; it was an integral element of Welshness, and as the involvement of local ministers in the city's Welsh publishing ventures well symbolizes, religion was inextricably entwined with the Welsh language and Welsh culture. Although not all the Welsh in Scranton were religious or attended services, religious attendance was widespread and, as in Wales, religion, in the words of Glanmor Williams, was 'a uniquely compelling force'.[18]

The Scrantonian Welsh imitated the Welsh in Wales in the frenzy with which they formed, and then built, chapels (or, in their American context, churches). By the late 1850s, all three leading Welsh denominations – Baptists, Congregationalists and Calvinistic Methodists – had established separate churches, and during the following three decades each grew rapidly in strength as Welsh immigration increased. In 1870 there were no less than seven Welsh churches in various wards of the city,[19] and their size and visual prominence alone reflected their importance. Nowhere was this more so than in Hyde Park itself. Here all three denominations had built magnificent edifices virtually next door to each other, each costing over $12,000 and capable of seating up to 800 people. In his *Hanes Cymry America* of 1872, Revd R. D. Thomas ('Iorthryn Gwynedd') marvelled at their impact on the landscape: 'Their spires rise up to Heaven! They can be seen plainly from Scranton, and from a great distance beyond the city.'[20]

All three denominations in the city flourished, but the Baptist cause was particularly strong. No doubt this was mainly due to the fact that the bulk of the Welsh immigrants in Scranton were from industrial south Wales, where Baptists were more numerous than in the rural areas.[21] Out of the seed of the original

---

[18] Glanmor Williams, 'Religion, language, and nationality in Wales', in *idem, Religion, Language and Nationality in Wales*, op. cit., pp. 1–33.
[19] *Webb's Scranton Directory*, 1870–1.
[20] R. D. Thomas, op. cit., p. 58.
[21] W. R. Lambert, *Drink and Sobriety in Victorian Wales c. 1820–1895* (Cardiff, 1983), p. 64.

Baptist Church formed in Slocum Hollow in 1845 flowered five large institutions, all on the West Side, with property worth around $250,000 and a total of 3,000 communicants. The first Welsh Baptist Church on South Main Avenue, Hyde Park (established in 1863), very quickly achieved a position of dominance over all the other Baptist churches in America. Not only was it the largest; by the time Revd Fred Evans ('Ednyfed') took up the pastorate in 1866, it was universally regarded as the most influential on the continent.[22] Within four years, as a result of his efforts and continued immigration, membership alone stood at 400, a figure unparalleled in the United States, whilst attendances averaged around 800.[23]

Although the religious community was divided into denominations, the similarities between them were perhaps more important than their differences over doctrine and church government. As Ieuan Gwynedd Jones has emphasized in his studies on Nonconformity in Wales, denominational splits may have clouded our appreciation of what each had in common. He suggests that the intense theological debates and controversies which raged in nineteenth-century Welsh newspapers had little relevance to the average chapel-goer, since they were ultimately the concern of a minority.[24] The same can be said of the Welsh churches in Scranton. In many ways, Welsh Nonconformity presented a united front and, consequently, religion was perhaps the most powerful of the forces which forged the community's societal cohesion and exclusive identity, especially as its impact was reinforced linguistically. Its importance in this respect is emphasized by the way religious beliefs either divided or failed to nurture a separate identity among other ethnic groups in the city. The German community was split along Protestant–Catholic lines, whilst English immigrants were far more diverse in their religion, and, lacking a separate language, they mostly attended American churches. Only the predominantly Catholic Irish were in a comparable position to

---

[22] *Seventy-Fifth Anniversary*, pp. 7–8; Murphy, *Hist. Hyde Park*, p. 53; B. D. Thomas (ed.), *Frederick Evans DD (Ednyfed): A Memorial* (Philadelphia, 1899), p. 61.

[23] *Dedication Service Souvenir, First Welsh Baptist Church* (Scranton, 1958), p. 3; *Seventy-Fifth Anniversary*, p. 13.

[24] Ieuan Gwynedd Jones, 'Religion and society in the first half of the nineteenth century', in *idem*, *Explorations and Explanations: Essays in the Social History of Victorian Wales* (Llandysul, 1981), pp. 217–35 (especially 231).

the Welsh; indeed relations between these two groups were strongly influenced by their religious animosities towards each other.[25]

The religious homogeneity of the Welsh alone made Nonconformity a strong unifying force, but its impact in this respect was heightened by the fact that the Welsh churches in Scranton were far more than ministers of Welsh-language 'moddion gras' ('means of grace') every Sunday morning and evening. In many ways, like their counterparts in Wales, they were communities in themselves. Each church had a number of auxiliary societies attached to it which catered for all ages and both sexes. As in Wales, the churches welcomed women's participation, particularly in their social activities, and the church was one of the few meeting places for women. The Baptist Church, for example, had a Women's Missionary Society, a Ladies' Aid Society, a Band of Hope and a Baptist Youth fellowship.[26] Similar groups were formed at the other churches.[27] By far the most important of the churches' vestry (or, to use its American terminology, lecture room) activities were the Sunday and Weekly Church or Bible Schools. The Welsh Congregational Church in Hyde Park organized such schools in Primary, Junior and Senior Departments and the latter was reputed to be the best in the city.[28] The First Welsh Baptist Church organized branch Sunday Schools in various wards of the city, and in the late 1880s it estimated that these had a total of over 750 members.[29]

The Sunday and Weekly Schools fulfilled an educational as well as a religious role. Many taught in English as well as in Welsh. The branch Sunday School which the Baptist Church established in a school house in ward 11 in 1871, for example, taught in both languages.[30] The emphasis on these occasions was on education and discussion. The weekly Baptist Bible School, held from the 1860s until well into the 1920s, read and debated the history and geography of the Bible and it discussed the Old Testament for the first six months of the year and the

---

[25] For a fuller discussion see Walker, op. cit., pp. 43–6.
[26] *Seventy-Fifth Anniversary, passim.*
[27] *Sixtieth Anniversary, passim*; Davy Edgar Jones, op. cit., *passim.*
[28] Murphy, *Hist. Hyde Park*, p. 55.
[29] *Seventy-Fifth Anniversary*, p. 3.
[30] Scranton *Morning Republican*, 24 Mar. 1871.

New Testament for the remainder.[31] Some of its debates could be hotly disputed affairs. In 1877 Phoebe Gibbons related two separate instances of the type of proceedings at these sessions. During a discussion on the Book of Samuel an intense disagreement arose over the question of whether Samuel was raised by the Witch of Endor. After some deliberation it was found that the question was taking up too much time and it was referred to disputants, two on each side. The controversy took up the remainder of the evening's business and it was eventually settled that Samuel was not raised (a conclusion with which the minister present did not agree!). Sometime during the early 1870s, too, the school argued the question of whether the world was created in six days, and it decided that the days concerned were not periods of twenty-four hours. After the debate a former preacher delivered a lecture on geology which put forward a similar analysis.[32]

The churches and their associated societies also organized a full calendar of social activities which further emphasized their importance to Welsh community life. They held various functions and outings and, in particular, promoted concerts and eisteddfodau, in some cases in order to clear debts or collect money for the families of victims of mining accidents.[33] Church choirs – both children's and senior – gave frequent performances, whilst it was the church buildings themselves which provided the venues not only for their own cultural events but also for many of those organized by non-religious societies.[34]

It seems that church activities were important in other aspects of life. Phoebe Gibbons was told that most of the courtship of the Welsh began, and often finished, whilst walking the streets after church:

> This street is thronged ... on Sunday nights in summer. At first the young men walk behind, but after a while one step is quickened or the other slackened, or both, and they come together, and form lively parties until ten or after. Courtships are brief and marriages early and happy.[35]

---

[31] Murphy, *Hist, Hyde Park*, p. 53.
[32] Gibbons, loc. cit., pp. 923–4.
[33] See, for example, *Drych*, 28 July 1870, 8 Jan. 1885, 21 Jan. 1886; *Scranton Republican*, 15 Aug. 1880, 28 July 1881.
[34] *Drych*, 22 Aug. 1867, 4 Apr. 1872. See also David E. Jones, loc. cit., pp. 339–40; *Seventy-Fifth Anniversary*, p. 12.
[35] Gibbons, loc. cit., p. 920. The evidence regarding ages of marriage among the

The Welsh churches' multiplicity of roles had a number of implications for the Welsh community. They created opportunities for the Welsh immigrants to experience and exercise leadership by organizing the affiliated societies, serving as teachers or superintendents in the Sunday Schools and participating in church government by acting as trustees and deacons. In this respect the church also created the conditions which enabled community leaders both to gain prominence and enhance authority. Many of the leading Welshmen in other spheres of community life also wielded influence in the churches: Benjamin Hughes was treasurer and a trustee of the First Baptist Church; H. M. Edwards was a trustee of the Hyde Park Welsh Congregational Church and taught in its Bible School, and the secretary and trustee of that section's Calvinistic Methodist Church was B. G. Morgan.[36]

In common with other immigrant groups, the Welsh established secular societies in Scranton. Improvement and benevolent societies which, like their counterparts elsewhere in the United States, also functioned as cultural organizations.[37] Among them were the various lodges of the Ivorites, notably the Teml Ifor Hael Lodge in Hyde Park, set up by Benjamin Hughes in 1867, which sponsored eisteddfodau and concerts. Proceedings were conducted in the Welsh language.[38] The most influential Welsh society in Scranton was the Welsh Philosophical Society, whose activities pervaded the cultural life of the community throughout the second half of the nineteenth century.

The Welsh Philosophical Society was established in 1857 and first met above Thomas Eynon's store on South Main Avenue in Hyde Park. Eynon himself was one of the founders, along with prominent Hyde Park mining men such as Benjamin Hughes,

---

Welsh in Scranton is contradictory. According to one Welshman interviewed by Phoebe Gibbons, both men and women who had not married before the age of 23 were considered 'old'. Ibid. Yet in a recent study based on a sample of Welsh families in Scranton in 1880, Bodnar found that the majority of Welsh wives had not married until their late twenties. Bodnar, loc. cit., p. 161.

[36] 'Sunday School history and biographical sketches of Scranton, Pennsylvania, members', in *Why We Are Protestants: History of the Welsh Calvinistic Methodists in Wales and America* (New York, 1893) (no pagination).

[37] Hartmann, op. cit., p. 156. For a survey of Welsh-American improvement and benevolent societies see ibid., pp. 156–61.

[38] *Drych*, 26 March. 1885; *Webb's Scranton Directory*, 1870–1; Murphy, *Hist. Hyde Park*, p. 63.

Thomas D. Davies and Thomas Phillips.[39] According to Thomas Murphy, the society was 'socially a leader. Every prominent Hyde Parker of Welsh blood was a member and membership was looked upon as a badge of standing.'[40] The society was set up 'to enable the Welsh working men of Hyde Park to meet at least once a week to investigate and debate questions relating more particularly to mines, mining, geology, natural philosophy and other kindred subjects'.[41] From the first its aim was to secure 'practical results' by aiding the upward mobility of its members. In this respect the society achieved a remarkable degree of success, to such an extent that by 1891, according to David Craft,

> A large number of the members of this society are now filling positions of profit and responsibility in the management of the mines. Some have become mine inspectors, others have become superintendents of mines, and many others mine foremen. The society has been the best possible preparatory school for its members, preparing them for higher and better positions.[42]

Attendance at the meetings seems to have been overwhelmingly male, although a Mrs Margaret Roberts was apparently a very prominent participant during the 1870s and 1880s.[43] The society's proceedings were conducted entirely in the Welsh language but, true to its commitment to education and improvement, from the mid-1870s onwards it organized classes for studying English grammar and spelling. It also issued circulars stressing the need for education because 'men started work at a young age'.[44]

Hardly surprisingly perhaps, mining was the major focus of the society's debates. This enabled many Welsh miners to

---

[39] *Scranton Republican*, 8 Feb. 1892; Craft, op. cit., p. 545.
[40] Murphy, *Hist. Hyde Park*, p. 65.
[41] Craft, op. cit., p. 545.
[42] Ibid., p. 546.
[43] *Drych*, 10 April 1884. Unfortunately very little is known about Mrs Margaret Roberts, who seems to have been a very strong-minded, independent character. Her contributions to the debates of the Welsh Philosophical Society were remarked upon by H. M. Edwards in 1910. *Druid*, 7 Oct. 1910. She also wrote articles in the *Drych*, many of them in support of the temperance movement, and in 1895 wrote a series describing the formation of the Women's Christian Temperance Movement, in which she seems to have been involved. One *Drych* correspondent was of the opinion that she stood as high as any man who had written for the newspaper on any subject. *Drych*, 8 Mar., 14, 21, 28 June, 12 July 1894, 14 Feb., 7 Mar. 1895.
[44] Ibid., 27 Apr. 1876; Scranton *Morning Republican*, 21 Feb. 1876; Scranton *Daily Times*, 15 Feb. 1877.

acquire an extensive knowledge of the subject, which would have been unattainable without the society's existence. It also debated other matters. Politics, ancient and modern history, poetry and music were all featured as were, on occasion, religious topics. In March 1871, for example, a meeting dealt with 'The Being of God: His Relation to our form of government', in which the debating skills of H. M. Edwards and the physically deformed W. Llewellyn Williams, 'with his diminutive four-foot stature and red hair', impressed the *Scranton Republican* reporter present.[45] Sometimes the society deliberated on some truly intriguing subjects. In 1893 a John E. Jones read a paper which queried whether there was a rainbow in the clouds before the Deluge.[46] Sadly, no records of the society's debates are extant. The sentiments expressed on the evening of 7 February 1891, when a meeting argued whether it was 'proper to call the Welsh people a nation being that they have no government of their own',[47] would undoubtedly have made interesting reading. Considering the scope of the society's proceedings, Craft was surely right to remark that 'the nature of the subjects investigated fully justified the title "philosophical society"'.[48]

The Welsh Philosophical Society embraced the same dichotomy of function that characterized other Welsh organizations in the city. As well as being an improvement society and a forum for intellectual discussion, it promoted a wide variety of concerts, literary gatherings and excursions.[49] Above all, from 1863 onwards, it held an annual eisteddfod on Christmas Day in order to defray its running expenses. These events were among the high points on the calendar of Welsh social and cultural activities in the city.[50]

The Welsh Philosophical Society's utilization of the eisteddfod and the widespread sponsoring of it by the Welsh churches and other Welsh organizations in Scranton reflect the emblematic

---

[45] Scranton *Morning Republican*, 5 Mar. 1871.
[46] *Scranton Republican*, 29 Apr. 1893.
[47] Ibid., 7 Feb. 1891.
[48] Craft, op. cit., p. 545.
[49] See, for example, Scranton *Morning Republican*, 3, 11 Mar. 1871; *Scranton Republican*, 6 Aug. 1880.
[50] *Drych*, 25 Apr. 1863, 10 Jan. 1878; Scranton *Morning Republican*, 7 Dec. 1876.

presence of that institution. The eisteddfod's popularity in Wales following its nineteenth-century revival was echoed across the Atlantic. Here, too, it gained the status of being, after the chapel, the premier Welsh institution, and eisteddfodau became integral elements in the cultural activities of most Welsh-American communities.[51] The Lackawanna Valley occupies a pioneering position in the Welsh-American eisteddfodic tradition because the first recorded eisteddfod in the United States was that held in Carbondale on Christmas Day, 1850. Some of those involved in organizing this occasion would later contribute greatly to the cultural life of the Welsh in Scranton, among them Thomas Eynon.[52]

The eisteddfod quickly took root in the new Welsh settlement lower down the valley. The first eisteddfod in Hyde Park took place in 1859, when the Welsh Philosophical Society held a meeting in Fellows Hall. In 1867 a two-day event was organized, undoubtedly the prototype for the prestigious large-scale 'National Eisteddfodau' which would be held sporadically in the city over the next forty years. According to one source the Merthyr-born composer who was raised in Danville, Pennsylvania, Joseph Parry, wrote one of his most famous works, 'Ar Don O Flaen Gwyntoedd', as a test piece for the chief choral competition at this event.[53] In that contest four choirs from the vicinity competed, including the Hyde Park Choral Union, conducted by Robert Jones, whose victory established the choral prestige which Scranton and Hyde Park would both enjoy and enhance during the next half-century.[54]

Eisteddfodau fulfilled a number of roles in the life of the Welsh community. They were important in developing and nurturing local literary and musical talent. Many of Scranton's early Welsh choirs were organized specifically to compete in eisteddfodau, notably the Cambro-Americans, the Pennsylvanians and

[51] Prys Morgan, *The Eighteenth Century Renaissance* (Llandybïe, 1981), pp. 63–6, 155; Hywel Teifi Edwards, *'Gŵyl Gwalia': Yr Eisteddfod Genedlaethol yn Oes Aur Victoria, 1858–1868* (Llandysul, 1980); idem, *The Eisteddfod* (Cardiff, 1990). For the eisteddfod in the U.S. see Hartmann, op. cit., pp. 146–9; Berthoff, *British Immigrants*, pp. 173–4.
[52] David E. Jones, loc. cit., p. 338.
[53] *Drych*, 26 Mar. 1868; David E. Jones, loc. cit., p. 339. There is some doubt regarding Jones's assertion. The work was included among Parry's entries for the composition competitions in the 1864 National Eisteddfod of Wales. Inexplicably, they failed to reach Wales. See Hywel Teifi Edwards, *'Gŵyl Gwalia'*, p. 228.
[54] David E. Jones, loc. cit., p. 339.

the Scranton Choral Society, whilst it was during these events that future eminent local soloists such as Eos Cynon, Llew Herbert and Lizzie Parry James first attracted attention.[55] As well as acting as a 'university of the poor', eisteddfodau were the most popular and effective of fund-raising activities for most Welsh organizations and not merely the Welsh Philosophical Society. In addition, for competitor and audience alike, and for both sexes, they were a rewarding leisure-time activity and festivals of endless entertainment, as Phoebe Gibbons's graphic, if rather bemused, account of the impact and character of the institution in Scranton in the 1870s emphasizes:

> Christmas is a great day among the Welsh and is observed by meetings of the 'Eisteddfod', a very ancient national gathering which can be traced back for nine hundred years . . .
>
> These gatherings are literary and musical. At Hyde Park it is announced in the Welsh paper, in the spring of that year, that the Philosophical Society will at the ensuing Christmas give prizes for the best essay or the best poem on given subjects and the best piece of original music for given words, also for singing and recitation . . .
>
> From the exercises of these gatherings women are not excluded. The Eisteddfods are very generally attended by the Welsh and are held in some large public hall, the greater part of the performances being in the Welsh language. Some of the observances have been described to me in simple language by one who has been a miner. He says that church choirs attend the eisteddfods, and some very difficult piece is selected for them to sing, the prize being about sixty to eighty dollars. Then there are singers alone and in parties of three. They get their poets there; they meet on Christmas morning about ten and adjourn about twelve and then give out subjects for the poets – likely the Lackawanna River, or some subject they had never thought of before. At two o'clock these poets will be called upon to recite these verses – two perhaps – and a small prize is given (about a dollar), principally for amusement . . . Another thing causes a good deal of laughter – they ask who will volunteer to sing a musical competition from the notes; some half a dozen will throw in their names . . . and then one will be called out . . . the other five will leave the room, while he picks up a difficult piece and begins to clear his throat and show his embarrassment, which is a subject of amusement to the spectators . . . and when all have finished the remarks of the judge upon each performance are also very amusing, the prize being only about 50 cents

[55] Ibid., pp. 339, 342.

... They hold these eisteddfods in Wales. The Welsh bards have for centuries back been accustomed to poetry.[56]

The frequency and popularity of eisteddfodau in Scranton led one Welsh commentator to draw the inevitable comparison with those eisteddfodau in the homeland to which Phoebe Gibbons referred. In the *Drych* in 1874, a correspondent writing under the pseudonym 'Exodus' outlined why the Scranton area was a south Wales reincarnate:

> Three big eisteddfodau within eight days of each other in the same County – and all of them attended by many people ... Luzerne County in America is almost like Glamorgan in Wales and Hyde Park is like Aberdare, Providence like Cwmdare and Heol y Felin and from there [go] over the Common to Olyphant and you are in Hirwaun ... This year Hyde Park Eisteddfod was like Aberdare Eisteddfod, Plymouth Eisteddfod like the old Pontypridd Eisteddfod and Pittston Eisteddfod like Mountain Ash Eisteddfod.[57]

The popularity of the eisteddfod and its uniqueness as a cultural event also made an impression on the city's non-Welsh population. In March 1871, for example, following a small eisteddfod in the Co-operative Hall, the *Scranton Republican* told its readers that all types of Welshmen had been present, 'mostly those with brains, religious and non religious, rich and poor, sober and a sprinkling of jesters all huddled in one room', and that William R. Williams had 'pocketed a quarter for something beyond our comprehension'.[58] Four years later, the same newspaper announced that a forthcoming church eisteddfod was scheduled to include a 'polysyllabic tournament' in which the Welsh would be caught in an 'orthographic epidemic'. It wondered whether Webster was to be the standard, but thought that this was unlikely owing to 'the language talked and the consonants selected'. The report quoted (wrongly) the word 'aunghufnewidiolediyaethau [*sic*]': 'a few words such as these will spread across the Atlantic,' it maintained.[59]

The impact eisteddfodau made on Scranton's Americans went beyond an occasioning of idle, if benevolent, amusement. With its emphasis on music, literature and self-improvement,

---

[56] Gibbons, loc. cit., p. 919.
[57] *Drych*, 12 Feb. 1874.
[58] Scranton *Morning Republican*, 11 Mar. 1871.
[59] Ibid., 11 May 1875.

the eisteddfod reinforced the positive, respectable image of the Welsh immigrants that was also created and confirmed by other aspects of their cultural life. The activities of the Welsh churches, the Sunday Schools, the Welsh Philosophical Society and the eisteddfod itself promoted, and were infused by, religiosity, utility and musical, literary, educational and intellectual endeavour. They complemented the efforts of the Welsh immigrant financial institutions to encourage home ownership and thrift. To the industrial and business élite in Scranton, who viewed the city's ethnically mixed population with unease, the widespread nurturing of these principles by the Welsh was proof that, despite their clinging to their national cultural traits, they were a worthy and valuable asset to Scranton. No single event did more to highlight the nature and the implications of this impact, or more symbolized the inextricable interrelationship between all the component parts of Welsh culture, than the 'American National Eisteddfod' held in September 1875. It was an episode which saw the mobilization of all cultural resources of the Welsh Athens of America to create what was arguably the most important cultural event organized by the Welsh in Scranton during the nineteenth and early twentieth centuries.[60]

The 1875 'National Eisteddfod' was held under the auspices of the Welsh Philosophical Society. Since its founding, the society had made strenuous efforts to establish its own library, but by the early 1870s appeals for voluntary contributions had yielded little more than a hundred books. In response to these relatively unrewarding results, the society acted boldly: it decided to hold a large-scale eisteddfod to raise funds.[61] The organizers – among them the familiar trio of Benjamin Hughes, Thomas D. Davies and H. M. Edwards – thought 'big'. It is perhaps a reflection of the manner in which the Welsh in Hyde Park saw themselves as leaders among the various Welsh communities in the United States that they called their event 'Eisteddfod Genedlaethol Cyntaf America'.[62] The title was justified: never

---

[60] According to H. M. Edwards, Hyde Parkers were still talking about the 'Eisteddfod on the Hill' (as the 1875 eisteddfod became known) over thirty years after the event. *Druid*, 21 Oct. 1909.
[61] *Scranton Republican*, 8 Feb. 1892; Craft, op. cit., p. 545.
[62] ('America's First National Eisteddfod'). *Drych*, 23 Sept., 1875.

before had an eisteddfod of this size and scope been held in the United States.

The two-day-long eisteddfod was held in a tent on the corner of Sumner Avenue and Price Street, Hyde Park. The tent was held up by six high poles with the American emblem flying on the top of each of them. It could be seen from the centre of Scranton, and apparently strangers who were unaware of the event thought Barnum's Circus in all its glory had come to town. Banners proclaiming slogans such as 'Oes y Byd i'r Iaith Gymraeg' hung across the streets in the vicinity of the tent whilst printed leaflets advertising the eisteddfod were posted on the walls of buildings throughout Hyde Park. Special trains were scheduled from all over the Wyoming and Lackawanna coalfields to coincide with the event. These promotional efforts were well-rewarded. The railway stations were full of people on both days and apparently Welsh was being spoken everywhere.[63] The eisteddfod tent, capable of seating 6,000, was full to capacity during all six sessions, and after the event a *Drych* editorial even commented that probably no other National Eisteddfod, either in Wales or America, had been so well attended in every session.[64] According to the *Scranton Republican*, the majority of both the audience and the competitors were women, and much of the success of the event, especially the musical items, was due to their presence.[65]

The eisteddfod was as prestigious as it was spectacular. Its proceedings were attended, at various times, by many distinguished and well-known Americans, among them Governor Hartanft of Pennsylvania, Moses Taylor of the D. & H., and Sam Sloan. After a speech by the last-named, it was announced that the D.L. & W. had donated $1,000 towards the eisteddfod's expenses (a donation Benjamin Hughes no doubt played no small part in securing).[66] Also present were Mayor Mckune of Scranton and a number of the city's dignitaries who had all been made vice-presidents especially for the occasion. Numerous prominent Welsh-Americans acted as speakers, adjudicators or conductors, including Horatio Gates Jones of Philadelphia,

---

[63] Ibid.; Scranton *Daily Times*, 16 Sept. 1875.
[64] *Drych*, 23 Sept. 1875.
[65] Scranton *Weekly Republican*, 22 Sept. 1875.
[66] *Drych*, 23 Sept. 1875; *Druid*, 28 Oct. 1909. According to H. M. Edwards, this was one of the incidents that made the 1875 eisteddfod famous.

WELSH CULTURAL LIFE IN SCRANTON 103

Edward Jones, the Olyphant coal operator, and Thomas J. Phillips, a Plymouth mine superintendent and one of America's most fervent 'eisteddfodwyr'.[67] Revd T. Cynonfardd Edwards, minister of the Edwardsville Congregational Church and perhaps the single most influential Welshman in late nineteenth and early twentieth-century America, also made an extended appearance. During it he personally accepted the eisteddfod's bardic chair, having won the competition with his poem on 'The Mayflower'.[68] Representatives of various newspapers were also present in force. Among them were reporters from the *New York Graphic*, *New York Herald*, *Scranton Republican*, *Scranton Times*, *Y Drych*, *Y Wasg* and Hyde Park's own *Baner America*. The latter published bilingual broadsheets during the two days of the event.[69]

Throughout the eisteddfod the emphasis was on the principles which the Philosophical Society strove to promote: education and self-improvement. The tent housed an exhibition on what purported to be the first Welsh book printed in America (wrongly, as recent research has shown).[70] It was apparently published in Philadelphia, written by an Abel Morgan and entitled *Cyd-Gordiad*. Abel Morgan himself, Horatio Gates Jones and Governor Hartanft were the subjects of three two-stanza poetry competitions, each with prizes of $5 donated by a Morris Hughes of Pittston. The tent's competition area was bedecked with mottoes, the most important being 'Goreu Arf, Arf Dysg' with its translation, 'The Best Weapon Is The Weapon of Learning'. The subject of the Welsh-language oratory competition was 'Ambition'. The *Scranton Times* reporter assumed that each of the three contestants for this particular laurel were good: 'our Welsh friends seemed to think so.'[71]

---

[67] Scranton *Daily Times*, 16 Sept. 1875. Revd T. J. Phillips was the father of Col. Reese A. Phillips, general inside superintendent of the D.L. & W. after 1900 and president of the Druid Society in Scranton. *Druid*, 6 June 1907; *Drych*, 7 Mar. 1907.

[68] For biographical details of Revd T. Cynonfardd Edwards (1848–1927), see *Dictionary of Welsh Biography*, p. 197.

[69] Scranton *Daily Times*, 16 Sept. 1875; Scranton *Morning Republican*, 16, 17 Sept. 1875; *Drych*, 23 Sept. 1875.

[70] The first Welsh book published in America was Ellis Pugh's *Annerch i'r Cymry* in 1721. See William Williams, 'The first three books printed in America', *National Library of Wales Journal*, II (Summer, 1942), pp. 109–20. The copy of Abel Morgan's book on display at the eisteddfod was owned by Horatio Gates Jones, one of the speakers. *Druid*, 28 Oct. 1909.

[71] Scranton *Daily Times*, 16 Sept. 1875.

America's first 'National Eisteddfod' was an outstanding success. The D.L. & W.'s donation and further donations towards prizes totalling $1,500 enabled the society to make a handsome $1,500 profit with which to purchase books, and the library was duly opened the following year.[72] But the eisteddfod did far more than fulfil its immediate purpose; to all observers it confirmed the quality and the value of the cultural life of the Welsh in the city. The *Drych* was fulsome in its praise and insisted that the eisteddfod was the best answer to those who said that the Welsh language was dying. It was also convinced that no other gathering, of whatever nature, had more elevated the Welsh in the eyes of the most important men in Pennsylvania. It had gained the Welsh greater recognition and shown their importance as citizens of the United States.[73] The newspaper's sentiments were echoed by influential non-Welsh opinion-makers. In his speech on the morning of the second day, Governor Hartanft proclaimed that the Welsh people in Pennsylvania were recognized as an intelligent, industrious and patriotic body of citizens. 'While they adhere to the traditions and customs of their native land,' he declared, 'they are not insensitive to the claims of their adopted country, and in the hour of her peril their blood and lives have been freely given to her service.' They had also contributed greatly to the successful development of the coal and ironfields.[74] The preparations for, and the actual proceedings of, the eisteddfod also stimulated the local Scrantonian press to stress the glory this particular eisteddfod would and did bring to the city. Three months before the event, the *Scranton Republican* proudly announced that the forthcoming eisteddfod would be the grandest ever attempted in the United States; different nationalities would be present and it would be the largest assemblage of people the city had ever known. The Hyde Park eisteddfod, it continued:

> ... will be a great credit not only to the Welsh people; it will reflect honor on this city. There is no class of people who place a higher estimate upon the advantages of intellectual culture than the Welsh and however limited the opportunities of a community composed of this nationality, it will abound in organisations and societies for music, literature, oratory

---

[72] Scranton *Morning Republican*, 25 July 1876; Craft, op. cit., p. 545.
[73] *Drych*, 23 Sept. 1875.
[74] Scranton *Weekly Republican*, 22 Sept. 1875.

and the lesser sciences. They are a reading people and one who has not mastered English is a rarity.[75]

The editorial also commented on the Welsh love for song and, all in all, it concluded that 'the tendency of such festivals is to elevate the whole community in public estimation and stimulate intellectual culture.'[76]

The *Scranton Republican* was not only accurate in its predictions, as the actual events of the eisteddfod showed. It also correctly identified the essence of Welsh cultural activity in Scranton during the heyday of its Welshness, and in so doing it articulated the fundamental paradox of the 1875 American National Eisteddfod and the flowering of Welsh culture in the city. That eisteddfod was a potent testimony to the importance the Welsh immigrants attached to their own ethnic culture, the extent of its strength and vibrancy, and the role that cultural factors played in creating and bolstering an exclusive Welsh identity. Yet the eisteddfod revealed, at the same time, that within the cultural bastion of Welshness there was, in some respects, a Trojan Horse which would ultimately help to undermine it. In a narrower sense, the very success of the 1875 eisteddfod forced the institution out of its exclusively Welsh limits and began the process whereby these events increasingly became festivals for the whole of Scranton and not merely for its Welsh inhabitants. In general, the eisteddfod's impact emphasized the similarities between the respectable, utilitarian and even 'middle-class' character of Welsh culture and the dominant White Anglo-Saxon Protestant (or Anglo-American) ideology of the host country. The culturally privileged position the Welsh immigrants enjoyed, and the perception of it among both the Welsh themselves and other ethnic groups, especially native-Americans, would both ease and hasten their assimilation. The sheer intensity of Scranton's 'Welsh' cultural experience and its inherent dialectic dictated that, for the Welsh, the impact and the actual process of their inevitable Americanization would be infinitely confusing in its complexities.

---

[75] Scranton *Morning Republican*, 10 June 1875.
[76] Ibid.

II CULTURAL CHANGE AND THE FORGING OF A WELSH-AMERICAN CULTURAL IDENTITY

During the last two decades of the nineteenth century profound changes occurred in the cultural life of the Welsh community, to such an extent that by the first decade of the twentieth century it bore little resemblance to that of a generation earlier. These changes reflected the rapid Americanization of the Welsh in both culture and language, and their assimilation into mainstream Scrantonian society. The thriving Welsh-language culture which had characterized the 'Welsh Athens of America' waned and virtually disappeared. Simultaneously a distinctively Welsh-American pattern of cultural behaviour, English – or, more accurately, American – in language and 'American' as much as 'Welsh' in nature, emerged to replace it. These changes were apparent in all areas of Welsh cultural life, but in the case of the most powerful bastions of Welsh-language culture, the Welsh churches, there were literally concrete indications that Welshness had entered a profound and ultimately fatal crisis.

The first brick-and-mortar proof that the magnificent edifice of Welsh Nonconformity was beginning to crack appeared on the streets of Scranton as early as 1871. In that year part of the congregation of the First Welsh Baptist Church in Hyde Park broke away and built their own church on Jackson Street. According to a history of the Baptist denomination in Scranton, the daughter church was formed by people from ward 4 and, ominously, 'the young people of the [mother] church who did not enjoy the Welsh language'.[77] During the following decade the fact that a growing number of Welsh people could not – or would not – speak the Welsh language led to major secessions within the Congregationalist denomination in the city. In 1881 the refusal to allow the introduction of English-language services in the Congregational Church in Hyde Park led to the defection of what became in the following year the Plymouth Congregational Church, with an initial membership of sixty-six. The mother church donated $5,000 to the new institution, which apparently thrived, and by the 1920s it was regarded as the strongest Congregational organization in the state.[78] Seven

---

[77] *Dedication Service Souvenir*, p. 3.
[78] *Sixtieth Anniversary* (no pagination); Murphy, *Hist. Hyde Park*, p. 55.

years later, the Providence Congregationalist Church suffered a similar fate to its counterpart in Hyde Park. In 1889 thirty-six members of the congregation withdrew to form an English branch, the Puritan Congregational Church. Again, the parent church furnished its daughter with all the necessary equipment and apparently placed it in better circumstances than any English church founded by Welsh churches in America.[79]

The secession of English-language churches reflected the steadfast commitment to Welsh-language services on the part of the mother churches. The amicability with which they granted financial aid and equipment concealed the intensity of the passions which the subject of English-language services aroused.[80] At the heart of the opposition to the introduction of English was the prevailing belief that the Welsh language was essential to religious feeling and expression, a mutuality which dated back to the growth of Nonconformity itself in Wales during the late eighteenth and early nineteenth centuries.[81] The identification of the Welsh language as the 'language of heaven' was mirrored across the Atlantic. In the *Drych* in 1883, when the question of English-language services was beginning to be a marked feature of its columns and those of the *Cambrian*, a writer named 'Caerddonian' declared:

> The religious language of the Welshman is the Welsh language. I admit that all languages are a medium but some media are more suitable than others. It is not possible to use a language more effectively in connection with religion than the Welsh language.[82]

Those who supported inclusion argued that unless the younger generation were allowed services in their own language, they would abandon religion altogether. This belief was shared by a historian of the Congregationalist denomination in Scranton, who in 1905 saw the struggle of the 1880s in almost apocalyptic terms:

[79] Davy Edgar Jones, op. cit., p. 33.
[80] Edward Hartmann has described the controversy, which raged in most Welsh-American churches in the 1880s, as a 'battle royal'. Hartmann, op. cit., p. 123.
[81] For the close links between Nonconformity and the Welsh language and the impact of the Sunday Schools on literacy and literature, see Glanmor Williams, 'Language, literacy and nationality in Wales', and 'Religion, language and the Circulating Schools of Griffith Jones, Llanddowror (1683–1761)', in *idem, Religion, Language and Nationality in Wales*, pp. 127–47, 200–16.
[82] *Drych*, 8 Mar. 1883.

> A strong feeling and great commotion seized most of the Welsh churches throughout the Valley . . . Christ understood it and knew well that a movement for the salvation of men could not be brought about without it. There must be pangs, agony and grief, great strife, revolutions and fierce battles in order to bring any new movement into existence. This is the reason for fierce fightings in our Valley some years ago and those fine English churches are the results.[83]

The secessions of 1871, 1882 and 1889 temporarily stemmed an attack which, to the mother churches, threatened the very nature of Nonconformity itself. Despite the loss of a part of its congregation, membership of the 'Old Church' in Hyde Park grew to a peak by 1890, double the 1870 figure.[84] Other Welsh churches in the city also witnessed growth. The Baptist Church, too, doubled its membership by 1890 and was able to make substantial renovations during 1889, including the installation of a large pipe-organ costing $22,000.[85] From the 1890s onwards, however, the Welsh-language churches experienced a sharp reversal of fortunes. They were increasingly faced with the problem of declining attendances. In the early years of the twentieth century the Baptist Church was said to be 'in a low financial ebb' through lack of members.[86] Moreover, as their Welsh-speaking congregations dwindled, these churches were themselves forced to hold occasional services in the English language, particularly morning services and those catering for children. Although Welsh-language services and Sunday School classes continued to be held in the city until at least the 1920s, by the first decade of the twentieth century the Welsh mother churches were in a desperate condition.[87] In 1925 a Welsh Baptist Church souvenir publication described how the arrival of Revd T. Teifion Richards to take up the pastorate in 1907 came at a crucial period:

> Many of the original Welsh-speaking members and workers had passed away depriving us of that great religious fervor which was characteristic of our Welsh forebears. Knowledge of Welsh was disappearing and the English language was increasingly being adopted.[88]

---

[83] Davy Edgar Jones, op. cit., p. 14.
[84] *Sixtieth Anniversary* (no pagination).
[85] *Seventy-Fifth Anniversary*, p. 13; *Dedication Service Souvenir*, p. 3.
[86] *Dedication Service Souvenir*, p. 3.
[87] *Drych*, 4 July 1907; *Sixtieth Anniversary*.
[88] *Seventy-Fifty Anniversary*, p. 15.

As the remembrancer's tone suggests, declining attendances in the Welsh churches were not solely the result of the waning of the Welsh language. Although some contemporary observers maintained that the younger generation were attending the English-language Welsh churches,[89] there is evidence to suggest that in Scranton, as elsewhere in the United States, fewer Welsh people were attending religious services in either language, mirroring the general drift away from religion which was a feature of American society as a whole during this period.[90]

In his study of the assimilation of the Utica Welsh community, Emrys Jones describes how the American-born children of Welsh immigrants rebelled not only against the Welsh language but also against religion itself. They embraced new 'worldly' cultural values which the older generation frowned upon.[91] In an industrial society like Scranton the trend would have been even more marked, particularly as the city offered numerous counter-attractions such as dance and music halls.[92] Moreover towards the end of the nineteenth century, many of the new Welsh immigrants who arrived in Scranton, especially those from the industrial areas of Wales from which the city derived the bulk of its Welsh population, were both non-Welsh-speaking and non-religious. As early as 1880 an American correspondent of the *Tyst a'r Dydd* declared:

> I am afraid . . . that present day emigrants do not have nearly as much religious zeal . . . There are widespread complaints in some places that those who have come from Wales in the last months are poor and unenthusiastic in religion, non-Sabbath-observing and heedless of their church covenant.[93]

The crisis in which Scranton's Welsh churches increasingly found themselves, therefore, was a lethal mix of the failure to keep their younger members (either because of a lack of Welsh

---

[89] In 1910 Dewi Cwmtwrch informed the *Drych* that 'hundreds of the children of the Welsh are in English churches.' *Drych*, 29 Dec. 1910.

[90] For a discussion of the general decline in religious observance in the United States see Maldwyn A. Jones, *The Limits of Liberty: American History 1607–1980* (New York, 1983), pp. 335–9.

[91] Emrys Jones, 'Some aspects of cultural change in an American Welsh community', *Transactions of the Honourable Society of Cymmrodorion* (1952), pp. 15–41, 27–8, 31–2. For similar conclusions see Revd Daniel Jenkins Williams, *The Welsh of Columbus, Ohio: A Study in Adaptation and Assimilation* (Columbus, 1913).

[92] See below, ch. 5, pp. 220–21.

[93] *Tyst a'r Dydd*, 23 Jan. 1880.

or a move away from religion altogether) with an inability to recruit new blood through immigration. It was not only a crisis of language; it was one of religion itself. In his description of a Welsh community very different from that in Scranton, namely Cambria, Wisconsin, in 1898, J. Glyndwr Davies remarked:

> The gradual depletion of the Welsh chapels in the United States has been too glibly ascribed to the disuse of the Welsh by the younger generation. That is only half the story. The drift away was also due to scepticism to a greater extent than has been realised.[94]

The decline of Welsh religiosity in Scranton, and the reasons why it occurred, were brought sharply into focus by an episode which temporarily halted the drift but which ultimately re-emphasized the increasing irrelevance of religion to a growing number of Welsh people in the city. Two years before Revd Teifion Richards arrived at the First Welsh Baptist Church, the Welsh churches in Scranton experienced – albeit briefly – a rekindling of that great religious fervour which the historian of that denomination nostalgically saw as being characteristic of older Welsh immigrants. During 1907 an intense revival broke out throughout the Wyoming and Lackawanna Valleys.[95] In May of that year Dewi Cwmtwrch informed the *Drych* of the close spiritual unity which existed between Welsh people – both Welsh- and non-Welsh-speaking – in Scranton. This had led to the holding of joint revival and prayer meetings. The revival was accompanied by a temperance crusade and a reawakening of interest – again briefly – in the Welsh language. In April Revd R. B. Jones, a local minister, organized daily prohibition meetings for a whole week in the city.[96] The Welsh-language churches began to hold children's services in Welsh as opposed to English, by then the usual practice, and these were reputed to be 'full of the living spirit'.[97] Moreover, the churches also organized classes to study the language. In March, the *Drych* reported that there was a strong desire to learn Welsh among the young people in the city.[98] By June, Revd John Hammond of

---

[94] J. Glyndwr Davies, 'Cambria, Wisconsin in 1898', *Transactions of the Honourable Society of Cymmrodorion* (1957), pp. 128–59 (especially 141).
[95] Revd T. Cynonfardd Edwards, *The Jubilee Memorial, 1868–1918, Welsh Congregational Church, Edwardsville, Pennsylvania* (Wilkes-Barre, 1918), p. 43.
[96] *Drych*, 18 Apr., 2 May 1907.
[97] Ibid., 4 July 1907.
[98] Ibid., 28 Mar. 1907.

the Ebeneser Welsh Calvinistic Methodist Church in Hyde Park was holding classes, and he informed the *Scranton Republican* that he expected large attendances, although in this he was ultimately to be disappointed.⁹⁹ The Baptist Church also organized similar classes, with its pastor, J. Cromwell Hughes, as teacher. There is an unmistakable tone of surprise in the accounts of the phenomenon which local reporters sent to the *Drych*. Dewi Cwmtwrch wistfully declared that it was a 'pity that it is not possible to get hundreds to join these classes'.¹⁰⁰ The classes, however, like the revival as a whole, were short-lived.

Despite its brevity, the revival was nevertheless a significant occurrence. It showed how far attendances at the Welsh churches and the Welsh language itself had declined by the early years of the twentieth century, and it also demonstrated the centrality of that language and temperance to the Welsh Nonconformist ethos. The fate of all three in Scranton during the late nineteenth and early twentieth centuries is a potent indication of how these central elements of 'Welshness' were increasingly under attack in a modern industrialized society. It is quite possible that the revival was a delayed transatlantic reaction to the 1904–5 religious revival in Wales, and in this respect it is all the more significant, since it was the same forces which created both. The revival in Wales was followed closely by the Welsh-American press, and, as in Wales, commentators highlighted the possibility that it would lead to a religious awakening and a greater respect and interest in the vernacular.¹⁰¹ Similar revivals occurred in many other Welsh communities in the United States in the 1905–7 period¹⁰² and the similarities between them all are striking. David Smith has suggested that the 1904–5 revival in Wales sometimes revolved around a sense of guilt among those who had 'rejected' a former way of life, and that it was, in part, a product of the geographical

---

⁹⁹ *Scranton Republican*, 5 June 1907.
¹⁰⁰ *Drych*, 4 July 1907.
¹⁰¹ *Cambrian*, XXV (Feb. 1905), pp. 47, 48, 49; *Cyfaill o'r Hen Wlad*, LXVIII (Feb. 1905), pp. 85–8, (Mar. 1905), p. 122, (June 1905), p. 511. For accounts of the 1904–5 religious revival in Wales see Basil Hall, 'The Welsh revival of 1904–05: a critique', in G. J. Cumming and Derek Baker (eds.), *Popular Belief and Practice* (Cambridge, 1972), pp. 291–301; C. R. W. Williams, 'The Welsh religious revival of 1904–05', *British Journal of Sociology* (1952).
¹⁰² *Cyfaill o'r Hen Wlad*, LXVIII (Mar. 1905), pp. 125–6; LXIX (Mar. 1906), p. 124; *South Wales Daily News*, 29 Dec. 1906.

divide between rural and industrial Wales. In a discerning phrase he describes revivalism as a 'frontier sport', and points out the way in which the United States resembled Wales not only in its general history but specifically in its penchant for evangelical protestant revivalism.[103] Revivalism was certainly endemic in Scrantonian society. In 1954 a Welsh Baptist publication recalled that in 1907, 300 applications for baptism had been accepted by the Welsh Baptist Church in that year. 'After all, these were the days of Billy Sunday,' it remarked. However, most of the new recruits soon drifted away from the church.[104] The 'Welsh' revival – in religious and linguistic terms – of 1907 may well have been the last gasp of Welshness in Scranton, the temporary yearning for salvation in the dislocation created by the emergency of a modern, secular, urban and industrial society. Its significance lies in its underlining that ultimately Welshness could not survive in this new environment.

During the late nineteenth and early twentieth centuries, therefore, the Welsh religious institutions were increasingly under attack. Religious expression became Americanized linguistically, but this was only a part of a much wider decline brought about by the growing embrace of new values among both first- and second-generation Welsh. The result was that the Welsh churches could no longer function as a powerful force in maintaining a separate Welsh identity. Not only were they weakened; the identity itself had changed.

The fate of the Welsh religious institutions in Scranton was in many ways a microcosm of the changes that were becoming apparent in other areas. Other cultural organizations whose proceedings remained in the Welsh language, like the Welsh Philosophical Society, declined and were disbanded. New Welsh societies were formed during the period, but their activities were conducted through the medium of English. These developments are again telling indicators of the decline in the use of the Welsh language in the community, at least in its

---

[103] David Smith, 'Wales through the looking glass', in *idem* (ed.), *A People and a Proletariat: Essays in the History of Wales, 1780–1980* (London, 1980), pp. 215–39 (especially 224–5).
[104] *Dedication Service Souvenir*, p. 3.

public life. As we have seen, there were important generational factors in operation here, and as the nineteenth century wore on, new immigrants from Wales tended to be non-Welsh-speakers. Because of the lack of evidence, it is difficult to evaluate the attitudes of first-generation Welsh-speakers towards the language and the extent to which – and, equally important, where – they continued to speak it. The reasons for, and the process of, linguistic change are made even more complex by the fact that the Welsh immigrants were bilingual, and this undoubtedly aided their rapid assimilation. They did not need to learn a new language, as was the case with most other immigrant groups. From the beginning, Welsh cultural institutions also emphasized the importance of a correct knowledge of English in their efforts to encourage education and self-improvement. After all, a knowledge of that language was essential in order to 'get on'.

It may well be that in Scranton, as Merfyn Jones has pointed out in his study of the Welsh in Liverpool,[105] for a time at least the use of Welsh came to be place-orientated and, to a lesser extent, person-orientated. Welsh may have continued to be the main language of the home at the same time as English was becoming the dominant language in public life, and here the attitude of the mother towards the preservation of the language was crucial to its maintenance. What little evidence there is suggests that very little Welsh was being spoken in Scranton at the turn of the century and that in general this was accepted as being inevitable and indeed desirable.[106] It is clear, too, that change in language use was inextricably entwined in a much wider process of cultural change. The new Welsh societies which were formed from the last decade of the nineteenth century onwards were not English-language carbon copies of earlier Welsh-language societies. They could not be. Although they retained some traditional aspects of Welsh culture, notably the eisteddfod, these new societies were markedly different in character and emphasis from their predecessors, indicating that

---

[105] R. Merfyn Jones, 'The Liverpool Welsh' in D. Ben Rees (ed.), *The Liverpool Welsh and their Religion* (Liverpool, 1984), pp. 20–43 (especially 29–30).

[106] In his reminiscences in the *Druid* in 1909, H. M. Edwards noted the decline in use of the Welsh language (see below, p. 87) and went on to maintain that 'the all-conquering Anglo-Saxon tongue will prevail universally. This will be as it should be.' Ibid., 21 Oct. 1909.

Welsh cultural behaviour was becoming 'Welsh-American' rather than 'Welsh'.

The Welsh Philosophical Society, despite its influence, was not immune to the forces that were changing the character of Welsh cultural life. Until the mid-1890s it continued to hold its debates in the Welsh language, but a drastic fall in membership forced it to switch to English. The adoption of English and a change of name – to the Hyde Park Literary and Scientific Association – failed to attract new members, whilst the society's library, its major achievement and 'the pride of Hyde Park', increasingly fell into disuse.[107] It was closed in 1897 through lack of funds. Apparently young people on the West Side were by this time patronizing the main Allbright Library in the centre of Scranton.[108] The Philosophical Society's books were donated to the Allbright Library on condition that a branch was established in the Welsh Philosophical Rooms. This was duly opened in 1898, whilst the society itself continued in a listless existence until 1907.[109] The fact that mining was no longer an outlet for Welsh occupational ambitions undoubtedly contributed to the society's decline. Equally its emphasis on intellectual debate and self-improvement was perhaps out of tune with an increasingly Americanized Welsh community which had developed other cultural and leisure time priorities and which, moreover, had achieved a marked degree of upward mobility. The final dissolution of the Welsh Philosophical Society marked the end of an era in the history of the Welsh presence in Scranton, one associated primarily with an intense involvement in the anthracite industry and a flourishing, if doomed, Welsh-language culture.

The experience of the Ivorites in the last two decades of the nineteenth century mirrored that of the Welsh-language churches. Two English-language lodges, the Thomas Jefferson and Robert Morris Lodges, were formed in 1893 and 1894, respectively, to complement the Welsh-language ones, which increasingly suffered a decline in membership.[110] Signifying

---

[107] Murphy, *Hist. Hyde Park*, pp. 65–7.
[108] *Scranton Republican*, 6 Mar. 1897.
[109] Ibid., 3 Dec. 1898; Murphy, *Hist. Hyde Park*, p. 67. Sometime during the 1920s or 1930s the Scranton Public Library inexplicably 'lost' the Philosophical Society's books. It is possible that they were sold illegally. Ex inf. the late Revd W. R. Lewis, Scranton.
[110] *Drych*, 17 May 1894; minute book, Robert Morris Lodge of the Order of American

perhaps their Welsh-American nature, the new lodges were named after Welshmen who had played prominent roles in American history rather than historical figures from Wales's past, as had been the custom when Welsh-language lodges were established.[111] The Robert Morris Lodge in Hyde Park was set up at a meeting of 'gentlemen of Welsh blood' with the object of being 'primarily Ivorite, but that the secondary purpose should be to make social features prominent'.[112] Its membership was limited to Welshmen and Welsh-Americans, and its officers, among them John Courier Morris and T. Ellsworth Davies, were described as being 'composed of the brightest young businessmen in Scranton'.[113] The lodge emerged as the most active of the Ivorite lodges in the city and it organized an annual eisteddfod throughout the 1890s and the first decade of the twentieth century.[114] After its 1897 eisteddfod the locally published *American Celt* periodical complemented the lodge on its efforts and declared that the eisteddfod as an institution, and especially a Scranton eisteddfod 'with 60,000 Welshmen [*sic*] within hail of a street car', should be the last place where the epitaph of the Welsh language ought to be proclaimed. Nevertheless, this particular event had been 'of a decidedly English character'.[115]

Apart from the appearance of English-language counterparts which coexisted alongside Welsh-language cultural organizations, two important new Welsh cultural societies were also set up in Scranton during the late nineteenth and early twentieth centuries: the Cymmrodorion Society and the Druid Society. The Cymmrodorion Society was set up in 1886 in order to 'celebrate St David's Day and to perpetuate ancient Welsh customs among the Welsh residents of the valley and their descendants'.[116] It did this by organizing grand prestigious banquets on or near 1 March, and these were held annually

True Ivorites, Scranton, 1894–1901, Lackawanna Historical Society, Scranton.
[111] Indeed, at the formation meeting of the Robert Morris Lodge there was a counter-proposal that the name of the new lodge be the Roger Williams Lodge. Minute book, Robert Morris Lodge, 16 Jan. 1894.
[112] Ibid.
[113] Ibid., 29 Jan. 1894; *American Celt*, I (June 1897), p. 98.
[114] Minute book, Robert Morris Lodge, *passim*; David E. Jones, loc. cit., p. 340.
[115] *American Celt*, I (June 1897), pp. 98–9.
[116] *Scranton Republican*, 2 Mar., 7 Apr. 1886; *Drych*, 11 Mar. 1886; *Williams' Scranton Directory*, 1890.

until the second decade of the twentieth century, when the Scranton St David's Society took up the same task.[117] Membership of the Cymmrodorion Society was as much a badge of honour in the Welsh community as that of the Welsh Philosophical Society. Throughout its existence, its officers were either long-standing *prominenti* like D. M. Jones, Lewis Pughe, Thomas D. Davies, Benjamin Hughes, Thomas R. Hughes and H. M. Edwards or, in later years, younger, leading Welshmen of the city, notably T. Ellsworth Davies and Reese G. Brooks.[118] Apart from organizing various outings, the St David's Day Banquets remained the sole focus of the society, despite attempts in the 1890s to promote a fuller calendar of events.[119]

The banquets themselves were sumptuous and select occasions – and indeed they were fully intended to be so. Elaborate preparations, involving the work of a number of subcommittees, went into their organization. At the 1892 event, for example, 'the attendance was large, the costumes of the ladies pretty, the enjoyment general, the menu delightful and the toast responses instructive as well as interesting.'[120] The guest lists were usually an impressive mixture of prominent Americans and Welsh from all over the world as well as hometown public figures. Had all the dignitaries who had been invited to the 1890 banquet accepted, then Mark Twain might well have sat down alongside Lord Penrhyn or Sir John H. Puleston M.P.[121] General Welsh attendance was also by invitation only, and although women were present at most of these gatherings, in 1905 the Cymmrodorion actually organized a 'stag' banquet. Outraged by the men's action, a number of 'young women of Welsh affiliation' in Hyde Park immediately formed a 'Daughters of Gwalia' committee and organized a very well-attended rival 'hen' dinner on the same evening. Attendance at this event was intended to be strictly for spinsters only because 'married women did not have control enough over their husbands who were members of the Cymmrodorion Society to

[117] Programme, St David's Society Annual St David's Day Dinner, 1914, Lackawanna Historical Society, Scranton.
[118] *Drych*, 11 Mar. 1886; *Scranton Republican*, 28 Jan. 1891; letterhead of Cymmrodorion Soc. See, for example, Thomas R. Hughes (sec.) to Robert Isaac Jones, 12 Feb. 1887, NLW MS 3292E.
[119] *Scranton Republican*, 29 Mar., 11 July 1892.
[120] Ibid., 2 Mar. 1892.
[121] Ibid., 4 Mar. 1890.

force them to hold a dinner like that of last year.'[122] However, the speakers at the event, at least, were married women. Toasts during the evening included 'Those Selfish Men' and 'Why We Will Never Marry a Male Member of the Cymmrodorion Society'.[123]

Feasting at the Cymmrodorion's banquets – often of bilingual cuisine[124] – was usually followed by speeches which more often than not extolled the virtues of the Welsh and praised their contribution to American society, both individually and as good, respectable American citizens. In 1892, the Governor of Pennsylvania, Lt.-Col. Watres, assured his audience that no history, whether local, state or national, which omitted the part taken by the Welsh would be complete because they had 'penetrated every civilized land . . . By their faith and their conduct the world has been led to a better living, to a nobler purpose and to a higher destiny.'[125] Speeches were interspersed with musical items and recitations. The proceedings, in general, were completely in the English language. Representatives of the various Scranton newspapers also attended and gave these events extensive coverage. No doubt this was encouraged because the nature of the banquets suggests strongly that they were celebrations not only of St David's Day but also of the status of the Welsh as a respected ethnic group and, indeed, the socio-economic status of leading members of the Welsh community. After the first Cymmrodorion banquet in 1886, a *Drych* reporter maintained that the event had 'added a great deal to the prestige of the Welsh in Scranton.'[126]

The Cymmrodorion Society's concentration on St David's Day celebrations reflects the emergence of that occasion as perhaps the most important date in the calendar of Welsh activities in Scranton. It had not always been so. Although noting that Welsh immigrants grew leeks in their gardens, Phoebe Gibbons was intrigued to discover in 1877 that 'while the Welsh in Wales celebrate the day with processions and

[122] *Scranton Republican*, 1 Mar. 1905.
[123] Ibid., 2 Mar. 1905.
[124] In 1914, for example, guests could wash down Blue Point Oysters/Llymeirch Aberystwyth and Potatoes Rissole/Cloran Sir Benfro with Pwns St David and Coffi LlanfairpwllgwyngyllgogerychwyrndrobwllLlandisiliogogogoch. Programme, Annual St David's Day Dinner, 1914, op. cit.
[125] *Scranton Republican*, 2 Mar. 1892.
[126] *Drych*, 11 Mar. 1886.

literary and musical meetings . . . among the people at large the celebration has died out here.'[127] Nevertheless, two years after the publication of Gibbons's article, St David's Day was celebrated for the first time in the Northern coalfield when a supper and concert were held in Hyde Park.[128] Thereafter, the event gained in importance, and not only on the part of the Cymmrodorion Society. During the 1880s and 1890s the Welsh churches in Hyde Park also organized celebrations to mark the occasion. In stark contrast to the more prestigious affairs held often simultaneously in the main part of the city itself, however, proceedings in the former were predominantly in Welsh.[129] St David's Day has remained as the most important and often the sole reflection of an awareness of a separate Welsh cultural identity to this day. Its growth in popularity in Scranton during the late nineteenth century reflected the trend whereby Welsh cultural activity was increasingly becoming focused on specific events and dates, as opposed to the frequent concerts and eisteddfodau which had been a characteristic of the community in its earlier years.

In some respects the increasing tendency of Welsh cultural activity to be both English in language and concentrated on specific occasions reached its apogee in the efforts of the Druid Society. Yet judging by its aims and the words of its more prominent members, this society was as much a mission as one which promoted cultural events. It was set up in 1907, and its creation reflected the emergence of a new generation of Welsh cultural leaders, notably T. Owen Charles, George Howell, Col. R. A. Phillips, Morgan Thomas and Albert Eynon. The ubiquitous H. M. Edwards was also actively involved.[130] In common with similar developments in some of the other larger Welsh communities in the United States, the Druid Society grew out of the belief that the Welsh ought to be more effectively organized as an ethnic group and have their own exclusive vehicle of expression.[131] To complement and support the society's activities, some of its leading members founded the

---

[127] Gibbons, loc. cit., pp. 918–19.
[128] *Scranton Republican*, 1 Mar. 1879.
[129] See, for example, ibid., 2 Mar. 1893.
[130] *Druid*, 23 May 1907; *Drych*, 7 Mar., 2, 9 May 1907. Dewi Cwmtwrch described H. M. Edwards's involvement in the Druid Society as the 'handle' between the old and new. *Drych*, 2 May 1907.
[131] See below, ch, 4, pp. 181–2.

Druid newspaper, with T. Owen Charles as editor, and this was published in the city until 1912, when it was bought by a consortium from Pittsburgh.[132] Like the *American Celt* (which was in existence for a few months during 1897) before it,[133] the fact that the *Druid* was an English-language newspaper is in itself an indication that English was by now the dominant language among the Welsh in Scranton. The newspaper not only indefatigably supported Welsh causes in the city (and the United States generally) and consistently urged the Welsh to be proud of their Welshness and be patriotic Americans. It also relentlessly boosted the size, strength and importance of the Welsh in Scranton and on one occasion an editorial even suggested that the city should have a consul in Wales because of its status among Welsh-American communities.[134]

If the Cymmrodorion Society's efforts showed a marked tendency towards exclusivity, the Druid Society's endeavours were unashamedly populist. Its object was, according to the *Druid*, 'to make one big Welsh family with its home in this city. A vigorous family which will do things, and that for the benefit of the members of the family'.[135] It intended that the proceeds from the events it organized should go towards aiding aspiring young Welsh men and women in their studies or careers, though how successful it was in this respect is difficult to determine.[136] Apart from its wider ambitions, the society held regular monthly literary and social meetings at which papers were read and addresses given. It organized a biennial eisteddfod from 1908 until 1914, and in the year of its founding it also introduced two new annual events into the calendar of Welsh cultural activities in the city – the Ladies' Night and the Welsh Day. Both were hailed as major innovations, and indeed their precedents were later followed by other Welsh-American communities.[137]

The Druid Society decided to organize the first Ladies' Night, held in June 1907, because 'hitherto the men have enjoyed a

[132] *Druid*, 23 May 1907.
[133] The *American Celt* was edited by a John Griffiths, and it was intended as a monthly magazine 'for the Welsh and other Celts in America'. Its contents were mainly devoted to various aspects of the history of the Welsh in America. Ibid., 1 (1897), *passim*.
[134] *Druid*, 20 June 1907.
[135] Ibid., 23 May 1907.
[136] Ibid., 23 May, 6 June 1907. There is no evidence in the *Druid* or elsewhere that the society set up scholarships or awarded grants to aspiring Welsh men and women in Scranton.
[137] Ibid., 23 May, 6 June, 2 July 1907, 12, 19 June 1908.

monopoly of social functions and now for the first time in the history of Scranton a night is to be set apart in honor of Welsh women young and old.'[138] It also sought the endorsement of Welsh women for the society's efforts – and asked them to show it by attending the gathering. Women were given free admission provided their husbands or partners wore the Druid Society's membership badge. The involvement of Welsh women in actually organizing this 'chivalrous idea' was, however, restricted to a Refreshments Committee.[139] The evening was very well attended by both sexes and consisted of speeches, musical items by the Jenny Lind Chorus, and a feast. It was presided over by H. M. Edwards, and the high point was apparently the speech of Lizzie Harris Howell (wife of George Howell, one of the society's trustees), who forcefully advocated that the Druid Society be far more than a cultural society.[140] Her speech is in fact one of the few records of the opinions of Welsh women in contemporary sources. 'Lectures, entertainments eisteddfodau and banquets were necessary for fun and funds,' she remarked, 'but for an organisation to be representative of our people . . . it must have for its chief purpose the doing of good.' She insisted that the 'noble mission' of the society should be the means of discovering and aiding

> the hidden talents of some poor Welshman and Welshwoman now in obscurity in order to add to the glory of our country and its people . . . Let me repeat with emphasis that in any effort to perpetuate the Welsh language, preserve its literature, make stronger our love for Wales, and give help to the worthy, you men of the Druid Society can rest assured that the Welshwomen will be ever ready to assist.[141]

Lack of evidence makes it difficult to determine whether the sentiments expressed by Mrs Howell during the first Ladies'

---

[138] Ibid., 6, 20 June 1907.
[139] Ibid., 6 June 1907.
[140] Ibid., 2 July 1907; *Drych*, 4 July 1907.
[141] *Druid*, 2 July 1907. Lizzie Howell also spoke at the Daughters of Gwalia's 'Hen' Banquet in 1905. On that occasion she spoke on the subject of 'Women' and insisted that if the lives of women were studied they would show that the development of the United States was as much indebted to women as to men, even though many of them 'worked quietly in their homes'. She also stated that there were great contrasts between women of earlier ages and those of the present day: 'Education, culture in the arts and sciences have been mighty clever to lift woman to her present condition of freedom and influence.' *Scranton Republican*, 2 Mar. 1905.

Night were shared by Welsh women in general.[142] To one Welshman in the audience, the fact that her speech was in English (it is not known if she could speak Welsh), and that the whole proceedings of the first Ladies' Night were conducted in that language, was a cause for great concern. Writing under the pseudonym 'Huw Llwyd', he complained bitterly to the *Drych* about what he had witnessed during the evening and accused the society, and H. M. Edwards in particular, of being hypocritical in their show of Welshness. As far as Edwards was concerned,

> he said he was a Welshman but he spoke English. This is a society for the Welsh. Its aim is to preserve the traditions and ceremonies of the nation. The need to keep the language was referred to many times; but why do not those who can speak Welsh use it among themselves and with their children. If they do this, they will go far in keeping the language alive.[143]

For all 'Huw Llwyd''s criticism, the constant eulogizing of the virtues of the Welsh language in the English tongue was a characteristic of the proceedings at the events organized by Welsh cultural societies in Scranton from the end of the nineteenth century onwards, be they St David's Day banquets, Ladies' Nights, Welsh Days or eisteddfodau. Dewi Cwmtwrch even maintained that the Druid Society was proof that it was not easy 'to steal a Welshman away from his nation, no matter what country he lived in or what language he spoke.'[144] The irony of it all was not lost on the Welsh bard Cyniesydd. During his visit to the United States in 1910 he attended that year's Welsh Day in Scranton and wrote a poem, 'Dydd y Cymry', about his experience:

> Dydd o hwyl a gwyllt rialtwch
> Dydd o sŵn ac yfed te
> Dydd yn feichiog o ddigrifwch
> Dydd digymar yw'r Welsh Day!
> Dydd yn wir a'i lond o asbri

---

[142] That the sentiments expressed by Mrs Howell were shared by many leading Welsh women in Scranton is perhaps demonstrated by the decision of the Scranton branch of the Welsh Women's Clubs of America (formed in 1920) to set up its own Welsh Home for the Aged in 1923. (It was considered that the Home the organization set up in Cleveland in 1919 was too far away for Scranton's Welsh.) *Druid*, 1 Nov. 1919, 1 June 1920, 1 Feb. 1923. See also Hartmann, op. cit., pp. 160–1.
[143] *Drych*, 11 July 1907.
[144] Ibid., 2 May 1907.

I roi clod i'r hen Gymraeg
A gwneir hyny gan y Cymry
Drwy barablu'n Saesonaeg!¹⁴⁵

If, to Cyniesydd at least, the Welsh Day highlighted the extent to which the Welsh in Scranton had become linguistically Americanized, in general these events, which were organized by the Druid Society, also demonstrated the 'American' character of their activities. The first Welsh Day in Scranton, and probably in America, was held at Luna Park in July 1907.¹⁴⁶ The Welsh Day soon became an important event in most of those cities and towns which had a sizeable Welsh element. In August 1909 Robert H. Davies ('Gomerian') of Pittsburgh commented in the *Druid* that 'Welsh Days are becoming a fad and are destined to become an important feature of the Cambrian's vacation period; in fact, the vacation is incomplete to the ardent Cymro unless he attends at least one of these reunion gatherings.'¹⁴⁷

Nowhere did the new phenomenon achieve more of a reputation for size and importance than in Scranton itself. Successful Welsh Days were held nearly every year from 1907 until well into the twentieth century. They were large and prestigious events. All were well attended – around 23,000 were present at the first Welsh Day (apparently the largest crowd in the history of Luna Park up to that time) – and each one gained a great deal of publicity and coverage in the local Scrantonian press.¹⁴⁸ Well-known Pennsylvanian personalities, both Welsh and non-Welsh alike, attended as guests of honour and delivered addresses. It is perhaps a reflection of the popularity and importance the annual event had achieved among the Welsh in

---

[145] Ibid., 18 Aug. 1910. 'A day of "hwyl" and wild merriment/A day of noise and drinking tea/A day that's pregnant with jollity/An incomparable day is the Welsh day!/A day that's true and full of eagerness/To give praise to the old Welsh language/And this is done by the Welsh/Through speaking in English!'

[146] *Druid*, 15 Aug. 1907. Some Welsh communities in the American West also claimed that they had first organized a 'Welsh Day'. Ibid., 26 Aug. 1909.

[147] Ibid., 26 Aug. 1909.

[148] *Druid*, 15 Aug. 1907. The reporting of Welsh Days by the local Scranton press was almost always favourable and was often reprinted by the *Druid*. After the first Welsh Day, the *Scranton Times* marvelled that 'the Welsh-American reunion and celebration... evidenced that there is one class of citizens who can meet... to the number of 20,000 and have a good time without intoxicating drink, fights, riots, stabbing affrays and murder.' To the *Scranton Tribune*, the same event had shown that the Welsh 'can safely be classed among the best Americans'. *Druid*, 15 Aug. 1907.

the city that the failure to organize one in 1915 was described by the *Druid* as 'humiliating'.[149]

The Welsh Days offered a wide variety of activities and attractions, among them certain vestiges of traditional Welsh cultural expression. Small eisteddfodau were usually held and these included literary competitions and, on at least one occasion, a competition for Welsh-language englynion. There were also other contests which were perhaps less mentally demanding for the competitors, such as competitions to find the largest Welsh families, the oldest Welsh couples, the oldest Welsh people born in America, and the tallest and shortest Welshmen in the audience. Most of the items on the programmes, however, were musical. In some cases, as in 1907, choral competitions were held, but generally the singing was confined to concert performances by combined mass choirs and soloists, intermingled with community singing of Welsh hymns and melodies and American patriotic songs. In the 1908 Welsh Day, following an earlier appeal by the *Druid*, thirty-six veterans of Caradog's 'Côr Mawr' of the early 1870s gathered on the platform to sing the hymn 'Crugybar'.[150]

The central feature of the Welsh Day was its emphasis on what the *Druid* described as 'patriotic demonstrations'.[151] It was these, above all, which signified the 'American' character of the event. During the second Welsh Day in 1908 President Theodore Roosevelt himself was scheduled to attend the evening session in order to light up a flaming red dragon as the audience sang 'My Country 'Tis of Thee', but he cried off at the last minute. However, he still took part by pressing a button in the White House in Washington which switched on the lights in Luna Park as a chorus of 1,000 Welsh voices sang the 'Hallelujah Chorus'. Earlier that afternoon a reception for Scranton's Welsh veterans of the American Civil War was held.[152] The patriotic nature of these functions was further reinforced by speeches which, like those at Cymmrodorion Society banquets and other events, continually emphasized the patriotism and loyalty of the Welsh. In 1911, for example, the

---

[149] Ibid., 15 Sept. 1915.
[150] Ibid., 15 Aug. 1907, 30 July, 27 Aug. 1908, 28 Aug. 1909.
[151] Ibid., 13 Aug. 1908.
[152] Ibid., 27 Aug. 1908.

governor of Pennsylvania paid a glowing tribute to Robert Morris, the 'financier' of the American War of Independence. As the *Druid* proudly proclaimed after the 1910 Welsh Day, the event 'is truly an American gathering where a continual note of loyalty is sounded to America. Here the eagle screams as loudly as at any Fourth of July gathering.'[153]

The Welsh Day encapsulated all the central features of a clearly discernible Welsh-American pattern of cultural activity which was apparent in the efforts of most other Welsh societies. Welsh cultural life had become dominated by occasions when Welshness was aired and, thereafter, to all intents and purposes, put by until the next time. In this respect it is perhaps significant that the Druid Society described the events it organized as 'big family reunions' since in many ways this was exactly what they were.[154] The kith and kin of Welshness had been dispersed by the forces of Americanization and assimilation, and their periodic returns to the hearth were moulded by their new cultural and linguistic 'American' identity. This ritualization of Welsh cultural activity was complemented and reinforced by the increasing emphasis on Welsh 'boosterism'. For speakers and audiences alike, the 'family' gatherings were incomplete without demonstrations of their American patriotism and proclamations and celebrations of their value both as Welsh people *and* as Americans.

The transformations in the character and activities of Welsh cultural societies, like the fate of the Welsh religious institutions, emphasized that by the end of the nineteenth century the nature of the cultural life which the Welsh had created and enjoyed a generation earlier had been irrevocably undermined. The existence and the efforts of the Cymmrodorion Society, the Druid Society and the English-language lodges of the Ivorites testified to the perseverance of a consciousness of Welshness and of a Welsh identity. Yet it was a Welshness which was articulated by American mouths and minds and, moreover, one whose expression was inextricably related to the fulfilment of external priorities. The ultimate proof that a separate and exclusive Welsh-language cultural identity was no longer in existence or required during the final years of the nineteenth

[153] Ibid., 27 July 1910; *Wales* (Nov. 1912), p. 318.
[154] *Druid*, 4 Aug. 1910.

century was that the very institution which the new Americanized Welsh societies retained as an integral feature of their activities – the eisteddfod – was itself transformed. In the 'Welsh Athens of America' the eisteddfod was the vortex of all the complexities of cultural and linguistic change and the impact of ritualization and 'boosterism'.

Throughout the late nineteenth and early twentieth centuries the eisteddfod continued, therefore, to play a major part in the cultural life of the Welsh community. Important 'National Eisteddfodau' were held in 1880, 1885, 1902, 1905 and 1908, whilst at a local level annual events sponsored by the various singing societies, Ivorites' lodges and the Welsh churches dominated the calendar of Welsh cultural activities in the city. Attendances at the larger events were high: during the 'National' of 1902, which was sponsored by the Scranton National Eisteddfod Association with H. M. Edwards as president, over 5,000 people witnessed the various competitions.[155] In general, eisteddfodau now attracted great attention, and not only among the Welsh, since their proceedings were extensively reported in the local press.

Despite, or perhaps because of, their multiplicity and undoubted popularity, eisteddfodau underwent major transformations in character during the last two decades of the nineteenth century. In common with other Welsh cultural activities in Scranton, proceedings at these events were increasingly conducted in English, and this was complemented by the growing inclusion of English-language subjects in the various literary competitions. Apart from an Americanization in language, the eisteddfod also experienced a marked change in focus. At the same time as the literary competitions became largely English-language contests, their status as an integral part of the eisteddfod's proceedings declined. Conversely, musical and particularly choral competitions became its primary function and many of the eisteddfodau held in Scranton from the 1880s onwards were purely musical in nature.

The decline in the status of literary competitions and their increasingly English nature can be detected in the four largest

[155] Ibid., 17 Feb. 1910.

eisteddfodau held in Scranton during the late nineteenth century. These were the three National Eisteddfodau of 1875, 1880 and 1885 organized by the Welsh Philosophical Society, and the Gwilym Gwent Eisteddfod of 1892 held to raise money for a monument to the local Welsh-American composer.[156] In 1875 all the literary competitions apart from one essay were in the Welsh language. They included a chair poem and a number of recitation, oratory and *englynion* competitions. Five years later, English had encroached much further into the literary competitions. There was one recitation and one oratory competition for each language, and one English poetry competition had been introduced; translation competitions were also included. In general, however, the number of literary competitions had declined. In 1885 even fewer such competitions were organized, and the majority were in English, whilst contests for poetic composition were conspicuously sparse. At the Gwilym Gwent Eisteddfod there were only four literary competitions – an English recitation, a Welsh-language elegy and two epitaph competitions, one for each language. Although a number of contestants entered in both the latter, none was deemed to be of a sufficiently high standard to deserve the respective prizes.

In contrast to the growing exclusion of literary competitions, those which were musical in nature, especially choral contests, grew in both number and importance. Whereas prizes for poetic composition rarely went above forty dollars, those for the choral competitions ran into hundreds. The latter were the focal points of eisteddfodau, and they occupied the bulk of the more important evening sessions. Moreover competitions were increasingly interspersed with non-competitive performances by choirs and soloists, perhaps further emphasizing that these events were celebrations of music, not of poetry or literature. The high point of the evening session on the first day of the 1875 National Eisteddfod was a performance by a combined choir of 'The Heavens are Telling' from Haydn's *Creation*, whilst in the Gwent Eisteddfod the famed Cymmrodorion Choir and a number of noted local soloists sang items but did not compete.[157]

---

[156] Scranton *Morning Republican*, 16, 17 Sept. 1875; *Scranton Republican*, 25 Nov. 1892; *Drych*, 18 Dec. 1879, 12 Mar., 19 Nov. 1885.

[157] Scranton *Morning Republican*, 16, 17, Sept. 1875; *Scranton Republican*, 29 Nov. 1889,

The increasing identification of the eisteddfod as a musical event in Scranton in the last two decades of the nineteenth century was reinforced by the appearance of eisteddfodau which were completely musical in nature. As early as 1884 an 'Eisteddfod Gerddorol' (Musical Eisteddfod) was held in Hyde Park,[158] whilst annual eisteddfodau organized by many of the Welsh choral societies were of a similar character. Notable here were the annual eisteddfodau of the Dr Parry Male Choir in the late 1880s and 1890s. That of 1889 was declared by the *Scranton Republican* to be 'not in accord with the traditional definition of the eisteddfod, for the contests were wholly musical.'[159] These musical eisteddfodau often included competitions for choirs from other nationalities. In 1894, for example, the Robert Morris Lodge of the Ivorites' Eisteddfod contained competitions for both Irish and German glee choirs.[160] Indeed, the overwhelming perception of the eisteddfod as a cosmopolitan musical occasion led other nationalities themselves to organize such events. The Scranton Catholic Choir Association held a musical festival in 1892 and over twenty church choirs, twenty-five singing societies and sixty-five soloists competed for prizes totalling well over a thousand dollars. They repeated their success a year later, when the St Peter's Cathedral Choir, with a Welshman, Joseph Roberts, conducting, won the chief choral competition.[161]

By the end of the nineteenth century, therefore, the Welsh bards, who in 1877 were described by Phoebe Gibbons as being accustomed to poetry for centuries, had become redundant in Scrantonian eisteddfodau. Despite its retention as an integral feature of the activities of most Welsh cultural societies, the institution was no longer an expression of an exclusive and separate Welsh identity. It had developed, and was perceived, as a cosmopolitan musical festival conducted in the English language, whilst its former function as an arena for Welsh bardic and literary endeavour had virtually disappeared. The transformation of the eisteddfod undoubtedly reflected the decline of a Welsh-language literary culture among the Welsh in

25 Nov. 1892.
[158] *Drych*, 7 Feb. 1874.
[159] *Scranton Republican*, 29 Nov. 1889; David E. Jones, loc. cit., p. 343.
[160] *Scranton Republican*, 23 June 1894.
[161] Ibid., 18, 21 Mar. 1892, 26 May 1893; David E. Jones, loc. cit., p. 340.

Scranton. The passing away of many of the city's Welsh bards, and the inability or refusal of the second generation to speak, let alone compose poetry in, Welsh inevitably led to a decline in the importance of poetic and literary competitions, and a greater emphasis on those for oratory and recitation. Although inheriting his father's muse, even the son of so eminent a Welsh-language littérateur as Dewi Cwmtwrch preferred English as the medium for his poetic expression.[162] Besides, as Emrys Jones has pointed out, it was not possible to adapt certain complex Welsh bardic metres to the English language.[163]

It might, therefore, be argued that the waning of a Welsh-language literary culture, and the wider decline of the language itself, alone necessitated a growing adoption of English both in the eisteddfod's general proceedings and in its literary competitions. However, there is evidence to suggest that the relationship between linguistic change and the eisteddfod's metamorphosis was far more complex, since it seems that 'English' eisteddfodau were an accepted feature of Scrantonian life even at the time when usage of the Welsh language was still widespread. In 1894, during a visit to the United States, Thomas Darlington, the scholar, linguist and inspector of schools, spoke at an eisteddfod in Scranton and later recorded his experiences in the *Wales* magazine.[164] He found that Welsh was spoken everywhere there and that eisteddfodau were major successes. In particular he was struck by the size of the audience at the eisteddfod he attended – some three to four thousand – and thought that Scranton was more Welsh than Utica (which he had previously visited), although he conceded that his impressions might have been influenced by the event. Nevertheless, 'less use was made of the Welsh language than might have been expected in view of the strength of the Cymric population of the city.' He had an explanation for this:

> The promoters of the Eisteddfod, wise no doubt to their generation, have evidently striven to give it a cosmopolitan character, which should serve to attract all elements of the heterogeneous population of the district. In

---

[162] Will S. Monroe, *Poets and Poetry of the Wyoming Valley*, Lackawanna Institute of History and Science Publications, No. 2 (Scranton, 1896), p. 11.
[163] Emrys Jones, loc. cit., p. 26.
[164] Thomas Darlington, 'The Welsh in America', *Wales*, 1 (Dec. 1894), pp. 349–52 (especially 351).

this aim they seem to have succeeded for the Eisteddfod is fast becoming a recognized Scranton institution, in which all good citizens, of whatever nationality, take pride and interest.

Darlington noted that at the eisteddfod he attended there was a competition confined to Catholic choirs, intended for the Irish, and a glee competition for the Germans. He recalled that the German barber who shaved him on the morning of the eisteddfod divided his attention between Darlington and a German,

> to whom he discoursed volubly in his guttural North German on the chances of the prize falling to the choir to which they both belonged. Listening to these enthusiastic foreigners, I felt that a new view of the Eisteddfod's mission was being opened out before me. As far as Wales itself is concerned, I am for the Eisteddfod's being made as Welsh as it is possible to be; but who knows that an Anglicised form of the Eisteddfod might not, to our very great advantage, take root among us in England as it is doing among the various nationalities in Scranton?[165]

It is possible that Thomas Darlington overestimated the amount of Welsh spoken in Scranton in the 1890s, although perhaps this does not undermine his conclusion that the emergence of 'English', cosmopolitan eisteddfodau was dictated by other considerations. In this respect his emphasis on the role played by the promoters of Welsh eisteddfodau poses the question of their motivation, since there is an apparent contradiction between maintaining the eisteddfod yet also making deliberate efforts to transform its essential character. Darlington's reminiscences suggest that the eisteddfod's metamorphosis must be seen in the context of relations between the Welsh and other nationalities in the city and the responses and attitudes of the Welsh themselves towards actually living in Scranton and becoming 'American'.

After the phenomenal impact and success of the 1875 National Eisteddfod, eisteddfodau in Scranton were increasingly regarded as important features of the cultural life of not only the Welsh, but also of the city in general. In some respects they were almost expected to be so and eisteddfodic promoters were urged to organize events with which all elements of the city's population could identify. In June 1883, in

---

[165] Ibid.

the wake of an Ivorites' eisteddfod, the *Scranton Republican* called on the promoters of the next eisteddfod to print programmes in English 'so all may understand'.[166] Its attitude reflects the pressures which were sometimes exerted on the Welsh, as on other immigrants, to 'Americanize' and to regard themselves as Scrantonians, not Welsh people.

Welsh eisteddfodic organizers responded favourably to these pressures – if indeed they regarded them as pressures. As Thomas Darlington observed correctly, eisteddfodau reflected the involvement of a wide cross-section of the city's population. Not only were competitions for other nationalities scheduled as part of these events; sponsorship was sought from all sectors of the Scranton economy. The patrons of the 1902 National Eisteddfod, for example, included most of the larger companies in Scranton as well as a number of prominent local public figures.[167] Generally, organizers of eisteddfodau have left little evidence regarding their own motivations but some insight into the deliberations that lay behind the 1902 National Eisteddfod can be gained from the personal reminiscences which H. M. Edwards (the chairman of the organizing committee) wrote for the *Druid* in 1910. The main purposes of the eisteddfod were 'to Americanize the old Welsh institution and . . . to exhibit to the people, particularly the English-speaking people, an ideal Eisteddfod. The committee did not for a moment consider the question of cost.'[168] Unfortunately he did not elaborate further on the reasoning behind these aims or indeed on how this particular eisteddfod was 'Americanized'. (In fact it differed little in character from its more recent predecessors.) However, he went on to describe the lavish preparations that were made, including the allocation of $1,500 of the $6,000 expenditure towards the expenses of prestigious adjudicators and artists. Among those invited was the famous German choir, the Arion Society of Brooklyn. The decision to feature the Arions was apparently the inspiration of David Prichard, the eisteddfod's secretary, 'who had influential German connections'. Its purpose was 'in part, to attract the attention of the Germans of

---

[166] *Scranton Republican*, 17 June 1883.
[167] Scranton Eisteddfod Association, *The National Eisteddfod, Scranton Armory, 29–30 May 1902: Official Program* (Scranton, 1902).
[168] *Druid*, 17 Feb. 1910.

Lackawanna and Luzerne Counties . . . to secure their presence at the Eisteddfod sessions; and, in part, to induce the Germans of New York and Brooklyn to introduce the Eisteddfod to their own people . . . to vary the monotony of their choral festivals'. (The latter aim was in fact accomplished when the Arion Society held its own eisteddfod in Brooklyn in November 1902.)[169]

The testimonies of Thomas Darlington and H. M. Edwards and the character of the larger eisteddfodau in Scranton at the turn of the century highlight the complexities of the processes of cultural and linguistic change which the forces of Americanization and assimilation brought to bear on the Welsh community. They suggest strongly that the Welsh (or at least those who were responsible for organizing the community's cultural life) were determined to retain some vestiges of a Welsh cultural identity but at the same time they openly embraced assimilation and were prepared to further it – indeed, they saw no contradiction between the two. Yet their motives were complex, because the eisteddfod's 'new mission' (as Darlington defined it) could not only demonstrate a willingness to 'Americanize' and assimilate, in this case by sharing their most important cultural institution with others; it could also be utilized to 'boost' the public profile of the Welsh. Cosmopolitan eisteddfodau emphasized the commitment of the Welsh to Scrantonian life. They could be interpreted as attempts by the Welsh to instil the perceived 'respectable' nature of their cultural life in other nationalities, especially the Irish (whose contemporary image was less esteemed among native-Americans than that of the Welsh), and perhaps even to 'Welsh-Americanize' them. Equally, the efforts of eisteddfodic organizers to make their events as prestigious as possible – notably the invitations to distinguished Americans to be guest speakers (Governor Hartanft in 1875, Sam Sloan in 1885, J. E. Barratt in 1892) and renowned musicians as adjudicators (W. J. Stephens of Harvard University in 1892, Walter Damrosch in 1902)[170] – further enhanced the importance of the institution to city life because it boosted civic pride. Fundamentally, cosmopolitan

[169] Ibid., 17, 24 Feb. 1910.
[170] *Scranton Republican*, 16 Sept. 1875, 25 Nov. 1892; *Drych*, 19 Nov. 1885; David E. Jones, loc. cit., p. 339.

and prestigious eisteddfodau enabled the Welsh to show off their value to Scranton and their image and existence as a civilizing and patriotic force in American society.

The close links between the 'new' eisteddfod and Welsh 'boosterism' suggest that the perception of the institution as a means of furthering the interests of the Welsh may have been partly responsible for its development. The impact of cultural and linguistic change on the nature of eisteddfodau in Scranton was complemented, to an extent, by the adaptation of the eisteddfod to suit those wider replacements, since the changes that occurred in its character were necessary if it was to fulfil its new role. The involvement of non-Welsh speakers, adjudicators and competitors naturally dictated an increasing use of the English language. Equally, in order to attract other nationalities emphasis had to be placed on musical competitions. As Rowland Berthoff has correctly pointed out, it was from the 1890s onwards that other ethnic groups took part in eisteddfodau or adopted the institution themselves, at least for a time. Otherwise, he remarks, 'what would they have made of the long-winded adjudications of Welsh poetry in its strict metres?'[171] In this respect the emergence of the eisteddfod as a primarily musical festival was an inevitable consequence of the possibly deliberate downgrading of its literary side. Yet music itself played a far more influential part in the institution's development. Ultimately the complexities of the emergence of the 'new' eisteddfod as a central feature of a 'Welsh-American' identity, and the wider relationship between cultural change and Welsh boosterism cannot be fully understood without a consideration of the centrality of music to the Welsh experience in Scranton.

Throughout the late nineteenth and early twentieth centuries, music, or more accurately singing, remained an integral feature of the cultural life of the Welsh community in Scranton. It was also an aspect which perhaps made the most permanent impression on the city in general. The Welsh contribution to the city's choral heritage is inestimable, and much of the vibrancy which can be detected in Scrantonian musical life during the period was the result of the activities of Welsh singing societies,

---

[171] Berthoff, 'Social order', p. 269.

soloists and conductors. Whilst describing Hyde Park's prestigious musical tradition in 1924, Thomas Murphy declared:

> No record of Hyde Park societies would be complete without mention of our great musical societies of the past. No organisations have added quite so much to the reputation of the city as have the singing clubs and societies which have been a part of the very existence of so many of our people. To the Welsh people must go the credit for these splendid organisations.[172]

The Scranton Welsh community bred a number of great choirs in all three choral categories, mixed, male and ladies. Among the male choruses which achieved a great reputation were the Dr Parry Male Chorus, the Scranton Glee Club, the Cymmrodorion Male Choir and the Welsh Prize Male Choir. Welsh ladies' choirs also made their mark: the Cymmrodorion Ladies, the Scranton Ladies' Choir and the Jenny Lind Chorus. But the choirs which achieved the greatest fame were the mixed choirs: the Hyde Park Choral Union, the Cambro-Americans, the Hyde Park Baptist Choir and, above all, the Cymmrodorion Choral Society, the Scranton Choral Union and the Scranton Oratorio Society.[173]

The community also bred a number of widely respected conductors whose reputation spread far beyond the Lackawanna Valley. By far the most important of these were Haydn Evans, Daniel Protheroe, John T. Watkins and David Jenkins. These conductors led Welsh choirs to a number of memorable eisteddfodic victories which brought great prestige to Scranton and reinforced the Scranton Welsh community's musical predominance. Among the triumphs were those of the Hyde Park Choral Union in the first National Eisteddfod in the city itself in 1875 and in the Philadelphia Centennial Eisteddfod four years later, the Scranton Choral Union's success in the Chicago World's Fair Eisteddfod in 1893, and the Scranton Oratorio Society's victories at St Louis in 1904, Brooklyn in 1906 and the 1913 Pittsburgh International Eisteddfod.[174]

The Hyde Park Welsh community took its own singing, and that of Wales, seriously. In the early 1870s it collected money to help the South Wales Choral Union to compete at the Crystal

---

[172] Murphy, *Hist. Hyde Park*, p. 65.
[173] David E. Jones, loc. cit., pp. 339–44.
[174] Ibid.; Murphy, *Hist. Hyde Park*, p. 65.

Palace in 1873, and mass celebrations were held in that section when news of the choir's victory was known.[175] Hyde Park's undoubted wealth of musical and vocal talent and the choral supremacy it enjoyed from the 1860s onwards instilled a consciousness of predominance over other Welsh communities in the United States, and even induced vanity. During the fuss over the choice of a conductor to lead the mass Welsh choir from Pennsylvania which was scheduled to perform at the Centennial Celebrations in Philadelphia in 1875, a letter in the *Scranton Republican* demanded to know what right Hyde Park had to represent the Welsh of the United States.[176] Within the community itself, inter-choral rivalry was an accepted and persistent feature of its musical life, especially around the time of eisteddfodau. There is no evidence that the intense identification with a particular choir ever led to a free fight, as occurred outside a Welsh church in Pittston in November 1878.[177] Nevertheless, the city experienced a number of internal choral battles, none more so than the fierce struggle for supremacy between the Cymmrodorion Choral Society and the Scranton Choral Union between 1888 and 1893.

The musical life of the community was by no means confined to eisteddfodau. Welsh choirs and soloists appeared in innumerable concerts, whilst from the 1880s onwards, when a distinct acceleration of musical activity among the Welsh and in the city as a whole can be detected, large-scale oratorio performances were given by, among others, the Hyde Park Baptist Choir.[178] Prime movers here were Daniel Protheroe and Haydn Evans, and the tradition was later continued by John T. Watkins. Welsh music teachers in the city – and there were many of them

---

[175] Scranton *Morning Republican*, 1 Aug. 1873; Gibbons, loc. cit., p. 919. There are in fact striking resemblances between the Welsh music-making scene in Scranton and that in Wales, especially the south Wales valleys. In Scranton, too, the choral societies were some of the few organizations in which women could participate on equal terms with men. The enthusiasm and occasional excesses of the supporters of Scranton's various choirs suggest that, as in Wales, the following at times took on a character similar to that of mass spectator sport. See Gareth Williams, ' "How's the tenors in Dowlais?" Hegemony, harmony and popular culture in England and Wales 1600–1900', *Llafur*, 5, No. 1 (1988), pp. 70–80; Peter Stead, 'Amateurs and professionals in the cultures of Wales', in Geraint H. Jenkins and J. Beverley Smith (eds.), *Politics and Society in Wales 1840–1922. Essays in Honour of Ieuan Gwynedd Jones* (Cardiff, 1988), pp. 113–34.

[176] Scranton *Morning Republican*, 30 Oct. 1875.

[177] Wilkes-Barre *Record of the Times*, 11 Nov. 1878.

[178] *Scranton Republican*, 19 Dec. 1891, 18 Mar., 27 June, 1 July, 19 Dec. 1892; David E. Jones, loc. cit., p. 339; *Seventy-Fifth Anniversary*, p. 12.

– organized concerts in order to show off the capabilities of their pupils, whilst most of the choirs held fairs to raise funds, at which they also sang. The Cymmrodorion Choir's fairs and tea parties were particularly imaginative, with stalls ranging from imitation Welsh kitchens, hosted by Welsh-costumed ladies, to Middle Eastern harems.[179]

At the same time as it increased in general importance, the nature of Welsh musical endeavour began to change. From the late 1880s and early 1890s onwards, the separate musical identity of Hyde Park began to break down as the musical life of the community merged into that of the city as a whole. The vibrancy of Welsh musical activity attracted the interest and attention of other groups in the city and, once again, attendances were by no means confined to Welsh people. Local newspapers, 'claimed' Welsh choirs and soloists, especially successful ones, as Scrantonians rather than Welsh people. In July 1889, for example, the *Scranton Republican* proudly announced that 'Shamokin wants the services of our phenomenal vocalists Llew Herbert and Eos Cynon.'[180] The increasing identification of the musical activity of the Welsh with that of the wider city was complemented by the growing participation of Welsh singers in Scranton-, as opposed to Hyde Park-based societies, in which other nationalities were also involved. Although only beginning in the late 1880s and 1890s, this development would eventually culminate in the situation of the 1920s, when far more Welsh people were involved in singing societies such as the Junger Männerchor than in the exclusively Hyde Park choirs.[181]

The undermining of the musical autonomy of the Welsh was a further indication of the weakening of a sense of a separate identity among the Welsh during the last years of the nineteenth century. It reflected the trends towards centralization and cosmopolitanism which were more than apparent in other areas of Welsh cultural life. Indeed, in 1892–3 the musical activity of the Welsh provided the arena for a confrontation which both encapsulated and symbolized the impact of the forces of social and cultural change on, and their ultimate triumph over, a

[179] *Scranton Republican*, 30 Mar., 1 July 1892, 9 June, 21 Aug. 1893.
[180] Ibid., 29 July, 2 Aug. 1889.
[181] David E. Jones, loc. cit., p. 340. Ex inf. Mrs Ceinwen Hughes, Scranton.

distinctive Welsh identity. The episode was one of those occasional epiphanies in the history of the Welsh in Scranton which revealed the true complexities of the experience. It was a struggle that culminated in the unique spectacle of two Welsh choirs from the same community competing against each other in the most important competition in one of the most prestigious eisteddfodau ever held.

The competition was the Chief Choral for Mixed Voices at the World's Fair Eisteddfod in Chicago on 9 September 1893; the first prize was an unprecedented $5,000. On that afternoon the 260 voices of the Scranton Choral Union, led by Haydn Evans, defeated the favourites, the 200-strong Cymmrodorion Choral Society, conducted by Daniel Protheroe, and two other choirs. Scores more of the Scranton Welsh, most of them supporters of the two choirs, were in the audience. (After the adjudication was announced there was little difficulty in identifying which group of followers was cheering frenziedly and which remained grimly silent.) Back in Hyde Park there was an even larger jubilant crowd outside Griffiths and Davies's Merchant Store, where a telegraph of the result was sent at 1.30 a.m. the following day.[182] The Choral Union's success was a memorable achievement and yet further proof of the Scranton Welsh community's choral predominance. Its unexpected triumph over its rivals, however, was but the final denouement of a bitter and often controversial battle that had raged between the two choirs for eighteen months and had absorbed the attention of, and even divided, the city as a whole.[183]

The Cymmrodorion Choral Society of Hyde Park, organized in 1887 by Daniel Protheroe and some of the most prominent members of the Welsh community, had first announced its intention of competing as early as October 1891.[184] By the following March, however, many members were having doubts because the choir had recently been beaten into second place in

---

[182] *Scranton Republican*, 9 Sept. 1893; *Drych*, 21 September 1893; W. D. Davies, *America a Gwledigaethau Bywyd* (Scranton, 1895), pp. 387–8. For an account of the World's Fair Eisteddfod see below, ch. 4, pp. 147–77.

[183] For a fuller account of this memorable episode in Scranton's history see the author's Daniel Protheroe, Haydn Evans and Welsh choral rivalry in late-nineteenth century 'Scranton, Pennsylvania', *Welsh Music*, IX, No. 3 (Spring 1991), pp. 25–34.

[184] *Scranton Republican*, 20 Oct. 1891. The officers of the Cymmrodorion included Col. Reese A. Phillips (vice-president), T. Ellsworth Davies (secretary) and John Courier Morris (corresponding secretary). Ibid., 21 Dec. 1891; David E. Jones, loc. cit., p. 341.

an eisteddfod in Wilkes-Barre after a controversial adjudication and had refused the prize.[185] In March, members of the World's Fair Eisteddfod committee met the choir and 'a large number of representative Welsh people of Hyde Park' to ensure that it would still fulfil its promise to compete. One committee member informed the meeting that it would be a lasting disgrace if Scranton were not represented in the competition. The choir unanimously reaffirmed its earlier decision, and this met with great enthusiasm and approval among the Welsh in Hyde Park and in the *Scranton Republican*.[186] A week later the newspaper even dismissed suggestions that a united choir should go from the city, under the directorship of an eminent musician from New York, as 'an insult to the musical genius and ability of our own city and the West Side'. The Cymmrodorion Choir, it maintained, was good enough on its own and deserved a clear field.[187]

The Cymmrodorion did not get one, however. During the same month, the Scranton Choral Union, under the leadership of Haydn Evans, announced that it also intended to compete.[188] An intense rivalry already existed between the two choirs. They had competed against each other at least twice during the previous three years, and on both occasions the Cymmrodorion had won. Whereas the Cymmrodorion choir was composed of an almost exclusively Hyde Park Welsh and Welsh-speaking membership, the Choral Union was a broader-based organization. Although the bulk of its members were Welsh, they were drawn from all over the city, and for the purposes of going to Chicago the choir recruited some outstanding Irish singers and members of Scranton's German singing societies. Apparently many of the Cymmrodorion's better known and more talented vocalists had recently defected to the Choral Union, and this naturally exacerbated tensions between the two choirs.[189] Both choirs were also so fanatically loyal to their respective conductors – both Protheroe and Evans were immensely popular figures in Scranton[190] – that efforts in December 1892 to

---

[185] *Scranton Republican*, 18, 28 Mar. 1892.
[186] Ibid., 21, 22 Mar. 1892.
[187] Ibid., 30 Mar. 1892.
[188] Ibid., 14 Apr. 1892.
[189] Ibid., 20 Mar. 1893; Hitchcock, op. cit., p. 469; Murphy, *Hist. Hyde Park*, p. 65.
[190] Of the two, Daniel Protheroe (1866–1934) was easily the better-established. Born

unite the two choirs in order to send a stronger choir to Chicago failed miserably. Apart from growing mutual antagonism, the rock that ultimately wrecked amalgamation was the inability of the two choirs to agree on whether Protheroe or Evans should conduct the combined choir.[191]

As the year of the Fair began, therefore, the people of Scranton, and particularly its Welsh inhabitants, faced a unique prospect: the spectacle of two choirs from the same city competing for the largest prize ever awarded in an eisteddfod. For the next eight months it was an endless topic of conversation, and the community as a whole, not merely its musical devotees, was split in two, since the division of musical loyalties became a matter of passionate debate, not least in the columns of the local press. Interest in the forthcoming encounter was further heightened by the fact that the Cymmrodorion Ladies Choir were also preparing to compete in one of the competitions for female choirs at the eisteddfod.[192]

If harmony was the speciality of both the Cymmrodorion and the Choral Union, during the run-up to the eisteddfod the music of inter-choral relations was strictly atonal. As efforts to seek a compromise continued unabated, the struggle between the two choirs turned into a battle of minds and hearts as well as voices, and psychological warfare was declared. In March 1893 the Choral Union resolved that 'in unison with a feeling of pride in the musical ability of the residents of the Lackawanna Valley and the Electric City in particular' it had become convinced that 'Scranton could not be creditably represented in the competition by two choirs.' Because of the failure of all efforts on the part of 'the mutual friends of the two leading choirs of the city' to unite them,

> it is evident that individual pride in the different choral societies must give way to the interest of Scranton to the end that the laurels which a

---

in Ystradgynlais, he made a tremendous impact on the musical scene in Scranton in the eleven years he lived in the city between 1883 and 1894. He was described by Thomas Murphy in 1924 as one 'who is still lovingly remembered by many Hyde Parkers'. Haydn Evans (1868–1916) was born in Aberaman and in 1892 was described as '*the* up and coming conductor in the area'. Murphy, *Hist. Hyde Park*, p. 65; *Scranton Republican*, 10 Dec. 1892. For biographical details, see Bill Jones, loc. cit., pp. 29–32; *Dictionary of Welsh Biography*, pp. 801–2 (Protheroe); *Welsh-American [Druid]*, 15 June 1916 (Evans).

[191] *Scranton Republican*, 10 Dec. 1892. At one civic function in the summer of 1892 the Cymmrodorion had actually refused to sing alongside the Choral Union. Ibid., 15 Oct. 1892.

[192] Ibid., 31 July, 9 Sept. 1893.

consolidated choir could bring to our city may not be carried to a community inferior to our own from a musical standpoint.[193]

Consequently, it proposed a preliminary contest on the test pieces, to be adjudicated by a panel of three, one selected by each choir and one agreed on by both. The winning choir would then compete in Chicago, augmented by the members of the loser, which would disband until after the competition.[194] The Cymmrodorion, out of either pride or confidence, refused this remarkable challenge, a decision which caused much controversy and criticism in the press.[195] One critic insisted that it was the Choral Union that deserved the support of the people of Scranton because its membership was open to all nationalities and was more representative of the city.[196]

The rivalry deepened and the excitement mounted as the event drew nearer. Never would the people of Scranton be more familiar with 'Worthy is the Lamb', 'Blessed are the men that fear Him' and 'Now the impetuous torrents rise', the competition test pieces, than they were during the rehearsal summer of 1893. The community as a whole moved in rhythmic sympathy with the choirs, mesmerized by the endless invisible triangles, vertical lines and squares drawn by the batons of Messrs Protheroe and Evans. But which one would be the 'Lamb' that would be sacrificed, Scrantonians wondered ceaselessly. (The state of the betting is not known, although the impression from contemporary accounts is that Hyde Park was expected once again to establish its supremacy.) Both choirs held fairs and concerts to raise funds to cover the expense of going to Chicago. Bravely, in June, the Choral Union sang the test pieces at a fund-raising event for a local church. (No doubt more than a few Cymmrodorion spies were present.) A large crowd also sat in on the Hyde Park choir's Sunday evening rehearsals until they were barred from doing so in July to enable it to concentrate more closely on the test pieces.[197] At such fever pitch was the atmosphere in Scranton the week before the competition that

[193] Ibid., 17 Mar. 1893.
[194] Ibid.
[195] Ibid., 20, 21 Mar. 1893; *Scranton Tribune*, 18 Mar. 1893. One Cymmrodorion supporter condemned the 'absurdity' of the Choral Union's challenge and thought that whoever conceived the idea 'should be on exhibition at the World's Fair as the greatest intellectual freaks extant'.
[196] *Scranton Republican*, 20 Mar. 1893.
[197] Ibid., 19 June, 5 July, 21 Aug. 1893.

many were seriously believing false rumours that a *third* choir from the city was planning to compete. This choir was allegedly rehearsing secretly between 11 p.m. and midnight so as to avoid detection, and was said to be composed of members of *both* the Cymmrodorion and the Choral Union.[198]

On their return to Scranton after the competition, the victorious Choral Union was given a tremendous welcome. The *Scranton Republican* thought its reception was even more ecstatic than that enjoyed by James G. Blaine when he visited the city during his presidential campaign.[199] Over 20,000 gathered and cheered as the choir paraded through the city before being given a civic supper.[200] No such scenes greeted the vanquished Cymmrodorion when they got home in the early hours of the following morning. They were met by a crowd of three hundred, testifying perhaps to the degree of commitment and loyalty amongst some, at least, of their supporters.[201] Apparently, although disappointed, they agreed that the Choral Union had deserved to win. Dewi Cwmtwrch later described relations between the two choirs as – almost in medical fashion – 'fair'.[202]

The legacy of September 1893 lived on for many years in Scranton. Twelve years later, the *Scranton Republican*'s music column referred to the animosity which still existed between Hyde Park and Scranton in musical matters. It noted that there were undoubted trends towards centralization actively at work in the musical life of the city and pointed out that most choirs now represented Scranton as a whole rather than the various sections, notably the West Side. The 1893 victory, it maintained, had been a victory for all of Scranton, not only Hyde Park; but bad blood still existed between them. This did not apply to all Hyde Parkers, since some of them were among the staunchest supporters of John T. Watkins's Scranton Oratorio Society. For some, however, it concluded, it was a question of Hyde Park forever, right or wrong.[203]

The columnist was being more perceptive perhaps than he or she realized. In many ways, the struggle between the Scranton

---

[198] Ibid., 28 Aug. 1893.
[199] Ibid., 3 Oct. 1893.
[200] Ibid., 10, 12, 16, 20 Sept., 3 Oct. 1893; *Drych* 21 Sept. 1893.
[201] *Drych*, 13 Sept. 1893.
[202] Ibid., 23 Sept. 1893; *Scranton Republican*, 13 Sept. 1893.
[203] *Scranton Republican*, 25 Feb. 1905.

Choral Union and the Cymmrodorion Choral Society in 1893 was a microcosm of what was occurring within the cultural life of the Welsh community in general. It was a battle between an exclusively Welsh and largely Welsh-speaking Hyde Park choir with a Welsh name, and a choir which was drawn from all over Scranton and included other nationalities yet was still primarily Welsh in its composition. The eventual outcome was a victory for the choir which represented the merging of Welsh cultural activity with that of the city as a whole. The symbolic nature of the contest gains even greater significance when it is located in the wider context of cultural change. It took place at the very time when other manifestations of Welsh-language culture were increasingly in crisis and were being replaced by a ritualized and centralized Welsh-American culture.

Yet if the dramatic struggle between the Scranton Choral Union and the Cymmrodorion Choral Society ultimately symbolized the fate of Welsh culture in Scranton, it undoubtedly also highlighted the importance of music to the Welsh in the city. The episode demonstrated, in action, the tremendous popularity of singing among both participants and spectators, and the seriousness with which they regarded their music-making and their choral rivalry. It more than confirmed, too, the superiority of Scranton's Welsh choral resources. Equally, the contest and its result brought sharply into focus the impact that the quality of Welsh musical endeavour made on the city in general and the role it played in reinforcing and enhancing the high cultural profile the Welsh enjoyed. The epic confrontation between the two choirs was categoric proof that 'Gwlad y Gân' had a powerful Scrantonian dimension and that, for the Welsh, singing was a vital and influential force.

The revelations of 1893 suggest that we may speculate further on the influence which the tremendous popularity of singing and its value to Welsh prestige may have exerted on the cultural experience of the Welsh in Scranton. Paradoxically, the musical activity of the Welsh may itself have played an important part in easing and hastening their assimilation. Music is an international language, or at least an area where the use of a foreign tongue does not necessarily impair enjoyment, and it blurs distinctions between different nationalities. Consequently, singing was by far the most accessible feature of Welsh cultural life during the late nineteenth century. This increased its appeal to other ethnic groups and, in turn, facilitated the process whereby Welsh musical activity became inseparable from that of the city as a whole. Yet there was one salient characteristic of Welsh singing in Scranton which enabled non-Welsh groups to identify with it even more closely: the nature of the music they sang.

In an interview with the *Rhondda Leader* in 1907, following yet another successful tour of Wales, Daniel Protheroe was asked about eisteddfodau in the United States. He replied:

> I know very well where people come from from their eisteddfod programmes. When numbers such as 'Round About the Starry Throne', 'Comrades in Arms', etc. are to be competed for, I know at once that the people come from South Wales, whereas if there is a preponderance of Welsh music and Welsh composers represented, they invariably come from North Wales. The Utica and Granville programmes, for instance, with but few exceptions, are all Welsh.[204]

Protheroe's vast experience of American eisteddfodau, and the fact that his formative musical years were spent in Scranton add weight to his testimony.[205] In Scranton, as in other areas of the United States and in south Wales, the repertoires of soloists and especially choirs were dominated by oratorio works with English-language librettos.[206] The Welsh in the city did not champion Welsh music; they sang pieces other nationalities would have recognized and sung, albeit perhaps to a higher standard. This further broke down the distinctiveness of the separate 'ethnic' cultures, perhaps as effectively as linguistic use – that is, speaking English, not Welsh or German. Both proceeded apace and on parallel lines.

If music-making aided the assimilation of the Welsh, the increasing importance of singing as the linchpin of a 'Welsh' identity and as a fulcrum of Welsh boosterism may have influenced the transformation, and perhaps even the fate, of the

---

[204] *Druid*, 24 July 1907.

[205] The accuracy of Protheroe's observations is confirmed by an impressionistic examination of the test pieces in musical competitions in eisteddfodau in Scranton and Utica. Based on the programmes of eisteddfodau in Scranton and Utica printed in the *Drych*, c. 1880–90.

[206] For a discussion of the importance of oratorio to the choral scene in Wales during the second half of the nineteenth century see Hywel Teifi Edwards, '*Gŵyl Gwalia*', pp. 270–7.

eisteddfod. As we have already seen, the reasons for the changes in the eisteddfod's character were complex. To speculate further on the impact of the popularity of singing on its transformation is to heighten the intricacies of this cultural development. During the second half of the nineteenth century the singing abilities of the Welsh were elevated to a national characteristic, and, as Hywel Teifi Edwards has shown, they played a major role in the development of the National Eisteddfod of Wales. He suggests that in Wales, the excellence of Welsh singers, and especially the choirs, was cultivated and utilized in order to show the worth of Welsh people, notably to their powerful English neighbours who were only too eager to deride Welsh cultural activities. From the 1860s onwards, choral competitions became the highlights and the central feature of the National Eisteddfod, to the detriment of competitions for poetry which had previously been its major focus. The adaptation of the institution to provide the platform on which the choral and vocal attributes of the Welsh could be proved and furthered was itself part of a much wider effort to make the eisteddfod 'the sales platform for the post-1847 image which was to uplift Wales in the eyes of its London critics'.[207]

A similar process occurred in Scranton. The choral prestige of the Welsh community was unmatched elsewhere in America, whilst the image of the Welsh as great singers prevailed widely in the city. As in Wales, non-Welsh adjudicators consistently marvelled at the standard Welsh choirs could attain even though they were amateur and often taught and led by non-professionals.[208] Welsh musical excellence was an important weapon in the armoury of Welsh 'boosterism', and it is perhaps feasible to suggest that the transformation of the eisteddfod was partly influenced by a desire among leading members of the Welsh community to provide an appropriate stage on which to show off Welsh vocal predominance. Yet if they did so, they may also have been responding to other pressures. According to one veteran eisteddfodic organizer at least, Scranton's Welsh male and female singers and their army of supporters and followers,

[207] Ibid., pp. 189–299; *idem*, 'Victorian Wales seeks reinstatement', *Planet*, 52 (Aug./Sept. 1985), pp. 12–24 (especially 13, 17–18).
[208] Both Carl Zerrahn and Walter Damrosch commented in these terms, apparently, after adjudicating in the 1875 and 1902 eisteddfodau, respectively, in Scranton. *Druid*, 28 Oct. 1909, 17 Feb. 1910.

whose devotion, enthusiasm and enjoyment created the effervescence of Welsh musical activity in the city, may have been the agents of the very changes that occurred. In 1910, comparing contemporary eisteddfodau with those held earlier in the nineteenth century, H. M. Edwards observed,

> The modern eisteddfod is largely musical . . . and the intense excitement and rivalry incident to choral contests and the great fervour to be found in audiences numbering many thousands were not features of the eisteddfodic gatherings of the former period . . . The eisteddfod has been popularized, and is now the means of recreation and amusement, as well as of education and instruction. The masses of the Welsh people in Wales and the United States have taken the eisteddfod into their own hands . . . Another reason for the change is based upon the love of the Welsh nation for music. The moment the people made the eisteddfod their own, music dominated the institution as it did the nation, and the singing of choruses, glees etc. became general.[209]

Yet even H. M. Edwards may have been behind the times. There are indications that the immense popularity of singing and the active promotion of the Welsh as a musical people may not only have influenced the development of the eisteddfod but may also ultimately have triumphed over it. Although the Gymanfa Ganu was a development of the 1920s and later,[210] by the first decade of the twentieth century there were signs that this would become the most popular form of 'Welsh' expression in the city. In an article concerning the eisteddfod scheduled as part of the 1908 Welsh Day, the *Druid* declared that were it possible,

> the committee would eliminate all the contests as it is plainly evident that everyone without dissent wants the Big Gymanfa and nothing else. They want to hear the two big choirs and they want to join in singing the glorious old hymns of Wales and the patriotic songs of our beloved adopted country. We promise that the contests will be disposed of as rapidly as possible and that the vast throng will be given every opportunity to sing to its heart's desire at the biggest musical festival of its kind to be held in America.[211]

The *Druid*'s apologia anticipated the eisteddfod's ultimate demise. To an extent, the 'ancient institution' had become an

---
[209] Ibid., 9 June 1910.
[210] Hartmann, op. cit., p. 149.
[211] *Druid*, 13 Aug. 1908.

almost irrelevant token, subordinate to the popularity of singing and the image of 'Welshness' as the bastion of song. Competition was unnecessary when, as the same newspaper declared after the event, 'The Welsh people of Lackawanna and Luzerne Counties have demonstrated to the world that Welsh singers were not prompted to sing for cash prizes only . . . They sing because they love to sing.'[212]

Within a generation, therefore, the vibrant Welsh-language cultural life of the 'Welsh Athens of America' had been superseded by a vast throng which sang 'My Old Kentucky Home' in the hills around Scranton.[213]

[212] Ibid., 27 Aug. 1908.
[213] Ibid., 27 July 1911.

IV
GILDING THE DRAGON: FAIRS, BARDS AND EMPIRE LOYALISTS

It was not only in the Lackawanna Valley that Welshness burned brightly, albeit briefly, in the United States during the nineteenth century. It flourished to a greater or lesser extent in most American communities where the Welsh settled in sufficient numbers to transplant and sustain it. The columns of the Welsh-American press are full of reports of Welsh cultural activities all over the United States. So, too, are they full of Welsh people's thoughts and opinions regarding their Welshness and their responses to the conundrum of what place their language and culture should have in their adopted country.

This book is not only about the Welsh in Scranton. It seeks to evaluate the nature of Welsh immigrant attitudes towards Wales and Welshness in the United States in general. As was stated in the Introduction, the written evidence we find in the Welsh-American press largely consists of the opinions of those who set the norms of Welsh-American life and who were most active in interpreting their Welshness and nurturing a consciousness of it. As such, the evidence reflects the preoccupations of what might be described as Welsh-American literary opinion and, as we shall see, it may not necessarily represent the views of the majority of Welsh immigrants. Nevertheless, it is necessary to analyse, on a much wider stage than the 'Welsh Athens of America' itself, what exactly was the nature of the Welshness nurtured and treasured in the United States during the golden age of Welsh involvement in American history. The writings and actions of leading Welsh-Americans, as recorded in the Welsh-American press and reflected in cultural activity, are permeated with definitions of what it meant to be Welsh in both Wales and America, and they offer a myriad of insights into those concerns. By focusing on episodes or 'moments', however, it is possible to prise open the Welsh-American turn of mind to reveal the essential lineaments which, it was believed, determined Welsh nationality. On two crucial occasions, the preoccupations of leading Welsh-Americans culminated in the holding of an event and the forming of an institution which were both key features of the Welsh experience in the United States: the World's Fair Eisteddfod at Chicago in 1893 and the foundation of the American Gorsedd during the second decade of the twentieth century. Both episodes provide clear illustrations of the nature of the Welshness nurtured in America.

I THE WORLD'S FAIR EISTEDDFOD, CHICAGO, 1893

The city of Chicago symbolized all that was 'new' in the late nineteenth century world. The child of the mating of the twin forces of industrialization and urbanization, by 1890 it had become, within a generation, the centre of both America's tentacled railway network and the world's foodstuffs trade, and the second largest city in the United States. During the penultimate decade of the nineteenth century Chicago's population had doubled to more than a million, nearly half of them immigrants. As far as the United States Congress was concerned, there could not be a better venue for the forthcoming World's Columbian Exposition, an event whose purpose was to commemorate the Four Hundredth Anniversary of the Discovery of America and to celebrate the emergence of the United States as one of the world's modern industrial nations.[1]

The World's Fair, as the Columbian Exposition was universally known, was conceived and executed on a massive scale, and it involved the construction of the monumental 'White City' especially for the event. When the Fair opened in May 1893, it covered 1,037 acres – four times the size of a similar event at Vienna twenty years earlier – and contained over four hundred buildings, including the enormous Transportation Building with its romanesque design and famous golden door. On display were a host of gadgets and appliances as well as the largest Ferris wheel in the world, all proudly proclaiming America's commercial and technological superiority. There were also panoramic theatrical and craft displays by most of the

---

[1] Ray Ginger, *The Age of Excess: The United States, 1877–1914* (New York, 1965), p. 161; Larzer Ziff, *The American 1890s: The Life and Times of a Lost Generation* (New York, 1966), p. 3.

world's nationalities. In the Women's Building, itself covering over two acres, women from the four corners of the globe showed off their culinary and needlework talents. Here, too, the impact of Welsh skill was more than evident: Miss Margaret Adams of Dolwyan, Felindre, Carmarthenshire, won the quilt-making competition with consummate ease.[2]

As a spectacle, the Fair was an unequivocal declaration, in the presence of representatives of all the world's nations, that the United States had come of age and the era of endless progress had arrived. Despite reservations, which the growing army of unemployed in the city exacerbated,[3] there was no denying the optimism and even the utopianism. In the words of Jay Martin, both the White City and the Fair as a whole 'celebrated the New, the vision of the urban future . . . [It] embodied the utopian impulses of the whole generation that had combined to create and celebrate it.'[4]

Nowhere, perhaps, was the faith in the future more evident than among the small enclave of Welsh immigrants who had made the United States their home. Firmly convinced of the value of their nationality to their adopted society, many Welsh-Americans saw a similar success story in their former homeland. Wales's growing economic importance and political assertiveness within the British imperial framework, accompanied by its 'national revival', was widely interpreted as being the beginnings of the true destiny of the Welsh people.[5] The Welsh, then, in Wales and the United States, had their own gospel of a contemporary maturity and a glorious future to preach and celebrate. If the opportunity were made available, what better time or place to do so than at the World's Fair itself?

Welsh-America *was* given its opportunity. The unlimited possibilities presented by the sheer spectacle and unprecedented auspiciousness of the Fair led to the holding of an event unparalleled in the history of the Welsh people. Of the twenty-seven million people who visited the Fair, there were forty

[2] Ibid., pp. 3–4; Jay Martin, *Harvests of Change: American Literature 1865–1914* (Englewood Cliffs, N.J., 1967), p. 243.; W. D. Davies, op. cit., pp. 346–8, 352–3.
[3] Ginger, op. cit., p. 162.
[4] Martin, op. cit., p. 242.
[5] See Kenneth O. Morgan, *Rebirth of a Nation: Wales 1880–1980* (Oxford and London, 1981), pp. 90–142; David Smith, 'Wales through the looking glass', pp. 215–26, and *idem*, *Wales! Wales?* (London, 1984), pp. 28–54.

thousand Welsh during 5–8 September alone.⁶ Their primary reason for being there, however, was to attend not the Fair itself, but an equally momentous occasion. During those four days, as one of the Fair's chief musical and literary attractions and as a special Prince Madoc Ap Owain Gwynedd feature, the Cymmrodorion Society of Chicago staged a Grand International Eisteddfod.⁷

The World's Fair Eisteddfod is an Alpine peak on the landscape of the Welsh experience in America.⁸ It was the largest eisteddfod ever held in the world up to that time, yet contemporary sources suggest that the event has an even greater significance. The eisteddfod dominated Welsh-America for two years before it was actually held. It involved preparations on an unprecedented scale and it triggered off a number of responses in the writings of leading Welsh-Americans. The eisteddfod was subjected to a rigorous post-mortem which attempted to evaluate it in the framework of the intense atmosphere of hope, expectation and even fear that it aroused. In all its three phases – preparation, the actual eisteddfod and its aftermath – the World's Fair Eisteddfod was both the child and the initiator of a number of teasing preoccupations among leading Welsh-Americans.

I.i PREPARATION AND EXPECTATION, JULY 1891–SEPTEMBER 1893

The announcement that the Cymmrodorion Society of Chicago would organize a Grand International Eisteddfod during the World's Fair was first made in June 1891.⁹ It was perhaps inevitable that the Cymmrodorion should choose an eisteddfod for the Welsh contribution to the Fair, given the institution's popularity in both Wales and the United States. From the outset, however, the organizers were determined that their event would be far more than just another eisteddfod. The

---

⁶ *Drych*, 5 Oct. 1893; Ginger, op. cit., p. 161.
⁷ W. D. Davies, op. cit., p. 354; *Druid*, 5 Sept 1907.
⁸ For a contemporary account of the World's Fair Eisteddfod, see W. D. Davies, op. cit., pp. 354–91. Our knowledge of the World's Fair Eisteddfod and its significance has been considerably enhanced by the recent publication of Hywel Teifi Edwards, *Eisteddfod Ffair y Byd, Chicago, 1893* (Llandysul, 1990). Edwards locates the Eisteddfod in the context of Welsh-American concerns regarding the role Welshness should play in immigrant life and comes to very similar conclusions to those in this chapter.
⁹ *Drych*, 18 June 1891; *Cambrian* XI (July 1891), p. 209.

unique nature of the Fair demanded an equally unique eisteddfod to match it. One of their very first actions was officially to involve Wales in their plans: they invited the National Eisteddfod of Wales to hold its 1893 event in Chicago simultaneously with that of the World's Fair.[10]

The invitation was sent to the National Eisteddfod's ruling body and other prominent Welsh people in Britain during the summer of 1891. However, Wales was unimpressed. At the Swansea National Eisteddfod later that year, Pontypridd, not Chicago, was chosen as the 1893 venue. In what may have been a classic case of sour grapes, Idriswyn, the Cymmrodorion's representative in Wales, accused the National Eisteddfod Association of ignoring Chicago's claim because they would not have had any influence over the management of the event. To their shame the Bardic Circle had acquiesced in the decision.[11] There is no evidence to suggest or disprove the validity of this assessment. Nevertheless one thing is certain: the driving force behind Idriswyn's reaction was undoubtedly disappointment, for by the time the application came to be considered, the World's Fair Eisteddfod's organizers, and Welsh-American literary opinion in general, had come to the conclusion that a joint eisteddfod was a matter of the utmost urgency. Despite its failure, the whole episode of the invitation is crucial to an understanding of the context in which the eisteddfod was held.

The organizers decided to invite the National Eisteddfod because they believed their event was so important that the involvement of all Welsh people, and not merely those living in the United States, was essential. Writing in the *Drych* in June 1891, William Ap Madoc, the general secretary of the World's Fair Eisteddfod, on whose initiative it had all come about, suggested that the event would be big enough 'to include the Welsh of both continents, as well as several thousands of foreigners . . . We believe the Welsh in America will make every effort to be worthy of the occasion and our nation. But this is not enough. We want bardic, musical and oratorical Wales to be with us to make an exhibition of our national excellences.'[12] His

---

[10] *Drych*, 18 June 1891.
[11] *Drych*, 17 Sept. 1891.
[12] Ibid., 18 June 1891.

conviction was elaborated upon in the actual written invitation itself:

> The civilized nations of the world will be represented in their . . . achievements in art and knowledge, and their literary and musical qualities. Will the Welsh Nation be behind in displaying their musical and literary excellences, and on such a notable occasion? No they will not is the voice of the Welsh in America . . . We are confident that the voice of Wales will say the same. No other nation can bring to the Columbian Exhibition an institution so musical, literary, ancient and of such character as the National Eisteddfod . . .
>
> The Hon. George R. Davies . . . is the General Director of the Fair and his special request is 'Bring the Old National Institution to Chicago in 1893 . . . so that the Welsh Name will be elevated and honoured in the eyes of the whole world'.
>
> Welsh of the Land of our Fathers . . . on this most significant and advantageous of occasions, accept the heartfelt invitation of the Welsh in America . . . and stimulate and strengthen the national feeling of Welsh hearts on both continents.[13]

The Chicago Cymmrodorion were not alone in perceiving the World's Fair Eisteddfod as being pregnant with possibilities. Shortly after the invitation was issued, a *Drych* editorial commended the efforts of the eisteddfod's committee and outlined why its initiatives in both holding the event and inviting the National Eisteddfod were welcome. After re-emphasizing the point that every civilized nation in the world would be showing off its achievements at the Fair, it maintained that it was even more important for the Welsh to do so since they had been far more reticent than other nationalities in this respect:

> Our long-standing defect until now has been to keep away too much from the sight of strangers . . . Although our achievements have been, in general, masterly, no-one knew about them outside our own circles . . . they did not earn us fame as a nation outside our little native country . . . But for some years now the National Eisteddfod in Wales has attracted some attention from outside Offa's Dyke. Insofar as it flowed over Wales' borders, the more honour both it and its organisers attained. The more publicity this old Welsh institution can gain the better . . . At this time, nothing will attract more publicity to the Eisteddfod than holding it in Chicago.[14]

---

[13] Ibid.
[14] Ibid., 2 July 1891.

Under the circumstances, continued the editorial, it was only fair that the National Eisteddfod should accept the invitation. This would put the seal of the whole nation on the Chicago event and give it a character which the Welsh in America alone could not achieve without the official recognition and co-operation of the Welsh in Wales. To support its argument the *Drych* pointed to the fact that the National Eisteddfod had recently been held in Liverpool and London: 'If it is possible to hold it in the middle of English speakers in London, why is it not possible to hold it in the middle of speakers of the same language in Chicago?' It hoped that the invitation would be accepted, for both patriotism and love of nationality demanded it:

> ... the Chicago Eisteddfod should ... be worthy of the nation and worthy of the circumstances. What Welshman would wish his unique national institution to appear weak in the middle of the boundless wonders and achievements of the Exposition. We must have an Eisteddfod which will be more than a thread in the quilt of the World's Fair; we must have one which will add to our brilliance as a nation.[15]

Although on this occasion the *Drych* did not outline exactly what these Welsh national characteristics which deserved to be celebrated were, numerous Welsh-American commentators had, during the previous twenty years, been more than eager to pinpoint them in speeches, articles and editorials. All usually emphasized the loyalty, religiosity and respectability of the Welsh, and the worth of their language and their literary and musical culture.[16] The feeling that these virtues deserved greater recognition had rapidly become a central preoccupation of Welsh-American literary opinion. Two months before its editorial supporting the invitation to the National Eisteddfod, the *Drych* had welcomed the appearance in *Cosmopolitan* of a very complimentary article on the Welsh by ex-Postmaster General

---

[15] Ibid. There are in fact striking resemblances between the World's Fair Eisteddfod and the National Eisteddfodau in Liverpool in 1884 and London in 1887 in terms of the preoccupations and the image of Welshness they reflected. See Hywel Teifi Edwards 'Victorian Wales seeks reinstatement'.

[16] In the *Drych* in January 1883, for example, a writer named 'Caerddonian' emphasized that the Welsh possessed many excellences which far outweighed their defects, and of which many nations would be proud. He listed loyalty, musicality, religiosity and the Welsh language as the major ones. Ibid., 8 Jan. 1883. See also Erasmus W. Jones, 'The Welsh in America', loc. cit.; Thomas L. James, loc. cit.; *Cambrian*, I (Jan./Feb. 1880), pp. 5–7, 25. See also Hywel Teifi Edwards, *Eisteddfod Ffair y Byd*, especially pp. 34–61.

Thomas L. James. The article, said the *Drych*, had brought 'a great deal of benefit to us as a nation . . . as it brings us to the attention of Americans in a respectable and appealing way; it will do so much to encourage the idea that it is honourable to be a Welshman . . . We must admit that many of Welsh blood have been negligent in this respect.'[17]

The same motivations that lay behind the doomed invitation to the National Eisteddfod also led to another initiative to involve Wales in the grand design. After the refusal of the invitation, the organizers made overtures to the Gorsedd of Bards of Great Britain regarding the possibility of holding official Gorsedd proceedings during the World's Fair Eisteddfod. In this they again received the support of correspondents to the Welsh-American press. One writer informed the *Drych* that it was 'of the greatest importance that the Chicago Committee lay a foundation stone for the International Eisteddfod . . . This is an excellent opportunity to transplant the Bardic Circle in the field of American literature.'[18] This time the application was successful. It was received favourably by Archdruid Clwydfardd, and as a result Hwfa Môn, as official representative, was enabled by special patent to preside over Gorsedd ceremonies at Chicago.[19] Although it was perhaps no substitute for the National Eisteddfod, Welsh-America had after all succeeded in securing its much sought-after official sanction from Wales. From now on the organizers could concentrate on preparations in the United States itself.

The organizers' determined efforts to make their event unique and as all-embracing as possible continued apace. The eisteddfod's Board of Directors was incorporated in November 1891 with a capital stock of $25,000 and 'patriotic' Welsh people were urged to take out shares in the 'grandest and most patriotic undertaking of the Welsh people'.[20] With Ap Madoc firmly at the helm, various committees were set up to organize the event and decide on competition subjects. The board and the

---

[17] *Drych*, 2 Apr. 1891; Thomas L. James, loc. cit. For biographical details of James, see *Welsh-American*, 15 Sept. 1916.
[18] *Drych*, 22 Oct. 1891.
[19] Ibid., 12 Nov. 1891; W. D. Davies, op. cit., pp. 360-1, 372-4.
[20] *Drych*, 18 Feb. 1892.

committees were composed of a number of the most prominent Welsh-American men – there were no women on any of the committees – in the Midwest, including, as the board's president, Samuel Job, the superintendent of the Pullman Iron and Steel Company, and W. E. Powell ('Gwilym Eryri').[21] By the beginning of 1892 a final programme of competitions had been published, with prizes totalling a mammoth $12,000; as we have seen, the chief choral competition alone offered an unprecedented $5,000 for the winning choir and $1,000 for the second. A team of eisteddfod 'missionaries' was appointed, and these visited most of the larger Welsh communities in the United States during 1892, drumming up support from potential competitors and spectators alike.[22]

Frequent progress bulletins in the Welsh press in America and in Wales during 1891–3 gave the impression that all arrangements were in hand. Nevertheless, it would not be smooth running all the way for the committee. Many Welsh adjudicators in Britain were invited to take part, but most regarded the committee's financial inducements as insufficient, and consequently they declined.[23] Also, despite the $5,000 prize, it was not able to tempt mixed choirs from Wales to compete in the chief choral competition, although it had initially announced that a number would in fact do so.[24]

The work of the committee was also tainted by scandals. The Liverpool agent Cymro Gwyllt, whom Glanmor Williams has described as a man who had 'his finger in every emigrational pie',[25] informed the *Drych* of the rumours in Wales which held that the committee had already 'sewn up' the major literary competitions.[26] More ominously perhaps, in July 1892 the *New York World* alleged that the committee was dominated by a cabal which ran things as it pleased, without any regard for accountability. The newspaper also accused some members of

---

[21] Ibid., W. D. Davies, op. cit., pp. 355–6. For biographical details of Job, see *Cambrian*, X (July 1890), pp. 193–4; Ebenezer Edwards, op. cit., p. 410.

[22] *Drych*, 18 Feb. 1892, 15 Dec. 1910; *Cambrian*, XIII (Sept. 1893), p. 257; *Scranton Republican*, 19 Mar. 1892.

[23] *Baner ac Amserau Cymru*, 9 Aug. 1893.

[24] *Cambrian*, XI (July 1891) p. 209; *Scranton Republican*, 19 Mar. 1892; *Drych*, 1 Sept. 1892.

[25] Glanmor Williams, 'A prospect of paradise', p. 224.

[26] *Drych*, 15 Oct. 1891. In fact, both the Chair and the Crown were won by competitors from Wales.

1. Anthracite mining in Scranton and the landscape it created. The D.L. & W.'s Hyde Park mine in 1910, with Hyde Park in the background. The distinctive breaker, where coal was prepared for the market, dominates the scene. *By permission of Lackawanna Historical Society.*

2. Breaker boys at work amid the dust and noise in the north-east Pennsylvania anthracite coalfield, about 1900. Many Welsh boys in Scranton began their working lives in this way at an early age. (See p. 30.) *By permission of Lackawanna Historical Society.*

3. The first Welsh Baptist Church, South Main Avenue, Hyde Park shortly after Revd T. Teifion Richards (inset) became its pastor in 1907. The photograph bears out Revd R. D. Thomas's testimony in 1872 that the spires of Welsh churches in Scranton 'rise up to heaven'. (See pp. 91–2.) *By permission of Lackawanna Historical Society.*

4. From the 1870s onwards larger eisteddfodau in Scranton attracted national attention. A choral competition at the Welsh Philosophical Society's second 'National Eisteddfod' in 1880, as recorded by Joseph Becker for *Frank Leslie's Illustrated*. *By permission of Pennsylvania Anthracite Heritage Museum.*

5. 'Welsh Days' were the highpoints of the year for the Scranton Welsh during the early twentieth century. Scene from the 1921 Welsh Day at Rocky Glen, Scranton, with H. M. Edwards (far left) officiating. *By permission of Lackawanna Historical Society.*

6. Cartoon entitled 'Voices from the "other side" '. The caption: 'It is a glorious fact that the further one goes into the ends of far America the grander and deeper is the expression of my countrymen's patriotism. The way that "Hen Wlad fy Nhadau" is sung in the remote districts is almost too expressive to bear; it almost breaks one's heart.' (Interview with Mr Ap Madoc.) *Western Mail*, 10 August, 1907.

7. For Welsh-Americans in 1893, all rails led to Chicago and the 'grandest and most patriotic undertaking of the Welsh people'. Railway companies were quick to take advantage of the tremendous interest the World's Fair Eisteddfod was attracting. (see pp. 148–77)

Facsimile of Certificate of Membership.

8. The Gorsedd had a trans-Atlantic dimension between 1913 and 1941. The American Gorsedd's Membership Certificate was adapted from that of the Gorsedd in Britain but its aims were distinctively Welsh-American.

9. The Scranton Choral Union: the underdogs who took on the mighty Scranton Cymmrodorion Choir at the World's Fair Eisteddfod in Chicago, September 1893, and emerged victorious. The choir defied predictions and won the Chief Choral Competition for Mixed Voices. (See pp. 135–40.) *By permission of Lackawanna Historical Society.*

10. Robert H. Davies (Gomerian) (1856–1947) of Pittsburgh, the driving force behind the American Gorsedd and editor of the *Druid* after 1916. His efforts to make Welsh-Americans be proud of their Welsh heritage were indefatigable.

11. Judge H. M. Edwards, (1844–1925) the most well-known Welshman in Scranton and possibly in America during the late nineteenth to early twentieth centuries. No Welsh cultural event in Scranton was complete without some involvement from 'H. M.'

12. America's first archdruid in his robes of office. Revd T. Cynonfardd Edwards (1848–1927) of Kingston, Pennsylvania served in this capacity between 1913 and 1919.

13. John F. Davies (1809–1882) the Scranton family's saviour when their dreams of becoming major industrialists turned sour in 1841–2. Davies was the Welshman who lit the fuse that set Scranton's industrial revolution alight. (See pp. 13–14.) *By permission of Lackawanna Historical Society*

financial mismanagement during a previous eisteddfod at Chicago: 'These are not the right sort of people at all to conduct an Eisteddfod at the World's Fair,' it concluded.[27] Apparently these sentiments were endorsed by some of the Columbia Exhibition's officers, and similar ones were articulated in the columns of the *Drych*. That newspaper described the discussion of accusations of this kind in non-Welsh newspapers as 'unfortunate', and stated that Welsh-Americans deserved to know all the facts in order to evaluate the true prospects of the World's Fair Eisteddfod.[28]

The *Drych*'s decisive intervention in the *New York World* scandal highlighted another development which marred the efforts of the organizers. They lost the support of Welsh-America's foremost newspaper. Initially, during the summer of 1891, the *Drych* had been enthusiastic regarding the venture, and it had even insisted that the success of the eisteddfod ought to be a matter of personal importance to every Welshman and woman on the continent.[29] However, from the end of 1891 onwards the newspaper cooled in its attitude. Although it continued to publish progress reports, it refrained from giving editorial support to the committee. Its change of heart was influenced by the increasing involvement of its great rival, the Chicago bilingual, *Y Columbia*, in the organization of the event. Writing two years after the eisteddfod, W. D. Davies suggested that the *Drych* was envious of the *Columbia* because the eisteddfod committee placed more emphasis on the services of the latter. As a result, the Utica newspaper was 'cooler in its zeal for the movement than the *Columbia*'.[30]

The disaffection of the *Drych* and the scandals of 1891–2 were undoubtedly developments which augured ill for the success of the eisteddfod. More generally, some doubts were expressed as to whether in fact the event would fulfil the ambitious aims attached to it by many influential Welsh-Americans. One of the eisteddfod committee's members informed *Baner ac Amserau Cymru* that many Welsh-Americans wondered whether the event would be a success, considering the appeal of other attractions at the Fair. Moreover, many regarded the size of the

[27] Ibid., 28 July, 1, 8 Sept. 1892.
[28] Ibid., 28 July, 4 Aug., 8 Sept. 1892.
[29] Ibid., 3 Sept. 1891.
[30] W. D. Davies, op. cit., p. 357.

United States and the scattered nature of the Welsh communities as a major barrier to a large Welsh attendance and participation.[31] These doubts, and the committee's various troubles, were perhaps made all the more worrying by the way in which the World's Fair Eisteddfod was being seen as a golden opportunity for the Welsh. After all there was a great deal at stake. Dafydd Rhisiart, a member of the committee, issued what can almost be interpreted as a warning: the Welsh, he said, would be showing themselves in front of all the nations of the earth, and all the newspapers of the world would be reporting on their excellences – and their defects.[32]

Yet if fear and scandal surrounded the World's Fair Eisteddfod during the two-year-long build-up to the momentous event, so, too, were there hope, optimism and expectancy, which also surfaced in the Welsh-American press. Revd Fred Evans ('Ednyfed') of Milwaukee, who would be one of the conductors at the eisteddfod, informed the English-language, Welsh-American periodical, the *Cambrian*, in July 1893 that an intense optimism prevailed for 'the greatest and grandest eisteddfod'. At the Chicago Festival Hall, he maintained, 'six or seven thousand may sit . . . and dream of Wales and Heaven as the song pure and sweet will rise to the God of Music.'[33] The eisteddfod attracted an increasing volume of literary attention, especially in the *Cambrian*, a magazine which since its first appearance in 1880 had been steadfast in its crusade to provide information on Welsh matters to non-Welsh speakers in the United States.[34] Although it passed little editorial comment, it gave a great deal of space to frequent progress reports and to wider explanations of the meaning and significance of the eisteddfod as an institution.

The more general articles on the eisteddfod in the *Cambrian* emphasized the antiquity of the institution and its centrality to the Welsh way of life. Ap Madoc reacted strongly in July 1891 to a Chicago newspaper which had referred to the 'national festival of the Welsh people' as 'games'. He described these

[31] *Baner ac Amserau Cymru*, 30 Mar. 1892.
[32] Ibid., 6 Apr. 1892.
[33] *Cambrian*, XIII (July 1893), p. 218.
[34] The *Cambrian* was published in Utica by the same printer as the *Drych*, T. J. Griffith, and was one of the very few long-running Welsh-American periodicals. It carried articles on the histories of the various Welsh communities, portraits of prominent Welshmen and Welsh-Americans, and religious discussions.

Welsh 'games' as 'intellectual ones', which involved 'exhilaration and excitement of intense competition'. 'Eisteddfod,' he maintained,

> is a word which sets the Welsh heart on fire. There is no English equivalent to it. This many centuries old institution is a most unique literary and musical feature of an ancient and active nation. They are the British literary Olympics and none the less so in their adopted land.[35]

Ednyfed also dwelt on a similar theme in an article published in March 1893. After first explaining how the word 'eisteddfod' was pronounced – a necessary direction, perhaps, considering the character of the *Cambrian*'s readership – he described it as, above all, a venerable institution. It was venerable not merely because it was old, but because it was honourable and honoured and loved by the Welsh people. It was also loved because it offered a pleasant opportunity for the Welsh and their descendants to meet on a festival day, to absorb its inspirational atmosphere, to gratify their love of music, and even to shed tears when 'Hen Wlad fy Nhadau' was sung. The latter, according to Ednyfed, was the best indication 'of the Welshman's love for his country, his language and his nation, and they can sing it infinitely better here than their brethren in old Gwalia.'[36]

But the eisteddfod was not only an 'ancient' Welsh institution which illustrated the antiquity of the Welsh people as a nation and, moreover, one which proved that the Welsh in the United States had maintained their Welshness. It was also a symbol of the worth of the Welsh to American society and a positive force in nurturing their good citizenship. This interpretation was the kernel of an article entitled 'An American view of the eisteddfod' which appeared in the *Cambrian* in July 1891:

> The most praiseworthy characteristic of our Welsh citizen is that his determination to renew native lore and sentiment and to familiarize the younger ones with historic verse and literary characters does not deter them in the least from their efforts to familiarize themselves with American institutions, to digest the true genius of our government and voluminous literary curriculum. The Welsh in this way are not displaying native prejudices and foreign practices but pure patriotic sentiment. Compare it with the record of certain classes of foreigners who are guided

[35] Ibid., XI (July 1891), p. 209.
[36] Ibid., XIII (Mar. 1893), p. 89.

by bigotry, dense ignorance and blinding prejudice. The eisteddfod is one of those practices which awaken nobler sentiments of the soul and the security of our government is thus made stronger. The religious inclination and the tendency to educate, prosper and progress of the Welsh is fully explained when Americans see the absorbing desire to practice and perpetuate the purity of verse and music.[37]

The article was originally published in the *Mankato Free Press* in February 1891, but it was reprinted by the *Cambrian* in the same issue which announced that the World's Fair Eisteddfod would be held. The sentiments expressed in the article were often articulated at Welsh society functions and in articles in the Welsh-American press and in the American press in general.[38]

The International Eisteddfod also attracted great interest in Wales. *Baner ac Amserau Cymru* consistently carried reports on developments and even reported the fears of some of the committee members.[39] During 1893 it became apparent that many in Wales were forming parties with a view to attending the eisteddfod. Emigration agents were quick to take advantage of the situation. 'Hurrah! Chicago and back for £16 14*s*', declared an advertisement for James Roberts, an agent at – of all places, considering the events of two years before – Pontypridd; he would provide free admission tickets, board, lodgings, and trips on Lake Michigan.[40] Even the National Eisteddfod in Pontypridd played its part and absorbed the spirit of Chicago 1893. It was held early in order to avoid clashing with its rival and ironically, or perhaps even predictably, the subject of its prize-essay competition was 'Welshmen who have emigrated and have risen to distinction in America and the British Colonies.'[41]

Many in Wales also echoed the manner in which those Welshmen who had emigrated and had risen to distinction in the United States regarded the World's Fair Eisteddfod. Idriswyn wrote a series of articles in the *News of the Week* articulating the hopes of the Welsh-Americans,[42] whilst as early as November 1891 the *Welsh Review* declared:

---

[37] *Mankato Free Press* (Iowa), 27 Feb. 1891, reprinted in *Cambrian*, XI (July 1891), p. 42.
[38] See, for example, *Drych*, 8 Jan. 1883; *Cambrian*, VIII (Feb. 1888), pp. 56–7.
[39] *Baner ac Amserau Cymru*, 30 Mar., 6 Apr. 1892, 9 Aug. 1893.
[40] *Tyst a'r Dydd*, 17 Mar., 23 Apr. 1893.
[41] *Baner ac Amserau Cymru*, 9 Aug. 1893; *Western Mail*, 14 June 1892.
[42] *Drych*, 17 Sept. 1891.

There is every prospect that Wales will make a presentable appearance in the World's Fair in 1893. There are many Welshmen in America and with natural fondness they look forward to a display of national resources which will give the old country a place at least among the rival nations of the world. A great eisteddfod will be held at which it is hoped that some of the leading spirits on this side of the water will be present.[43]

By September 1893 the stage was set. For two years the World's Fair Eisteddfod had dominated the actions and pens of many leading Welsh-Americans. On the eve of the great event, Ap Madoc predicted that

amid the progress shown in the World's Fair, the Welsh people of the world, under the immediate leadership of their Chicago countrymen, are to inaugurate a new era in the national Welsh institution known as the Eisteddfod. It has been planned on such a scale and manner as has never been seen before.[44]

The general secretary's words undoubtedly reflect the optimism with which some sections, at least, of Welsh-American literary opinion looked forward to the eisteddfod, an optimism which at times took on a utopian tinge. The intense anticipation and the committee's efforts give the impression that the eisteddfod was being seen as the platform on which to show the value of being Welsh and to proclaim that the future of Welshness was secure. In many ways, Welsh-American writers applied the literary gloss to the undercoat that the eisteddfod's organizers' ambitious preparations painted on the bare woodwork of the immense utopian vision of the World's Fair.

I.ii 'THE GRANDEST AND MOST PATRIOTIC UNDERTAKING OF THE WELSH PEOPLE'

The World's Fair Eisteddfod opened at midday on Tuesday 5 September 1893 with a ceremony at the specially constructed Gorsedd Circle. It was an auspicious occasion in itself: it was the first time Gorsedd proceedings were held outside the British Isles. Apparently thousands witnessed the event and the parade along Midway Plaisance. It was also a fitting overture to the immense significance of the opera which took place between

---
[43] *Welsh Review*, 1 (Nov. 1891), p. 66.
[44] *Cambrian*, XIII (Sept. 1893), p. 257.

those first trumpet calls at the Gorsedd and the final exultant 'Hallelujah' at the end of Handel's famous chorus which closed the eisteddfod three and a half days later.[45] The 'Wales' which was being celebrated was reflected in a number of symbolic acts and images. Indeed, from the grand choral performances right down to competitors' pseudonyms, the whole eisteddfod reeked of the 'national revival' which was taking place in contemporary Wales, and of the integral part leading Welsh-Americans believed they were playing in it.

The World's Fair Eisteddfod was attended by an auspicious gathering of Welsh dignitaries from all over the world. Some of those 'leading spirits' in Wales to whom the *Welsh Review* had referred two years earlier certainly were present in both mind and body. Indeed, although the National Eisteddfod Association of Wales had been wary, the participation of adjudicators, bards, choirs and soloists more then testified to the homeland's recognition of the Welsh-Americans' endeavours. Among those who sent adjudicators across the Atlantic were Professor John Rhys of Oxford, O. M. Edwards and Beriah Gwynfe Evans, whilst Pencerdd Gwalia and Hwfa Môn offered their critical services in person. Poets from Wales snapped up the bardic honours. The Revd E. Rees ('Dyfed') of Cardiff and Watcyn Wyn of Ammanford were the chaired and crowned bards, the former actually in attendance, and both were honoured in true eisteddfodic fashion by *englynion* composed by Welsh-America's foremost bards.[46] Furthermore, four choirs from Wales competed; they succeeded in enrapturing audiences and critics alike.

The impact of the homeland choirs ensured that the eisteddfod was a classic affirmation of the image of Wales as the 'Land of Song'. Three choirs from Wales competed in the male voice competition: the Gwent Glee, the Rhondda Glee and the Penrhyn Male Choir. Apparently, their impact was stunning: each performance was followed by hundreds of people in the audience rising to their feet, shouting, and waving hats and scarves. W. D. Davies, who witnessed the competition, thought it was the 'most glorious "treat" the Welsh of the United States

---

[45] W. D. Davies, op. cit., p. 360; *Cambrian*, XIII (Oct. 1893), p. 312; *Drych*, 2 Nov. 1893.
[46] W. D. Davies, op. cit., *passim*.

had ever had'.[47] The Rhondda Choir and the Penrhyn Choir came first and second respectively, whilst the former, under its conductor, Tom Stephens, confirmed its speciality of capturing choral laurels outside Offa's Dyke, first established at the London National Eisteddfod six years previously.[48] The quality with which Clara Novello Davies's Cardiff Ladies Choir won the Female Choir competition at Chicago astounded all,[49] whilst even the man who was largely responsible for establishing Wales's choral prestige, the hero of the South Wales Choral Union's victories at the Crystal Palace in 1872–3, was present. In a tremendous scene during the Wednesday afternoon session, a member of the audience stood up in the middle of an adjudication and shouted 'Dacw Caradog' ('There's Caradog'). The audience rose as one, amid wild cheering, clapping and stamping of feet, which completely disrupted the proceedings. Caradog was persuaded to go on to the stage, and, on being introduced, received a tumultuous ovation which apparently had a visible effect on him. He told the crowd that this was the most sublime moment of his life, to have had the honour to be in America at such a notable time. His appearance in Chicago was crowned by his being given the honour of conducting the mass eisteddfod choir's triumphant rendering of the 'Hallelujah Chorus' which closed the eisteddfod.[50]

The greatest event in Welsh-American history was also the greatest gathering of Welsh-American dignitaries. The eisteddfod not only paraded representatives of the 'national revival' in the homeland; it also brought into the limelight many of those Welsh-Americans who embodied the virtues which Welsh blood was believed to offer the adopted country, and who were playing a vital role in Welsh-American circles and in American life in general. The cream of Welsh-America contributed either as guests of honour, conductors, adjudicators or committee members. Representing the part Welsh people had played in the industrial and commercial development of the United States, for example, was the Hon. David Richards, the 'coal king' from Knoxville, Tennessee, who presided over the Wednesday

[47] Ibid., p. 364.
[48] Ibid., pp. 363–4; *Drych*, 21 Sept. 1893.
[49] *Scranton Republican*, 7 Sept. 1893; *Drych*, 21 Sept. 1893; W. D. Davies, op. cit., p. 384.
[50] *Scranton Republican*, 7 Sept. 1893; W. D. Davies, op. cit., pp. 370–1, 390.

proceedings. Also scheduled to chair sessions were Anthony Howells, United States Consul at Cardiff, Judge Noah Davis of New York and Thomas L. James, ex-Postmaster General of the United States. Actually, all three cried off, although the latter was included in the ranks of a host of other 'eminent' Welsh-Americans who acted as adjudicators.[51]

Many of those whose lives had been dedicated to fostering the 'Welshness' of the immigrants were also involved. One of the vice-presidents was W. E. Powell ('Gwilym Eryri'), bard and preacher of the gospel of Welsh emigration, and 'founder' of the Welsh settlement of Powell, S. Dakota. He had used his position as general immigration agent for the Chicago, Milwaukee and St Paul Rail Road Company to travel around the West publicizing the eisteddfod, and he was admitted to the Gorsedd during the week.[52] The conductors during the eisteddfod were the famous three 'E's – the powerful trio of Revd T. Cynonfardd Edwards, a future archdruid of the American Gorsedd, H. M. Edwards of Scranton, a future deputy archdruid, and Revd Fred Evans ('Ednyfed') of Milwaukee.[53] Apart from being among Welsh-America's foremost men of letters, all three had unrivalled reputations as eisteddfodic conductors. Indeed, the manner in which they controlled the various sessions in Chicago was a source of pride to many commentators after the event.[54] But the towering presence which put all these notables in the shade at Chicago was that of William Ap Madoc, whom the *Western Mail* once described as a 'literary and musical genius ... a charming conversationalist and a great and amiable gentleman whose face fairly beams with intelligence'.[55]

The success of the eisteddfod rocketed the already influential standing of Ap Madoc in Welsh-American cultural life into the

---

[51] Ibid., pp. 358, 362, 369, 374; *Drych*, 21 Sept. 1893. For biographical details of David Richards (1824–1906), see *Cambrian*, XXVI (Apr. 1906), pp. 181–2. For Judge Davies (1818–1902), Associate Justice of the Supreme Court of New York, 1873–86, see *Cambrian*, XVI (Feb. 1896), p. 65–7; Hartmann, op. cit., p. 215. For Anthony Howells (1832–1910?), a Massillon, Ohio, coal operator and State Treasurer 1877–9, see *Cambrian*, XII (Feb. 1892), pp. 33–5; Hartmann, op. cit., p. 200.

[52] *Drych*, 9, 15 Dec. 1910; W. D. Davies, op. cit., p. 373. For biographical details of W. E. Powell (1841–1910), see *Drych*, 15 Dec. 1910.

[53] W. D. Davies, op. cit., p. 358. For biographical details of Revd Fred Evans (1840–99), see B. D. Thomas, op. cit.

[54] *Drych*, 21 Sept. 1893. All three had also conducted at a number of National Eisteddfodau in Wales. *Cambrian*, XV (Sept. 1895), p. 285; B. D. Thomas, op. cit., pp. 110–11; *Dictionary of Welsh Biography*, p. 197.

[55] *Western Mail*, 9 Aug. 1907.

realm of legend. His contribution to that event was immense: he was its instigator, general secretary, and the president or a member of a number of its various committees. And as if organizational exertions were insufficient to sap his mental and physical stamina, for months before the event he had been rigorously rehearsing the eisteddfod's choir, which he also conducted in performance during the festival.[56] Outside the World's Fair arena he was a publisher, editor, musician and bard. Here undoubtedly was the man who most embodied the spirit of the World's Fair Eisteddfod.

William Ap Madoc (1844–1916) was born in Maesteg, south Wales, and had emigrated to the United States in the early 1870s.[57] Between 1872 and 1874 he edited and published in conjunction with T. Solomon Griffiths of Utica, *Blodau'r Oes a'r Ysgol*, a magazine for children written from a religious and temperance standpoint. But it was in the musical field that he excelled. Throughout his life he was a champion of Welsh music, constantly urging Welsh soloists, choirs, and eisteddfod organizers to include Welsh songs and Welsh folk music in their repertoires and competitions. He was, too, a firm advocate of choral training, immovable in his determination to ensure that Welsh choral singing not only retained its superiority but also improved its standard. He wrote regular music columns in the *Drych* and, after 1899, the 'Musical notes' section in the *Cambrian*, all lively commentaries on Welsh musical affairs.[58] Professionally, he was musical director of the Chicago High Schools, a musical instructor at that city's William H. Sherwood School of Music and the cantor at Chicago All Souls Church. A keen eisteddfodwr, and a firm believer in the inseparability of that institution and 'Welshness', Ap Madoc became one of the founders of the American Gorsedd towards the end of his life.

Next to the World's Fair Eisteddfod itself, Ap Madoc's greatest triumph perhaps was his visit to Wales in July–August 1907, which was almost ambassadorial in character. His reception and his activities confirmed both his own standing and the nature of the wider lineaments of 'Welshness' which he

---

[56] W. D. Davies, op. cit., pp. 355–6, 371, 376, 385.
[57] For biographical details of Ap Madoc see *Cerddor*, XXXVIII (Nov. 1916), pp. 122–3; *Welsh-American*, 1 Sept. 1916.
[58] See, for example, *Drych*, 30 May 1907; *Cambrian*, XIX (Feb. 1899), p. 65.

represented, and which had created the World's Fair Eisteddfod. He acted as a conductor and delivered a lecture 'of a truly elevating character' on 'The Welsh in America' at the Swansea National Eisteddfod of that year.[59] During his visit he was interviewed by the *Western Mail*, which informed its readers that he had acted as adjudicator or conductor at 126 eisteddfodau in America, a fact which 'tells its own tale of the virility of the Celtic spirit across the sea'. Furthermore, the report continued, it was on Ap Madoc's initiative that the World's Fair Eisteddfod had come about, 'an event which did more than anything to bring the Welsh people into prominence in the States'.[60] In response, the Welsh-American took the opportunity of stating his own opinion of the extent of Welsh feeling in the United States:

> Wherever I have gone I have marvelled at the Welsh patriotism to be found there, yearning for expression in some form or another. It is a glorious fact that the further one goes into the ends of far America, the greater and deeper is the expression of my country's patriotism. The way that Hen Wlad fy Nhadau is sung in the remoter districts is too expressive to bear; it almost breaks one's heart.[61]

Ap Madoc's remarks inspired a remarkable cartoon in the following day's *Western Mail*.[62] On Ap Madoc's itinerary during the summer of 1907 a luncheon was given in his honour by the Cardiff Welsh Society at the Park Hotel. He was entrusted with delivering a patriotic message from the people of Wales to the Welsh in America:

> To you personally, we offer our profound thanks for the ceaseless service you are rendering Cymru, Cymro a Chymraeg in the vast new world of the United States ... Tell the Cambrians of America that we are making for a Greater Wales; greater educationally, greater in our ideals and greater in our appreciation of all that goes to make a prosperous people. Tell them we are exceedingly encouraged ... by the constant interest which is being taken in our national movements by the 'Britons across the sea' in America.[63]

---

[59] *South Wales Daily News*, 2 Aug. 1907.
[60] *Western Mail*, 9 Aug. 1907.
[61] Ibid.
[62] See illustration section (no. 6).
[63] *Druid*, 5 Sept. 1907.

Those who sat through all twelve sessions of Ap Madoc's brainchild, and attended the various associated meetings held during its course, could have been left in little doubt that it was this same 'Greater Wales' and its 'national movements' which were being celebrated at Chicago in September 1893. Apart from the significance of those involved, the actual proceedings are full of telling imagery and symbolic acts which pinpoint exactly the essential elements of the 'Welshness' the eisteddfod promoted.

Not surprisingly, perhaps, religion and education, and their centrality to the 'national revival' of the Welsh, figured prominently. Both were honoured by being made subjects in the list of literary competitions; both, too, were the focus of auxiliary meetings held during the week. The eisteddfod took place at the same time as the Welsh-Americans played host to the Fair's World's Religious Congress. On the Sunday preceding the first eisteddfodic session, a large congregation of Welsh people from both Wales and the United States, and representing a number of denominations, assembled in a Welsh church in Chicago to hear a sermon delivered by the Gorsedd's envoy, Revd Rowland Williams ('Hwfa Môn'). Welsh religious services were also held throughout the week in various locations in the city for the benefit of those attending the eisteddfod.[64]

Not the least significant of the symbolic gestures made during the event was that which arose out of the meeting of the International Congress of Cymmrodorion held on the Wednesday morning. Chaired by Cynonfardd, the meeting was attended by representatives from north and south Wales, London and Liverpool, as well as the United States. They gathered to hear an address on 'Education in Wales' by W. Cadwaladr Davies of London. Davies began by stating that the national revival in Wales was the creation of the religious and literary feeling which constituted the root of the Welsh race. For centuries after the Romans had left Britain, he told his audience, Wales was noted for its bards and colleges. All this was lost, however, when Wales lost its independence: the colleges were destroyed, the bards fled and the eisteddfod and the Gorsedd went under a cloud. But, maintained Davies, the national

[64] W. D. Davies, op. cit., p. 359.

imagination was retained. He proceeded to outline the revivals in religion and in the eisteddfod during the late eighteenth century. Although antipathetic at first, both had been essential to the development of the nation. The educational movement which had caught the imagination of Welsh people in Wales during the previous twenty years was the child of the eisteddfod on the one hand and the Sunday School on the other. To loud applause, the speaker then announced that this movement had reached its apogee with the government's decision to grant the Welsh people a national university.[65]

Dramatically, Davies then showed his audience a copy of the charter, and amid an enthusiastic response he declared it was a significant fact that this announcement was being made for the first time at the World's Fair Eisteddfod and in the New World. It proved, he said, that in their 'national revival' the Welsh were being true to the imagination which was at the root of Welsh life. The great danger of the British nation was the overemphasis on the commercial spirit; the World's Fair Eisteddfod however was a protest against the materialism of the age and proof that the Celtic element would flower in the future of the New World as it did in that of the Old.[66]

Fired by his speech, the meeting passed unanimously a motion that the eisteddfod should extend its thanks to W. E. Gladstone and his ministry for passing the University Act and congratulate them on their record of reform measures. At one of the eisteddfod's sessions later that day, a declaration to this effect was read and greeted by a standing ovation from the audience, preceded and followed by fanfares by the Gorsedd's trumpeters.[67]

But it was not only in the auxiliary meetings that the nature of what was being celebrated was fully apparent. Even competition subjects, competitors' pseudonyms and the titles of the various concert items during the eisteddfod seemed to symbolize the central tenets of the 'national revival' blossoming in contemporary Wales: religion, loyalty, respectability, education and the sense of historic nationhood. There were tributes to those 'national heroes' who had been rediscovered during the

[65] Ibid., pp. 365–8.
[66] Ibid., p. 367.
[67] Ibid., pp. 378–9.

late eighteenth and nineteenth centuries: the 500-strong eisteddfod choir, accompanied by an orchestra of sixty, sang Pencerdd Gwalia's dramatic cantata 'Llewellyn' and D. R. Williams of Braddocks, Pennsylvania, won the competition for writing an operatic libretto on the life of Owain Glyndŵr.[68] Dyfed adopted the pseudonym 'Lazarus', as if to signify the resurrection of the Welsh nation; the official World's Fair Eisteddfod song was 'Gwlad y Menyg Gwynion' ('The Land of the White Gloves'). The subject of the Crown poem was 'Jesus of Nazareth', whilst that of the Chair competition was 'George Washington'. Such was the ecstatic reception received by the renowned London tenor Ben Davies after his rendition of 'Our Queen' that he was obliged to sing it again.[69]

It was the three prize-essay competitions which perhaps reflected most acutely the preoccupations that had created the World's Fair Eisteddfod. Their subjects were 'The Keltic [sic] contribution to England's fame and power', 'The extraction and career of Welshmen who have distinguished themselves in various fields of learning', and most crucial of all, 'Welshmen as civil, political, and moral factors in the formation and development of the United States republic'.[70] The winner of the latter, Revd Ebenezer Edwards of Minersville, Pennsylvania, writing under the pseudonym 'William Penn', received $300 and a handsome buggy, as well as a warm appreciation from the audience when he appeared on the stage. The glowing adjudication he was given demanded the immediate publication of his essay, although this did not in fact take place until 1899.[71] Nevertheless, despite its late appearance, the work was a child of the World's Fair Eisteddfod, and not merely because it was brought into being by a particular competition at that event. Indeed, if William Ap Madoc was the personification of the 'Welshness' which permeated the eisteddfod, then its bible was Edwards's essay. In one volume, the Minersville minister provided his countrymen with apparent proof that the Welsh had been, were, and would continue to be of inestimable value to their adopted country.

[68] Ibid., pp. 371–2, 386. See also Prys Morgan, *The Eighteenth Century Renaissance*, pp. 67–100, 119–20.
[69] W. D. Davies, op. cit., pp. 374, 376–7, 386–7, 388.
[70] *Drych*, 18 Feb. 1892; *Cambrian*, XIII (Sept. 1893), p. 257.
[71] Ebenezer Edwards, op. cit., p. 1; W. D. Davies, op. cit., pp. 374–5.

To the adjudicators of the competition, Revd W. C. Roberts of New York and Thomas L. James – both of whom incidentally received glowing tributes in the text – Edwards's efforts was 'a treasure of valuable information'.[72] This valuable information consisted of the identification of large numbers of individuals of Welsh blood who the author believed had played a prominent part in American life. They proved the author's contention that the contribution of the Welsh to the American republic had been immense and that the latter was largely indebted to Wales and Welshmen. *Facts about Welsh Factors*, as the published essay is perhaps rather unimaginatively entitled, is almost a history of America based on the Welsh, for apart from its concentration on individuals, Welshmen even dictate the author's structure. His second section, for example, that dealing with the period from 1789 to the time of writing, is subdivided into six chronological periods, representing what the author terms 'our bridge of history'. Each span of the bridge rests on the administrations of Presidents who were of Welsh blood, i.e. Jefferson, John Quincy Adams, William Harrison, James Garfield and Benjamin Harrison.[73]

The early chapters of the essay deal with the colonial Welsh settlers, the Welsh signatories of the Declaration of Independence and the part Welsh people played in the War of Independence. There are biographies of Roger Williams, William Penn, John Adams and Thomas Jefferson in a chapter entitled 'Factors of special forcefulness and efficiency'. In the remainder of the essay Edwards presented a long list of Welshmen who he believed had played important roles in the various fields of education, science, invention, politics, religion and industry, to lead to the conclusion that 'those whose ancestors were prominent factors in the formation are valuable factors in the development of the Republic'. Yet such was the author's belief in the richness of the Welsh contribution that 'here as elsewhere in our essay we can gather but a few sheaves and give these as examples of a well-nigh incredibly full crop.'[74] Besides, the Welsh contribution was continuing, culminating in the role that Welsh men – the fact that it was men deserves

---

[72] Ebenezer Edwards, op. cit., p. 3.
[73] Ibid., pp. 10, 176, 179, 190, 217, 245, 319, 355.
[74] Ibid., pp. 15–156, 179, 362–3.

stressing as not one woman is included – were playing in contemporary life, following on the great contribution of their ancestors. An appendix to the work contains biographies of 'our representative men', whose portraits are included through the text. Among them are Samuel Job, H. M. Edwards, T. Cynonfardd Edwards and William Ap Madoc.[75] It is these men who were regarded by Edwards as the leading Welshmen of the day, the men who were major civil, political and moral factors in the United States.

Facts about Welsh Factors, with its almost overwhelming tone of sycophancy and self-righteousness, is a classic expression of what might be termed the cult of the eminent Welsh-American. Many of the individuals Edwards focused on were descendants of Welsh people and were less than one-eighth Welsh. Nevertheless, despite the small proportion of Welsh blood, such men could still be regarded as Welsh. Throughout the essay, the existence of Welsh blood is deemed sufficient to 'prove' Welshness and the maintenance of Welsh traditions. As the author declared, 'Welsh blood . . . does not cease to be Welsh wherever found.'[76] Ultimately, the essay is far more than a list of individuals; it is a celebration of Welsh characteristics. The Welshmen whom Edwards regarded as having achieved prominence had done so not only through their own efforts, but also *because* they were Welsh.

It is perhaps not surprising, therefore, that certain judgments regarding the nature of Welsh characteristics emerge from the text. Commenting on the part played by Welshmen in commerce, Edwards maintained that the 'honest Welshman' is appreciated in these days of 'shameless trickery. Not every man bearing a Welsh name is worthy of the distinction implied in this aphorism . . . nevertheless there stands the proverbial saying and for some reason the Welsh are considered specially trustworthy.' Naturally, in dealing with the prominent part Welshmen had played in American religious affairs, Wales was asserted to have 'astonished the world by the number and power of its preachers. There is no spot on the globe so glorious in this regard. Here, as in the Fatherland, the people have believed that there are no

---

[75] Ibid., appendix G, pp. 406–17.
[76] Ibid., pp. 10–11.

such ministers as the Welsh.'[77] The implication is obvious: Wales furnishes so many good preachers because the Welsh are such a religious people.

Yet if their characteristics had helped Welsh people to play a prominent part in American life, to Edwards this was fundamentally a reflection of the 'fact' that Wales's ancient traditions lay behind the formation of the American republic in the first place. According to the author, Welshmen played a prominent part in 'establishing and favoring that civil and religious liberty which has brought impenetrable glory to our Republic'. They did so because they were Welsh:

> ... the U.S. Government enjoys the heritage of the ancient Kymry [sic] ... The memory of Welsh free institutions still lingered in the hearts of Welshmen, [and] they came hither to escape the tyranny of the English church and state and to plant the standard of freedom upon this Western Hemisphere ... The laws of ancient Britons ... guaranteed the equality of civil and religious rights and served the pursuit of life, liberty and happiness. The 'free' principles – civil, political and moral – which distinguished these colonies did but reflect what had for ages existed and flourished among the Cymry.[78]

In this passage Edwards articulated a belief which was rapidly becoming a central tenet of Welsh-American writing and one which would be increasingly proclaimed by speakers at Welsh cultural events. It provided the most potent weapon of all in the battle to prove the value of Welshness in America: history. Not only had the Welsh bred individuals who had aided the growth of the United States; their traditions were at the core of its existence and, as such, their prominent part in its future was also secure. Here was the necessary American dimension to the vision of Wales as an ancient nation which was at last achieving its historical destiny.

The significance of Edwards's essay lies as much in the nature of its reception as in its content. Although Carl Wittke would later dismiss the work as 'a veritable hodge-podge of names ... without scientific merit or organisation',[79] few leading Welsh-Americans of the late nineteenth century would have agreed with his criticism. Edwards's seemingly endless list of names

---

[77] Ibid., p. 333.
[78] Ibid., pp. 157, 158–9.
[79] Carl Wittke, *We Who Built America* (New York, 1939), p. 313.

provided his countrymen with assimilable proof. That seasoned campaigner in the fields of Welsh emigrational and evangelical endeavour, Benjamin Chidlaw, welcomed the essay heartily. 'As a Welshman,' he wrote, 'I feel it a pleasure to find historic evidence of the patriotism and public services of Welshmen.' To a *Drych* correspondent, the work was a 'matter of the utmost interest and importance to the nation'.[80]

By concentrating on the value and importance of his work to the Welsh, Edwards's admirers not only reflected the prevailing image of Welsh patriotism and their good citizenship in America. Their comments also confirm that these concerns were central to the whole phenomenon of the World's Fair Eisteddfod. The author himself emphasized it. His purpose in writing, he declared, was merely to ensure that the Welsh people were given due acknowledgement for the 'fact' of their glorious contribution. The essay title, he continued, 'has been placed on the International Eisteddfod program because this fact has lacked the full recognition it deserves.'[81]

I.iii POST-MORTEM

After the World's Fair Eisteddfod, the Welsh-American press carried a number of observations on what had taken place. In general it was seen as having been a major success, though dissenting voices were raised. There were in fact a number of complaints regarding purely organizational matters. The Festival Hall had been too large, and it was difficult for those in the rear to hear what was taking place on the stage. Presidents often failed to turn up, and there had also occurred an embarrassing incident when the *Drych*'s reporter was refused entry to one session as the committee had neglected to offer him a pass. Even the Gorsedd proceedings came in for some criticism from a correspondent to that newspaper. He described the parade as a 'funny scene' and a shame to enlightened Welshmen, and thought it was worrying to see so many who professed to be the leaders of the nation in morals and religion supporting such 'paganism'.[82]

[80] Ebenezer Edwards, op. cit., p. 1.
[81] Ibid., p. 169.
[82] *Drych*, 21, 28 Sept., 2 Nov. 1893.

In general, however, the eisteddfod was regarded as having fulfilled all the hopes centred on it. The *Cambrian*, in a lengthy review, thought it had compared favourably with most of the National Eisteddfodau held in Wales and had been successful 'in all aspects . . . Never before had there been in America such an assembly of Welsh people, so representative and cosmopolitan in character.' In stark contrast to the *Drych*'s corespondent, it singled out the Gorsedd proceedings. These had been 'novel and picturesque' and 'an useful spectacle for advertising the Eisteddfod.' The apparent success of the event induced the reviewer to see a glorious future for the institution, if the example set by Chicago was followed:

> Association in the bonds of Welsh nationality is one of the most enjoyable features of the Eisteddfod and might be made one of its most beneficial features, if time and opportunity were afforded for the exchange of ideas and discussion of topics of general and practical interest. It can be a means of infusing new ideas and a new spirit into the national life and of shaping the destiny of Cymru Fydd . . . the Chicago Eisteddfod is to be commended for introducing this feature.[83]

The review concluded by expressing the hope that all the money and work which had gone into the eisteddfod would result in 'the general advancement of Welsh nationality in all knowledge and virtue'.[84]

Many commentators regarded the World's Fair Eisteddfod as proof that, despite living in the United States, the Welsh-Americans were nevertheless still Welsh to the core. One committee member was adamant that never had so much Welsh been spoken in America as during those four days, although others offered contrary opinions on the matter. By holding the event, most agreed that the Welsh-Americans, and Ap Madoc and the committee in particular, had done a lasting service to their nationality.[85] W. D. Davies, who devoted a substantial section of his book *America a Gweledigaethau Bywyd* to the eisteddfod, outlined three reasons why it had been a success in this respect. First, it had been the grandest eisteddfod the world had ever seen. Secondly, it had raised the status of the Welsh people as an ancient literary and musical nation in the eyes of

---

[83] *Cambrian*, XIII (Oct. 1893), p. 312.
[84] Ibid.
[85] *Drych*, 21, 28 Sept. 1893.

the world. Finally, the Welsh had needed four days at least to show off their national virtues, whereas for other nationalities one day had been sufficient.[86]

Most reviewers were convinced that the event had also confirmed the musicality of the Welsh. The *Drych* thought the eisteddfod had been an outstanding musical success, whilst the standard of the choral singing – with its implicit reaffirmation of the image of Wales as 'Gwlad y Gân' – was the source of a great deal of satisfaction.[87] Indeed, so successful had the event been in this direction that one commentator suggested that the Welsh had achieved immortality and had raised themselves to the pinnacle of world choral singing by surpassing anything any other nation could muster.[88] Two years after the eisteddfod, a *Cambrian* correspondent writing under the pseudonym 'Cambro-American' recalled the impact of the visiting Welsh choirs:

> It was the first time that any considerable body of singers from Wales had paid this country a visit and at once attention centered on them... They competed in the eisteddfod and were victorious to a degree that must have been gratifying to themselves and their friends at home besides strengthening the reputation of Wales as a land of song and that of her people as a race of singers.

The choirs had travelled throughout the eastern United States, staying with 'the best people of the country' and using the opportunity to impart knowledge on all manner of things pertaining to Wales. The upshot was that this sequence of events had made the wider American public take note, and 'Cambro-American' could write with pride that

> the past year has witnessed the establishment in several English journals of high standing in certain sections of the East . . . of regular correspondence from principal points in Wales, which is found to interest many readers. The amount of reading matter descriptive of Wales and her people which has found its way into current American journals during the past year has certainly been surprisingly large . . . Welsh-Americans can never become too well acquainted with the history of Wales and her

---

[86] W. D. Davies, op. cit., p. 391.
[87] *Drych*, 14, 21 Sept. 1893; *Cambrian*, XV (Apr. 1895), pp. 103–4.
[88] *Drych*, 21 Sept. 1893.

people and there are many lessons to be learned and much pleasure to be derived from continuous study of the subject.[89]

To many observers, then, the World's Fair Eisteddfod had fulfilled its promise. Not only had the Welsh people gained greater attention; the impression they had made had been more than favourable. The event had vindicated the prediction of one member of the eisteddfod's committee, who in 1892 informed *Baner ac Amserau Cymru*: 'The Welsh spirit is very alive in this country and gets more so annually; and the Eisteddfod to be held here next year will be the biggest symbol of this.'[90]

The committee member pinpointed what was ultimately one of the most significant features of the entire phenomenon of the World's Fair Eisteddfod. During all three of its phases – the intense preparations, the event itself and its aftermath – Welsh-American literary opinion had regarded it as being an unparalleled opportunity to prove that the 'Welsh spirit' could both survive in American society and play an integral part in it. All three phases encapsulated potent illustrations of what that 'Welsh spirit' was. The eisteddfod was a celebration of a particular idea of Wales, one which revolved around a sense of historic nationhood, complete with its own national characteristics. It was also a celebration of the American dimension to this idea of Wales. The momentous events at Chicago were imbued with the necessity of proclaiming to America the importance, the value and the loyalty of Welsh-Americans and of showing that their nationality was as much a vital force in the United States as Wales was perceived to be in the British empire.

The World's Fair Eisteddfod was thus not only a symbol of the 'Welsh spirit' to which the committee member referred; it was also itself a proclamation that the future of the spirit was secure. In many ways, the relationship between Welshness and the eisteddfod was a microcosm of the wider relationship between American culture and the World's Fair. The White City was regarded by many as being the fulfilment of the promises of modern times and as a symbol of the solution to urban evils.[91] Likewise, at Chicago Welsh-American literary opinion saw the eisteddfod as proof that its own definitions of

---

[89] *Cambrian*, XV (Apr. 1895), pp. 103–4.
[90] *Baner ac Amserau Cymru*, 6 Apr. 1892.
[91] Martin, op. cit., pp. 240–1.

Welshness could be an integral part of the modern, industrial New World.

Yet, ultimately, it was all an illusion. In the same way as the plaster of the White City was constantly crumbling,[92] so did the magnificent edifice of 'Welshness' erected and celebrated at Chicago visibly show the weathering the elements of Americanization and industrialization had battered against it. The Welsh immigrant group was not immune to the dramatic and rapid changes that had transformed America from the Civil War onwards. By 1893 an industrial society had been created in the United States. New forces – the rise of wealth, the growth of the city and the impact of mass immigration, technology and scientific scepticism of hitherto universally accepted beliefs and modes of thought – had irrevocably changed America so completely and rapidly that they instigated recurrent crises in American culture. These new forces had to be confronted and understood in terms of the past if a culture was to move forward at all.[93]

The Welsh immigrants, like all those living in America, were subjected to the instability which these forces created. Their own trauma was compounded by the undeniable fact that modern America had thrust Welshness into a crisis. In the industrial areas especially, as we have seen in the case of Scranton, the Welsh had experienced rapid and profound cultural changes resulting in the decline of the Welsh language and religious observance, and the embracing of lifestyles far removed from the more respectable and accepted notions of what it meant to be Welsh.[94]

The cracks were more than evident during the eisteddfod itself. In cultural terms, the fragility of Welsh-American musical and literary prowess in comparison with that of the homeland had been only too apparent. Reflecting perhaps the decline of Welsh-language literature in America, not one Welsh-American had won a literary competition in that language. To one commentator, the Welsh-Americans had been taught an

---

[92] Ibid., p. 242.
[93] Martin, op. cit., pp. 2–11. See also Ginger, op. cit., pp. 3–153; Herbert G. Gutman, *Work, Culture and Society in Industrializing America* (New York, 1977); Robert H. Wiebe, *The Search for Order, 1877–1920* (London, 1967).
[94] See, for example, *Drych*, 12 Mar. 1874, 7 Feb. 1875, 9 June 1881; *Cambrian*, II (Sept./Oct. 1882), pp. 228–9; III (Mar./Apr. 1883), p. 91.

important lesson by the Welsh in Wales, since the latter had been victorious in every competition they entered. He was of the opinion that competitors from Wales, and particularly the choirs, had saved the eisteddfod: 'But you musicians, bards and littérateurs in America, wake up, wake up. What would our Eisteddfod have been without the bards, singers and littérateurs of Wales? That is a question which should be thought about.'[95]

The relative poverty of Welsh culture in America, which the World's Fair Eisteddfod had brought sharply into focus, symbolized the wider crisis which 'Welshness' was facing by the early 1890s. There were also other indications during the event which highlighted the extent to which the central tenets it celebrated were under attack. The position of the Welsh language at the eisteddfod was at best ambivalent. There were frequent complaints that not enough Welsh had been spoken and that the event had been much 'too English'.[96] The committee itself was accused of being so, and many had walked out of the International Congress of Cymmrodorion meeting because it was being conducted in the English language. Some observers took the attitude that they might as well be thankful for the amount of Welsh that was actually spoken, considering the circumstances.[97] One committee member even took one of his children with him to the eisteddfod in order to converse with him in Welsh in the hope of attracting other Welsh speakers. He did this in response to what he saw as one of the biggest defects of the Welsh in America: it was as hard to come across a Welsh-speaker as it was to find a needle in a haystack.[98]

There were other major contradictions. Despite the image of Welsh religiosity which permeated the event, the eisteddfod's organizers had been among those who had actively campaigned for the Sunday opening of the Fair, as well as other amenities such as the saloons, much to the disgust of some Welsh commentators.[99] The eisteddfod made a loss and the committee was forced to pay its debts out of its members' own pockets.[100] The audiences had been far less than expected, whilst the Revd

[95] *Drych*, 21 Sept. 1893.
[96] Ibid.; *Baner ac Amserau Cymru*, 30 Mar. 1892.
[97] *Drych*, 21 Sept. 1893.
[98] *Drych*, 7 Sept. 1893.
[99] *Tyst a'r Dydd*, 17 Feb. 1893.
[100] *Drych*, 14 Sept. 1893.

D. P. Jones of Scranton informed the *Drych* that he was not at all surprised that this had been so. In his opinion the World's Fair had not been a good time to hold an eisteddfod, if indeed a favourable time was ever possible. Echoing doubts which had occasionally surfaced in the press in the run-up to 1893, he thought the Welsh were too scattered over the United States to have been able to attend in large numbers, and consequently they had been only in the shadows of the Fair.[101]

The event, too, produced a number of delicious ironies. It was a Prince Madoc Ap Owain Gwynedd feature and the brainchild of a man named Ap Madoc, but it was also the occasion for the long-delayed publication of Thomas Stephens's magisterial demolition of the Madoc myth.[102] The biggest irony of all was the teasing paradox of the eisteddfod's venue. It was held in the city which was the embodiment of all the forces which were attacking 'Welshness'. In June 1895 the magazine of the Welsh Christian Endeavour Societies in America, *Yr Ymdrechydd*, outlined why the city was such a good field for missionary work. Chicago apparently had 60,000 opium eaters, 40,000 homeless girls, 30,000 'professional politicians', 10,000 gamblers, 60,000 who spent their lives in saloons and brothels, 7,000 tavern keepers, 28,000 workers in saloons, 10,000 thieves and 1,900 vagrants.[103] It was hardly the ideal setting for an event which proclaimed Welsh respectability, morality and religiosity. Moreover, there were indications that the definitions of 'Welshness' which the World's Fair Eisteddfod embodied did not necessarily apply to the Welsh in Chicago itself. A correspondent named 'Siva' informed the *Drych* in May 1892 that there were twelve thousand Welsh people living in the city, yet membership of its Welsh churches stood at only a thousand. Where, the writer asked, were the other eleven thousand?[104]

The ambivalence as to whether the World's Fair Eisteddfod had been a success or not, and the contradictions apparent during the event itself, emphasized that it was a divided Welsh-America that took the stage at Chicago in September 1893. Indeed, if the World's Fair was, as Jay Martin has maintained,

---

[101] Ibid., 5 Oct. 1893.
[102] Gwyn A. Williams, *Madoc*, p. 201.
[103] *Ymdrechydd*, I (June 1895), p. 168.
[104] *Drych*, 19 May 1892.

'the catalyst for the expression of the contradictions, the hopes and fears of American culture itself',[105] the eisteddfod, which its spectacle brought into being, was the creation of the hopes, contradictions and fears of 'Welshness'. The 'grandest and most patriotic undertaking of the Welsh people' was born out of the collision of faith in the national destiny of the Welsh people and the increasing realization that the essential elements of their Welshness were under attack.

II THE AMERICAN GORSEDD

Looking back on the momentous events of the World's Fair Eisteddfod in December 1912, Ap Madoc declared that at Chicago 'the dreamers dreamed a dream too soon. In fact they, the dreamers, were considered too visionary, if not gone stark looney.'[106] He was referring to the possibility of establishing a permanent Gorsedd in America, which had been discussed at the time but which had not materialized. His remarks were inspired by what was to him a 'patriotic purpose' and 'a sign of awakened interest in the language and literature that have stood the test of time through centuries'.[107] Ap Madoc's 'dream' had in fact come true. Following a successful mission to Wales on the part of the prominent Pittsburgh Welshman, Robert H. Davies ('Gomerian'), it had been announced that the Gorsedd of Bards of Great Britain had granted permission for a permanent American Gorsedd to be established at the Pittsburgh International Eisteddfod during the following year. Archdruid Dyfed himself would preside over the proceedings, a decision which was perhaps influenced by the memory of his triumph at Chicago twenty years earlier.[108]

---

[105] Martin, op. cit., p. 243.
[106] *Druid*, 5 Dec. 1912.
[107] Ibid.
[108] Ibid., 26 Sept. 1912, 9 Jan. 1913. Robert H. Davies ('Gomerian') (1856–1947) was one of the most active figures in Welsh-American cultural and literary life. As well as recorder of the Gorsedd, he owned the American Printing Company which specialized in Welsh publications, he was the Pittsburgh correspondent for both the *Drych* and the *Druid*, and he became the editor of the latter following the death of his close friend, T. Owen Charles, in 1916. He was also secretary of the Pittsburgh St David's Society for over a quarter of a century and a prominent member of the Oakland Welsh Calvinistic Methodist Church. For biographical details, see *Cambrian*, XXIII (Oct. 1903), pp. 430–2; *Drych*, 3 Aug. 1911, 15 Nov. 1947; *The Royal Blue Book: Prize Productions of the Pittsburgh International Eisteddfod, July 2, 3, 4 and 5 1913* (Pittsburgh, 1916), pp. 73–5.

The ceremony would duly take place in July 1913, and with the investing of Revd T. Cynonfardd Edwards as America's first archdruid, the American Gorsedd was established as a permanent feature in Welsh-American life.[109] Within only six years of its inauguration the American Gorsedd had been markedly transformed. Proclaimed by the *Druid* as 'an epochal event in the history of the Welsh people in America', there emerged on the Welsh-American scene a new-look Gorsedd with aims and ambitions which intended it to be the single most important Welsh organization in America. Dedicated to providing a national organization to unify the Welsh people throughout the United States and Canada and, more immediately, to organize and co-ordinate the proposed visit of David Lloyd George, the new Gorsedd now embraced two major, long-standing campaigns.[110] Its appearance was accompanied by an intense wave of optimism among many leading Welsh-Americans. Writing in July 1919, its new National Organizer predicted that the American Gorsedd 'will become the medium for . . . enabling Welshmen to achieve greater things . . . and consequently to bring them as a people to greater recognition.'[111] His words are strikingly reminiscent of the preoccupations that characterized the World's Fair Eisteddfod over a quarter of a century before. Bearing in mind the way in which at Chicago one manifestation of a Welsh cultural tradition became the vehicle for expressing certain ideas regarding the value and nature of being Welsh in America, we can examine to what extent the Gorsedd was the fresh creation or the stale culmination of similar concerns.

II.i THE AMERICAN GORSEDD, 1913–1919

Until 1919 the American Gorsedd's existence had been rather vague and sporadic. At the inaugural ceremony in July 1913, a number of prominent Welsh-Americans were invested as officers and members. Among them were seasoned campaigners who had played an integral part in the memorable events in Chicago

---

[109] Ibid., 17 July 1913; Hartmann, op. cit., pp. 149–51.
[110] *Druid*, 1 Jan. 1919.
[111] Revd Ebenezer Pugh Thomas, *Glimpses of the Gorsedd: A Brief Sketch of the History and Progress of the American Gorsedd* (Pittsburgh, 1919), pp. 6–7.

twenty years earlier. Apart from T. Cynonfardd Edwards, his namesake H. M. was chosen as deputy archdruid, and Ap Madoc too enrolled as a member. The Gorsedd also contained a number of other personalities who were prominent in contemporary Welsh-American literary circles. They included Gomerian himself, as recorder, T. Owen Charles, the editor of the *Druid*, and Henry Blackwell, the New York publisher, bookseller and compiler of Welsh-American biographies who would in the following year launch his own short-lived magazine, *Cambrian Gleanings*. In general, the Gorsedd's membership signified the involvement of most of the premier Welsh-Americans of the time.[112]

More members were initiated during the Gorsedd's next appearance, at the San Francisco International Eisteddfod of 1915, although it was prominent Scrantonian and Pittsburgh Welshmen, such as Ben Phillips, John T. Watkins and Col. Reese A. Phillips, who were the dominant element in the new recruits.[113] In 1916 the Gorsedd published the *Royal Blue Book: Prize Productions of the Pittsburgh International Eisteddfod*, an anthology of the winning literary compositions at that eisteddfod, which also contained biographical sketches of the winners and the Gorsedd officers.[114] By 1917 many of the Gorsedd's members had come to the opinion that an expansion of the scope and aims of the organization, and an attempt to make it a more effective force in Welsh-American life in general, were necessary. Consequently a special meeting was held in Pittsburgh in May 1917 to discuss the matter.[115]

At this meeting, many members apparently expressed their belief that in its present form the Gorsedd accomplished little work of permanent value, particularly as it met only at irregular

[112] *Druid*, 26 June, 17 July 1913; *Drych*, 10 July 1913; E. P. Thomas, op. cit., p. 8; *Royal Blue Book*, pp. 24–7; *Cambrian Gleanings*, 1 (Jan. 1914), title page. For biographical details of Henry Blackwell (1851–1916), see *Dictionary of Welsh Biography*, pp. 38–9. For T. Owen Charles (1866–1916), see *Welsh-American*, 15 Oct. 1916.

[113] *Royal Blue Book*, pp. 27–8; E. P. Thomas, op. cit., p. 8.

[114] The *Royal Blue Book* was compiled by Gomerian and published by his American Printing Company.

[115] *Welsh American*, 1 June 1917. In April 1914 the *Druid* was renamed *Welsh-American* in order to appeal to second- and third-generation Welsh. It reverted to the name *Druid* in June 1918 because of anxiety over the popular hysteria over 'hyphenated Americanism' that accompanied United States involvement in the First World War. The newspaper ceased publication in 1937. *Druid*, 5 Sept. 1912; *Welsh-American*, 1 Apr. 1914, 1 June 1918; Hartmann, op. cit., pp. 130, 151.

intervals. It was resolved that the organization should progress 'along modern lines, though retaining the salient features of the Ancient Gorsedd'. There were diverse opinions as to the exact form modernization should take, although there was apparently unanimity over the need both to be efficient and progressive, and to take up the challenge of unifying the Welsh people of the United States and Canada in a single organization.[116] The latter was a new departure. The *Blue Book* had stated that the Gorsedd's aims included federating Welsh-American literati and forming 'a bond that should eventually bring together the bards and minstrels of this country into a well-knit organization.'[117] The meeting also decided that the Gorsedd should not merely be a cultural institution. It was to be a national organization which would represent and promote the interests of all Welsh people in America in all walks of life. This, it was felt, was the best way forward to make the Gorsedd modern, progressive and efficient. In order to achieve its new goal the meeting sanctioned a number of initiatives, including the decision to establish a central headquarters and to appoint a committee of five with full powers to draw up a constitution and select a 'Gorsedd missionary'. The latter would be responsible for visiting the various Welsh communities in America and organizing an auxiliary Gorsedd in each in order to keep in touch with all the Welsh people scattered over the continent.[118]

The May 1917 meeting was a crucial one for the development of the American Gorsedd. In deciding that the organization should strive to weld together the various Welsh societies and organizations in the United States into a unified cohesive force, the organizers embraced a challenge which had long occupied the thoughts of many leading Welsh-Americans, among them members of the Gorsedd itself. Originally the ideas regarding the desirability of a national organization had emerged some years before the Gorsedd had been established. Throughout the late nineteenth century, Welsh commentators had urged those of their nationality to form societies in their communities.[119] By the first decade of the twentieth century, however, a national organization had become a frequent topic of discussion, both in

[116] *Welsh-American*, 1 June 1917.
[117] *Royal Blue Book*, p. 10.
[118] *Welsh-American*, 1 June 1917.
[119] *Drych*, 12 Mar. 1874, 2 Jan. 1890, 8 Oct. 1891.

the columns of the Welsh-American press and in meetings of Welsh societies, particularly those in Pennsylvania.[120]

Although these discussions contained a wide range of suggestions regarding the necessity for a national Welsh-American organization and the form it should take, a number of common priorities did emerge. Most commentators were agreed that the Welsh should have a national organization in the same way as other nationalities in the United States, and that such an organization should be geared towards furthering the interests of Welsh people through promoting their business interests, aiding their general improvement and providing an insurance scheme.[121] Equally, there was a general consensus of opinion that a national organization was needed in order to ensure that the Welsh in the United States did not lose their individuality. Welsh people had played, and were playing, a great part in American life, and it was essential therefore that an organization be formed not only to help the Welsh in the future but also to nurture an awareness of the greatness of their past.[122] Governor Arthur L. Thomas of Utah informed the *Druid* in June 1911 that without unity, valuable information regarding the history of the Welsh in the United States would be lost. This would be a great tragedy as the Welshman ought to be 'proud of his race, for every page of American history, from the day of the first settlement down to the time of the Revolution, and during and since the Revolution, is illumined by the work accomplished by Welshmen'.[123] Echoing Thomas's words, all commentators were adamant that a national organization of the Welsh people in America ought to be as much a patriotic American society as one intended to foster a sense of Welsh national identity and a pride in its ancestry. Such an organization was needed in order to promote the view that in contemporary America it was possible for the Welsh to be both patriotic Americans and enthusiastic Welsh people, since they were complementary and strengthened each other.[124] As a Robert Jones of Seattle informed the *Druid*, a Welsh national organization would be of great value to the United States as 'the

[120] Ibid., 25 Apr., 20 June 1907; *Druid*, 28 May, 5 Nov. 1908, 5 Jan. 1911, 26 Sept. 1912.
[121] *Druid*, 28 May 1908, 1, 15 June 1911.
[122] Ibid., 28 May 1908, 15, 22 June 1911, 26 Sept. 1912.
[123] Ibid., 1 June 1911.
[124] Ibid., 28 May 1908, 1 Jan., 15 June 1911; *Drych*, 25 Apr. 1907.

Welsh in America have ever been law abiding and patriotic citizens'.[125]

Although the history of the efforts to form a national organization is largely one of words rather than of actions, two abortive federation schemes were in fact launched in the early years of the second decade of the twentieth century. These failures were perhaps a necessary prelude to the Gorsedd's decision to take up the cause of unification in 1917. The first scheme was organized by a number of individuals integrally involved with the *Druid*, among them Gomerian, T. Owen Charles and John Courier Morris. In August 1911 the newspaper announced that a committee had been elected to work out details for a federation plan, and it would submit proposals to the various Welsh-American societies in the United States.[126] Although the initiative was preceded by a lengthy debate in the *Druid*'s columns, in which leading Welsh-Americans expressed great enthusiasm on the matter,[127] the newspaper carried no further references to the committee's progress, which suggests that the plan died a quick death.

A similar fate befell the other national organization which briefly appeared on the Welsh-American scene. In December 1912 a number of 'Patriotic Welsh' from New York City, among them Henry Blackwell, met at the Union Square Hotel to establish 'Cymdeithas Genedlaethol Gymreig yr America' ('The Welsh National Society of America').[128] The new society was intended to be a non-religious, non-political organization and its aim was to affiliate the various local societies of the Welsh-American people. Apparently those attending the meeting had felt for a long time that there was a need to unify the Welsh in New York, and throughout the United States, in the manner of other nationalities. They were concerned that there was no institution in the city where the Welsh could meet and keep away from dubious places of temptation, and that it was difficult

---

[125] *Druid*, 29 June 1911. The arguments in favour of a national organization were also being put forward to support the setting up of community-based Welsh organizations, as we have already seen in the case of the Scranton Druid Society. The Pittsburgh St David's Society was another of a number of societies established in 1907–8 which sought, at a local level, to promote aims similar to those of a national organization. *Druid*, 20 June, 13, 20 Oct. 1907, 16 Apr. 1908; *Drych*, 25 Apr. 1907.

[126] *Druid*, 3 Aug. 1911.

[127] Ibid., 1, 15, 22 June 1911.

[128] *Drych*, 26 Dec. 1912; *Druid*, 26 Dec. 1912.

to provide jobs for newly-arrived Welsh immigrants. The society hoped to remedy this state of affairs by setting up a headquarters for the Welsh in New York, where Welsh cultural events, particularly eisteddfodau, could be held, where visitors, and especially David Lloyd George (who at the time had not cancelled his visit), could be received, and which in general would be open to help Welsh people. The main driving force behind the organization was John W. Davies, a 46-year-old lawyer, originally from Denbigh, north Wales. Davies had been afraid that no one would turn up at the meeting and was surprised to find it full, enthusiastic and willing to contribute financially. Despite the initial enthusiasm, however, the society seems to have collapsed almost immediately.[129]

II.ii THE 'NEW' GORSEDD OF 1919

The work of the committee set up in May 1917 came to fruition on St David's Day 1919. A grand banquet and concert were held in order to dedicate formally the new Pittsburgh headquarters which occupied an entire floor of a large building in the centre of the city and consisted of executive offices, an assembly room and a library replete with literature 'of Welsh interest'. Here, too, the offices of the *Druid* would now be located, 'thus centralizing Cymric interests under the same roof and making the Gorsedd home a mecca for all Welsh pilgrims, where a cordial welcome will be extended to all worthy Cambrians'.[130] From these rooms would be launched a massive campaign to establish a strong cohesive body that would represent the interests of Welsh people all over the American continent. In the short term, the intention was to host a meeting of representatives from various localities to formalize arrangements for the forthcoming visit of David Lloyd George, which was scheduled to take place after the termination of the Paris Peace Conference.[131]

At the dedication ceremonies the new constitution and declaration of aims of the American Gorsedd were also unveiled.

---

[129] *Drych*, 26 Dec. 1912. Although the society set up a working party and fixed a date for a meeting during the following month, no subsequent reports of it appeared in the press.
[130] *Druid*, 1 Jan., 15 Mar. 1919; *Drych*, 13, 20 Mar. 1919.
[131] *Druid*, 1 Jan. 1919.

Whereas entry into the Gorsedd had till then been by examination only, membership was now thrown open to all Americans of Welsh extraction. The new rules were described as the result of a 'practical' desire 'to extend the rights and privileges of this time-honored institution to all worthy compatriots eligible for membership'. Undoubtedly they were designed to attract greater numbers and to be compatible with the Gorsedd's aim of becoming a national organization. Five classes of membership were introduced: Active; Life; Junior; Associate; and Honorary. The first two were open to all Welshmen and Welshwomen and their descendants, whilst those under sixteen could enrol as junior members. People who were directly related to the Welsh, either by marriage or adoption, were eligible for associate membership. Despite the broader categories, however, the Gorsedd was still a restricted organization. Membership was open only to those who were physically and mentally normal and of good moral character. All applications also had to profess a belief in a Supreme Being, and, in the words of the constitution, the associate membership 'shall be composed of persons of the Caucasian race'.[132]

The 'new' Gorsedd presented a new set of aims and objectives. There were three: to unify all Americans of Welsh origin and to blend their interests through the study of past achievements; to establish a National Eisteddfod in America as a 'university of the poor'; and to provide the Welsh people scattered all over the United States in communities and mining camps with Welsh-language religious services and 'to impress on them the claims of American patriotism'. The Gorsedd also proposed to encourage the Welsh-American Women's Clubs in their efforts to establish a home for the aged and unfortunate among the Welsh in the United States.[133]

As well as the changes in the constitution and aims, the reconstructed Gorsedd possessed a new archdruid, Revd William Surdival of Middlesport, Ohio, and a new deputy archdruid, Revd Ebenezer Pugh Thomas of Pittsburgh. During the previous year they had replaced Cynonfardd and H. M. Edwards respectively. The withdrawal from active service of the two north-east Pennsylvanian stalwarts did not signify a

[132] E. P. Thomas, op. cit., pp. 7, 14.
[133] Ibid., p. 10.

disassociation from the Gorsedd's efforts on their part, since both remained involved, with Cynonfardd as archdruid emeritus and the judge as vice-archdruid.[134] Revd E. P. Thomas was also appointed as the Gorsedd's national organizer, and as an indication of the importance of his post, perhaps, he was allocated one of the two executive offices in the Gorsedd Home (the other was occupied by Gomerian).[135]

The 'new' Gorsedd of 1919, therefore, differed from the original institution established six years earlier in a number of important respects. Central to its transformation were the hopes and motives of its leading members, and these were set out in two publications which appeared during the summer of 1919. In May the *Druid* published an 'American Gorsedd Supplement' to publicize the Gorsedd's first annual conclave, to be held in Pittsburgh the following month. The supplement contained photographs of previous gatherings and commentaries on the meaning and purpose of the organization.[136] Two months later, the Gorsedd itself published a pamphlet, *Glimpses of the Gorsedd: A Brief Sketch of the History and Progress of the American Gorsedd*, edited by the national organizer, who in his prefatory note declared that its aim was to 'enlighten and encourage in the quest for a wider knowledge of the history and literature of the Cymric race and to point to the Gorsedd as a means of unifying the Welsh people, leading them . . . to a clearer vision and a larger conception of the truth'.[137] In a section entitled 'The mission of the Gorsedd', he outlined why such a greater awareness of Welsh history and culture was needed and why the Gorsedd was the best means of securing it. In fact, this section was the clearest statement of the organizers' thoughts, since others who wrote for both publications merely elaborated on the central tenets of Thomas's argument.

Thomas began by suggesting that at the time of writing, a knowledge and consciousness among Welsh people of their history and attributes were not only desirable but essential:

> We have been so busy watching the current of events that we have drifted far from the fundamentals . . . Our great need today is a knowledge of

---

[134] Ibid., p. 2.
[135] Ibid.; *Druid*, 1 Jan. 1919.
[136] *Druid*, 1 May 1919.
[137] E. P. Thomas, op. cit., p. 3.

history and a more familiar acquaintance with the past, for history is not antiquarianism. It is not the study of a dead past, but rather of living and vital things, of noble deeds and pulsating achievements. Nothing will be more helpful in this epochal period of world history especially to us as Welsh people, in order to take our place in the vanguard which has always been ours in all stages of the world's progress, than to possess a clear conception of our source of greatness as a people, and those agencies that tend to the highest development of the Welsh race.[138]

It was important, too, that the Welsh people in America should foster a consciousness of the greatness of their past because

> every American of Welsh blood can afford to be proud of his or her own lineage ... This is the aim of this booklet, for we would have you be proud of our great leading spirits, past and present, both in British and American history ... [proud] of our statesmen, heroes, divines and the race that has produced a Lloyd George, who is the living, propelling incarnation of modern democracy.[139]

Thomas continued by insisting that in order to ensure this an organization was needed, and in his opinion the only one which could accomplish the task was the American Gorsedd:

> Never before in the history of the Welsh people has there been an organisation that was sufficiently universal and practical to meet the expectations and aspirations of our versatile people. Societies have come and gone. They have ceased to be.[140]

Thomas believed that the American Gorsedd was destined to succeed where others had failed because of its attributes as an ancient, but living, Welsh institution and its relevance to contemporary America. For centuries the Gorsedd had encouraged self-improvement and upheld the salient Welsh characteristics of love of truth, liberty and democracy. Also, it had fostered unity: 'The Ancient Gorsedd was the dynamic of our people in olden times and the source of light and inspiration in social, religious and national spheres. It was also the power that held and guided them.' The potential which the traditional role of the Gorsedd offered, Thomas maintained, was heightened by the adaptation of the organization to suit American

---
[138] Ibid., pp. 5–6.
[139] Ibid., p. 6.
[140] Ibid.

conditions. The Gorsedd could encourage unity among the Welsh and nurture their characteristics and simultaneously promote American patriotism, for ultimately all these goals were completely compatible:

> The trend of the age is towards unity and organisation and the highest kind of Americanism is that which marks the identity of nobility of the units that make up the complete whole. A man who is proud of his race and honors its past greatness, honors the nation of which his race is an integral part. Here at last is established an institution which possesses every attribute to weld our people and unite our scattered forces.[141]

By virtue of its impeccable Welsh credentials and its 'American' character, the national organizer was convinced that the Gorsedd was ideally suited to usher in a new era for Welsh-Americans and he foresaw a glorious future for the organization:

> The Ancient Gorsedd of Great Britain, translated into practical and vigorous American ideals, is destined to add lustre and beauty to our democracy. It is an institution that will carry us back along the avenues of history and literary renown, imbuing us with a spirit of patriotism, creating within us a nobler sentiment, deepening the spirit of humanitarianism and awakening within us the desire for the pursuit of literature, science and the arts as well as arousing our spiritual and religious aspirations.[142]

Such was the writer's belief that the Gorsedd mission was a noble and important one that he was equally sure it would attract the support of Welsh people all over the United States. Addressing the readers of the pamphlet directly, Thomas declared that:

> with the red blood of ancient Britons coursing in your veins you will soon ask 'What must I do to become a member of the American Gorsedd?' ... And furthermore you will readily lend your aid to the perpetuation of these noble principles, cherished and gallantly defended by our progenitors from the dawn of history and which have been and are the bulwark of civilisation.[143]

The National Organizer's elucidation of the purpose and the ambitions of the reconstructed Gorsedd was also emphasized by

[141] Ibid.
[142] Ibid.
[143] Ibid., p. 5.

others involved in the organization. Thomas's almost utopian vision of what the Gorsedd could achieve was stressed even more strongly by the archdruid, Revd William Surdival:

> The message and spirit of the American Gorsedd will eventually reach every hamlet on this continent where Cymric spirit and blood is found. Its spirit of goodwill and friendship will cover the land. The poor and the aged will have this Gospel preached unto them, and the destitute and needy will be cared for . . . It will help instil into the hearts of our young men and women the spirit of higher ambition and studiousness, and to strengthen and deepen our loyalty thereby making us better and more useful Americans as well as to help usher in the new era of permanent peace and universal brotherhood. To prove yourself one hundred per cent efficient in this period of reconstruction, get in line with the men and women of the American Gorsedd.[144]

The interrelationship between being Welsh and patriotic Americans, which Surdival highlighted here, was far more complex than certain preconceptions regarding the contemporary behaviour of Welsh-Americans. The Gorsedd organizers' interpretation of a Welsh past in Wales, with its emphasis on national antiquity and traditional characteristics, was complemented by an interpretation of the history of the Welsh in America which saw them as having played a major role in the development of the United States. In part, this revolved around the contribution of Welsh-American heroes, those famous statesmen and divines to whom the national organizer referred in his pamphlet. They illustrated Welsh patriotism, and their deeds symbolized what 'Welsh' characteristics had to offer America. Fundamentally, however, there was an even more crucial historical dimension. The 'Welsh' characteristics of loyalty and love of truth, liberty and democracy were seen as being the principles on which the American republic itself had been founded. 'I know of no reason,' wrote H. M. Edwards, 'why there should not be an American Gorsedd. While the Gorsedd is an ancient Welsh institution, it is founded on principles clearly recognized among the foundation stones of American democracy.'[145] Thus, if the Gorsedd was a vehicle to promote the organizers' own definitions of Welshness, it was also one which embodied their definitions of Americanism. In this

[144] *Druid*, 1 May 1919.
[145] Ibid.

way, to be more 'Welsh' was to be more 'American'. Equally, to be more 'American' was to be more 'Welsh', and underlying this belief was the assumption – and it is one that is perhaps implicit in the very adaptation of the Welsh Gorsedd to contemporary America – that the Welsh in America were more 'Welsh' than the Welsh in Wales.[146] In many ways they had to be so in order to be more 'American'.

Ultimately, therefore, in terms of the 'Welshness' – and equally the 'Americanism' – it nurtured and its emphasis on unity, there was little that was novel in the 'new' Gorsedd. But what was new was that these long-term concerns had now been channelled into the American Gorsedd and had then become coloured by the belief that only that organization could achieve them. The commentaries of, and on, 1919 suggest a conviction on the part of the Gorsedd organizers that their efforts would find sympathetic ears among Welsh-Americans. Surdival was of the opinion that the purpose of the institution would appeal 'to every Welshman in the land and . . . should impel them to seek the opportunities the Gorsedd offered'.[147] Perhaps the Gorsedd organizers were inspired by a belief that they were giving concrete expression to widely held and accepted notions regarding the nature of Welshness. Yet we should note the frequent use of the imperative 'should' and the constant emphasis on 'worthy' Welsh people (any emphasis reinforced by the stipulation of specific conditions of membership).[148] In effect, the organizers were telling the Welsh in America how to be Welsh and how to regard their Welshness and, equally, their American status. By so doing, however, they were implicitly recognizing that there were many Welsh people who either no longer saw themselves as being Welsh or did not identify with the Gorsedd's conception of it. It is in this context, perhaps, that

---

[146] The belief that the Welsh in America were more Welsh than the Welsh in Wales was often articulated during the early twentieth century. The columns of the *Druid*, in particular, suggest that Welsh-Americans were firmly convinced they had better choirs, better preachers and spoke more and better Welsh. *Druid*, 23 May 1907, 23 June, 3 Aug. 1910, 18, 25 Jan. 1911. One even suggested that America had created a 'higher type' of Welshman. *Druid*, 27 Feb. 1908. The same sentiments were sometimes echoed by visitors from Wales. In 1913 Glyndwr Richards, conductor of the Mountain Ash choir which had successfully toured America in 1911, informed the *Merthyr Express* that Welsh-Americans were 'ten times more Welsh than they were at home. They are Welsh to the core.' *Cambrian*, XXXIII, No. 1 (Jan. 1913), p. 6.

[147] *Druid*, 1 May 1919.

[148] Ibid., 1 Jan, 15 Feb., 1 Apr., 1 May 1919.

the emphasis on history gains its true significance. The 'drifting away' which the national organizer detected was a withdrawal from a self-consciousness of a Welsh identity. The primary purpose of the Gorsedd, then, was to rekindle an awareness of Welshness, but it was a Welshness that was specifically defined.

The subsequent fate of the American Gorsedd after 1919 would show that its attempts to instil its own vision of a Welsh-American identity were destined to fall on stony ground. In that year, however, those involved in the organization were imbued with an unmistakable air of confidence that success was inevitable. Writing in the *Druid* after attending the Gorsedd's first annual conclave in June 1919, the secretary of the Welsh-American Women's Clubs, Mrs J. L. Vopalecky, declared that the event had 'put more pep and determination in us . . . for . . . whatever we set out to do, we will accomplish.'[149] 'Whatever stands in our way . . . will be overcome, if we so will it,' insisted Revd E. P. Thomas, 'for where there's a will there's a way.'[150]

The attitude of these commentators was not solely a consequence of their firm faith in the auspicious nature of the institution, the appeal of its aims and its suitability to the American environment. At a deeper level, it was inspired by much wider developments. The national organizer concluded his *Glimpses of the Gorsedd* pamphlet with an explicit identification of the ultimate, and vital, motivating force which, above all, created the aura of inevitability:

> When the Hunnish hosts ran across Belgium, Lloyd George rose as a mighty wall and the peace-loving, musically inclined and religiously inspired little nation, whose hands were not trained to war and a stranger to military systems, rose out of its peaceful slumber as a mighty giant, answered the call of its great leader and proved to the world that no obstacles and difficulties were too great for the Welsh to overcome. Thus all opposition to the unification of all Americans of Welsh origin . . . will be overcome.[151]

The national organizer's citation of David Lloyd George and of Wales's involvement in the First World War was by no means an idle comparison. It was central to the heady atmosphere which permeated the various commentaries on the Gorsedd

---
[149] Ibid., 15 June 1919.
[150] Ibid., 1 May 1919.
[151] E. P. Thomas, op. cit., p. 16.

during 1919. The organizers' confidence in the future and their historical vision were inspired and influenced by a particular interpretation of contemporary events which saw Wales – and Lloyd George – as having played a major role in winning the war. This itself was an extension of the general belief that the Welsh people were an ancient nation who at last were achieving their historical destiny, as the career of David Lloyd George showed, and who were certain of an even greater future. If the aims and purpose of the American Gorsedd reflected old preoccupations which can be detected in the actions and thoughts of leading Welsh-Americans over a number of years, its emergence in its reconstructed form was infused with the immediate circumstances, or the apparent proof, of Wales's 'arrival' as one of the world's premier nations.

According to Bob Owen, Croesor, the doyen of Welsh-American biographers, it was David Lloyd George who actually suggested to Gomerian that a permanent American Gorsedd should be established.[152] If this is so, then it is a fitting symbol of the tremendous influence the Welsh statesman, and all he represented, wielded on those who attempted to expand the Gorsedd into a national organization. In this respect it was no accident that the Gorsedd took up the cause of his visit, for his career was both a symbol and a creator of the 'Welshness' which lay at the heart of the organization. Yet it was not only the Gorsedd's organizers who praised, and added significance to, the cult of Lloyd George; he was the darling of all sections of Welsh-American literary opinion. Indeed, by the end of the first decade of the twentieth century, Lloyd George's position as the centrepiece of the pantheon of Welsh-American heroes had been firmly secured.

Lloyd George's prestige in Welsh-American circles was immense. Some measure of the extent of his stature can be seen in the almost frenzied efforts of various Welsh-American organizations – including the Gorsedd itself – to induce him to visit the United States. In many ways, the saga of the Lloyd George visit, like that of the national organization, is a sub-plot

---

[152] Bob Owen, entry on Gomerian in *Y Bywgraffiadur Cymreig, 1941–1950* (London, 1970), p. 10.

of the whole drama of the American Gorsedd. He first made known his intention to cross the Atlantic in 1909, when he accepted an invitation by the Lackawanna County Druid Society to attend its Welsh Day the following year, and also to visit a number of other cities in the eastern United States. However, he never arrived.[153] In 1910 the Scranton Druid Society renewed their invitation but although it was initially accepted, Lloyd George later cancelled – as he did again two years later.[154] In June 1917 the *Welsh-American* (that is, the *Druid*) reported that it had received assurances from Lloyd George that he would make his journey when the war was over. It suggested that as he was an ardent eisteddfodwr, 'the greatest eisteddfod in the annals of America' should be arranged in his honour.[155] Two years later the Gorsedd announced that Lloyd George's wife had made public his intention finally to visit, this time after the Paris Peace Conference had ended.[156] However, it was not until 1923, after the collapse of his government, that the long-expected visit actually took place.[157]

The persistence with which Welsh-American societies and individuals pursued Lloyd George was matched by their eagerness to shower him with accolades and adulation. He was the focus of innumerable speeches, articles, essays and lectures throughout America during the early twentieth century. His own speeches and writings were continually reported and quoted, even in novels,[158] for Lloyd George was far more than an object of Welsh-American praise and admiration. He was a motivating force, and as Revd E. P. Thomas's concluding remarks in his pamphlet well illustrated, his name was frequently invoked as a rallying cry and as an example to inspire greater efforts among Welsh-Americans.[159]

---

[153] *Druid*, 23 Dec. 1909, 16 June 1910; *Drych*, 20 Jan. 1910.
[154] *Druid*, 23 June, 15 Sept., 1910, 24, 31 Oct. 1912.
[155] *Welsh-American*, 1 June 1917.
[156] *Druid*, 1 Jan. 1919.
[157] Ibid., 1 Nov. 1922, 1, 15 Oct., 1, 15 Nov. 1923. See also below, Concl., pp. 243–4.
[158] T. Owen Charles included an extract from one of Lloyd George's speeches and a portrait of him in the preface to his novel *Dear Old Wales: A Patriotic Love Story* (Pittsburgh, 1912). Charles declared that the speech, which dealt with the commitment of the Welsh to freedom of conscience, had been the most important incentive for writing the novel.
[159] In July 1910, for example, a *Druid* editorial declared that Lloyd George had put 'ginger' into Welsh life and Welsh sentiment. Welsh-Americans, it continued, should follow his example because with more 'ginger' and 'snap' they would accomplish greater

Much of the esteem which Lloyd George enjoyed in America was undoubtedly inspired by his successful career and his rise from obscurity to become, ultimately, Prime Minister of Great Britain and leader of the victorious Allies. As the *Druid* remarked in an editorial as early as December 1909, Lloyd George was 'one of the greatest men in history – one who has risen from such a lowly estate to such high office, and one who, moreover, has covered the Land of the Gospel with glory'.[160] Success brought publicity, and this alone endeared him to a Welsh-American literary opinion eager to attract greater recognition for the Welsh, either in Wales or in the United States. Added to this was the nature of his politics, which appealed to Welsh-Americans who were undoubtedly 'progressive' in their outlook, and his constant proclamation of his Welshness. The *Druid*, in January 1910, quoted with pride from one of his electoral addresses:

> I owe everything to Wales. My Welsh training is my best inheritance. I am, first of all, a Welshman . . . My love for the people I owe to my ancestors. Democracy has been in our blood for twelve centuries and it will take more than twelve centuries to get it out. Wherever I find my fellow-countrymen in this land, or other lands, I always find them fighting stalwartly for freedom and liberty.

The *Druid* insisted that the passage be noted by all those 'who hesitate to answer when asked if they are Welsh'.[161] In an editorial especially written for the newspaper in May 1912, Revd J. Gwawrfryn Evans of Vaughansville, Ohio, declared:

> The spirit of the Ancients is now embodied in Hon. David Lloyd George and in the newer Wales of today – Cymry Fydd – the spirit of chivalry, Druidic learning, Christian doctrine and true patriotism is the spirit now regnant among the Welsh people throughout the world.[162]

Lloyd George's actual political beliefs and his ministerial activities, as well as his political fortunes, were closely followed and wholeheartedly supported. His 'People's Budget' and especially his struggle with the House of Lords over the Parliament Act of 1911 earned widespread congratulation in

results. Ibid., 21 July 1910.
[160] Ibid., 23 Dec. 1909.
[161] Ibid., 27 Jan. 1910.
[162] Ibid., 16 May 1912.

the Welsh-American press.[163] To the *Druid*, the latter was a 'long-neglected task' and by so doing he had 'relieved the oppressive burdens of the poor, lightened the load of the weary and heavy laden'.[164] In September 1912, in its first editorial after being purchased by a Pittsburgh consortium, the same newspaper stressed the wider context of Lloyd George's efforts in the name of progress:

> There is a general awakening, from a long period of lethargy . . . both at home and abroad among our people. For generations we have had our place among the vanguard in matters spiritual, but in the material elements we have proved lacking. In the Homeland, the Welsh have, under the able leadership of David Lloyd George, become a power – they are no longer immured within the confines of Offa's Dyke as of old, but are to be found warring aggressively beside the erstwhile enemy for a better world in which to live.[165]

The *Druid*'s intermingling of the fortunes of Lloyd George and of Wales emphasizes that the most important aspect of Lloyd George's career to Welsh-American literary opinion was as a symbol of the increasing indispensability of Wales to the British empire, and, inextricably related to it, the reawakening of the Welsh people to fulfil their destiny. At a St David's Day celebration in Salt Lake City in 1910, Governor Arthur L. Thomas inspired ecstatic applause from the seven hundred present when he declared how interesting it was to read of the part that Welsh statesmen, and especially Lloyd George, were playing in British life.[166] In its report of the investiture ceremony of the Prince of Wales in 1911, the *Cambrian* took the opportunity to congratulate Wales on its impact on the British empire:

> Wales has been ignored, despised and almost forgotten by England . . . but of late Wales has been a necessity . . . and a bright light has shone upon the Empire from the mountains of Wales. The eyes of Britain have been opened to the worth of the principality physically, educationally, religiously and politically . . . Wales has a message for the world from away back and occasionally she does something for the benefit of the world. She gave birth to the modern David, beloved throughout the

---

[163] *Cambrian*, XXX, No. 3 (Feb. 1910), p. 7; No. 11 (June 1910), p. 7; *Druid*, 29 Apr. 1909, 6 Jan. 1910; *Drych*, 20 Jan., 22 Dec. 1910.
[164] *Druid*, 30 Mar. 1911.
[165] Ibid., 26 Sept. 1912.
[166] *Drych*, 24 Mar. 1910.

Israel of beneficient [sic] statesmanship. Wales not only supplies England with waters and preachers, but is beginning to furnish her with political teachers.[167]

During 1919, following the Allied victory in the First World War, the eulogizing of David Lloyd George reached it apogee and took on what can only be described as epidemic proportions. Indeed, if 1919 was the year of the 'Red Scare' and of Chief Justice Palmer, in Welsh-American circles it was the year of Lloyd George mania. Banquets to celebrate his birthday were organized by Welsh societies throughout the United States.[168] At one such event in Oakland, California, George Douglas, reputed to be an eminent political and literary critic, pronounced Lloyd George as 'the greatest world figure of today'.[169] The Revd R. R. Davies of Wilkes-Barre, a future national organizer of the American Gorsedd, toured the various Welsh communities in America delivering a lecture on the subject of Lloyd George. Hardly surprisingly perhaps, this had first been heard during the Gorsedd Home celebrations in March 1919.[170] One Welsh-American ardently recommended it to the readers of the *Drych* as a 'tonic for your bodies and your souls'.[171] The *Druid*, in wondering which Welsh town would be the capital of Wales after the Home Rule it now thought was inevitable was actually granted, declared that a brand-new capital should be built in mid-Wales and called Georgetown.[172]

The *Druid*'s faith that Home Rule for Wales was a foregone conclusion was reiterated on a number of occasions during 1919–20, and it vividly illustrates the assumption that it was not only Lloyd George but Wales itself which was now regarded as being in the vanguard of world affairs. To the newspaper, Wales deserved Home Rule for two reasons: it had been loyal to the British empire, in stark contrast to the rebellious Irish, and, of greater importance, it had won the war for Britain.[173] In January 1919 the *Druid* proclaimed with pride that 'Wales has been running the British Empire during the most critical period

[167] *Cambrian*, XXXI, No. 16 (Aug. 1911), p. 3.
[168] *Drych*, 23 Jan. 1919; *Druid*, 1 Feb. 1919.
[169] *Druid*, 1 Feb. 1919.
[170] *Drych*, 20 Mar., 15 May 1919.
[171] Ibid., 20 Mar. 1919.
[172] *Druid*, 15 Mar. 1919.
[173] In July 1919 the newspaper declared: 'If disloyal Ireland has a claim to Home Rule, what of the demand for autonomy of loyal little Wales?' *Druid*, 1 July 1919.

of its history. And who will have the temerity to assert she has not made a good job of it.'[174]

The *Druid* could only have come to this conclusion, however, because during the previous five years Welsh-American literary opinion had already defined the war as being an opportunity for the Welsh nation to show its importance and loyalty to the British polity. In America itself, Welsh support for the Allies was widespread, as was the condemnation of the German empire in the Welsh-American press. In May 1915, for example, the *Welsh-American* carried a strongly worded editorial against German butchery, to accompany its report that three members of the Gwent Male Chorus had lost their lives as a result of the sinking of the Lusitania.[175] Nor was it only verbal support. The *Welsh-American*'s Welsh Relief Fund appeal – which included a Cymric Denial Day on 21 December 1914 – collected nearly $8,000 within the first six months of the war, whilst during 1915 the Welsh tea merchant, George T. Matthews, donated 10 per cent of his parcel post sales to buy gifts for Welsh soldiers. Largely owing to T. Owen Charles's efforts, a number of Welsh Soldiers' Relief Societies were established throughout the United States, and these and various other Welsh-American organizations collected large amounts of money and clothing.[176]

The enthusiasm with which Welsh-Americans aided the Welsh war effort was complemented by the extensive coverage the Welsh-American press devoted to developments in the struggle. Until the United States itself entered the war in 1917 and attention switched to Welsh-American soldiers, its columns were dominated by news of Welsh people at the various fronts and, increasingly, as the war wore on, their obituaries. Indeed, support for the war effort became almost a central tenet of the 'Welshness' defined by Welsh-American public opinion, and manifestations of it were widely reported and praised. In this respect, during the first two years of the war Welsh-American newspapers and periodicals jubilantly reported the number of

[174] Ibid., 15 Jan. 1919.
[175] *Welsh-American*, 15 May 1915.
[176] Ibid., 15 Sept., 16 Nov., 1, 15 Dec. 1914, 1 Jan., 1, 15 Feb., 1 June 1915, 1 July 1916, 15 Dec. 1917. T. Owen Charles also donated the proceeds from *Dear Old Wales* to the fund. His commitment to raising money for distress funds in Wales was indefatigable. Largely through his efforts, Welsh-Americans had earlier contributed nearly $4,000 to aid the families of the victims of the 1913 Senghenydd Colliery explosion. *Druid*, 8 Jan. 1914, 1 July, 15 Nov. 1916; *Welsh Outlook*, IV (Jan. 1917), p. 6.

Welshmen who had displayed their patriotism by joining the colours. In September 1914, for example, the *Cambrian* told its readers that over four hundred miners had enlisted from Clydach Vale in the Rhondda in the first month of the war alone.[177] Within Wales, the vast majority of the Welsh were pro-war,[178] but it is the manner in which the Welsh-American press reported the phenomenon which is significant here. The ultimate proof of all they had said lay in the number who had volunteered to fight for the empire. In their eyes, to support the war effort was to be Welsh; to oppose it was un-Welsh. In October 1914 the *Cambrian* declared: ' "Pacifistaid" is a vernacular journal's Welsh for Pacifists. This is dreadful, unless, indeed, it is a sly hint that the Welsh language – or Wales – has no need of the term.'[179]

This adaptation of 'Welshness' to suit the immediate circumstances of the war, or, more accurately, the Welsh-American interpretation of it, is perhaps confirmed by the fact that one key event which conflicted with the prevailing image of the Welsh as the empire's most fervent – and active – loyalists was not reported in the Welsh-American press. In 1915 the miners of south Wales defied both their own leadership and the wartime government's anti-strike regulations and came out on strike in order to increase their wages. In this they were successful, for Lloyd George, the Minister of Munitions, was forced to accede to their demands.[180] No doubt there were a number of reasons why these developments were ignored, although clearly the 'unpatriotic' actions of the miners tarnished the perception of the Welsh as the bulwark of the British empire during its greatest crisis.

It was in the midst of this potent brew of both historical and contemporary perceptions that Wales was providing the ultimate proof of its loyalty and value to the British empire and at the same time fulfilling its destiny that David Lloyd George became Prime Minister of the United Kingdom in December 1916. The *Welsh-American* was not slow to see the significance of

---

[177] *Cambrian*, XXXIV, No. 18 (Sept. 1914), p. 8.
[178] Morgan, *Rebirth of a Nation*, pp. 159–62. For a discussion of the Welsh involvement in the war and its impact on Wales, see ibid., pp. 159–79.
[179] *Cambrian*, XXXIV, No. 20 (Oct. 1914), p. 9.
[180] See R. Page Arnot, *South Wales Miners. A History of the South Wales Miners' Federation*, vol. II: *1914–1926* (Cardiff, 1975), pp. 50–87.

the development within the framework of the prevailing image of Wales which it and other sections of Welsh-American opinion had erected and perpetuated during the war years. Despite the gravity of the situation, an editorial in December 1916 welcomed Lloyd George's elevation to the premiership and declared:

> But it may not be out of place to recall that the Principality came into her own once before when Harry of Monmouth became Henry VII [*sic*]. And she has come into her own again now that an infinitely greater son of hers heads not alone Britain, but the liberty-loving hosts of the world.[181]

Yet despite the optimism of 1919, and the seemingly categoric proof that their historical vision had been vindicated, the hopes of the Gorsedd's organizers would not be fulfilled. The subsequent history of the institution emphasized its failure to become an effective national organization and substantially to increase its membership beyond the two hundred it had secured by 1919.[182] Plans to double its membership were unveiled in December 1920, and a new national organizer, Revd R. R. Davies (the author of the famous lecture on Lloyd George), was appointed to undertake a vigorous campaign to recruit new members. However, despite being acclaimed as a wise choice,[183] Davies fared no better than his predecessors. Throughout its existence until 1941, the Gorsedd never had more than three hundred members, and these were drawn principally from the Pittsburgh area. Although it held various conclaves and eisteddfodau in the eastern Ohio–western Pennsylvania area during the 1920s and 1930s, and officially received Lloyd George when he visited the United States – finally – in 1923, attempts to establish a subsidiary Gorsedd at Youngstown failed miserably. The Gorsedd remained little more than a Welsh society for Pittsburgh, sponsoring St David's Day banquets and Welsh Days.[184]

The fact that the Gorsedd was never able to expand out of the Pittsburgh area was one of its central and, ultimately, one of its most debilitating features. Although it attracted both officers

---

[181] *Welsh-American*, 15 Dec. 1916. Harry of Monmouth in fact became Henry V.
[182] Hartmann, op. cit., pp. 150; E. P. Thomas, op. cit., p. 7.
[183] *Druid*, 15 June, 15 Dec. 1920.
[184] Ibid., 15 Oct., 1 Nov. 1922, 1 Apr., 1 Oct., 1 Nov. 1923; Hartmann, op. cit., pp. 150–1.

and members from all over the United States, it was primarily the creation of leading Welsh-Americans in Pittsburgh and those associated with the *Druid*. Like the Pittsburgh International Eisteddfod of 1913 and the purchasing of the *Druid* by W. B. Jones and James J. Davis's consortium during the previous year, the Gorsedd can be regarded as a reflection of the self-perception among that city's Welsh community leaders that they were the prime upholders of Welshness in America. But their enthusiasms were not shared by other sections of the Welsh-American press, and the acclaim which the *Druid* showered on the Gorsedd from its initial appearance in 1913 was not matched by either the *Drych* or the *Cambrian*. The former merely reported its existence and passed no editorial comment, whilst, for the most part, the accounts which appeared in the newspaper were written by those actively involved in the Gorsedd.[185] As far as can be detected, the *Cambrian* was completely silent on the matter. The reticence of the Utica-based constituents of the Welsh-American press symbolized the wider lack of interest on the part of that Welsh community. Few Utica Welsh were either members of the Gorsedd or included in the 'Loyal Legion' list of subscribers to the *Royal Blue Book*.[186] Ultimately the American Gorsedd was an attempt by leading Welshmen in Pittsburgh, and their allies in the Wilkes-Barre–Scranton area, to impose their own definitions of Welshness on the remainder of the Welsh in the United States. Although their assumptions regarding the nature of Welsh nationality were widely held in Welsh-American literary circles, what differentiated the Gorsedd was that these preoccupations came to be channelled into a perceived ancient, national Welsh institution. Both the original Gorsedd and its reconstructed version were the products of the more industrialized, and consequently more rapidly Americanized, sections of Welsh-America.

Yet even in its own heartland, Welsh support for the Gorsedd was limited. The Gorsedd Home did not become the flourishing mecca of Welshness it was intended to be and, ironically, there were indications that this would in fact be its fate even during 1919. Within only a few months of its opening, one of the *Drych*'s Pittsburgh correspondents lamented:

[185] *Drych*, 10 July 1913, 20 Mar. 1919.
[186] *Royal Blue Book*, pp. 24–8, 451–64.

Everything is quiet here in the world of Welsh matters. After the establishing of the Gorsedd and the obtaining of such comfortable rooms in which to meet, we thought that everything would be at its peak amongst us. Hopefully we will see a new lease of life before long.[187]

The failure of the American Gorsedd to attract widespread support in Pittsburgh itself suggests that the majority of the Welsh there were unresponsive to the preoccupations which obsessed its leading members and which had been infused into the institution. Undoubtedly, this was also the fundamental reason for its failure throughout the United States. Ultimately, the greatest obstacle to the fulfilment of the Gorsedd's ambitions was the fact that it was the expression of the concerns of a minority.

---

[187] *Drych*, 3 July 1919.

V
THE CRACKED MIRROR

If the minority achieved resounding, though ephemeral, success in projecting their valued ethnic traits to audiences beyond their own Welsh communities, it was none the less within their own local social structures that their minoritarian presence swelled to a sense of élitism. In so far as Scranton, our exemplum, is concerned, this did not, generally, imply dovetailing into a native or American élite whose own exclusive organizations, such as the Scranton Club and the Lackawanna Historical Society, underpinned their economic attainment (reflected in the ramifications of the Scranton family and the financing of banks and other companies) and their social status (fashionably housed in removed residential districts). According to Folsom, in 1880 only forty individuals in Scranton qualified for such economic or élite status (the two were interchangeable).[1] Of these, only two, Lewis Pughe and Benjamin Hughes, were Welsh.[2] It was, then, more sensible and perhaps gratifying to mirror such élite certainties within their own peer groups. Throughout the late nineteenth century the internal structure of the Welsh community was hierarchical. As we have seen, mining officials, professionals and businessmen were invariably the church deacons, eisteddfod organizers and the officers of the various cultural societies. In their behaviour and lifestyle Welsh community leaders were quite capable of aping Scranton's ruling élite, as in the grand and prestigious Cymmrodorion Society's St David's Day banquets.

[1] Folsom, op. cit., pp. 43–67. All these individuals held three or more directorships or partnerships in Scranton, Folsom's criteria for an 'economic leader'.
[2] Ibid., pp. 54–5. Hughes's interests lay primarily in the Welsh financial institutions, where he was president of the Cambrian Mutual Fire Insurance Company and the West Side Bank, though he was also a director of the Hyde Park Gas Company and president of the Schuylkill Anthracite Royalty Company which had coalmines in the Southern coalfield. In contrast, Pughe's financial interests were in the city's main banks. His only involvement in the Welsh community seems to have been his membership of the Cymmrodorion Society, which perhaps confirms the latter as a 'Welsh élite' organization. Ebenezer Edwards, op. cit., pp. 406–7; Murphy, *Hist. Hyde Park*, p. 43; Throop, op. cit., pp. 149–52; *Scranton Republican*, 23 Jan., 28 Feb. 1890.

From the 1840s evidence of the Welsh in Scranton, at any level, addressing each other is sparse because the material (speeches, letters, exhortations) would have been delivered in Welsh (thereby preventing inclusion in the local Scrantonian press). Nevertheless, by the early 1870s the self-consciousness is quite evident and, as we have seen, grows and grows. In 1871 H. M. Edwards published an essay entitled 'The defects of the Welsh nation in America'.[3] Edwards, whose whole life would be a paean of praise to the unity of Protestantism, Yankeedom and their Welsh equivalents, did not dwell on the negative in order to castigate but rather to boost Welsh pride in religious observance, respectability and their inter-community vehicle, the Welsh language. It is an early example of the constant refrain which the élite minority would impress, to good effect, on the public behaviour of the Welsh well into the twentieth century. However, the attendant chorus, which was required to respond only in a certain, increasingly prescribed fashion, did not always do so. The crises in the anthracite industry and in political activity testify to this. Even more telling, if more elusive, is the existence, known but not always acknowledged, of a Welsh subculture whose traits were also becoming more and more American, but doing so via the agency of an unwanted, threatening popular culture.

There is evidence, then, to suggest that there were other aspects of the cultural life of the Welsh immigrants which scarcely bear out the image of that all-embracing Welsh respectability that community leaders strove to emphasize in their actions and words. Beneath the veneer flourished alternative 'definitions' of Welshness which were expressions of a cultural behaviour whose priorities were far removed from more acceptable features. If the Welsh immigrants brought with them their language, religion and eisteddfod, they also brought with them aspects of the culture of an industrial society which was equally prevalent in contemporary Wales and which equally gave meaning and identity to their lives. Many would deplore these other manifestations of Welshness; more ignored them. Nevertheless, drink, insobriety, 'dubious' amusements and

---

[3] H. M. Edwards, 'Diffygion y genedl Gymreig yn America', loc. cit. The essay was originally written for a competition at the 1871 Youngstown Eisteddfod and was awarded joint first prize.

sports, lawless and violent behaviour and sexual abuse flourished among the Welsh even in the 'Welsh Athens of America'.

I THE SAMARIA OF WELSH-AMERICA

In the early 1870s, in the heyday of its 'Welshness', the morality of the Welsh immigrants in Scranton – or rather their lack of it – was in fact the 'talking point of the country' and the subject of great anxiety among sections of the Welsh both in the city itself and in other parts of the United States.[4] Some observers publicized their concern in the *Drych*, and two major exposés were printed in its columns. The first appeared in July 1870 in an article written by a resident of the city under the pseudonym 'Huw o'r Ddôl'. After deriding the efforts of the Welsh Philosophical Society and denying the existence of any real bards in the city, he went on to discuss the morality of the Welsh immigrants:

> But what of the morals of Hyde Park? In many respects they are second to those of Sodom, and the equal of Gomorrah. The Welsh saloons here are as numerous as the frogs of Egypt. On Main Street some kind of Welshman ... keeps a bar room at nearly every other house. If you ... want to see Welsh grogshops, whisky holes, gin mills, rum cellars etc., go to Lackawanna Avenue, Scranton and Main Street, Hyde Park. You can see sons and daughters, husbands and wives, forever half-drunk, fooling, idling around and singing in Welsh until they are a disgrace even to the half-civilized Irish. If you want to see disrespect on the Lord's Day, if you want to hear the language of the fiends of hell pouring ... out of Welsh mouths, go for half an hour along the streets and into the Welsh saloons in Hyde Park.[5]

Huw o'r Ddôl was in no doubt as to who was to blame for this state of affairs: 'Welshmen and Welshwomen from Tredegar, Rhymney, Dowlais, Merthyr, Aberdare etc., those that have recently arrived from there or within the last two years. The scum of the works of Wales has been shipped to Hyde Park in recent years.' He called for missionaries from Wales to come

---

[4] *Drych*, 18 Aug. 1870.
[5] Ibid., 28 July 1870. 'Huw o'r Ddôl' suggested that the Welsh Philosophical Society was a meeting place for 'the occasional man and several children' and that its proceedings were dominated by those members who spoke the most nonsense and told the funniest jokes.

over in order to sober up the Welsh men and women of Scranton and wondered for how long the Welsh churches and the Good Templars would tolerate these conditions. He pleaded to the 'respectable' and the 'half a dozen other public men' in the city to ask 'What should be done in order to sober up our countrymen?' The author was adamant that church members could not teach morals to the world by frequenting barber shops on Sundays and the saloons during the week. No Welshman should drink alcohol; women ought to keep away from the saloons and young men ought to join the temperance brigades. Only then, maintained the writer, would Hyde Park return to what it had once been.[6]

A year later the morality of the Welsh in Hyde Park was once more under intense scrutiny in the *Drych*. In August 1871 a letter from Davenport, Iowa, complained bitterly about the anti-temperate character of Hyde Park and took Dewi Cwmtwrch to task for apparently saying it was a shame that the Welsh drank in German taverns. To the Iowan, drinking in any tavern was disgusting.[7] The letter occasioned the writing of an article by 'Pittstonian' entitled 'The Welsh in Hyde Park: Temperance and politics', which appeared in the newspaper the following month. This congratulated the *Drych* for the way it supported the temperance movement and also criticized Dewi Cwmtwrch:

> What, is the drunkenness produced in the Welshman's tavern less sinful than that produced in a German tavern? I am afraid that the Welsh of Hyde Park are prepared to commit every wrong, violence, injustice etc. . . . as long as it has a Welsh form. The saloon keepers of Hyde Park are all-right because they are Welsh. It is his own children [presumably those of Dewi Cwmtwrch] who are damaging the character of the Welsh nationality.[8]

'Pittstonian' continued by describing the prevalence of drunkenness among the Welsh in the Scranton area and some of their amusements and pastimes:

> From Olyphant down to Plymouth it is reckoned that Welsh saloons are a hundred or more. From Olyphant to Plymouth it is reckoned that thousands of Welsh are regular beer and whisky drinkers, and hundreds are public drunks, who have learned in Aberdare, Rhymney, Merthyr

[6] Ibid.
[7] Ibid., 17 Aug. 1871.
[8] Ibid., 7 Sept. 1871.

etc., to drink beer like water, to get drunk like tinkers, to swear and curse worse than the fiends of the bottomless pit. Here you can see girls and their sweethearts, and wives with their husbands in the Welsh saloons in the same accursed fashion as in Wales. Are there not here Welsh in the ring as prize-fighters? Are there not here Welsh who breed dogs and cocks and who amuse themselves with dog fights and cockfights on the Sabbath? Are there not here Welsh saloons which are open from morning until midnight on the Lord's Day? . . . Cannot there be counted scores of women of our nationality with their infants at their breasts parading and loafing in the streets?[9]

The article urged Welshmen to keep away from the saloons and spend their spare time reading the Bible instead of walking the streets and talking nonsense with every troupe of wasters they met. On Sundays they should go to church, not play pitch and toss, throw quoits and take part in long-jump and foot-race competitions. The author thought it was worrying to see church members in Welsh saloons at 10 or 11 o'clock on a Saturday night, their heads too ill to go to chapel on Sunday morning, and their eyes red for a week. In Hyde Park there were three Welsh pulpits, which taught morality, and thirty taverns, the schools of the devil, which taught the Welsh and their children to drink and get drunk, curse and swear and gamble and fight. 'Pittstonian' warned that if the Welsh of Hyde Park were thinking of nominating Welshmen for office, they should remember that Welsh temperance supporters would vote only for those who were thorough abstainers. The writer maintained that half the prominent men in Welsh causes in Hyde Park were anti-temperance.[10]

These accounts paint a markedly different picture from most other contemporary Welsh reports and the overpowering image of respectability contained in them.[11] Because of their conflicting evidence it would be wise to treat them with caution. In

---

[9] Ibid.
[10] Ibid.
[11] Contemporary Welsh accounts of the Welsh-American community in Scranton by and large concerned themselves only with the strictly 'Welsh' aspects of its cultural life. In his *Hanes Cymry America* of 1872, Revd R. D. Thomas dealt solely with the churches, their ministers, the Welsh Philosophical Society, local Welsh-language publications and the community's most prominent individuals, bards and musicians. Twenty years later, in a book actually published in the city, W. D. Davies confined himself to similar matters. The perception of a thrifty, religious, respectable and cultured Welsh community was also reiterated by editorials in the press and by other non-Welsh observers. R. D. Thomas, op. cit., pp. 57–9; W. D. Davies, op. cit., p. 73; Gibbons, loc. cit., *passim*.

common with temperance writing in Wales, their primary purpose was to shock, to shame, to warn Welsh readers to keep away from the saloons and to urge temperance reformers to greater efforts. Both accounts also reflect the manner in which the 'drink problem' was being viewed in contemporary Wales. The pub (or in this case the saloon) was seen as an evil, a hot-bed of vice and a creator of poverty. Its role in providing badly needed recreational facilities, and the wider social and working conditions that engendered drunkenness, were ignored.[12] As 'One from the Place' informed the *Drych* in May 1871, a few months before the second tirade was published, 'What is the chief cause of poverty among the Welsh in America but the taking to of intoxicating drink?' He urged temperance reformers in Hyde Park to start working at once because they were 'under a cloud at present'.[13]

Given their sensationalist nature and the reason for their being published, the revelations of both Huw o'r Ddôl and 'Pittstonian' probably contain a certain amount of exaggeration. Nevertheless, there is more than sufficient evidence to conclude that they are a fairly accurate assessment of a section, at least, of the Welsh immigrants in Scranton. The fact that they were written at all is in itself an indication of the scale of the problem as far as temperance supporters were concerned. The allegations regarding widespread drunkenness and immorality – of which both churchgoers and non-churchgoers, and women as well as men, were equally guilty – were not denied by those who commented on them in the *Drych*, suggesting perhaps that their veracity was accepted. Indeed, most commentaries supported the disclosures. In response to 'Huw o'r Ddôl''s article, a letter by 'The Voice of Many' confined itself to refuting the attack on the Welsh Philosophical Society and complaining bitterly about the actions of 'traitors from the town itself'.[14] Another, however, sent an anti-temperance verse by Milton to the newspaper and dedicated it to 'the bad Welsh of Scranton' because of 'their hypocritical and mocking behaviour'.[15] More significantly, perhaps, a David Crouk maintained that before condemning those who should not be condemned, ' would it not

[12] See Lambert, op. cit., especially pp. 13–19, 23–33, 119–20, 250.
[13] *Drych*, 11 May 1871.
[14] Ibid., 1 Sept. 1870.
[15] Ibid., 18 Aug. 1870.

be beneficial to understand why some people have gone to keep saloons here?' As we have already seen, he went on to insist that many Welsh had been forced to open saloons after they had been thrown out of work because of the oppression of the 'bosses'.[16]

Besides, there is sufficient evidence from contemporary local sources, especially the local press, to confirm that not only in the early 1870s but also throughout the late nineteenth and early twentieth centuries drink and drunkenness were prevalent among the Welsh. Despite the Pottsville *Miners' Journal*'s assertion in 1870 that there were no Welsh saloons in Hyde Park, there were in fact a number of them both in that section and in Scranton itself in that year.[17] Nor were they only a feature of Scranton's frontier years of industrial growth. There were almost as many Welsh saloons in 1900 as there had been in 1870, and the tradition of Welsh people opening saloons in the city continued until the 1930s.[18] Nor is this surprising, perhaps, given the way in which the public house was one of the two major foci of most communities in nineteenth-century Wales and that the saloon occupied an equally central role in American industrial society.[19] 'Yf dy gwrw efo dy Garwr' ('Drink your beer with your Loved One'), urged an advertisement for Bennett's Saloon in Scranton in *Y Ford Gron* in 1867, and there were many Welsh immigrants who followed the advice at both his and the numerous other establishments available.[20] Even Phoebe Gibbons acknowledged that the Welshman drank beer, although she maintained 'he does not drink as much here as at home, for he has bidden his native land farewell with the intention of making money.'[21]

As W. R. Lambert has pointed out, the existence of drinking establishments is not necessarily an indication of drunkenness.[22]

[16] Ibid. See also above, ch. 2, p. 42.
[17] *Webb's Scranton Directory*, 1870–1. See also above, ch. 1, p. 22.
[18] *Taylor's Scranton City Directory*, 1900. A family of Welsh immigrants from Aberaman opened the 'College of Beer knowledge' in the Scranton area in the 1930s. Ex inf. Mr Tom Evans, Aberdare.
[19] Lambert, op. cit., p. 23. For the importance of the saloon in American society and its role as a distinctive working-class leisure institution see Roy Rosenzweig, *Eight Hours For What We Will: Workers and Leisure in an Industrial City* (Cambridge, 1983), pp. 35–64, 94–100, 183–90.
[20] *Ford Gron*, I (Feb. 1867), advertisement.
[21] Gibbons, loc. cit., p. 918.
[22] Lambert, op. cit., p. 20.

Nevertheless there are a number of reports which suggest that insobriety was rife among the Welsh in Scranton, as the temperance crusaders maintained. Often these involved arrests: a John Davies was fined for being drunk on Pennsylvania Avenue in February 1871; a month later, a William Jones of Hyde Park was arrested for a similar offence.[23] Incidents such as these were common, whilst some lost their lives because they were inebriated. One of the two drunks who suffocated after going to sleep on a cinder tip on Christmas Night 1870 was David Hopkins, a single 28-year-old Welshman who had emigrated to Scranton from Ynyspenllwch, Swansea, eighteen months earlier.[24] Throughout the late nineteenth century local newspapers continued to reflect the persistence of arrests for drunkenness among Scranton's Welsh inhabitants: a David Lewis fined for that offence in August 1889; a John E. Jones of 508 North Main Avenue, Hyde Park, arrested for recklessly driving a buggy into a crowd of children and cursing a police officer whilst drunk the following month; a James Davis of Providence arrested for being drunk and sleeping on the street that same September; a Mary and David Roberts arrested for drunkenness one Sunday afternoon during the following August.[25] The regularity of such cases is perhaps even more significant if the testimony of a local priest in 1877 is to be believed. He told Phoebe Gibbons that 'the Irishman does not drink more than the Welshman, but perhaps he is more frequently seen intoxicated in public.'[26]

One of the major arguments of 'Huw o'r Ddôl' in his article in the *Drych* in 1870 was that the drink problem in Hyde Park had surfaced in the previous two years, implying that it was once devoid of what were for the 'scum' of industrial Wales the realities of life. It is difficult to reconcile his assertion with other evidence available. Although there was a marked increase both in Welsh industrial immigration and in the number of Welsh saloons in the city after the end of the Civil War, there were nevertheless at least three Welsh saloons in Hyde Park alone in 1865.[27] Earlier industrial immigrants brought a culture similar

---

[23] Scranton *Morning Republican*, 17 Feb., 18 Mar. 1871.
[24] *Drych*, 5 Jan. 1871.
[25] *Scranton Republican*, 17 Aug., 6, 24 Sept. 1889, 6 Oct. 1890.
[26] Gibbons, loc. cit., p. 918.
[27] *Scranton City Directory*, 1865.

to that of the people whom 'Huw o'r Ddôl' would later castigate. Commenting on the Welsh in Carbondale in 1840, the *Carbondale Advance* declared: 'Intemperance is known among them and we fear sometimes prevails to an unhappy extent.' The correspondent maintained that their preference was for strong ale and beer, not spirits, reflecting perhaps the fact that contemporary Wales was a predominantly beer-drinking country.[28] Drink was an integral part of the cultural life and tradition of pre-industrial Wales, which spread in the late eighteenth and early ninteenth centuries to the new industrial towns, where it flourished in the prevailing social and working environment.[29] In regarding the insobriety of Hyde Park in the early 1870s as an aberration, capable of being purged if sufficient work was done, 'Huw o'r Ddôl' echoed the way in which temperance reformers viewed the problem in Wales. They recognized that it was the industrial areas which presented the biggest challenge, yet failed to see that what was emerging both in south Wales and in the United States was a different culture for a new society.

Throughout the late nineteenth century castigation in the press was often accompanied by concerted campaigns to 'clean up' the Welsh in Scranton. In common with other groups in the city the Welsh did have their temperance organizations both independent of, and as auxiliaries to the various churches.[30] In fact the disclosures in the *Drych* in 1870–1 led to – or perhaps were complemented by – action at a local level. In September 1870 a conference of Good Templars, including representatives from Hyde Park's Welsh-language sections, Teml Cambro-America and Teml Gwalia Bellevue, met in that section of the city in order to consider the state of the Welsh in Luzerne County. It condemned those 'religious men who profess to be supportive of peace and sobriety' and who signed liquor licences, and it decided that their names were to be published in newspapers. It also agreed to raise a levy to pay for other lecturers to visit the area to help the district deputy, S. D. Williams, a Welshman who had recently been appointed

---

[28] *Carbondale Advance*, 11 June 1840; Lambert, op. cit., p. 7.
[29] Lambert, op. cit., pp. 5, 7–13.
[30] *Drych*, 23. Feb. 1871, 25 Jan. 1872, 7 May 1885; Scranton *Morning Republican*, 29 Mar. 1871; Murphy, *Hist. Hyde Park*, p. 69.

'to work among his own people'.³¹ The report of the conference sent to the *Drych* declared that Williams would undoubtedly face a lot of opposition; in fact, he had had some already. It also claimed that *Baner America* had 'either refused or negligently forgot' to print the report: 'Is this what they call supporting the virtuous institutions of our country?'³² These allegations perhaps confirm other contemporary accusations regarding the hypocrisy of some leading Welsh citizens in Scranton, including prominent members of the churches, and the lip-service they paid to temperance causes.

Campaigns over liquor licences also caused controversy on other occasions. In 1884 Revd John W. Williams, minister of the First Welsh Baptist Church, sued Revd Jonathan Edwards for libel following his claim that Williams was ambiguous in his support for the temperance movement.³³ Edwards was a staunch and active Prohibitionist, and apparently because of this, four members left the Plymouth Welsh Congregational Church when he was appointed its minister later that year. As a result, his church became even more active in the cause of temperance, and this attracted many new members 'despite its enemies – the taverners and their friends'.³⁴ None of the Welsh ministers in Scranton, however, seems to have taken as overt a stand against saloon licences as Revd T. Cynonfardd Edwards in Edwardsville, near Wilkes-Barre. In 1905 his efforts led to the dynamiting of his church, with the compliments of the local saloon keepers, an outrage which must have been particularly galling as a few years previously he had been defeated at the polls by a Prohibition candidate.³⁵ Although no such dramatic episodes coloured the religious history of the Welsh in Scranton, it is possible that local ministers were active in this field.

Yet temperance workers faced an uphill task in a north-east Pennsylvania coalfield society in which one former Welsh minister fell dead in a Minersville street because of intemperance in 1863, or where, in 1871, three Plymouth Welshmen

---

³¹ *Drych*, 1 Sept. 1870. As part of the scheme, Revd Thomas Roberts lectured at various venues in the Lackawanna Valley in early 1871. Scranton *Morning Republican*, 17 Jan. 1871.
³² *Drych*, 1 Sept. 1870.
³³ *Scranton Republican*, 4 Jan., 24 Feb. 1884.
³⁴ *Drych*, 7 May 1885. See also ibid., 14 Dec. 1882 and 1 Feb. 1883 for other controversies over liquor licences.
³⁵ T. Cynonfardd Edwards, op. cit., pp. 22–41; *Drych*, 15 Nov. 1888.

tried to force liquor down the throat of a member of the Temple of Honor, one of them biting off a portion of the victim's ear.[36] It was an equally daunting task in Scranton itself, where one of the city's Welsh policemen assaulted a fellow officer in 1893 after he had been called a Prohibitionist.[37] Such episodes undoubtedly highlight the centrality of drink and insobriety in the lives of the Welsh. They also illustrate the close relationship which often existed between drunkenness and another feature of the culture of the Welsh immigrants: lawless, violent and sometimes murderous behaviour. If the prevalence of drunkenness alone demonstrated that notions of Welsh respectability were rather fragile, the roughness of Welsh immigrant life in Scranton more than confirmed it.

As well as drinking with their wives, their countrymen, the Irish and the Germans, Welshmen also fought with them. Lawless behaviour was by no means a Welsh speciality; it was a characteristic of the society as a whole, especially during its frontier years and, as Berthoff has pointed out, it was also a badly policed region.[38] The use of both firearms and fists was widespread. The *Shenandoah Herald* complained bitterly in 1875 of what it termed as the 'promiscuous' shooting which took place on the streets, notably on pay-day nights. All nationalities were guilty.[39] This could apply to any of the north-east Pennsylvania coalmining towns, even the 'metropolis' of Scranton itself, for violence was not unique to the rawer and more disorganized coal patches of the Southern coalfield. Nor, apparently, was it restricted to adults: the *Scranton Times* reported in 1876 that small boys in Patagonia, Hyde Park, were carrying revolvers and terrifying women, and it hinted at the existence of gang warfare among the young.[40] Luckily for Johnnie, son of William Jones of Eynon Street, Hyde Park, it was only a toy gun which he discharged to break a window of the Welsh Baptist Church in 1889, an act which resulted in his arrest. He was no doubt following the example of the youths who had smashed all the windows of the Welsh Congregational

[36] Pottsville *Miners' Journal*, 7 Mar. 1863; Scranton *Morning Republican*, 23 Mar. 1871.
[37] *Scranton Republican*, 7, 11 Jan., 16, 25 Mar. 1893.
[38] Berthoff, 'Social order', p. 266.
[39] *Shenandoah Herald*, 17 July 1873.
[40] Scranton *Daily Times*, 15 June 1876.

Church a few months earlier.[41] Fortunately, too, for Edward Thomas, being shot accidentally by Thomas Reese, a fifteen-year-old from Providence, in the French Roof Hotel in the same year did not prevent him taking his mining examinations.[42]

When guns were used in earnest, loss of life or severe injury was always a strong possibility. In an incident on the corner of Main and Hampton Streets, Hyde Park, a drunken Robert Jones first struck William Griffiths with the butt of his revolver and then followed Griffiths into his house. On being ejected by Griffiths and an Edward Davis, Jones shot Davis in the leg, severely wounding him. The cause of the affray was apparently a heated discussion about the ownership of a dog which Griffiths and Jones kept in Mrs O'Connor's saloon on Luzerne Street. Jones was described as being 'demented' even when sober.[43]

Recent research on the Molly Maguires has brought to light the existence in the anthracite coalfield both of Welsh anti-Irish gangs, such as the Modocs and the Chain Gang, and of disreputable Welsh characters who all too quickly resorted to crime, violence and even murder.[44] One Welshman who gained quite a reputation in the Southern coalfield during the early 1870s was William M. Thomas, whose succession of assaults, robberies and frequent bouts of drunkenness seem to have earned him the well-deserved nickname 'Bully Bill'. His attacks on Irishmen led to an attempt by the Mollies to assassinate him in June 1875; this failed when a bullet narrowly missed his jugular vein. Thomas had recovered sufficiently by August to get involved in yet another drunken shoot-out with an Irishman, this time a James Duggan, in a street in Mahanoy City. Both fired many shots, one lodging in 'Bully Bill's' cheek and another killing a German miner who happened to be in the street awaiting his wife. Thomas was arrested, but no charges were brought. Nor did this experience chasten him. At the height of the Molly Maguire trials, he and another Welshman, Jesse Major (a cousin of George Major, the Welsh burgess of

---

[41] *Scranton Republican*, 10 Sept. 1889.
[42] Ibid., 8 Aug. 1889.
[43] Ibid., 7, 8 Oct. 1889.
[44] Broehl, op. cit., *passim*. The Modocs and the Chain Gang were tantalizingly obscure organizations set up by Welsh and Protestant German miners in Mahanoy City to counter Molly Maguire violence and terrorize the Irish. It is possible that the name 'Modocs' may have derived from 'Madocs'. Pottsville *Miners' Journal*, 27 Nov. 1874; Broehl, op. cit., pp. 164–5, 181, 182; Aurand, op. cit., p. 108.

Mahanoy City who had been shot dead in a fight between the Mollies and the Modocs in 1874) started brawling and ended up in gaol. Apparently the fight started when Major slapped a woman, and this had aroused Thomas's chivalrous feelings, since he claimed never to hit women.[45]

It is quite possible that there were characters like 'Bully Bill' Thomas among the Welsh in Scranton. Certainly there were infamous 'bruisers' within the community, such as 'Big' John Thomas and 'Red' Sam Morgan. They were apparently long-standing and bitter enemies who fought each other at every available opportunity. In May 1872 they decided to settle the matter once and for all. A ring was formed quickly and a hundred people gathered around as the combatants went about their task. The wife of one of them attempted to stop the fight but was badly beaten up herself in the process and had to be taken home. However, her misfortune did suceed in bringing the encounter to a close.[46]

Much of the lawlessness had undertones of ethnic hostility. During times of industrial strife tempers often ran high, as the violent tactics the Welsh miners and their wives adopted during the 1871 strike clearly demonstrated. In June of that year, for example, a disagreement inside John P. Jones's saloon on Franklin Avenue escalated into a free fight between a crowd of Welsh and a crowd of Germans.[47] As Berthoff has pointed out, however, intra-group conflict was probably more frequent than inter-group conflict, but the latter tended to attract greater attention in the local press.[48] To some Welsh bruisers the ethnicity of their victims seems to have been of little consequence. In May 1893 a William Lewis took on the 'famous' McNally brothers outside the 'notorious speak easy' on the corner of Fellows and Fourteenth Streets. Lewis came off the worse and in his rage shot a fourteen-year-old Welsh boy, John Thomas, who with around two hundred others had gathered to witness the scene.[49] Nor was it only Welsh males who had a tendency towards violent conduct. In July 1889 Officers John Thomas and Thomas Lewis arrested a Mrs Roberts and a Mrs

[45] Broehl, op. cit., pp. 181, 213–18, 228, 331; *Drych*, 12 Mar. 1885.
[46] Scranton *Morning Republican*, 5 May 1872.
[47] Ibid., 20 June 1871.
[48] Berthoff, 'Social order', pp. 266–7.
[49] *Scranton Republican*, 3 May 1893.

Lewis and her child after a drunken disturbance in Mrs Bratton's saloon in Sweetland Street, Hyde Park.[50]

The Welsh had quarrels within their own families. Wife-beating was not unknown, and occasional scandals of a sexual nature surfaced in the press, indicating that the image of Welsh respectability could not be all-embracing even if it was intended to be so. Within the space of two months in 1889 the *Scranton Republican* reported at least three cases of Hyde Park Welshmen assaulting their wives or other members of their families. In September John E. Jones of Sweetland Street was arrested for deserting his wife and ill-treating her. That same month David Pearce, a frequent offender apparently, was arraigned for abusing his family and disturbing neighbours at their home in Sumner Avenue. His behaviour included tearing the clothes off his wife, a well-known fortune-teller in the city. The following month William Evans of Jackson Street was gaoled for assaulting his sister when drunk and for resisting arrest.[51]

Bigamy, desertion and adultery were other features of the society. Nor is this surprising, perhaps, considering that for long periods of time marriage ties stretched across the Atlantic and the boarding system presented opportunities unimaginable within the confines of the nuclear family.[52] One of the most striking aspects of the reports of Poor Board meetings in Scranton throughout the late nineteenth century is the number of claims for allowances by women on the grounds of desertion by their husbands. The *Scranton Republican* reported in May 1901 that 50 per cent of cases at such meetings involved women, mostly young wives with large families.[53] Welsh wives were no exception to the general pattern. At the meeting of the Poor Board in July 1889 – at which a few prominent Scranton Welshmen sat in judgement, as it were – both Mrs Mary Ann Jones and Mrs May Price of Hyde Park applied for allowances

---

[50] Ibid., 27 July 1889.
[51] Ibid., 27 Sept., 24 Oct., 16 Aug. 1889. Our written record of the Welsh in Scranton reveals little regarding the tensions which undoubtedly did exist between family members and which could sometimes lead to disturbances. For a study of this theme in the context of south-west Wales see Russell Davies, 'Voices from the void: social crisis, social problems and the individual in south-west Wales, *c*. 1876–1920' in Geraint H. Jenkins and J. Beverley Smith (eds.), *Politics and Society in Wales 1840–1922. Essays in Honour of Ieuan Gwynedd Jones* (Cardiff, 1988), pp. 81–91.
[52] Berthoff, 'Social order', p. 287.
[53] *Scranton Republican*, 4 May 1901.

as they had been deserted by their husbands.[54] For some Welsh male immigrants, starting a new life in America sometimes involved starting with a new wife, even if she was neither the first nor legally entitled to be the second. In a community which kept a watchful eye on, and perhaps an even more acute ear for, such developments, the custom of 'horning' both took seed and flourished. The Scranton Carlithargian Band blew their brass instruments outside Charles Jenkins's house on his wedding night in September 1881 because it was rumoured he already had a wife in Wales.[55] Thomas Morgan and Mary J. Lewis were reported to have had a 'lovely wedding' in Hyde Park in March 1878, but the celebrations were marred later by small boys horning and throwing stones. One of them, Benjamin Davis, was arrested.[56] The 'sensation of the day and the topic of conversation in Minooka' in August 1891 was the elopement of Mrs Henry Davis, a woman in her forties, with a 26-year-old former boarder, George Andrews. Apparently, the liaison had been going on for some time and had occasioned a great deal of local gossip. As well as taking six of her seven children, Mrs Davis also took all portable items in the house, including carpets, pictures, beds and chairs. The deserted husband, Henry Davis, described as 'a man who bears on his face the miners' diploma, blue marks, the result of an accident discoloring every feature', was the inside foreman at the National mine and the couple had formerly lived in Hyde Park before moving nearer to Davis's place of work two years earlier.[57]

Paternity suits involving Welshmen occasionally came before the courts. Thomas T. Evans, of Evans & Thomas, Grocers, Hyde Park, was arraigned in January 1893 on charges of being the father of the four-month-old child of Miss Theodosia Morgan. Miss Morgan had emigrated from Wales three years earlier, and the couple had become intimate after she had begun to buy provisions from the defendant's store. For his defence, Evans was able to draw on the best resources available in the Hyde Park Welsh community. His attorney was the eminent H. M. Edwards, and the insurance agent, Daniel J. Evans,

---

[54] Ibid., 6 July 1889.
[55] Ibid., 9 Sept. 1881.
[56] Ibid., 25 Mar. 1878. 'Horning' as a form of community protest has strong echoes of 'rough music' or 'charivari'. See Rosemary Jones, loc. cit.
[57] Ibid., 12 Aug. 1891.

testified to his good character. After an examination of the baby, the jury failed to agree. It was rumoured that the jury's vote was eleven to one in favour of Miss Morgan and that the sole dissenter was himself soon to be the defendant in a similar case. To the *Scranton Republican* the episode was 'another clear illustration of the depravity that exists on the West Side'.[58] Adultery, too, was by no means uncommon among the Welsh. John T. Jones, proprietor of Jones' Hotel on Lackawanna Avenue, was charged with being criminally intimate with a Miss Emma Brown. Mrs Jones appeared before the Poor Board and expressed her intention of suing for desertion.[59] Even ministers of religion were not above immorality, no doubt to the horror of the local Welsh churches. A young preacher from Rhymney, John Hindes, attempted to have intercourse with a Mary Ellen Davies in June 1883. After failing, he drank a bottle of laudanum and almost lost his life. Not surprisingly perhaps, he was expelled from his church and was reputed to be joining the Mormons.[60]

The Welsh in Scranton indulged in pastimes and amusements other than eisteddfodau and musical and literary gatherings organized by the Welsh churches and various societies. In some cases, such as prize fighting and cock-fighting, these consisted of traditions brought from Wales, relics of that pre-industrial culture which had been transferred to the new industrial areas of south Wales and which to more respectable Welsh opinion reeked of idleness and immorality.[61] In others, new American recreations, notably baseball, were embraced.

As we have already seen, the participation of the Welsh in dog-fighting, cock-fighting and prize fighting was scathingly condemned in the adverse reports in the *Drych* in the early 1870s on the morality of the Welsh community, especially as such contests often took place on Sundays. Welsh people were both spectators and gamblers at these events whilst, despite their illegality, some Welshmen were at the centre of the limelight.

[58] Ibid., 26, 28 Jan. 1893. See also Russell Davies, 'Voices from the void'.
[59] Ibid., 8 Feb. 1890.
[60] *Drych*, 21 June 1883.
[61] See Martin Barclay, 'Aberdare, 1880–1914: class and community' (unpublished University of Wales M.A. Thesis, 1985) for details of foot racing, cock-fighting and mountain fighting in Aberdare in the late nineteenth century. Like Scranton, Aberdare was hailed as 'Athen Cymru' and, like Scranton, there was a constant effort to keep the lid on an explosive world of popular culture (pp. 83–7).

Welsh prize-fighters were numerous in the 1860s and 1870s, no doubt willing to risk arrest in pursuit of the often considerable financial rewards and status – or notoriety – which victory brought. Some fights could be marathon affairs. The Welshman and the Englishman who fought on the outskirts of Scranton in July 1860 pummelled each other for a remarkable 195 rounds before the latter was declared the winner.[62] Two years later, a Welshman named Reese, aged twenty-four and weighing 190 lb, took on an Englishman named Elliot, aged forty-five and weighing 145 lb, in Hyde Park. Despite his age and weight Reese needed 102 rounds and nearly two hours to defeat his opponent.[63] The Scranton Welsh community could also breed its potential champions. The *Scranton Republican* reported in June 1882 that David Lewis, alias 'Dai Benlas', a former Welsh resident of the city, wanted to fight the well-known prize-fighter, Tom Wallis of Colorado.[64] Whether the contest actually took place, however, is not known.

Other sporting pursuits also offered opportunities for the Welsh to be spectators, gamblers or participants. A pay-day in September 1889 was the occasion for a jumping match between Evan Edmunds and Daniel Lewis, two Hyde Park Welsh miners. The winner received a prize of three dollars.[65] Stakes at foot races were often much higher. John Jones defeated George German in a foot race at the West Side Park in June 1890 and was $150 dollars the richer for this win.[66] In July 1889 a number of athletic contests took place at the Bellevue Baseball Ground, including a foot race between two Welshmen and a quoits game between a Welshman and an Englishman.[67] Another popular game among the Welsh was billiards. Scranton had a number of billiard saloons which catered for all nationalities, whilst Reynold's Billiard Rooms occupied a central location in Hyde Park in the years after the Civil War.[68] Even the Robert Morris Lodge of Ivorites installed a pool table in their meeting place in

---

[62] Wilkes-Barre *Record of the Times*, 4 July 1860.
[63] Ibid., 2 July 1862.
[64] *Scranton Republican*, 14 June 1882.
[65] Ibid., 6 Sept. 1889.
[66] Ibid., 27 May 1890.
[67] Ibid., 6, 12 July 1889.
[68] Scranton *Morning Republican*, 29 Apr. 1871; *Webb's Scranton Directory*, 1870–1; *Williams' Scranton Directory*, 1890.

1900, though it insisted that the new facility was to be governed by strict rules.[69]

It was baseball which rapidly emerged as the major sport for Welsh immigrants, and especially their children, and a Welsh-American football team, the Welsh Stars, was certainly in existence in Scranton in 1889.[70] Welsh immigrants may have started to play baseball as soon as they arrived in the city. As early as 1867, Hyde Park had an OKBBC baseball team, which had at least six Welsh members.[71] Welsh players were involved in the baseball matches which followed the drill practices of the local militia during the 1871 strike, whilst Welsh teams representing wards 4 and 5 often played each other.[72] Baseball offered the opportunity for the Welsh to mix with other nationalities – and in some cases the chance of a free-for-all fight.[73] Some Welsh even became good at the game. In 1883 Gomer Price of Hyde Park refused an offer to play ball for a team in Leadville, Colorado, for $100 a month, an invitation which resulted from the good impression he had made there the previous summer. The Hyde Park Welsh community also bred in John Hopkins one of the foremost baseball players in Plymouth, Pennsylvania, in the late nineteenth century.[74] Even the summer 'Welsh Days' during the early years of the twentieth century had their scheduled baseball matches, further reflecting the 'American' character of those occasions and the societies which organized them. In 1910, for example, a team of Scranton 'Druids' took on a similar team from Olyphant.[75]

The growing embrace of the 'Great National Game' and the sporting culture of their adopted land illustrates the acculturation and Americanization of the Welsh. Like rugby or soccer in Wales, the rapid growth of organized sport in general and its mass popularity echoed the vast social and cultural changes wrought by industrialization. American historians have increasingly emphasized the role of baseball as a far more effective unifier of American nationality than school or history

---

[69] *Scranton Republican*, 28 Jan. 1900.
[70] Ibid., 24 Aug. 1889.
[71] *Pittston Gazette*, 3 Sept. 1867.
[72] Scranton *Morning Republican*, 15 Mar., 4 Apr. 1871.
[73] Ibid., 20 Mar. 1871.
[74] *Scranton Republican*, 17 June 1883, 30 Sept. 1889.
[75] *Druid*, 16 June 1910.

texts. By playing baseball and – though the nature of the evidence makes it difficult to detect – even more so by being in the crowd at the ballgame, the Welsh in Scranton became American.[76]

The Welsh danced, too, despite Phoebe Gibbons's claim in 1877 that 'dancing is generally considered a heinous sin among the Welsh' and that 'the ministers denounce balls and dancing as they would manslaughter or murder.'[77] The *Scranton Republican* noted in March 1901 that the Friday night dancing classes at Mears Hall in Hyde Park attracted 'a strong Welsh presence' – presumably of both sexes.[78] Nor were the musical activities of the Welsh restricted to choirs, hymns and classical music. Half of the members of the Providence Brass Band formed in June 1870 were Welsh (the other half were Irish), and so too were the majority of the thirty original members of the 'Home Guards' band formed in 1885.[79] All but one of the founders of the Fife and Drum Corps in Hyde Park in the last decade of the nineteenth century were also Welsh, whilst the Druid Society established a Druid Brass Band in 1907.[80]

As in the case of baseball, the nature of contemporary sources of evidence makes it difficult to assess whether Welsh people frequented the music-halls in Scranton. Unlike the eisteddfod, which is a cultural event directed primarily at one paticular ethnic group, music-halls, like baseball, cater for the public in general. The problem of the lack of sources in this respect is compounded by the fact that we are dealing with people who rarely leave written evidence of the way they led their lives. Nevertheless, like the Welsh in Wales, most Welsh in Scranton undoubtedly partook of the entertainment offered by the music-hall and, later, the cinema.[81] The growing popularity and

---

[76] See David Quentin Voight, *American Baseball*, vols. I and II (Pennsylvania State University Press reprint, 1983); Rosenzweig, op. cit., pp. 189–90; Maldwyn A. Jones, *The Limits of Liberty*, pp. 334–5. For rugby in Wales see David Smith and Gareth Williams, *Fields of Praise: The Official History of the Welsh Rugby Union, 1881–1981* (Cardiff, 1980). See also David Smith, 'Back to the future', *Planet*, 56 (Apr./May 1986), pp. 14–25, (at 22–24), for the importance of the history of organized sport and popular culture generally in Wales.

[77] Gibbons, loc. cit., p. 918.

[78] *Scranton Republican*, 30 Mar. 1901.

[79] Scranton *Morning Republican*, 21 Mar. 1871; *Drych*, 7 May 1886.

[80] *Scranton Republican*, 9 May 1893; *Druid*, 26 Sept. 1907.

[81] One music-hall theatre in Scranton even occupied the old Welsh Baptist Church on Pennsylvania Avenue after 1907. *Drych*, 2 May 1907.

importance of commercialized forms of amusement and their role in changing cultural and leisure patterns in America during the late nineteenth and early twentieth centuries are also being emphasized by historians. The music-hall, the amusement park and, above all, the cinema were potent instruments in creating a new national mass culture shared by workers, immigrants and the middle class.[82] One Welsh-American popular entertainer, at least, made a lucrative career out of the music-hall. Born in Rhondda and brought up in Plymouth, Pennsylvania, George 'Honey Boy' Evans was described in 1910 as the 'king-pin of minstrel land' and the highest-paid minstrel artist in America.[83]

By 1910, George 'Honey Boy' Evans was more representative than Joseph Parry. Certainly, on the streets of his native Rhondda in 1910, it was music-hall songs and popular ditties that the striking colliers and the women folk of mid-Rhondda were singing. The 'definition of community' that was proceeding under the guise of an industrial dispute in Tonypandy[84] was just as apparent in Scranton. When the Welsh-American newspapers discussed Tonypandy, however, it was with as much scorn and concern as their Welsh equivalents had done. The riots of mid-November 1910 were the work of the irresponsible, of hooligans and of strangers. The *Druid* regretted that 'the most notorious scenes in the history of the South Wales Coalfield' had marred the 'good name' of the district but reassured its readers that no malice had been intended. Nevertheless, it condemned the actions 'of irresponsible youths who were prompted more by a desire for mischief than the wanton destruction of property'.[85]

The reality of Wales was unacceptable to many within the 'old country': how much more so to those who needed Wales, as they imagined it, to act as an example to their fellow-Americans and as a counterbalance to the disturbing lives of their fellow-Welsh-Americans. In the end the development of Wales would be such as to leave some Welsh-Americans in no doubt that they

---

[82] See Rosenzweig, op. cit., pp. 171–222. For the impact of the early commercialized leisure industry in the Rhondda Valley, see David Smith, 'Tonypandy, 1910: definitions of community', *Past and Present*, 87 (May 1980), pp. 158–84, 169–72. See also Stead, loc. cit.

[83] *Druid*, 14 July 1910. Evans penned the popular hit 'In the Good Old Summertime'.

[84] See David Smith, 'Tonypandy 1910', loc. cit.

[85] *Druid*, 24 Nov. 1910.

were more 'Welsh' than those who lived in Wales. At this point of climax in Welsh-America's progress, it was still possible, indeed vital, to highlight the 'modern' or progressive aspects of contemporary Welsh life that could be deemed to have evolved properly from Welsh tradition. The history made no sense if it could not be shown, in the present state of Wales, to speak for a Welsh-American future.

II A WALES FOR AMERICA

In January 1908, the *Druid* printed a long article from an unnamed correspondent who attributed the recent marked decline in the slate industry in Wales to the disastrous effects of the 1900-3 Penrhyn dispute.[86] According to the writer, the lock-out had enabled foreign competition to gain a foothold in the home market which it had succeeded in retaining, to the detriment of the north Walian industry. The writer maintained that a conciliation board could possibly have averted the conflict and prevented its ruinous consequences. The article was accompanied by an editorial on the same subject which declared that the fate of the slate industry emphasized the importance of an awareness among employers and employees of the necessity of arbitration and conciliation. Strikes meant ruin for all. When both sides in a dispute failed or refused to reach an agreement, a strong hand such as that of Lloyd George ought to intervene and insist on arbitration in order to prevent the ruin of industry and 'the breaking up of hundreds of happy homes'. The editorial continued by contrasting the disastrous effects of the Penrhyn lock-out with the situation prevailing in the coal industry in south Wales:

> Mabon, the successful leader of the organised hosts of South Wales is the great Apostle of Peace and Conciliation and what a different and happier picture is presented in the thickly populated Vales of Glamorgan, where a board of conciliation has been at work for years. Wages are higher than ever and have, in fact, reached the maximum limit, advance after advance being conceded by the employers with comparative cheerfulness.

---

[86] Ibid., 23 Jan. 1908. For details of the 1900-3 Penrhyn dispute, see R. Merfyn Jones, *The North Wales Quarrymen, 1874-1922* (Cardiff, 1982), pp. 210-66.

> Mabon teaches us that a strike must be absolutely the last resort when everything else has failed and he also preaches that there shall be no such thing as 'fail'.[87]

The *Druid*'s comparison between the apparent success of conciliation in south Wales and the consequences of the lack of it in the north highlights the way in which the Welsh-American press, and that newspaper in particular, took the opportunity to praise the value of conciliation on every possible occasion. The extolling of its virtues and those of William Abraham M.P. ('Mabon'), with whom it was identified, was central to the Welsh-American perception of a 'Welsh' response to industrial relations.

In stark contrast to the tone and extent of the coverage of industrial disputes (which was relatively sparse, and commentaries on them even more so), the success of Conciliation Board agreements or settlements in general between the south Wales miners and the coalowners were frequently and glowingly reported. The imbalance in the reporting is perhaps in itself an indication that conciliation was regarded as the dominant and most influential factor in relations between masters and men in south Wales. The *Druid* also explicitly articulated its views on the desirability of conciliation and its importance to Wales on a number of occasions. In September 1907 an editorial announced that industrial peace had been secured in south Wales by a recent Conciliation Board agreement. Strikes had brought disaster in the past, it maintained, but now the miners had come to realize that such conflicts were ruinous. As long as capital and labour were loyal to each other, prosperity was guaranteed. The Conciliation Board had brought higher wages and increased confidence and stability.[88] A year later another editorial in the same newspaper proudly proclaimed that the triumph of conciliation had heralded 'the dawn of peace in the South Wales coalfield' because a crisis which had threatened a strike had been averted. It was an object lesson in the peaceful method of settling disputes and the newspaper congratulated both sides on realizing that

---

[87] *Druid*, 23 Jan. 1908.
[88] Ibid., 5 Sept. 1907. For details of the Conciliation Board, first set up in 1903, and its agreements, see R. Page Arnot, *South Wales Miners: A History of the South Wales Miners' Federation*, vol. 1: *1898–1914* (Cardiff, 1967), pp. 76–104, 113–23, 139–55, 162–81, 264–71, 277.

their respective standpoints were not, and should not be, incompatible:

> The interests of both are essentially mutual and vitally involved are the interests of the community... Both realized that not only their interests, but their duty, lay in putting in force the machinery for peace which the Conciliation Board offers.[89]

Because it secured peace and prosperity, conciliation was in the best interests of all sections of the community, not only capital and labour. By implication, it was also in the best interests of Wales. In this respect the *Druid* was undoubtedly defining industrial relations – and with it Welsh interests – in the context of the Liberal, Nonconformist philosophy of consensus which prevailed in Wales during the late nineteenth and early twentieth centuries.[90] Yet in emphasizing the harmony between the interests of capital and labour, it is perhaps significant that the *Druid* introduced the word 'duty'. It suggests that consensus was regarded as an ideal that all Welsh people should accept and strive for, and a framework within which all should act for the common good. Consensus was thus defined as the national interest and, as such, it was an integral element of 'Welshness'. Implicitly, any behaviour outside it or contrary to it was un-Welsh or, to use David Smith's phrase, 'potentially anti-national'.[91]

If, according to Welsh-American literary opinion, conciliation and consensus should be lauded and encouraged, those who above all represented these ideals were certain to be included in its pantheon of heroes. It is in this context that the eulogizing of Mabon and the almost compulsory inclusion of his name and opinions in Welsh-American writing on industrial relations and disputes in Wales need to be seen.[92] Mabon was undoubtedly a popular figure among the Welsh in the United States. During 1901–2 he spent three months touring Ohio, Pennsylvania and New York State, lecturing, preaching and

---

[89] *Druid*, 25 Mar. 1908.

[90] For a discussion of the close links between the Liberal Party and radical Nonconformity and their role as the most powerful force in Welsh social, political and cultural life during the late nineteenth and early twentieth centuries, see K. O. Morgan, *Rebirth of a Nation*, pp. 26–58, 94–122, 134–42.

[91] David Smith, *Wales! Wales?*, p. 29.

[92] For the life and career of William Abraham (1842–1922), see E. W. Evans, *Mabon: A Study in Trade Union Leadership* (Cardiff, 1959).

delivering addresses. Welsh-Americans in those states gave him an outstanding reception, whilst his tour through the Wyoming and Lackawanna Valleys, the heartlands of the Welsh, was a particular triumph.[93] As a Welsh-speaker, lay preacher, teetotaller, bard, singer and keen eisteddfodwr, Mabon represented all the virtues that the Welsh-American press saw as being essentially 'Welsh'.[94] But above all it was his active labours on behalf of conciliation which earned him tributes that were second only to those showered on Lloyd George.

Mabon was the arch-exponent of the necessity for capital and labour to work together. It was a gospel he took with him to the United States in 1904–5, when, as a delegate of the Trades Union Congress, he spent most of his time advocating conciliation as a means of avoiding disputes in American industry.[95] To Welsh-American literary opinion he was the most obvious example of the working man's responsible leader, one who constantly worked for peace, stability, improvement and, in their definition, progress. 'We should not overlook the personal character,' declared the *Cambrian* during his visit in 1902, 'and his national labors on the lines of civilization ... in his position as Miners' President and a representative of labor he is pre-eminently a man of peace and a persistent advocate of arbitration.'[96]

Apart from congratulating Mabon for his views on industrial relations, the Welsh-American press was equally keen to articulate what it saw as the logical consequence of his endeavours. In January 1911 a *Druid* editorial welcomed his recent appointment as a Privy Councillor and took the opportunity to assess the miners' leader's significance in contemporary Welsh life.[97] His appointment, it declared, was long deserved. He had filled, and was filling, a unique role in the affairs of labour since his unswerving sense of right and justice made him the trusted adviser of both employer and employee.

---

[93] *South Wales Daily News*, 3 Jan. 1902; *Cambrian*, XXII (Jan. 1902), p. 49; E. W. Evans, op. cit., pp. 67–8. Mabon's welcome occasioned H. M. Edwards to remark that no Welshman had been received with greater enthusiasm. See also *Cyfaill o'r Hen Wlad*, LXV (Jan. 1902), p. 47, for Mabon's own account of the visit and a glowing tribute to Welsh-Americans.

[94] *Cambrian*, XXIII (Nov. 1903), p. 439; E. W. Evans, op. cit., pp. 44–5.

[95] Ibid., p. 68.

[96] *Cambrian*, XXII (Jan. 1902) p. 49.

[97] *Druid*, 12 Jan. 1911. For Mabon's appointment, see E. W. Evans, op. cit., p. 95.

According to the newspaper, there could not be a more suitable adviser to the king on labour matters or in judging and prescribing the needs of the miner. However, although it maintained that the right to adopt the prefix 'Rt. Hon.' was a great triumph,

> what title or honor could this king confer on him that is not overshadowed by the name that will forever live amongst the Welsh people – the name that has the love and respect not only of his own people, but of all people who recognise merit and worth . . . [The] name of Mabon will live when that of the Rt. Hon. William Abraham is forgotten.[98]

The eulogizing of Mabon and his centrality to Welsh life were therefore essential elements in promoting an image of Wales in which all people worked together in order to further the national interest. But if he represented Welsh interests so comprehensively, how was the increasing undermining of his influence and the growing militancy among the miners in the south Wales coalfield from the turn of the century onwards to be explained?[99] It was a question that worried one correspondent to the *Drych* during the Cambrian Combine Strike. The correspondent wondered why Mabon was under attack from within the ranks of the miners when it was clear he was the best leader they could ever hope for.[100] It is in this context, perhaps, that the true significance of a *Druid* accusation that the Cambrian Combine Strike had been caused by greedy and ambitious miners lies. In November 1910 an editorial maintained:

> It is feared that the present trouble has been precipitated largely by men who are all anxious to depose the leaders so that they may secure their positions and salaries. That selfish personal ambition should bring about such suffering and sorrow to thousands is most deplorable.[101]

---

[98] *Druid*, 12 Jan. 1911.
[99] For discussions of the major social and industrial upheavals in the coal industry in the years leading up to the First World War and the dramatic and irrevocable social, economic and political changes which engulfed the coalfield and undercut 'Mabonism' and consensus, see Martin Barclay, op. cit.; Hywel Francis and David Smith, *The Fed: A History of the South Wales Miners in the Twentieth Century* (London, 1980), pp. 1–28; Kenneth O. Morgan, 'The new liberalism and the challenge of labour: the Welsh experience, 1885–1929', *Welsh History Review*, VI (1973), pp. 288–312; R. Page Arnot, op. cit., vol 1; David Smith, 'Tonypandy 1910', loc. cit.; L. J. Williams, 'The road to Tonypandy', *Llafur*, 1, No. 2 (Summer 1973), pp. 41–2.
[100] *Drych*, 29 Dec. 1910.
[101] *Druid*, 17 Nov. 1910.

Ultimately, the definitions of Welshness nurtured by leading Welsh-Americans in their actions and words could not accommodate the internal conflicting forces in Wales that were challenging the prevailing Welsh liberal social philosophy of a community of interest.[102] Consequently, indications of behaviour which clashed with the accepted image, or signs of alternative cultural and political traditions, had to be dismissed as the work either of those acting out of dubious motives or of 'alien' or un-'Welsh' influences. During the 1898 six-month lock-out in the south Wales coalfield, the *Cambrian* implied such an explanation when it reported that the population of Rhondda 'at working times appears homogeneous and Welsh to a remarkable degree, but during the present strike, the foreign element seems to be much in evidence.'[103] Two years later the same magazine asserted that 'it has been well observed that the Welsh language contains no word for strike in the industrial sense of the word. The word, like the practice, was imported from England.'[104]

The Welsh-American belief that a propensity to strike was not a feature of the Welsh character was influenced by assumptions regarding Welsh docility, and these were themselves bound up with one of the linchpins of the defined 'Welshness': loyalty. As Hywel Teifi Edwards has shown, promoting the image of 'Cymru Lân, Cymru Lonydd' ('Pure Wales, Placid Wales') became a major priority of leading spokesmen in Wales from the mid-nineteenth century onwards.[105] They strove to show England that Welsh people, in contrast to the increasingly intransigent Irish, were loyal, untroublesome subjects of the British Crown. The epitome of this image, as the same historian has pointed out, was *Punch*'s description of the Welshman as the

---

[102] These conflicting interests were most forcefully demonstrated by the succession of industrial disputes and disturbances in the coal industry and other sectors of the economy from the end of the nineteenth century onwards. As David Smith has suggested, the inescapable paradox of the period was that the very economic vitality that made possible the flowering of the 'national revival' was also undercutting the social basis on which the notion of Welsh unity was dependent. It created powerful combines and a Welsh proletariat, and forced a cleavage between industrial Wales and the rural areas which provided the template for 'Welsh' values. See *idem*, 'Wales through the looking glass', loc. cit., pp. 220–33.
[103] *Cambrian*, XVIII (July 1898), p. 328.
[104] Ibid., XX (Oct. 1900), p. 469.
[105] Hywel Teifi Edwards, *Gŵyl Gwalia*, pp. 379–98; *idem*, 'Victorian Wales seeks reinstatement', pp. 12–17.

'Jolly Little Brick'. In their efforts to achieve this, aspects of a radical political tradition among the Welsh, notably Chartism and the Rebecca Riots, were all too often deliberately ignored by the country's leading spokesmen.[106]

A similar process occurred among the Welsh in America, where the need for an image of loyalty and docility was perhaps even more important, given their status as an immigrant group. Indeed, the World's Fair Eisteddfod and the American Gorsedd can be seen as major efforts to nurture this image and to encourage the belief that, as a Josiah Perry informed his audience at a St David's Day banquet in New York in 1888, 'no-one has heard of a Welsh anarchist.'[107] It is not perhaps surprising, therefore, that a similar erasing of certain unpalatable aspects of Welsh history could also occur among the writings of Welsh observers in America. A striking illustration of this was a letter which a certain Aneurin Jones of New York wrote to the *Cambrian* and the *New York Times* in 1902, to complain of distortions which had appeared in the latter's review of O. M. Edwards's *Wales*. Apparently the reviewer had maintained that during the nineteenth century in Wales, Chartism and the Rebecca Riots had been the first signs of political discontent. To Jones this was

> ... an entirely false accusation. The leaders of Chartism were English and Irish ... but it extended partly to Wales and the only Welshman among the Chartists was Zephaniah Williams of the 'Frost, Williams and Jones' indicted as leaders in the attack on the Westgate, Newport ... which ended all Chartist agitation. To call the Rebecca movement a Welsh political discontent is wrong. That movement had not the least political aspect, neither was it national, but a local complaint against the commissioners of highways, principally in the counties of Glamorgan and Carmarthenshire in consequence of the toll-gates being too numerous, neither were there any riots connected with it but the quiet removal of the objectionable toll-gates by night.[108]

There are undoubtedly elements of truth in Jones's assertions. There are also revealing historical omissions and distortions, notably the extent of the support which Chartism, using

---

[106] *Idem, Gŵyl Gwalia*, pp. 379–98. See also David Smith, 'Wales through the looking glass', loc. cit., p. 220.
[107] *Cambrian*, VIII (Feb. 1888), pp. 57–8.
[108] Ibid., XXII (July 1902), p. 329.

physical force, attracted in Wales, and the violence which accompanied the Rebecca attacks on toll-gates and the ransacking of Carmarthen workhouse in 1842.[109] Evidently Jones's belief was that Welsh people had not engaged, and did not engage, in violent or even peaceful action and, moreover, that such behaviour was an inherently un-Welsh activity. The Welsh-American defining of what it meant to be Welsh was accompanied by a clear conception of what Welshness was not.

The attitude of Welsh-American literary opinion towards industrial disputes in Wales, therefore, suggests that it echoed the belief in the Liberal–Nonconformist consensus, with its emphasis on the common interests of all Welsh people, which prevailed in the homeland in the nineteenth and early twentieth centuries. Strikes and disturbances such as those at Tonypandy and elsewhere were direct challenges to the perceived mutuality of Welsh interests, and they clashed with the image of a peaceful, loyal, docile Wales. These clear manifestations of deviance from defined notions of Welshness consequently had to be explained as aberrations, the work of foreign elements, and in terms of individuals acting out of dubious motives.

The explanation and ultimate dismissal of contrary behaviour as being un-Welsh were not confined to the turbulence of industrial relations in Wales. Although they are scattered and fragmentary, there are sufficient incidents and commentaries throughout contemporary Welsh-American sources to support the conclusion that in fact the denial of the epithet 'Welsh' was a stock response to any adverse criticism of the nature of Welshness as defined by Welsh-American literary opinion. In February 1911, for example, a *Druid* editorial focused on the question of the contemporary state of religion in Wales. It noted that a number of Welsh ministers were openly expressing fears that Welsh religiosity was waning and chapel attendance was beginning to decline. The newspaper, however, had its own interpretation of the situation:

> There is a suspicion that these same preachers who yelled about irreligious Wales were hungry for notoriety. Their hunger has been

---

[109] For the Rebecca disturbances, see David J. V. Jones, *Rebecca's Children: A Study of Rural Society, Crime and Protest* (Oxford, 1989). For Chartism, see idem, *The Last Rising; The Newport Insurrection of 1839* (Oxford, 1985).

appeased, but at great cost – at the cost of their reputation as fair-minded men, messengers of truth, ambassadors of love and – not the least – patriots of the Land of the Gospel.[110]

The editorial continued by proclaiming that on Sundays in Wales the streets were deserted during the hours of divine service because everyone was at worship. There was little profanity on the streets and in public places compared with other countries, whilst, in general, according to official statistics, Wales was the most crime-free country in the world, earning it the title of 'Gwlad y Menyg Gwynion' ('The Land of the White Gloves'). According to the *Druid*, the main factor which determined this state of affairs was the intense religiosity of the Welsh people.[111]

In dismissing the reports of anxious ministers as the product of unwholesome, and ultimately un-Welsh, motives and accompanying its denunciation with a categoric restatement of the religiosity of the Welsh, the *Druid*'s editorial illustrated a pattern which can be detected in much of the Welsh-American writing seeking to accommodate contrary evidence. Indications which threatened the dominant image of what it meant to be Welsh – whether factual or not – were often greeted with forthright denial, usually of an abusive nature, and followed by an even more outspoken reaffirmation of the image. Similarly, any criticism, from whatever quarter, of Welsh people or Welsh things was treated in like fashion. Besmirching the name of Wales was regarded as an affront, and it occasioned contemptuous indignation – and abusive rejoinder. In September 1910, for example, the *Druid* reacted violently to an editorial in the *New York Times* which suggested that the decision to hold the investiture ceremony of the Prince of Wales at Caernarfon the following year had caused great friction between north and south Wales. The editorial was dismissed as having been written by 'a monocled Saxon who cannot see that any good can come from Wales', and was denounced for its 'sneering, contemptuous references to Gwalia Wen'.[112] Indeed the English often suffered stab-wounds from Welsh-American knives if they dared to tarnish the glorious sheen of Welshness.

[110] *Druid*, 9 Feb. 1911.
[111] Ibid.
[112] Ibid., 1 Sept. 1910.

An article in the *Saturday Review* in 1912 which dismissed Welsh claims to be a musical nation only showed, according to the *Druid*, 'the incapability of the Saxon of judging the Cymro sympathetically'. Besides, it retorted, there was 'more music in one inch on top of Snowdon than in any square mile in England'.[113]

Attacks on Welshness by non-Welsh people could ultimately be dismissed as the product of ignorance. When dissenting voices were raised by Welsh people, however, the vilification directed at Anglo-Saxon criticism was muted in comparison. Complaints about the blind adoration of all things Welsh, which was one of the most striking features of the Welsh-American press during the late nineteenth and early twentieth centuries, were sometimes reported. More often than not the impression is conveyed that such comments were given space in order to enable abusive refutation. An illuminating episode in this respect was the impact of a letter written to the *Druid* by William Howells of Garfield, Utah, in February 1909. Howells wrote to complain about the vast amount of fulsome praise which its correspondents, especially John Courier Morris of Scranton and John T. Richards of Philadelphia, showered on the Welsh. Their attitude, he believed, was both offensive and unjustified:

> In my opinion there is nothing more nauseating as [*sic*] this ever constant overwhelming praise of the Welsh and of Welsh things simply and solely because they are Welsh and not on account of any intrinsic merit they possess. Doubtless there are many people other than Welsh reading your paper and I can well imagine how absurd and silly such egotism must appear to them. Personally I was born in Carmarthenshire and am thoroughly Welsh in sentiment, yet I must confess I feel chagrined at the display of nonsense and absurdities such praise must evoke to intelligent readers.
>
> Unfortunately the Welsh people have never had the chance of developing their talents until within very recent years . . . consequently this extravagant flattery of things Welsh is uncalled for and, furthermore, not warranted by facts . . . [since] the various 'Dago' countries have produced men and are producing men of greater international renown.
>
> Facing these facts, for goodness sake let us be a little more modest and less assuming in our self-esteem . . . We Welsh make big pretence of being intensely religious, referring continually to Wales as being 'Gwlad y Breintiau Mawr' . . . Considering this presumptuous [*sic*] claim which

[113] Ibid., 26 Sept. 1912.

practically amounts to God's chosen race, the fact is . . . we are not a whit better than we ought to be.[114]

Howells's plea for reason and moderation was anathema to a newspaper such as the *Druid* which dedicated itself to boosting Welsh interests incessantly and proclaiming the excellence of Welsh people on every possible occasion.[115] Its reaction was swift and uncompromising. The editor, T. Owen Charles, was first off the mark, advising Howells to take some dyspepsia tablets to make him feel better.[116] The following week, John T. Richards took the opportunity, during his reporting of the Philadelphia Cambro-American League's celebrations of the anniversary of the birth of the great 'Welsh' statesman, Abraham Lincoln (the previous issue of the *Druid* had trimphantly announced that he was of Welsh blood), to confirm his editor's diagnosis of Howells's complaint and to offer the same antidote. He was convinced that 'the difficulty in all probability with Mr Howells lies in the fact that no-one has perceived in him signs of greatness and heralded this to the Welsh of this and other countries.' Furthermore, Richards stated that he was only too pleased to be placed in the same category as that 'artistic writer', J. Courier Morris.[117] The latter, in response to the allegations, merely called Howells a 'slob' who produced manure.[118]

Though minor, this literary altercation was nevertheless characteristic of the way Welsh-Americans reacted to unfavourable criticism of either their conduct or nationality. Rather than attempting to counter Howells's arguments, the responses were aimed at him personally. The impression given is that the correspondents of the *Druid* (and others like them who created the atmosphere of comprehensive hagiography that disgusted Howells) had sufficient confidence to deem an argued response as being either unnecessary or irrelevant. The validity or invalidity of Howells's accusations were, perhaps, of minor concern compared to the general need to defend or glorify the Welsh. To those doing their utmost to make the wider American

[114] Ibid., 11 Feb. 1909.
[115] In July 1907, for example, the *Druid* insisted that the solution to the problem of corruption in the Scranton municipal government and the need for an honest mayor was easy: 'Elect a Welshman'. Ibid., 20 June, 2 July 1907.
[116] Ibid., 11 Feb. 1909.
[117] Ibid., 18 Feb. 1909.
[118] Ibid., 25 Feb. 1909.

public aware of the importance of the Welsh element in the United States, who urged all those with Welsh connections to 'pull together' (a phrase the *Druid* often used)[119] to achieve this, Howells's words were an affront and even dangerous. He had dared to speak out against the prevailing consensus in what was ultimately to be regarded as an act of treachery. Consequently, unworthy motives were attributed to him – in this case indignation at his own failure to be regarded as great – just as those who were deemed responsible for the Cambrian Combine dispute or for spreading rumours of 'irreligious Wales' were condemned for allowing personal ambition to come before the common good. Once identified as a 'traitor', Howells was a justifiable target for insult.

The forthright manner in which the newspaper's correspondents and editor abused Howells also typifies the *Druid*'s style of journalism. Its tone is undoubtedly far removed from the two other major Welsh-American organs, the *Cambrian* and the *Drych*. The *Druid* was a more Americanized journal with a brasher, blustering and ultimately 'American' style. Humbert Nelli has pinpointed the tendency of Italian immigrant newspapers in the United States to imitate the American press in adopting innovations such as bold headlines and including sensational news stories.[120] This was certainly true of the *Druid*, and in its denunciations, at least, it was clearly sensationalizing. The *Western Mail* was perhaps being more perceptive than it realized when it bemusedly reported in August 1907 that 'when a Welshman goes into journalism in the United States he out-Yankees the Yankees.'[121] The notice referred to a recent editorial in the *Druid* on the subject of a letter it had received from a Scrantonian Welshman belittling the Druid Society's first Ladies' Night. After calling the letter-writer a 'notorious ingrate' and a 'cur', amongst other things, the *Druid* concluded: 'He calls himself a Welshman; God forbid. He is a social skunk.'[122]

---

[119] For example, 'All pull together and every man, woman and child will be proud of the day and the strength displayed at Luna Park' was one of the *Druid*'s exhortations to the Welsh to attend the first Scranton 'Welsh Day' in 1907. Ibid., 23 May 1907. See also ibid., 26 Sept., 3 Oct., 14 Nov. 1907, 23 Dec. 1909, 26 Sept. 1912.
[120] Humbert S. Nelli, *The Italians in Chicago, 1880–1930* (New York, 1970), p. 167.
[121] *Western Mail*, 6 Aug. 1907.
[122] Ibid.; *Druid*, 24 July 1907. It is quite possible that the newspaper was reacting to the letter 'Huw Llwyd' wrote to the *Drych* to complain about the 'English' character of the

In his study of modern American literature, *Waiting for the End*, Leslie Fiedler has analysed the type of writing which was a characteristic of late nineteenth- and early twentieth-century immigrant or minority groups. Although he was referring specifically to Jewish-American literature, his words have an equal relevance to the commentaries of Welsh-Americans. 'Regional' writing or 'sub-literature', he notes, is

> ... intended to represent the values and interests of a group which feels itself penalised, even threatened, by the disregard of the larger community. From one side such writing constitutes a literature of self-congratulation and re-assurance, intended to be consumed by an in-group which knows it is abused and suspects that it is hardly noticed by those who abuse it; from another it aims at becoming a literature of public relations, intended to 'sell' that in-group to certain outsiders, who, it is assumed, will respond favourably only to 'positive' i.e. innocuous or untrue images of the excluded group.[123]

Welsh-American writing lies firmly in these categories. There were few novelists, short-story writers or even dramatists among the Welsh in late nineteenth- or early twentieth-century America, despite occasional urgings in the Welsh-American press that they should write more imaginative literature.[124] Those works that were produced, like T. Owen Charles's *Dear Old Wales: A Patriotic Love Story*, and articles in the Welsh-American press in general, are undoubtedly the literature of self-congratulation and glorification. They were intended to reinforce specific images of Wales and Welshness and their meaning in an American context, as well as to parade those virtues before the wider American public.[125] As we have seen, the feeling that Welsh people and their attributes were being ignored or not sufficiently appreciated was a major preoccupation of Welsh- American writing and one which inspired

---

'Ladies' Night'. See above, ch. 3, p. 121.

[123] Leslie A. Fiedler, *Waiting for the End: The American Literary Scene from Hemingway to Baldwin* (New York, 1964), pp. 82–3.

[124] In the *Cambrian* in 1899, for example, a correspondent insisted: 'To take and maintain its proper place among the intellectual and highly civilised nations of the earth ... the Welsh race must produce a Walter Scott, whose literary genius shall reveal to the world in the coming language (English) the achievements of our Welsh heroes as Scott immortalised those of the Scottish race.' Ibid., XIX (Aug. 1899), p. 360.

[125] T. Owen Charles, op. cit.; Revd Erasmus W. Jones, *Llangobaith: A Story of North Wales* (Utica, 1886); David Pugh Griffiths, *The Last of the Quills: A Story of Welsh Life* (Binghampton, 1902); Revd Jonathan Edwards, *The Career of Cadogan Cadwgan* in *Royal Blue Book*, pp. 251–361.

the holding of cultural initiatives at both a local and a national level.

Fiedler continued his analysis by outlining what occurred when ethnic writers moved beyond celebration:

> Regional writing ceases to be sub-literary, however, not when those it portrays are made to seem respectable, but when they are representative (in all their peculiarity) of the larger community... But this only begins to happen when regional writers stop being apologists and become critics, abandon falsification and sentimentality in favour of treating not the special virtues of the group from which they came, whether those virtues be real or fancied, but the weakness it shares with all men. Such writers seem often to their fellows, their very friends and parents, traitors – not only for the very harsh things they are led to say about those fellows, friends and parents in the pursuit of truth, but also because their desire for universality of theme and appeal leads them to begin tearing down from within the walls of a cultural ghetto, which, it turns out, has meant security as well as exclusion to the community that nurtured them.[126]

Welsh-America did not produce a writer to whom Fiedler's analysis could be applied. Perhaps it could not, given that the size of the Welsh immigrant group and its rapid assimilation prevented the emergence of an alternative cultural, political and literary tradition. In Wales itself, however, during the second decade of the twentieth century, there emerged a writer who did perhaps break out of the sub-literary tradition of Welsh congratulatory writing and whose work was greeted with a reaction similar to that which Fiedler suggested was the fate of other such writers. If Welsh-America could not produce a Caradoc Evans it could – and did – contribute to his condemnation. Indeed, the manner in which it did so embraced all the essential elements of the way Welsh-American literary opinion reacted to interpretations of Welshness which conflicted with its own.

Few Welsh writers have received as hostile a reception as Caradoc Evans.[127] The publication of his first volume of short stories, *My People*, in 1915 created an intense furore which would recur after the appearance of each of his works. Non-Welsh

---

[126] Fiedler, op. cit., p. 83.
[127] For biographical details of Caradoc Evans (1878–1945) and discussions of his work, see John Harris (ed.), *Fury Never Leaves Us: A Miscellany of Caradoc Evans* (Bridgend, 1985), pp. 9–45; T. L. Williams, *Caradoc Evans* (Writers of Wales Series, Cardiff, 1970).

critics generally regarded his creative output favourably. In Wales, however, his portraits of a sly, cramped Welsh peasantry were seen as a direct attack on Nonconformist values and notions of Welsh respectability and morality in the rural areas as enshrined in the mythologized image of 'y werin'.[128] Undoubtedly, Evans's writing was a challenge to the prevailing Welsh consensus for, as recent commentators have pointed out, the obverse side of Evans's denunciation of the Welsh peasantry was his own hopes for a proletarian Wales.[129] This was most forcefully expressed in 'The Welsh miner', an article published in the *New Witness* in December 1916 which dealt with the south Wales miners' strike of 1915, a series of events which were not reported in the Welsh-American press. In the article, Evans congratulated the miners on their rebellion not only against the coalowners but also against their religious and erstwhile political leaders, and saw it as a sign of hope for the end of the dominance of Liberal-Nonconformity.[130]

As far as can be detected, the uproar which surrounded the publication of *My People* in 1915, including the attempt to ban the book, was not covered by the Welsh-American press. This is perhaps surprising as even in the United States the book had run to two editions and had been well received.[131] In stark contrast, however, the appearance in America of Evans's second volume of short stories, *Capel Sion*, early in 1919 (it had originally been published in Britain in 1916)[132] attracted a great deal of attention in the *Druid*, though not in other Welsh-American journals or periodicals. The two February issues of the newspaper in that year carried three reviews, two by George W. Bowen, a Scranton Welsh poet originally from Aberdare, Glamorgan, and one by John Courier Morris, the *Druid*'s former long-standing Scranton correspondent, now living in Buffalo. The book and its author were also the subject of a major

[128] John Harris, 'Introduction' to the Seren Books edition of Caradoc Evans's *My People* (Bridgend, 1987), pp. 7–47; M. Wynn Thomas, '*My people* and the revenge of the novel', *New Welsh Review*, 1 (Summer 1988), pp. 17–22; T. L. Williams, op. cit., pp. 1–2, 20–6.

[129] Dai Smith, 'A novel history', in Tony Curtis (ed.), *Wales: The Imagined Nation. Essays in Cultural and National Identity* (Bridgend, 1986), pp. 131–58 (especially 132); Harris, 'Introduction', loc. cit., pp. 25, 38–41.

[130] Caradoc Evans, 'The Welsh miner', *New Witness*, 7 Dec. 1916, reprinted in Harris, op. cit., pp. 154–6.

[131] Harris, op. cit., p. 31.

[132] Caradoc Evans, *Capel Sion* (London, 1916); Harris, op. cit., p. 31.

editorial and a number of the newspaper's 'Passing comments', all presumably written by the editor, Gomerian. These commentaries are unique in the sense that apart from a brief reference to *My Neighbours*, Evans's third book, in the following year, they are probably the only existing source of evidence of the reaction of Welsh-Americans to the work of Caradoc Evans up to 1920.[133]

The fifteen stories in *Capel Sion* were similar in theme to those in the author's first book, although throughout this volume the chapel emerges as the central source of evil in Welsh rural society. Its is depicted as a shrine of hypocrisy and as an authoritarian, avaricious power which fed on the ignorance of its members and condoned their sins and vices as long as its material benefits were not affected. Like his previous effort, the author's new collection was widely acclaimed in London and, later, in the United States, though not in Welsh-American circles. In Wales, however, as T. L. Williams has suggested, *Capel Sion* added 'fifteen splashes of petrol on to the flames of *My People*'.[134] Judging by the titles alone of the reviews which appeared in the *Druid*, Welsh-Americans shared their countrymen's condemnation of the book. George Bowen's contributions carried the headlines 'Caradoc Evans, Human Scavenger: Defiles the Welsh Nation and Besmirches the Reputation of His Own Kith and Kin. The Book a Travesty of Truth', and 'Capel Seion [*sic*] is a Hideous Libel on the God Fearing People of Beloved Wales: His Screed is Merely Slush', in the 1 and 15 February issues respectively. The editorial in the former was entitled 'Ananias Redivivus'.[135] Apart from echoing the condemnation which Caradoc Evans's work evoked in Wales, the *Druid's* reviewers also framed their criticism in a manner which bore striking resemblances to that of their fellow-critics in the homeland. Indeed, if anything, the Welsh-American reaction was more hysterical.

The nature of the Welsh critical response to Caradoc Evans's literary output in general has been acutely analysed in a number

---

[133] *Druid*, 1, 15 Feb. 1919, 15 Apr. 1920. George Bowen ('Ap Gwalia') was a mine foreman in Scranton. Born in 1867, he had worked underground since the age of ten. It is not known when he emigrated. In 1928 he published a collection of poems and short stories, *Diamonds of the Mines* (Scranton, 1928), p. v.

[134] *Capel Sion, passim*; T. L. Williams, op. cit., pp. 79–82 (especially 79).

[135] *Druid*, 1, 15 Feb. 1919.

of recent studies.[136] A genuine literary criticism was eschewed in favour of an outraged moral reaction which inhibited a rational discussion of his work for the rest of his life. Evans's critics treated his early works as sociological studies rather than the imaginative creations of an artistic mind. Instead of assessing his literary merit, his shocked Welsh readers took refuge in indignant condemnation, accusing him of despicable misrepresentation. Evans himself further fanned the flames of controversy by consistently maintaining that he was telling the truth, but, as T. L. Williams has pointed out, the main weapon of the satirist is distortion.[137] Evans drew on the more unsavoury aspects of Welsh Nonconformity and life in south-west Wales (and of Welsh life in London in *My Neighbours*),[138] but those aspects were nevertheless present. Historians have amply documented the discrepancy between the real and the ideal, especially regarding avarice and sexual promiscuity, and also how the rigidity of the Nonconformist code could encourage hypocrisy in these matters.[139] But contemporary Welsh critics, who regarded Evans's work as a second 'Treason of the Blue Books', were only too keen to neglect the factual basis which underpinned Evans's nightmare society.[140]

Fundamentally, however, as John Harris has pointed out, the crime of Evans's 'literature of the sewer' lay not so much in what was said as in the fact that he had written and published in English: 'to expose national defects before a gloating English readership was unforgivable.' Evans's satire 'cut across the psychic and emotional roots of the Welsh establishment. That establishment, all-powerful in the life of the nation and confident of popular support, branded Evans as anti-Welsh: to attack institutionalized Liberal-Nonconformity was to attack

[136] Harris, 'Introduction', loc. cit., pp. 37–47; M. Wynn Thomas, loc. cit., pp. 18–19; T. L. Williams, op. cit., pp. 2, 4.

[137] T. L. Williams, op. cit., pp. 2, 4.

[138] See John Harris, ' "Neighbours": Caradoc Evans, Lloyd George and the London Welsh', *Llafur*, 5, No. 4 (1991), pp. 90–8.

[139] T. L. Williams, op. cit., pp. 4–10; Harris, 'Introduction', loc. cit., pp. 16–29; Russell Davies, ' "In a broken dream": some aspects of sexual behaviour and the dilemmas of the unmarried mother in south west Wales, 1887–1914', *Llafur*, 3, No. 4 (1983), pp. 24–33: *idem*, 'Inside the "House of the mad": the social context of mental illness, suicide and the pressures of rural life in south west Wales c. 1860–1920', *Llafur*, 4, No. 2 (1985), pp. 20–35. See also David A. Pretty, *The Rural Revolt That Failed: Farm Workers' Trade Unions in Wales, 1889–1950* (Cardiff, 1989), who suggests that in his stories Caradoc Evans was 'understating his case'.

[140] T. L. Williams, pp. 2, 10.

the nation. His was the dissident's knotty position, and in speaking to the outside world he committed the dissident's further crime.'[141]

In common with outraged reviewers in Wales, Caradoc Evans's Welsh-American critics interpreted *Capel Sion* as an attempt by the author to paint an accurate picture of west Walian life. A central theme in the reviews was, consequently, the insistence on the falsity of his characterizations. All were agreed that Caradoc Evans had lied. 'The book itself,' declared George Bowen, 'is baseless fiction, a compendium of lies, a catalogue of vibrant noises, a cataclysm of nonsense, a roaring farce.'[142] According to the Scranton poet, Evans had attempted to portray the life of the peasantry in west Wales, but his effort was an ignominious failure. Instead, he had provided a false picture and, in particular, he had misrepresented the sincerity of their religious beliefs. To Bowen, the result was a cruel and unwarranted insult:

> His sardonic depiction and his brutal parody of the humanities of the simple plain people of the soil is a disgrace ... a brazen insult and a gross injustice to every warm-blooded Welshman. Oh the effrontery of this poltroon of prose and poetry who murders truth with the same dagger as Macbeth murdered Duncan at Cawdor Castle! A born liar, he defiles a nation as Nero defiled Rome. He transforms simple piety into blackest hypocrisy, humble devotion of the true God into savage superstition, purity into immorality, God into a heathen deity, heaven into hell, Wales, my Wales, into a land of savages where truth, love, honor and virtue are unknown – a land where we cannot distinguish its people from the common beasts of the field.[143]

The ease with which George Bowen lapsed into a counter-vision to be juxtaposed against that of the author was characteristic. No concrete proof that Evans was 'lying' was offered. Instead each reviewer, and George Bowen in particular, replaced Evans's perceived interpretation with their own versions of the 'truth' about the Welsh peasantry and Wales itself. In many ways, the issue was black or white – no grey areas were possible. To the *Druid*, Evans was 'the biographer of a non-existent people in a Welsh No-Man's Land' and one who cared

---

[141] Harris, 'Introduction', loc. cit., pp. 40, 45.
[142] *Druid*, 15 Feb. 1919.
[143] Ibid., 1 Feb. 1919.

little that 'by distorting and magnifying the peccadilloes of a remote rural district, he bespattered with his crude, filthy brush the length and breadth of a land which is second to none in spirituality and moral decency.'[144] The question of the truth was paramount. George Bowen was appalled that some Welsh critics (whom unfortunately he did not name) had praised the book's literary merit but had not dealt with the truthfulness of the subject matter.[145] Yet, presenting *Capel Sion* as an attempt at accuracy, the Scranton poet's denial was inextricably entwined with rhetorical restatements of his own equally universal idealization of the character of the west Walian peasantry and of their religiosity. His second review concluded with an emotive rallying call:

> Live on O ye people of West Wales. God bless your humble, honest lives. Live on, as ye have lived, in close communication with God and nature, undisturbed by the wild ravings of this mad maniac. Let Capel Seion and Capel Horeb resound with the beautiful harmonies of your pure hearts. Sing again those soulful hymns I love so dearly . . . Peace and plenty be with you for you are worthy of open vindication.[146]

The reviewers' insistence on the falsity of *Capel Sion* was matched by their equally adamant assertions that Evans had written the book for dubious and despicable motives. The *Druid* dismissed his effort as:

> . . . a craving for notoriety, a desire for 'filthy lucre' . . . His cherished ambition was to produce something that would attract attention, cause talk, engender controversy and appeal to the ignorance and incredulity of readers far removed from the locale of the writer's masterpieces.[147]

The newspaper's words pinpointed the concern which lay at the heart of both the reviewers' efforts to discredit Evans and their sense of outrage. Not only were the author's motives unwholesome; ultimately, they were also infinitely dangerous. The *Druid* declared in one of its 'Passing comments' that although a man's good deeds were limited, 'there is no limit to the mischief a man of Caradoc Evans' calibre can accomplish'.[148] The crucial point was that Evans had written in

---

[144] Ibid.
[145] Ibid., 15 Feb. 1919.
[146] Ibid.
[147] Ibid., 1 Feb. 1919.
[148] Ibid., 15 Feb. 1919.

English. By writing in that language, and therefore making his work available to a wider public, he had endangered the good name of the Welsh people. As George Bowen lamented,

> ... he has seen fit to publish his book in the English language, for the readers of the English speaking world who are ignorant of the traditions of our beloved country, its people and its wealth of legendary and literary lore. I as a Welshman vehemently protest against his ... patchwork of literature being foisted upon English readers, the ignorant among whom will undoubtedly accept it as a standard authority on Wales and its good people.[149]

The belief that *Capel Sion* could do irreparable harm to the public image of Wales perhaps explains why the reviewers' reaction was so vehement and so extensive. In many ways, a hostile backlash was essential in order to reaffirm the truth. George Bowen himself stressed the urgency of it: 'When a writer publishes a book whose palpable fallacies influence the public mind perniciously, it is the paramount duty of all lovers of the truth immediately to challenge it'.[150] Undoubtedly, the reviewers saw themselves as the defenders of the true character of Wales and of the Welsh. Indeed Courier was of the opinion that George Bowen deserved 'the thanks of the people here and in the homeland' for his review.[151] Yet what they were actually protecting was *their* 'truth', the definitions of Welshness which the *Druid* and the American Gorsedd strove to encourage and publicize. All three reviewers were leading members of the Gorsedd, and it is in this context also that the significance of the appearance of the reviews in the *Druid* ultimately lies.[152]

For his deceit and his endangering of the good image of the Welsh, in the view of his Welsh-American critics Caradoc Evans deserved all the venom they could muster. All three commentators vilified him mercilessly. Courier was shocked that 'such a filthy scoffer existed and lived in one of the most Christianized and civilized countries in the world' and, in praising Bowen's first review, painted a fanciful picture of the Scranton poet 'on horseback, whip in hand, lashing unmercifully the base defiler ... from pillar to post'.[153] Evans was a

[149] Ibid.
[150] Ibid.
[151] Ibid.
[152] *Royal Blue Book*, p. 24; *Druid*, 1 May 1919.
[153] *Druid*, 15 Feb. 1919.

traitor: on separate occasions the *Druid* called him a Judas and the 'Ham' of the Welsh nation.[154]

Caradoc Evans had forfeited any claims he might have had on the American Gorsedd by virtue of being both Welsh and Caucasian. Response to his widely publicized stories which were well received outside Wales can be understood only when the power of his image-making is placed against the images of Wales and Welshness which had been so ardently promoted in Wales and Welsh-America for half a century past. Reality could always be ignored or massaged into shape. Imaginative reworking of actuality was the ground on which the struggle for control of reality took place – its nature was always a separate thing. Caradoc Evans really was the arch-fiend for he not only accused his splendidly self-bedecked compatriots of nakedness; he dared to give them fig leaves for their nudity. The insensate denunciation of him by Welsh opinion in America was a direct reflection of the sanctity of Wales in their American minds. How they would have wished, at their apogee of Welshness, to have praised an internationally renowned Welsh author who used the English tongue as they did! But they looked in his mirror, and it cracked.

[154] Ibid., 1 Feb. 1919.

CONCLUSION

It would have made quite a spectacle. In 1910 the *Druid* demanded that the forthcoming investiture ceremony of the Prince of Wales be held not in Caernarfon or Cardiff but during the Druid Society's Welsh Day in Scranton. Scranton was the best place to host the event because, it declared, 'We are the largest real Welsh community in the world.'[1] When Caernarfon was chosen as the venue, the newspaper haughtily riposted that Caernarfon should reciprocate by sending Lloyd George to Scranton so that he could be proclaimed as the 'uncrowned king of the Welsh people' at the following year's 'Big Welsh Day'. The Scranton Welsh would much prefer the latter to 'the investing of a dozen princes'.[2]

On the cold, drizzly evening of Tuesday, 2 November 1923, the second dream came true. As they stepped out of their private train on to Lackawanna Station, David Lloyd George, his wife, and daughter Megan were greeted by a crowd of around 15,000. After being officially met by George Maxey, H. M. Edwards and Mayor Durkan, they walked to a waiting automobile through an arch formed by the raised bayonets of 300 soldiers whilst a choir of 300 selected voices sang 'Hen Wlad fy Nhadau'. The following day Mrs Lloyd George and Megan were given a reception by the Scranton Welsh Women's Club, and in the afternoon the husband and father delivered an address on 'Peace' to a full-to-capacity Armory whilst 5,000 gathered outside, unable to get in.[3]

Lloyd George's visit had been planned for over a year, but before his arrival the same streets along which his triumphant parade would advance had to be cleansed of an unwelcome, sullied shadow. If the arch-hero of the Welsh-American élite who regarded Scranton as the largest real Welsh community in the world was intending to visit in 1923, so also, it was

[1] *Druid*, 23 June 1910.
[2] Ibid., 15 Sept. 1910.
[3] Ibid., 15 Nov. 1923.

rumoured, was their arch-villain. On hearing that Caradoc Evans was planning a lecture tour of the United States, Theophilus Bowen, the *Druid*'s Scranton correspondent, assured the newspaper's readers,

> I do not believe in mob rule ... but I verily believe that if a body like the Ku Klux Klan got hold of the likes of Caradoc Evans it would prove a wholesome and beneficial lesson to prostituters of their own nation and defamers of their blood and flesh. And should Caradoc Evans put into effect his threat to invade the United States on a lecture tour in which he ridicules the Welsh people and portrays them as the most villainous on earth, rest assured there are enough Welshmen in the anthracite regions to make it so hot for him that he will conclude he has eventually reached the place for which he is destined.[4]

Caradoc Evans did not visit Scranton or the United States, but Lloyd George did. And even he almost did not make it – yet again. In mid-October it was announced that because of ill-health Scranton and Boston would be eliminated from his itinerary.[5] But there he was at Lackawanna Station at last – and after he left an era came to an end. This was one of the last occasions when Scranton would feature prominently in the history of the Welsh: the final time was in 1942 when, most appropriately, John Ford's film *How Green was my Valley* was premièred in the city. Apparently, those with Welsh connections turned out in force to see it and, like the miners in the movie, they went home singing.[6]

The fact that Scranton could realistically have been omitted from the itinerary of Lloyd George's visit in 1923 showed that the premier position it had enjoyed among Welsh communities in the United States during its heyday had already been lost. By 1942 the decline of its Welshness and even Welsh-Americanism had set in even deeper. The inexorable processes of acculturation and assimilation increasingly undermined the more tangible manifestations of Welshness that remained. The Welsh presence became a third, fourth and (by now) fifth – and generally indifferent – generation. Although there was some fresh Welsh emigration to the area (and to the United States in general) after the First World War, new recruits were far fewer

[4] Ibid., 15 Apr. 1923.
[5] Ibid., 15 Oct., 1 Nov. 1923.
[6] Ex inf. Mrs Ceinwen Hughes, Scranton.

in number than their predecessors had been the previous century. Severe depression in Wales and in the United States in the 1930s brought the golden age of Welsh emigration to an abrupt and bitter end, just as it ravaged the Welsh communities in the heavy industry heartlands of both countries. In Scranton the Welsh were forced to move in search of work, with disastrous and inescapable consequences for their already beleaguered ethnic institutions. 'Not dead but gone to Akron or Detroit' was perhaps the Scrantonian Welsh equivalent of that bitter epitaph of the savage inter-war years in south Wales when nearly a quarter of the population moved to England: 'Not dead but gone to Slough'. In the United States as whole, as the twentieth century progressed, one by one the Welsh churches closed, eisteddfodau became rarities, societies collapsed and even the *Drych* switched to English. By then the distinctive character of the nineteenth-century Welsh immigrants had become dissolved in what Rowland Berthoff has described as 'the "Anglo-Saxon" generality of middle-class America'.[7] The trickle of Welsh who have crossed the Atlantic since the resumption of emigration after the Second World War have left a very different Wales from the one their predecessors both treasured and imagined.

Two months before he threatened to muster a Welsh-American lynching party for Caradoc Evans in 1923, Theophilus Bowen, the *Druid*'s Scranton correspondent, visited his home town's Young Men's Hebrew Association and was asked, 'What does it mean to be Welsh in the city of Scranton?' He replied: 'The Welsh people have been potent factors in the development of Scranton and for the past forty years have been prominent in professional, industrial, social and political circles.' He went on to complain that despite this, 'they do not have a home to hang their hat in,' implying that the Welsh (unlike the Hebrew Association) were too little interested to organize a permanent home where they could hold functions and meetings.[8] He was right in both respects. There can be little doubt that the Welsh were a powerful force in Scrantonian society throughout the late

---

[7] Berthoff, 'The Welsh', p. 1017.
[8] *Druid*, 15 Feb. 1923.

nineteenth and early twentieth centuries. There is little doubt, too, that to most of them, the lack of a 'Welsh temple' in the city was of little relevance.

In conclusion, we can perhaps rephrase the Hebrew Association's question and ask what it meant to be Welsh in Scranton – and indeed in the United States – during the late nineteenth and early twentieth centuries. In many respects, it was a running paradox: to be Welsh in Scranton – as in America – was to be confused. And, of course, there was not a single Welsh experience; there were many. As the foregoing pages have attempted to show, the various Welsh experiences in the city were infinitely complex, and far more complex than the picture lovingly nurtured by a Welsh-American tradition of writing which confines itself to accounts of Welsh societies and cultural activities and to ceaseless indulgences in the cult of the eminent Welsh-American.

This book has argued that in Scranton during the late nineteenth and early twentieth centuries Welsh community leaders were successful in promoting a public image of the Welsh which saw them as models of American citizenship by virtue of their perceived national characteristics and contemporary conventional morality. The Welsh social élite both regarded themselves as an élite and were one. They saw American élite status as desirable and saw their own élite status as a means of gaining entry into the former. But that was not possible. Consequently they needed self-definition as 'Welsh', as they saw it, in order to maintain the élite status they accorded themselves. They were an élite because they represented a cultural ethnicity which was respected by non-Welsh groups, especially the native-American or Yankee élite, and by the Welsh themselves, who felt superior to immigrants who could not assimilate as easily into the Anglo-Saxon norms of American life. The higher contemporary profile of these 'natural' leaders granted their Welshness or Welsh-Americanism official status and ensured their unrepresentative presence in our surviving written sources of evidence. Their Welshness was the American version of the 'official' Welshness that prevailed, as some historians have argued, in late nineteenth-century Wales.[9]

---

[9] See, for example, David Smith, 'Wales through the looking glass' and *Wales!*

CONCLUSION

Because the Welsh élite were in a minority, however, they were compelled to influence, control, organize, castigate and denounce those 'other' Welsh who spoilt things by living their lives without concern for these minoritarian preoccupations. The bulk of the Welsh in Scranton responded only fitfully, and the defined sense of Welshness was directly challenged during crises in the anthracite industry (notably during the 1871 strike) and by political activity. The élite kept stubbing their toes against the real Americanization of the Welsh through economic involvement and, even more telling, through a vibrant popular culture. This new culture took off from the 1880s onwards and was the agency through which the majority became American. The result was that the élite's self-justifying inclusion in élitism – whether Welsh or American – inevitably led to their own exclusion from a wider Welsh-American reality. The 'Wales in America' nurtured by the élite minority in Scranton and elsewhere in the United States, could not accommodate these alternative definitions of Welshness, and it was by-passed by the real experience of the Welsh in America and, simultaneously, by that of the Welsh in Wales.

Wales in America 'succeeded' during the late nineteenth and early twentieth centuries because Wales itself was so strong an image and a reality. The very confidence that underpinned the 'national revival' in Wales was equally prevalent across the Atlantic, and it infused the image-making of the Welsh élite in the United States. Indeed, the advantaged position of the Welsh and their growing economic success in America were the foundation on which the make-up artists of the late nineteenth- and early twentieth-century world could apply the Welsh-American cosmetic. Wales's own changing world after the 1920s made the decline of 'Wales in America' inevitable. In Wales, industrial south Wales (or American Wales, as Sir Alfred Zimmern described it)[10] became a monster that had to be 'written out'. And in America, as Gomerian forcefully reminded a *South Wales News* reporter during his visit to Wales in 1927:

> You in Wales have nothing like the spirit of we Welsh people over there. Why, we think nothing of travelling three or four hundred miles and even

---

Wales? passim; Hywel Teifi Edwards, 'Victorian Wales seeks reinstatement', *passim*.

[10] See Sir Alfred Zimmern, *My Impressions of Wales* (London, 1927).

more to attend an eisteddfod, while you folk over here hesitate to cover a distance of thirty miles. The indifference of you people over here is simply amazing. Take again the Welsh and their own language. Over in America it is flourishing... You are not nearly so patriotic as we are, nor do you seem to care so much for Welsh traditions and customs. What you Welsh people here want is to cultivate more aggression. I cannot understand your servility as far as the English are concerned... What you want is to assert yourselves. Let the world know that our country is as good as any, and better than most, and that we are proud of it.[11]

For some Welsh-Americans, it seems, an ideal Wales had now come to indict the Welsh themselves. Yet Gomerian's condemnation was but one more manifestation of the same Welsh-American turn of mind that could also, in 1910, genuinely proclaim Scranton as the largest 'real' Welsh community in the world. Their sensibilities perceived the necessity for, and seriously believed the existence of, a 'real' Welshness – which, ultimately, they themselves had defined. The expression and defence of that ideal Welshness inevitably made the Welsh in America more 'Welsh' than the Welsh in Wales. The remarkable success story of the 'nationality across the Atlantic', as celebrated by the *Herald Cymraeg* in 1872, had reached the apogee of its imagination. The bastions of 'real' Welshness had gone in search of, and found, Uncle Sam.

[11] *South Wales News*, 30 July 1927.

APPENDICES

1 BRITISH EMIGRATION TO THE UNITED STATES, 1820–1950

	Wales	England	Scotland	Ireland	Not specified
1820–1830	170	15,837	3,180	54,338	8,302
1831–1840	185	7,611	2,667	207,381	65,347
1841–1850	1,261	32,092	3,712	780,719	229,979
1851–1860	6,319	247,125	38,331	914,119	132,199
1861–1870	4,313	222,277	38,769	435,778	341,537
1871–1880	6,631	437,706	87,564	436,871	16,142
1881–1890	12,640	644,680	149,869	655,482	168
1891–1900	10,557	216,726	44,188	388,416	67
1901–1910	17,464	388,017	120,469	339,065	
1911–1920	13,107	249,944	78,357	146,181	
1921–1930	13,012	157,420	159,781	220,591	
1931–1940	735	21,756	6,887	13,167	
1941–1950	3,209	112,252	16,131	26,444	
Total	89,603	2,753,443	749,905	4,618,552	793,741

Source: R. T. Berthoff, *British Immigrants in Industrial America*, p. 5.

2 POPULATION OF THE UNITED STATES BORN IN WALES, 1850–1970

Year	No. born in Wales
1850	29,868
1860	45,763
1870	74,533
1880	83,302
1890	100,079
1900	93,586
1910	82,488
1920	67,066
1930	60,205
1940	35,360
1950	30,060
1960	23,469
1970	17,014

Source: U.S. Bureau of the Census, *Historical Statistics of the United States from Colonial Times to 1957* (Washington, D.C., 1960), p. 66; John Williams, *Digest of Welsh Historical Statistics*, vol. 1, p. 76.

3 DISTRIBUTION OF POPULATION OF THE UNITED STATES BORN IN WALES, 1900, BY STATES

State	No. born in Wales
Pennsylvania	35,453
Ohio	11,481
New York	7,304
Illinois	4,364
Wisconsin	3,356
Iowa	3,091
Utah	2,141
Indiana	2,083
Kansas	2,005
Colorado	1,955
California	1,949
Massachusetts	1,680
Missouri	1,613
Washington	1,509
Minnesota	1,288
New Jersey	1,195
Vermont	1,056
Montana	935
Nebraska	922
Michigan	838
Idaho	732
Maryland	674
Connecticut	650
South Dakota	549
West Virginia	482
Oregon	401
Wyoming	393
Kentucky	337
Texas	313
Alabama	306
Tennessee	300
Virginia	267
Rhode Island	256
Maine	199
Indian Territory	175
Florida	169
North Dakota	147
Arizona	136
Nevada	128
Louisiana	126
Arkansas	113
New Mexico	105

Appendix 3 continued

State	No. born in Wales
Oklahoma	94
District of Columbia	82
New Hampshire	68
Georgia	65
Delaware	43
Alaska	41
Mississippi	30
Hawaii	21
North Carolina	20
South Carolina	8
Total	93,744

Source: U.S. Bureau of the Census, *Twelfth Census of the United States, 1900*, vol. 1, p. 735.

Note: The total figure cited in the table in the Census is 93,744 (incorrect addition). The correct total of 93,648 includes figures for Alaska and Hawaii (cf. figure for 1900 in Appendix 2 which excludes those states).

4 DISTRIBUTION OF POPULATION OF THE UNITED STATES BORN IN WALES, 1900, BY COUNTIES (WITH CHIEF CENTRE)

County (with chief centre)	No. born in Wales
Luzerne, Pa. (Wilkes-Barre)	8,578
Lackawanna, Pa. (Scranton)	7,708
Allegheny, Pa. (Pittsburgh)	5,245
Oneida, N.Y. (Utica)	2,536
Schuylkill, Pa. (Pottsville)	2,100
Cook, Ill. (Chicago)	1,917
Lawrence, Pa. (Newcastle)	1,690
New York City	1,686
Mahoning, O. (Youngstown)	1,627
Cuyahoga, O. (Cleveland)	1,592
Trumbull, O. (Warren)	1,205
Philadelphia, Pa.	1,033
Rutland, Vt. (Poultney)	979
Cambria, Pa. (Johnstown)	946
Northampton, Pa. (Bangor)	832
Westmoreland, Pa. (New Kensington)	703
Salt Lake, Utah (Salt Lake City)	695
Lehigh, Pa. (Slatington)	692
Washington, N.Y. (Granville)	675
Franklin, O. (Brown Township)	649
Mercer, Pa. (Sharon)	611
Madison, Ind. (Anderson)	590
Stark, O. (Alliance)	579
Northumberland, Pa. (Shamokin)	568
King, Wash. (Seattle)	567
Kings, N.Y. (Brooklyn)	561
Belmont, O. (Martin's Ferry)	530
Tuscarawas, O. (Sugar Creek)	530
Macon, Mo. (Bevier)	503
Carbon, Pa. (Lansford)	459
Lyon, Kan. (Emporia)	451
Clearfield, Pa. (Houtzdale)	449
Summit, O. (Akron)	448
Columbia, Wis. (Columbus City)	442
Jefferson, Pa. (Horatio)	433
Blue Earth, Minn. (Mankato)	428
Jackson, O. (Oak Hill)	426
Arapohoe, Col. (Denver)	423
Grant, Ind. (Gas City)	416
Berkshire, Mass. (Pittsfield)	407

Source: U.S. Bureau of the Census, *Twelfth Census of the United States*, 1900, vol. 1, *passim*.

Note: Only counties with over 400 people born in Wales are listed.

5 DISTRIBUTION OF POPULATION OF THE UNITED STATES, BORN IN WALES, 1990. (each dot represents 500 persons.)

6 THE NORTH-EAST PENNSYLVANIA COALFIELD
(coal deposits in black)

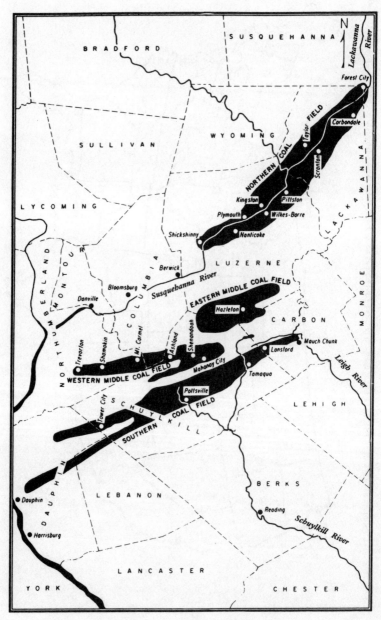

Based on a map in *The Guns of Lattimer* by Michael Novak (Basic Books Inc., 1978).

7 SCRANTON: POPULATION, 1860–1980

1860	9,209
1870	35,092
1880	45,890
1890	75,215
1900	102,026
1910	129,867
1920	137,783
1930	143,433
1940	140,405
1950	125,536
1960	110,786
1970	102,699
1980	87,370

Source: United States Censuses, 1860–1980.

8 SCRANTON: FOREIGN-BORN POPULATION, 1870–1920

Born in	1870	1880	1890	1900	1910	1920
Wales	4,177	3,616	4,890	4,621	4,137	2,714
England	1,444	1,558	3,065	3,692	3,022	2,313
Ireland	6,491	6,772	8,343	7,193	5,302	3,365
Scotland	366	301	576	576	557	480
Germany	3,056	3,153	5,587	5,363	4,325	2,612
Italy	7	12	367	1,312	3,549	3,433
Russia	7	37	488	3,181	8,568	5,363
Austria	–	–	–	–	3,184	2,863
Hungary	–	–	–	–	1,214	888
Poland	–	–	–	–	–	3,276
Others	339	408	2,257	3,035	1,264	1,280
Total Foreign Born	15,887	15,857	25,573	28,973	35,122	28,587

Source: United States Censuses, 1870–1920.

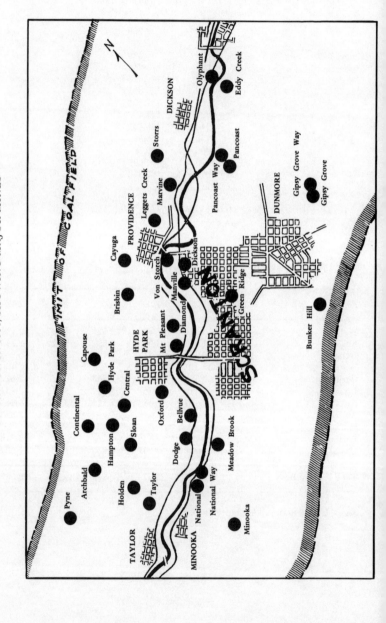

9 SCRANTON IN 1914, SHOWING MAJOR MINES

10 DISTRIBUTION OF FOREIGN-BORN POPULATION OF SCRANTON, 1910, BY WARDS

Foreign-born white: Born in:	1	2	3	4	5	Ward 6	7	8	9	10	11
Austria	35	186	104	17	186	324	269	335	35	9	123
Canada	19	31	4	13	5	5	12	3	41	23	5
England	549	284	34	320	268	87	43	25	108	64	39
Germany	94	108	22	165	105	72	35	51	92	404	559
Hungary	33	87	12	3	37	113	46	79	26	10	43
Ireland	298	424	386	219	305	319	203	69	223	84	110
Italy	34	373	22	48	455	36	1	141	6	249	39
Russia	1,242	1,499	668	364	468	224	163	198	71	13	640
Scotland	149	62	9	15	18	10	18	10	27	45	5
Sweden	6	2	–	26	43	–	–	2	4	1	1
Switzerland	2	8	–	4	3	1	2	1	7	47	22
Turkey	1	–	–	1	90	–	–	4	–	–	–
Wales	826	346	29	672	621	320	10	12	43	23	19
Other foreign countries	22	21	3	13	14	8	2	62	34	20	5
Total Population	10,962	10,529	4,161	7,969	9,322	4,747	2,757	2,490	5,675	5,524	5,557

Appendix 10 continued

Foreign-born white: Born in:	Ward											TOTAL
	12	13	14	15	16	17	18	19	20	21	22	
Austria	17	42	65	78	49	207	517	67	90	287	142	3,184
Canada	8	20	8	3	28	37	1	3	10	17	3	299
England	46	239	91	182	87	139	24	48	106	196	43	3,022
Germany	110	153	51	165	72	134	13	1,172	553	142	53	4,325
Hungary	11	18	32	4	38	91	358	29	7	133	4	1,214
Ireland	345	231	121	261	110	255	119	361	579	217	63	5,302
Italy	10	34	947	32	57	8	55	238	647	81	36	3,549
Russia	22	257	140	196	626	122	147	103	434	607	354	8,568
Scotland	8	40	12	12	12	46	8	11	11	27	2	557
Sweden	—	1	2	5	2	6	—	10	3	—	—	114
Switzerland	5	6	5	10	—	9	1	69	5	3	5	215
Turkey	—	2	122	12	7	5	2	2	—	17	—	265
Wales	25	69	57	576	16	43	8	25	38	211	148	4,137
Other foreign countries	4	22	6	18	20	34	—	15	7	6	25	361
Total Population	3,376	6,635	4,294	6,122	3,649	6,831	2,729	9,222	7,705	7,099	2,512	129,867

Source: U.S. Bureau of the Census, *Thirteenth Census of the United States,* 1910 pp. 610–11

BIBLIOGRAPHY

1. MANUSCRIPT COLLECTIONS
2. NEWSPAPERS
3. PERIODICALS
4. OFFICIAL PUBLICATIONS
5. WORKS OF REFERENCE
6. MISCELLANEOUS PRIMARY SOURCES
7. OTHER BOOKS
8. ARTICLES
9. THESES

1. MANUSCRIPT COLLECTIONS
Lackawanna Historical Society, Scranton
Jones Musical Collection, containing the programmes, press clippings and other professional materials used by Dr David E. Jones (1867–1947), music critic for the *Scranton Tribune*
Delaware, Lackawanna and Western Railroad Company (Coal Department) Papers
Hudson Coal Company Service Records
Minute Book, Robert Morris Lodge of the American Order of True Ivorites, Scranton, 1894–1901
'The Welsh' Miscellaneous File, containing photographs, press cuttings and souvenir programmes of Welsh cultural activities, mostly in Scranton

National Library of Wales, Aberystwyth
MSS. 2834 B: Account of a Tour of the USA by David Samwel, 1889
MSS. 3191–7 C: Letters from Various Welsh-Americans to David Davies, 1881–5
MSS. 3292–3 E: Miscellaneous Letters from Welsh-Americans, *c.* 1863–85
MSS. 4861 D: Letters to Henry Blackwell re Proposed Visit of T. Marchant Williams, 1913
MSS. 5631 B: Letters from Evan M. Williams to Relatives in Wales, 1872
MSS. 5940 A–6D, 9251–78 A: Henry Blackwell MSS

Scranton Public Library
Manuscript Census Returns, Scranton: 1870, 1900 (microfilm)

University of Pittsburgh
Archives of Industrial Society, Miscellaneous Ethnic Groups Folder, 'The Welsh': Press Cuttings, Bibliographia

Yale University
American Federation of Labor Records, the Samuel Gompers Era (microfilm)
Terence Vincent Powderly Papers, Scrapbooks (microfilm)

2. NEWSPAPERS
i) Welsh-American
The Druid (The Welsh-American, 1914–18)
Y Drych
Ninnau
Y Wasg

ii) Welsh
Baner ac Amserau Cymru
Glamorgan Free Press
Llanelly and County Guardian
Pontypridd Chronicle
South Wales Daily News (South Wales News from 1919)
South Wales Voice
Tarian y Gweithiwr
Y Tyst a'r Dydd
Western Mail

iii) American
Carbondale Advance
Cardondale Journal
Labor Standard
Miners' Journal (Pottsville)
Record of the Times (Wilkes-Barre)
Scranton Republican
Scranton Times
Scranton Tribune–Republican
Shenandoah Herald
United Mine Workers' Journal
Workingmen's Advocate

3. PERIODICALS
i) Welsh-American
The American Celt
Blodau'r Oes a'r Ysgol
The Cambrian
Cambrian Gleanings
Y Cenhadwr Americanaidd
Y Cyfaill o'r Hen Wlad
Y Ford Gron
Y Glorian
Y Lamp
Yr Ymdrechydd

ii) Welsh
Bye Gones
Y Cerddor
Cymru
Cymru Fydd
Y Geninen
Y Llenor
The Red Dragon
Y Traethodydd

Wales (1894–7, ed. O. M. Edwards)
Wales (1911–14, ed. J. Hugh Edwards)
Welsh Chips
The Welsh Outlook
The Welsh Review
Ysbryd yr Oes

4. OFFICIAL PUBLICATIONS
Censuses of the United States 1860–1920
U.S. Bureau of the Census, *Historical Statistics of the United States from Colonial Times to 1957* (Washington, D.C., 1960)

5. WORKS OF REFERENCE
Blackwell, H., *A Bibliography of Welsh-Americana* (2nd edn., Aberystwyth, 1977)
Bodnar, J. E., *Ethnic History in Pennsylvania: A Selected Bibliography* (Harrisburg, 1974)
Y Bywgraffiadur Cymreig, 1941–50 (London, 1970)
Dictionary of American Biography, 20 vols. (London, 1928–36)
Dictionary of Welsh Biography down to 1940 (London, 1959)
Jenkins, R. T. and Rees, W., *A Bibliography of the History of Wales* (2nd edn., Cardiff, 1962)
Lewis, I., 'Welsh newspapers and journals in the United States', *National Library of Wales Journal*, II (Summer 1942)
Owen, Bob, 'Welsh American newspapers and periodicals', *National Library of Wales Journal*, VI (Winter 1950)
Idem, *Bywgraffiadau Cymry Americanaidd* (n.p., 1960)
Thernstorm, S. et al. (eds.), *Harvard Encyclopaedia of American Ethnic Groups* (Cambridge, Mass., 1980) (includes entry on the Welsh by Rowland Berthoff)
Williams, J., *Digest of Welsh Historical Statistics* (2 vols., Cardiff, 1985)

6. MISCELLANEOUS PRIMARY SOURCES
Bowen, G. W., *Diamonds of the Mine* (Scranton, 1928)
Boyd's Wilkes-Barre City Directory, 1871–2
Casson, H. N., 'The Welsh in America', *Munsey's Magazine*, XXV (September 1906)
Charles, T. O., *Dear Old Wales: A Patriotic Love Story* (Pittsburgh, 1912)
Idem, 'The Welsh in two worlds', *National Magazine* (July 1913)
Chidlaw, B. W., *Yr American, yr hwn sydd yn cynnwys Nodau ar Daith o Ddyffryn Ohio i Gymru* (Llanrwst, 1840)
Idem, *The Story of My Life* (Philadelphia, 1890)
Clarke, J. A., *The Wyoming Valley* (Scranton, 1875)
Conway, A. (ed.), *The Welsh in America* (Cardiff, 1961)
Darlington, T., 'The Welsh in America', *Wales*, 1 (December 1894)
Davies, W. D., *America a Gweledigaethau Bywyd* (Scranton, 1895)
Davis, J. J., *The Iron Puddler: My Life in the Rolling Mills and What Came of It* (New York, 1922)
Eames, A. et al. (eds.), *Capt. David Evans of Talsarnau, 1817–1895: Letters from America* (Gwynedd Archive Service, 1976)
Edwards, E., *Facts about Welsh Factors: Welshmen as Factors in the Foundation and Development of the U.S. Republic* (Utica, 1899)
Edwards, H. M., 'Diffygion y genedl Gymreig yn America', *Glorian*, 1 (1872)

BIBLIOGRAPHY

Edwards, T. Cynonfardd, *The Jubilee Memorial, 1868–1918, Welsh Congregational Church, Edwardsville, Pennsylvania* (Wilkes-Barre, 1918)
Evans, Caradoc, *My People* (London, 1915)
Idem, Capel Sion (London, 1916)
Idem, My Neighbours (London, 1919)
Evans, W. D., *Dros Gyfanfor a Chyfandir* (Aberystwyth, 1883)
Evans, W. R., *Welshmen as Civil, Political and Moral Factors in the Formation and Development of the United States Republic* (Utica, 1894)
Idem, (ed.), *Hanes Sefydliadau Cymreig Siroedd Jackson a Gallia Ohio* (Utica, 1896)
Gibbons, P. E., 'The miners of Scranton', *Harpers New Monthly Magazine*, LV (1877)
Griffiths, D. P., *The Last of the Quills: A Story of Welsh Life* (Binghampton, 1902)
James, T. L., 'The Welsh in the United States', *Cambrian*, XII (1892)
Idem, 'The eisteddfod in Wales and in the United States', *Frank Leslies Monthly* (April 1895)
Jenkins, J. E., *O Gymru i Galiffornia* (Llanelli, 1893)
Jones, D. E. (ed.), *One Half Century of Work. History of the Providence Welsh Congregational Church of Scranton* (Scranton, 1905)
Jones, E. P., *Ymfudiaeth: Ymweliad a Dakota, 1885* (Bangor, 1885)
Jones, E. W., *Llangobaith: A Story of North Wales* (Utica, 1886)
Idem, 'The Welsh in America', *Atlantic Monthly*, XXXVII (1876)
Jones, R. G. et al., *Powys, Kansas: Cymdeithas Dirol ac Ymfudol America* (Utica, 1871)
Letter Carriers of Scranton, Pennsylvania, *Postal Guide* (Scranton, 1897)
Monroe, W. S., *Poets and Poetry of the Wyoming Valley* (Scranton, 1896)
Morgan, M. O. ('Morien'), *A Souvenir: The Visit of the Iron and Steel Institutes of Great Britain and Germany to America* (Cardiff, 1890)
Morgan, W. P., 'The Welsh in the United States', *Wales*, III (January 1896)
Nichols, F. H., 'The children of the coal shadow', *McClure's*, XIX (February 1902)
Owens, J. E., 'The Welsh in politics', *North American Review*, CLVII (November 1893)
Platt, J. C., *Reminiscences of the Early History of 'Dark Hollow', 'Slocum Hollow', 'Harrison', 'Lackawanna Iron Works', Scrantonia and Scranton Pa.* (Scranton, 1896)
Portrait and Biographical Record of Lackawanna County, Pennsylvania (New York, 1897)
Rood, H., 'The mine laborers in Pennsylvania', *Forum*, XIV (1892–3)
The Royal Blue Book: Prize Productions of the Pittsburgh International Eisteddfod, July 2, 3, 4 and 5, 1913 (Pittsburgh, 1916)
Scranton City Directories
Scranton Eisteddfod Association, *The National Eisteddfod, Scranton Armory, 29–30 May 1902: Official Program* (Scranton, 1902)
Steinke's Story of Scranton. Who's Who and Why in Cartoons (Scranton, 1914)
Stoddard, D. J., *Prominent Men of Scranton and Vicinity* (Scranton, 1906)
Taylor, C. (ed.), *From Wales to Wisconsin: Selections from the Plas yn Blaenau Papers* (Aberystwyth, 1973)
Idem, (ed.), *Samuel Roberts and his Circle: Migration from Llanbrynmair, Montgomeryshire, to America* (Aberystwyth, 1974)
Thomas, B. D. (ed.), *Frederick Evans DD (Ednyfed): A Memorial* (Philadelphia, 1899)
Thomas, E. P., *Glimpses of the Gorsedd. A Brief Sketch of the History and Progress of the American Gorsedd* (Pittsburgh, 1919)
Thomas, H. E., *Mel Myfyrdod: Pregethau, Traethodau, Barddoniaeth ac Amrywiaethau* (Utica, 1882)
Thomas, R. D., *Hanes Cymry America* (Utica, 1872)
Thomas, M. M., *Sing in the Dark. A Story of the Welsh in Pennsylvania* (Philadelphia, 1954)
Throop, B. H., *A Half Century in Scranton* (Scranton, 1895)
Virtue, G. U., 'The true history of the coal trouble', *Nation*, XII (1871)
Idem, 'The anthracite coal combination', *Quarterly Journal of Economics*, X (1895–6)

BIBLIOGRAPHY 263

Why We Are Protestants: History of the Welsh Calvinistic Methodist Churches in Wales and America (New York, 1893)
Williams, D. J., *The Welsh of Columbus Ohio: A Study of Adaptation and Assimilation* (Columbus, 1913)
Williams, E., *Traethawd ar Hanes Cymry Colorado o'r Sefydliad Boreuaf hyd yn Awr* (Denver, 1889)
Williams, R. E., *Glimpses of Wales and the Welsh* (Pittsburgh, 1894)

7. OTHER BOOKS

Arnot, R. P., *South Wales Miners: A History of the South Wales Miners' Federation, vol. I: 1898–1914* (Cardiff, 1967)
Idem, *South Wales Miners: A History of the South Wales Miners' Federation, vol. II: 1914–1926* (Cardiff, 1975)
Ashton, E. T., *The Welsh in the United States* (Hove, 1984)
Aurand, H. W., *From the Molly Maguires to the United Mine Workers: The Social Ecology of an Industrial Union, 1869–99* (Philadelphia, 1971)
Baber, C. and Williams, L. J. (eds.), *Modern South Wales: Essays in Economic History* (Cardiff, 1986)
Baines, D., *Migration in a Mature Economy: Emigration and Internal Migration in England and Wales, 1861–1900* (Cambridge, 1985)
Idem, *Emigration from Europe, 1815–1930* (London, 1991)
Berthoff, R. T., *British Immigrants in Industrial America, 1790–1850* (Cambridge, Mass., 1953)
Billinger, R. D., *Pennsylvania's Coal Industry* (Gettysburg, 1964)
Bodnar, J. E. (ed.), *The Ethnic Experience in Pennsylvania* (Lewisburg, 1973)
Idem, '*The Transplanted*'. *A History of Immigrants in Industrial America* (Bloomington, 1985)
Broehl, W. G. Jr., *The Molly Maguires* (London, 1964)
Browning, C. H., *The Welsh Settlement of Pennsylvania* (Philadelphia, 1912)
Craft, D. et al., *History of Scranton, Pennsylvania* (Dayton, 1891)
Curtis, T. (ed.), *Wales: The Imagined Nation: Essays in Cultural and National Identity* (Bridgend, 1986)
Davies, P. G., *The Welsh in Wisconsin* (Madison, 1982)
Davies, R. R. et al. (eds.), *Welsh Society and Nationhood: Historical Essays Presented to Glanmor Williams* (Cardiff, 1984)
Davies, W. H., *The Right Place, The Right Time* (Llandybïe, 1972)
Dedication Service Souvenir, First Welsh Baptist Church, Scranton (Scranton, 1958)
Dodd, A. H., *The Character of Early Welsh Emigration to the United States* (Cardiff, 1953)
Drury, P. J. (ed.), *The Irish in America: Emigration, Assimilation and Impact* (Cambridge, 1985)
Dubovsky, M. and Van Tine, W., *John L. Lewis: A Biography* (New York, 1977)
Edwards, H. T., '*Gŵyl Gwalia*': *Yr Eisteddfod Genedlaethol yn Oes Aur Victoria, 1858–1868* (Llandysul, 1980)
Idem, *Eisteddfod Ffair y Byd, Chicago, 1893* (Llandysul, 1990)
Idem, *The Eisteddfod* (Cardiff, 1990)
Erickson, C. J., *American Industry and the European Immigrant, 1860–1885* (Cambridge, Mass. 1957)
Idem, *Invisible Immigrants: The Adaptation of English and Scottish Immigrants in Nineteenth Century America* (London, 1972)
Evans, C., *A History of the United Mine Workers of America, 1860–1890* (Indianapolis, 1914)
Evans, D., *Bywyd Bob Owen, 1885–1962* (Caernarfon, 1978)
Evans, E. W., *Mabon: A Study in Trade Union Leadership* (Cardiff, 1959)

Fiedler, L. A., *Waiting for the End: The American Literary Scene from Hemingway to Baldwin* (New York, 1964)
Fleming, D. and Bailyn B. (eds.), *Dislocation and Emigration: The Social Background of American Immigration* (Cambridge, Mass., 1974)
Folsom, B. W., Jr., *Urban Capitalists: Entrepreneurs and City Growth in Pennsylvania's Lackawanna and Lehigh Regions, 1800–1920* (Baltimore, 1981)
Foner, P. S., *The Great Labor Uprising of 1877* (New York, 1977)
Francis, H. and Smith D., *The Fed: A History of the South Wales Miners in the Twentieth Century* (London, 1980)
Ginger, R., *The Age of Excess: The United States, 1877–1914* (New York, 1965)
Glenn, T. A., *Welsh Founders of Pennsylvania* (2 vols., Oxford, 1913)
Greene, V. R., *The Slavic Community on Strike: Immigrant Labor in Pennsylvania Anthracite* (Notre Dame, Ind., 1968)
Idem, American Immigrant Leaders, 1800–1910: Marginality and Identity (Baltimore, 1987)
Greenslade, D., *Welsh Fever: Welsh Activities in the United States and Canada Today* (Cowbridge, 1986)
Gutman, H. G., *Work, Culture and Society in Industrializing America* (New York, 1977)
Handlin, O., *The Uprooted* (Boston, 1951)
Hansen, M. L., *The Immigrant in American History* (Cambridge, Mass., 1948)
Hareven, K. (ed.), *Anonymous Americans: Explorations in Nineteenth Century Social History* (Englewood Cliffs, 1971)
Harries, F. J., *Welshmen and the United States* (Pontypridd, 1927)
Harris, J. (ed.), *Fury Never Leaves Us: A Miscellany of Caradoc Evans* (Bridgend, 1985)
Hartmann, E. G., *The Welsh Baptist Association of Northeastern Pennsylvania, 1855–1955* (Plymouth, Pa., 1955)
Idem, Americans from Wales (Boston, 1967)
Idem, Cymry yn y Cwm: The Welsh of Wilkes-Barre and the Wyoming Valley (Wilkes-Barre, 1985)
Harvey, K. A., *The Best Dressed Miners: Life and Labor in the Maryland Coal Region, 1835–1910* (Ithaca and London, 1969)
Harzig, C. and Hoerder D. (eds.), *The Press of Labor Migrants in Europe and North America 1880s–1930s* (Bremen, 1985)
Higham, J., *Strangers in the Land: Patterns of American Nativism, 1860-1925* (New York, 1963)
Hitchcock, F. L., *History of Scranton and its People* (2 vols., New York, 1914)
Hobsbawm, E. J. and Ranger, T. (eds.), *The Invention of Tradition* (Cambridge, 1983)
Hoerder, D. (ed.), *American Labor and Immigration History, 1877–1920s: Recent European Research* (Chicago, 1983)
Jenkins, G. H. and Smith J. B. (eds.), *Politics and Society in Wales, 1840–1922. Essays in Honour of Ieuan Gwynedd Jones* (Cardiff, 1988)
John, A. V., *Our Mothers' Land: Chapters in Welsh Women's History, 1830–1939* (Cardiff, 1991)
Jones, D., *Memorial Volume of the Welsh Congregationalists in Pennsylvania* (Utica, 1934)
Jones, D. J. V., *The Last Rising: The Newport Insurrection of 1839* (Oxford, 1985)
Jones, I. G., *Explorations and Explanations: Essays in the Social History of Victorian Wales* (Llandysul, 1981)
Idem, Communities: Essays in the Social History of Victorian Wales (Llandysul, 1987)
Jones, M. A., *American Immigration* (Chicago, 1960)
Idem, Destination America (London, 1976)
Idem, The Limits of Liberty: American History, 1607–1980 (New York, 1983)
Jones, R. M., *The North Wales Quarrymen, 1874–1922* (Cardiff, 1981)
Klein, P. S. and Hoogenboom, A., *A History of Pennsylvania* (University Park, 1980)
Korson, G., *Minstrels of the Mine Patch: Songs and Stories of the Anthracite Industry* (Philadelphia, 1938)

BIBLIOGRAPHY

Lambert, W. R., *Drink and Sobriety in Victorian Wales c. 1820–1895* (Cardiff, 1983)
Lewis, E. D., *The Rhondda Valleys* (Cardiff, 1959)
Lewis, T. H., *Y Mormoniaid yng Nghymru* (Cardiff, 1957)
Logan, S. C., *A City's Danger and its Defense or Issues and Results of the Strike of 1877 containing the Origin and History of the Scranton City Guard* (Scranton, 1887)
McCarthy, C. A., *The Great Molly Maguire Hoax: Based on Information Suppressed Ninety Years* (Wyoming, Pa., 1969)
Martin, J., *Harvests of Change: American Literature, 1865–1914* (Englewood Cliffs, 1967)
Marx, L., *The Machine in the Garden: Technology and the Pastoral Idea in America* (New York, 1964)
Mattes, P. V., *Tales of Scranton* (Scranton, n.d.)
Miller, D. and Sharpless, R. E., *The Kingdom of Coal: Work, Enterprise and Ethnic Communities in the Mine Fields* (Philadelphia, 1985)
Minchinton, W. E. (ed.), *Industrial South Wales, 1750–1914. Essays in Welsh Economic History* (London, 1969)
Montgomery, D., *Beyond Equality: Labor and the Radical Republicans, 1862–1872* (New York, 1967)
Morgan, K. O., *Lloyd George* (London, 1974)
Idem, Wales in British Politics, 1868–1922 (3rd edn., Cardiff, 1980)
Idem, Rebirth of a Nation: Wales, 1880–1980 (Oxford and London, 1981)
Morgan, P., *The Eighteenth Century Renaissance* (Llandybïe, 1981)
Morris, J. H. and Williams, L. J., *The South Wales Coal Industry, 1841–1875* (Cardiff, 1958)
Murphy, T. E., *Old Home Week Souvenir and History of Hyde Park* (Scranton, 1924)
Idem, History of Lackawanna County (Scranton, 1928)
Idem, History of the West Side Bank of Scranton, Pennsylvania, 1874–1949 (Scranton, 1949)
Nelli, H. S., *The Italians in Chicago, 1880–1930* (New York, 1970)
Pelling, H., *American Labor* (Chicago, 1960)
Platt, F., *Early History of Scranton and First Presbyterian Church* (Scranton, 1948)
Powderly, T. V., *The Path I Trod* (New York, 1947)
Pretty, D. A., *The Rural Revolt That Failed: Farm Workers' Trade Unions in Wales, 1889–1950* (Cardiff, 1989)
Rees, D. B. (ed.), *The Liverpool Welsh and their Religion. Two Centuries of Welsh Calvinistic Methodism* (Liverpool, 1984)
Roberts, E. W., *The Breaker Whistle Blows: Mining Disasters and Labor Leaders in the Anthracite Region* (Scranton, 1984)
Roberts, P., *The Anthracite Coal Industry* (New York, 1901)
Idem, Anthracite Coal Communities (New York, 1904)
Rosenzweig, R., *Eight Hours for What we Will: Workers and Leisure in an Industrial City* (Cambridge, Mass., 1983)
Roy, A., *A History of the Coal Miners of the United States* (Columbus, 1905)
Salay, D. L., *Hard Coal, Hard Times: Ethnicity and Labor in the Anthracite Regions* (Scranton, 1984)
Schlegel, M. W., *Ruler of the Reading: The Life of Franklin B. Gowen, 1836–1889* (Harrisburg, 1947)
Seventy-Fifth Anniversary of the First Welsh Baptist Church, Scranton, Pennsylvania, 1850–1925 (Scranton, 1925)
Shepperson, W. S., *Samuel Roberts: A Welsh Colonizer in Civil War Tennessee* (Knoxville, 1961)
Sixtieth Anniversary of Church Charter, First Welsh Congregational Church, Scranton, Pennsylvania 1864–1924 (Scranton, 1924)
Smith, D. (ed.), *A People and a Proletariat: Essays in the History of Wales, 1780–1980* (London, 1980)
Smith, David, *Wales! Wales?* (London, 1984)

Smith, David and Williams, Gareth, *Fields of Praise: The Official History of the Welsh Rugby Union, 1881–1981* (Cardiff, 1980)
Taylor, P. A. M., *Expectations Westward* (Edinburgh, 1965)
Thistlethwaite, F., *The Anglo-American Connection in the Early Nineteenth Century* (Philadelphia, 1959)
Thomas, B., *Migration and Economic Growth: A Study of Great Britain and the Atlantic Economy* (Cambridge, 1954)
Idem, (ed.), *The Welsh Economy: Studies in Expansion* (Cardiff, 1962)
Idem, *Migration and Urban Growth* (London, 1972)
Voight, D. Q., *American Baseball* (2 vols., Pennsylvania State University Press Reprint, 1983)
Wallace, A. F. C., *St. Clair: A Nineteenth Century Coal Town's Experience with a Disaster-Prone Industry* (New York, 1987)
Warne, F. J., *The Slav Invasion and the Mine Workers: A Study in Immigration* (Philadelphia, 1904)
Wiebe, R. H., *The Search for Order, 1877–1920* (London, 1967)
Williams, D. J., *One Hundred Years of Welsh Calvinistic Methodism in America* (Philadelphia, 1937)
Williams, David, *Cymru ac America: Wales and America* (Cardiff, 1946)
Idem, *A History of Modern Wales* (2nd edn., London, 1977)
Williams, Glanmor, *Samuel Roberts, Llanbrynmair* (Cardiff, 1950)
Idem, *Religion, Language and Nationality in Wales* (Cardiff, 1979)
Williams, Glyn, *The Desert and the Dream* (Cardiff, 1975)
Williams, G. A., *Madoc: The Making of a Myth* (London, 1980)
Idem, *The Search for Beulahland: The Welsh and the Atlantic Revolution* (London, 1980)
Idem, *The Welsh in their History* (London, 1982)
Idem, *When Was Wales* (Harmondsworth, 1985, paperback edition)
Williams, R. B., *Y Wladfa* (Cardiff, 1962)
Williams, T. L., *Caradoc Evans* (Cardiff, 1970)
Wittke, C., *We Who Built America* (New York, 1939)
Yearly, C. K., *Britons in American Labor: A History of the Influence of the United Kingdom Immigrants on American Labor, 1820–1914* (Baltimore, 1957)
Ziff, L., *The American 1890s: The Life and Times of a Lost Generation* (New York, 1966)
Zimmern, A., *My Impressions of Wales* (London, 1927)

8. ARTICLES

Beddoe, D., 'Munitionettes, maids and mams: women in Wales, 1914–1939', in A. V. John (ed.), *Our Mothers' Land: Chapters in Welsh Women's History 1830–1939* (Cardiff, 1991)
Berthoff, R. T., 'The social order of the anthracite region, 1825–1902', *Pennsylvania Magazine of History and Biography*, LXXXIX (July 1965)
Bodnar, J. E., 'Socialization and adaptation: immigrant families in Scranton, 1880–1890', *Pennsylvania History*, XVIII, No. 2 (1976)
Conway, A., 'Welsh emigration to the United States', in D. Fleming and B. Bailyn (eds.), *Dislocation and Emigration: The Social Background of American Immigration* (Cambridge, Mass., 1974)
Davies, J. G., 'Cambria, Wisconsin, in 1898', *Transactions of the Honourable Society of Cymmrodorion* (1957)
Davies, R., ' "In a broken dream": some aspects of sexual behaviour and the dilemmas of the unmarried mother in south-west Wales, 1887–1914', *Llafur*, III, No. 4 (1983)
Idem, 'Inside the "house of the mad": the social context of mental illness, suicide and the pressures of rural life in south-west Wales c. 1860–1920', *Llafur*, IV, No. 2 (1985)

BIBLIOGRAPHY

Idem, 'Voices from the void: social crisis, social problems and the individual in south west Wales, c. 1876–1920', in G. H. Jenkins and J. B. Smith (eds.), *Politics and Society in Wales, 1840–1922. Essays in Honour of Ieuan Gwynedd Jones* (Cardiff, 1988)

Edwards, H. T., 'Victorian Wales seeks reinstatement', *Planet*, No. 52 (August/September 1985)

Ellis, D., 'The assimilation of the Welsh in central New York', *Welsh History Review*, VI, No. 2 (1973)

Erickson, C. J., 'The encouragement of emigration by British trade unions, 1850–1900', *Population Studies*, III (December 1949)

Falzone, V. J., 'Terence V. Powderly: politician and progressive mayor of Scranton, 1878–1884', *Pennsylvania History*, XLI, No. 3 (July 1974)

Hall, B., 'The Welsh revival of 1904–05: a critique', in G. J. Cumming and D. Baker (eds.), *Popular Belief and Practice* (Cambridge, 1972)

Harris, J., 'Introduction' in Caradoc Evans, *My People* (ed. J. Harris, Bridgend, 1987)

Idem, ' "Neighbours": Caradoc Evans, Lloyd George and the London Welsh', *Llafur*, IV, No. 2 (1991)

Hopkin, D. R., 'Welsh immigrants to the U.S. and their press', in C. Harzig and D. Hoerder (eds.), *The Press of Labor Migrants in Europe and North America, 1880s–1930s* (Bremen, 1985)

John, A. V., 'A miner struggle? Women's protests in Welsh mining history', *Llafur*, IV, No. 1 (1984)

Jones, B., 'Daniel Protheroe, Haydn Evans and Welsh choral rivalry in late-nineteenth century Scranton, Pennsylvania', *Welsh Music*, IX, No. 3 (Spring 1991)

Jones, Dot, 'Counting the cost of coal: women's lives in the Rhondda, 1881–1911', in A. V. John (ed.), *Our Mothers' Land: Chapters in Welsh Women's History, 1830–1939* (Cardiff, 1991)

Jones, E., 'Some aspects of cultural change in an American Welsh Community', *Transactions of the Honourable Society of Cymmrodorion* (1952)

Jones, M. A., 'The background to American immigration from Great Britain in the nineteenth century', in D. Fleming and B. Bailyn (eds.), *Dislocation and Emigration: The Social Background of American Immigration* (Cambridge, Mass., 1974)

Idem, 'From the old country to the new: the Welsh in nineteenth century America', *Flintshire Historical Society Publications*, 27 (1975–6)

Jones, R. A. N., 'Women, community and collective action: the *Ceffyl Pren* tradition', in A. V. John (ed.), *Our Mothers' Land: Chapters in Welsh Women's History, 1830–1939* (Cardiff, 1991)

Jones, R. M., 'The Liverpool Welsh', in D. B. Rees (ed.), *The Liverpool Welsh and their Religion* (Liverpool, 1984)

Kneller, P., 'Welsh immigrant women as wage earners in Utica, New York', *Llafur*, V, No. 4 (1991)

Lewis, W. D., 'The early history of the Lackawanna Iron and Coal Co.: a study in technological adaptation', *Pennsylvania Magazine of History and Biography*, XCVI (October 1972)

Morgan, I., 'Welshmen in America', *Wales and Monmouthshire*, 1, No. 2 (1935)

Morgan, J. J. 'Atgofion am America', *Yr Eurgrawn Wesleyaidd*, CXXIII, Nos. 2 and 4 (February and April 1931)

Owen, Bob, 'Bedyddwyr Cymraeg yr Unol Daleithiau', *Trafnodion Cymdeithas Hanes Bedyddwyr Cymru* (1954)

Idem, 'Ymfudo o Sir Frycheiniog i'r Amerig, 1785–1860', *Brycheiniog*, VII (1961)

Roberts, G., 'Wales outside Wales', *Wales and Monmouthshire*, 1, No. 1 (1935)

Idem, 'Welshmen in contemporary America', *Wales and Monmouthshire*, 1, No. 6 (1936)

Roberts, M., 'The American Welsh', *Wales*, VII, No. 30 (November 1948)

Rodechko, J. E., 'Irish-American society in the Pennsylvania anthracite region, 1870–1880', in J. E. Bodnar (ed.), *The Ethnic Experience in Pennsylvania* (Lewisburg, 1973)

Schlegel, M. W., 'The Workingmen's Benevolent Association', *Pennsylvania History*, X (1943)
Smith, David, 'Tonypandy 1910: definitions of community', *Past and Present*, No. 87 (May 1980)
Idem, 'A novel history', in T. Curtis (ed.), *Wales: The Imagined Nation* (Bridgend, 1985)
Idem, 'Back to the future', *Planet*, No. 56 (April/May 1986)
Smith, T. L., 'New approaches to the history of immigration in twentieth century America', *American Historical Review*, LXXI, No. 4 (July 1966)
Stead, P., 'Amateurs and professionals in the cultures of Wales', in G. H. Jenkins and J. B. Smith (eds.), *Politics and Society in Wales, 1840–1922. Essays in Honour of Ieuan Gwynedd Jones* (Cardiff, 1988)
Thomas, M. W., 'My people and the revenge of the novel', *New Welsh Review*, No. 1 (Summer 1988)
Van Vugt, W. E., 'Welsh emigration to the U.S.A. in the mid-nineteenth century', *Welsh History Review*, 15, No. 4 (December 1991)
Walker, S. E., 'Varieties of working-class experience: the workingmen of Scranton, Pennsylvania, 1855–1885', in M. Cantor (ed.), *American Working-class Culture: Explorations in American Labor and Social History* (Westport, Conn., 1979)
Williams, C. R., 'The Welsh religious revival of 1904–05', *British Journal of Sociology*, 1952
Williams, David, 'Some figures relating to emigration from Wales', *Bulletin of the Board of Celtic Studies*, VII (1935)
Idem, 'The Welsh Mormons', *Welsh Review*, VII, No. 2 (Summer 1940)
Idem, 'The contribution of Wales to the development of the United States', *National Library of Wales Journal*, II (Summer 1942)
Williams, Gareth, ' "How's the tenors in Dowlais?" Hegemony, harmony and popular culture in England and Wales, 1600–1900', *Llafur*, V, No. 1 (1988)
Williams, Glanmor, 'The idea of nationality in Wales', *Cambridge Journal*, VII, No. 3 (December 1953)
Williams, Glyn, 'The structure and process of Welsh emigration to Patagonia', *Welsh History Review*, VIII, No. 1 (June 1976)
Williams, J. A., 'The influence of the Welsh on the history of Pennsylvania', *Pennsylvania History*, X (April 1943)
Williams, L. J., 'The road to Tonypandy', *Llafur*, I, No. 2 (1973)
Williams, T. L., 'The birth of a reputation: early reactions to the work of Caradoc Evans' *Anglo-Welsh Review*, 19, No. 44 (1970)
Williams, W., 'The first three books printed in America', *National Library of Wales Journal*, II (Summer 1942)
Idem, 'More about the first three books printed in America', *National Library of Wales Journal*, III (Summer 1943)

9. THESES

Barclay, M., 'Aberdare, 1880–1914; class and community' (M.A., University of Wales, 1985)
Blatz, P. K., 'Ever-shifting ground: work and labor relations in the anthracite coal industry' (Ph.D., Princeton University, 1987)
Evans, P. D., 'The Welsh in Oneida County' (M.A., Cornell University, 1914)
Gallaher, P. J., 'Scranton: industry and politics, 1835–1885' (Ph.D., Catholic University of America, 1964)
Gottlieb, A. Z., 'The regulation of the coal mining industry in Illinois with special reference to the influence of British miners and British precedents, 1870–1911' (Ph.D., University of London, 1975)

Jones, W. D., 'Wales in America: Scranton and the Welsh, c. 1860–1920' (Ph.D., University of Wales, 1987)
Knowles, A. K., 'Welsh settlement in Waukesha County, Wisconsin, 1840–1873' (M.Sc., University of Wisconsin, 1989)
Walker, S. E., 'Terence V. Powderly – labor mayor: workingmen's politics in Scranton, 1870–1884, (Ph.D., Ohio State University, 1973)

INDEX

Abbott, Philip, 3
Aberdare, 66, 100, 204, 205, 217n
Abraham, William, M.P. ('Mabon'), 222–3, 224–6
Adams, John, 168
Adams, John Quincy, 168
Adams, Margaret, 148
adultery, 215, 216, 217
Akron, 245
Allegheny Co. (Pa.), xx, 252
American Celt, 115, 119 and n
American football, 219
American Gorsedd, 147, 163, 178–201, 228, 241, 242
  (1913–19), 179–84
  failure of, 199–201
  formation, 178–9
  Gorsedd Home (Pittsburgh), 184, 186, 196, 200
  'new' Gorsedd of 1919, 184–92
  at World's Fair Eisteddfod 1893, 153, 159, 162, 171, 172
American Institute of Mining Engineers, 34
American National Eisteddfod *see* eisteddfod
American Printing Company, 178n
Americanization, 105, 106–45 *passim*, 200, 219–20, 233, 247
Ancient Order of Hibernians, 12
anthracite coalfield, north-east Pennsylvania, xx, 2, 5–6, 7, 29, 33, 34, 36, 44, 52, 79n, 80, 85, 211, 212, 254
  see also anthracite industry; Lehigh coalfield; Schuylkill coalfield; Wyoming–Lackawanna coalfield
anthracite industry, north-east Pennsylvania,
  accidents in, 1, 44–6
  chain of command, 31n
  decline of 9
  growth of 5–7,
  recomposition of work-force in, 83–5
  in Scranton, 1, 3, 4, 5–6, 7 and n, 8, 9, 16–17, 18, Chapter II, *passim*
  Welsh in, 16–17, 18, Chapter II, *passim*, 247

see also anthracite mines; strikes
anthracite mines
  Archbald, 48
  Bellevue, 32
  Boston, 30
  Brigg's Shaft, 65, 67
  Church, 57
  Continental, 46, 48
  Diamond, 7, 17, 34, 37, 42
  Greenwood, 38
  Hyde Park, 48
  Lackawanna, 37
  Lansford, 37
  Mount Pleasant, 17, 24
  Oxford, 32, 33
  Storrs, 33
  Tripp's Slope, 58
Ap Madoc, William, 150, 153, 156–7, 159, 162–5, 169, 172, 177, 178, 180
Archbald, 8, 18
Arion Society (Brooklyn), 130–1
athletic contests *see* foot racing
Austrian Empire, immigrants from, 11, 255, 257–8
Avondale Mine Disaster (1869), 1, 44–5

ballads, anthracite mining, 44
Band of Hope, 93
Baner ac Amserau Cymru, 158
Baner America, 27, 42, 61–2, 62n, 74, 76, 88–9, 103, 211
Baner y Gweithiwr, 89 and n
banks, 2, 8, 26
  see also under names
Baptists, 18, 41, 45 and n, 55, 91–2, 106
  see also First Welsh Baptist Church
Barratt, J. E., 131
baseball, 60, 217, 219–20
Bellevue (Scranton), 57, 68
Benjamin, Isaac (Bardd Coch), 88
Bible Schools, 93–4
bigamy, 215
billiards, 218–19
Blackwell, Henry, 180, 183
Blodau'r Oes a'r Ysgol, 163
'bossism', Welsh, 35–43
Boston, 244

INDEX

Bowen, George W., 236, 237 and n, 239, 240, 241
Bowen, Morgan, 38
Bowen, Theophilus, 244, 245
breaker boys, 30, 81
  see also children, employment of
Brooklyn, 130, 131, 133, 252
Brooks, Reese G., 116
Brynffynnon Welsh colony (Tenn.), xvi
Bushnell, General, 60 and n

Caernarfon, 230, 243
Cairns, Michael ('Fenian'), 67, 68, 69, 71
California, xx, 250
Calvinistic Methodists, 41, 55, 91
  see also Hyde Park Welsh Calvinistic Methodist Church
Cambria (Wis.), 110
Cambrian, 107, 156, 157, 158, 163, 172, 195, 198, 200, 225, 227, 233
Cambrian Combine dispute (1910–11), 226, 233
  see also Tonypandy 'Riots'
Cambrian Gleanings, 180
Cambrian Mutual Fire and Insurance Co., 26, 202n
Cambro-Americans (choir), 98, 133
Canada, 179, 181
  Canadian immigrants, 257–8
Capoose, 3
Caradog see Jones, Griffith Rhys
Carbondale, 6–7, 8, 14, 15, 18, 98, 210
Carbondale Advance, 210
Cardiff, 243
Cardiff Ladies Choir, 161
Cardiff Welsh Society, 164
Catausaqua, 13, 14n
Catholicism, 11, 12, 92–3
Chain Gang, 213 and n
Charles, T. Owen, 118, 119, 178n, 180, 183, 193n, 197 and n, 232
  Dear Old Wales: A Patriotic Love Story, 143n, 197n, 234
Chartism, 228, 229
Chicago, 147, 150, 165, 177, 252
  see also World's Fair, Chicago (1893)
Chicago, Milwaukee and St Paul Rail Road Company, 162
Chidlaw, Benjamin, 171
children, employment of, 30, 46–7
  see also breaker boys
choirs, 23, 94, 98, 99, 126, 127, 129, 130–1, 132–4, 134n, 135, 140, 141, 154, 160–1, 173–4, 190n, 220, 243

  see also under names; singing
churches, 1, 2, 5, 15, 17–18, 20, 27, 28, 42 and n, 56, 59, 87, 91–5, 106–12, 114, 177, 206n
  see also under denominations and names
cinemas, 220–1
Citizen Party, 79
Cleveland, 121n, 252
Clifford Township (Susquehanna Co.), 14
Clwydfardd, Archdruid, 153
coal mining
  in bituminous coalfields in U.S.A., xx, 80
  see also anthracite industry;
cock-fighting, 206, 217
Columbia, Y, 155
Company G., 77th Regiment, 71
company stores, 5, 41, 42n
Conciliation Board (south Wales coal industry), 223, 224
Congregationalists, 17–18, 41, 91, 93, 106, 107
  see also under church names
Co-operative store (Scranton), 25
Cosmopolitan, 152
courtship, 94
Cyfaill o'r Hen Wlad, Y, 90
Cymanfa Ganu, 1, 144
Cymdeithas Genedlaethol Gymreig yr America, 183–4, 184n
Cymmrodorion Choral Society, 126, 133, 134, 135, 136–40, 141
Cymmrodorion Ladies Choir, 133, 138
Cymmrodorion Male Choir, 133
Cymmrodorion Society (Chicago), 149, 150, 151
Cymmrodorion Society (Scranton), 115–18, 119, 120n, 123, 124, 202 and n
Cymric Denial Day, 197
'Cymro Gwyllt', 154
Cynon, Eos, 99, 135
Cynonfardd, see Edwards, Revd T. Cynonfardd

Daily Democrat (Scranton), 60, 71n
Damrosch, Walter, 131, 143n
dancing, 220
Daniels, William B., 20
Danville (Pa.), 13
Darlington, Thomas, 128–9, 130, 131
Davies, Ben, 167
Davies, Clara Novello, 161

INDEX

Davies, Henry D., 74
Davies, Hon. George R., 151
Davies, J. Glyndwr, 110
Davies, John W., 184
Davies, Revd Joseph E. ('Ieuan Ddu'), 88
Davies, Revd R. R., 196, 199
Davies, Robert H. ('Gomerian'), 122, 178 and n, 183, 186, 192, 237, 247–8
Davies, T. Ellsworth, 81 and n, 115, 116, 136n
Davies, Thomas D., 26, 32, 33, 81, 96, 101, 116
Davies, W. Cadwaladr, 165–6
Davies, W. D., 155, 160, 206n
America a Gweledigaethau Bywyd, 172
Davies, Dr William Rowland, 25
Davis, Benjamin, 67, 68
Davis, Enoch, 55, 69
Davis, Gomer C., 26
Davis, James J., 200
Davis, John F., 13–14, 27
Davis, Lewis C., 21
Davis, Judge Noah, 162
Delaware and Hudson Canal, 6
Delaware and Hudson Railroad Co., 7, 14, 15, 52
Delaware, Lackawanna and Western Railroad Co., 4, 7, 11, 16, 29, 32, 33–4, 52, 103n, 104
Democratic Party, 11, 59, 60, 71n, 73, 75, 78, 79
desertion (by Welsh husbands and wives), 215–16, 217
Detroit, 245
'Dewi Cwmtwrch' *see* Powell, David C.
Dickson City, 8
doctors, 2, 25, 27, 81
dog-fighting, 206, 217
domestic servants, xvii, xviii, 27, 47
Dowlais, 204
dressmakers, xviii, 27
Dr Parry Male Choir, 127, 133
Druid, 119 and n, 122n, 123, 144, 178n, 179, 180n, 184, 186, 190n, 193n, 194, 195, 196–7, 198–9, 200, 221, 222–4, 225, 226, 229–30, 231, 232 and n, 233 and n, 236, 237, 239, 240, 241, 242, 243, 245
Druid Brass Band, 220
Druid Society of Lackawanna County *see* Scranton Druid Society
drunkenness, 90, 203, 214–12
Drych, Y, xx, xxii, 96n, 102, 103, 104, 107, 142n, 151, 155, 163, 171, 173, 178n, 200, 204, 205, 233, 245
Dunmore, 3
'Dyfed' *see* Rees, Revd E.

Ebeneser Welsh Calvinistic Methodist Church, 111
'Ednyfed' *see* Evans, Revd Fred
education, 24–5, 96, 103, 165–6
Edwards, Revd Ebenezer ('William Penn'), 167
Facts about Welsh Factors, 168–71
Edwards, Judge Henry M., 2, 25, 26, 38, 69, 87, 88, 89, 95, 97, 101 and n, 102n, 113n, 116, 118 and n, 120, 121, 125, 130, 131, 144, 162, 169, 180, 185, 189, 203 and n, 216, 225n, 243
Edwards, Revd Jonathan, 211
Edwards, O. M., 160
Edwards, R. J., 24
Edwards, Revd T. Cynonfardd, 103, 162, 165, 169, 179, 180, 185–6, 211
Edwardsville, 45n, 211
Edwardsville Congregational Church, 103
eisteddfod, xv, 41, 49, 87, 88, 94, 97–100, 101, 115, 119, 120, 121, 123, 125–32, 134, 142 and n, 143–5, 149, 156–7, 166, 184, 185, 193, 202, 203, 217, 245, 248
American National Eisteddfodau (in Scranton): (1875), 101–5, 129, 131, 133, 143n; (1880), 125, 126; (1885), 125, 126, 131; (1902), 125, 130, 131, 143n; (1905, 1908), 125
Carbondale (1850), 98
Philadelphia Centennial (1879), 133
Pittsburgh International (1913), 133, 178, 180, 200
San Francisco International (1915), 180
Scranton: (1867), 98; Gwilym Gwent (1892), 126, 131; Robert Morris Lodge of the Ivorites (1894), 127, (1897), 115
St Louis (1904), 133
see also National Eisteddfod of Wales; World's Fair Eisteddfod
elections, 60n
Luzerne County (October 1871), 75
Scranton mayoral election (1872), 75, (1878), 79
Electric City Bank, 26
Ellis, Revd Morgan A., 69, 89, 90

274 INDEX

emigration, Welsh to United States, xv–xxii, 15, 209, 244–5, 249
  see also Welsh
England, xvi, 21, 129, 167, 249,
English, 11, 12–13, 19, 50, 65, 66, 79n, 83, 85, 92, 230–1, 255, 257–8
Evans, Beriah Gwynfe, 160
Evans, Caradoc, 235–6, 237–8, 241–2, 244, 245
  Welsh-American reviews of writings of, 235–42
Evans, D. D., and Co., 22
Evans, Daniel J., 25, 216
Evans, Revd E. B., 25
Evans, Revd Fred ('Ednyfed'), 88, 89, 90, 92, 156, 157, 162
Evans, George 'Honey Boy', 221
Evans, George B., 20
Evans, Haydn, 133, 134, 136, 137 and n, 138, 139
Evans, Reese T., 42
Eynon, Albert, 19, 118
Eynon, Thomas, 19, 95, 98

Fife and Drum Corps, 220
First Welsh Baptist Church, 55, 92, 93, 95, 106, 108, 110, 112, 211
foot racing, 206, 217n, 218
Ford Gron, Y, 89
Ford, John, 244
Forest City, 32
Free Props Act, 33
funeral directors, 2, 22, 44

gambling, 217–18
Garfield, James, 168
Garrety, William, 68
Geary, Governor, 58, 68–9
Germany, 197
Germans, 11, 12, 19, 50, 55, 57, 60, 61, 64 and n, 65, 73, 79n, 83, 92, 127, 129, 130–1, 137, 205, 212, 213 and n, 214, 255, 257–8
Gibbons, Phoebe, 28, 47, 49, 52, 53, 63, 94 and n, 98, 100, 117, 127, 208, 209, 220
Gladstone, W. E., 166
Glimpses of the Gorsedd: A Brief Sketch of the History of the American Gorsedd, 186, 191
'Gomerian', *see* Davies, Robert H.
Good Templars, 205, 210–11
  Teml Cambro-America, 210
  Teml Gwalia, Bellevue, 210
Gorsedd of Bards of Great Britain, 150, 153, 165, 178, 188
  see also American Gorsedd
Grant, General Ulysses S., 76
Granville (N.Y.), 142, 252
Greeley, Horace, 76
Greenback-Labor Party, 76, 78, 79, 89
Griffiths, T. Solomon, 163
Gwent Glee Choir, 160
Gwent Male Chorus, 197

Hammond, Revd John, 110
Harris, Howell, 36–7
Harrison, Benjamin, 168
Harrison, William, 168
Hartanft, Governor, 102, 103, 104, 131
Herald Cymraeg, Yr, xv, xvi, 248
Herbert, Llew, 99, 135
'Home Guards' band, 220
Home Rule for Wales,
  Druid's views on, 196 and n
'horning', 216
'How Green Was My Valley' (film), 244
Howell, George, 24, 118, 120
Howell, Lizzie Harris, 120–1, 121n
Howells, Anthony, 162
Howells, William, 231–3
Hughes, Benjamin F., 16, 26, 32, 33, 34–5, 35n, 40, 45, 56, 74, 95, 101, 102, 116, 202 and n
Hughes, Evan, 45
Hughes, Revd J. Cromwell, 111
Hughes, John ('Irlwyn'), 88
Hughes, Thomas R., 25, 116
Hungarians, 83, 85, 255, 257–8
'Hwfa Môn' *see* Williams, Revd Rowland
Hyde Park (Scranton), 1–2, 3, 7, 17–27, *passim*, Chapter II, *passim*, Chapter III, *passim*, 204–21 *passim*,
  Welsh 'bossism' in, 40–3
  Welsh businesses in, 19–24, 27,
  Welsh settlement in, 17–18
  see also Scranton; Welsh
Hyde Park Baptist Choir, 133, 134
Hyde Park Choral Union, 98, 133
Hyde Park Deposit Bank, 26
Hyde Park Literary and Scientific Association, 114
Hyde Park Welsh Calvinistic Methodist Church, 68, 95, 111
Hyde Park Welsh Congregational Church, 93, 95, 106
'hyphenated Americanism', 180n

INDEX

'Idriswyn', 150, 158
Illinois, xx, 250
indentured servants, xvi
Indiana, xx, 250
Indian Territory, 84, 250
insurance agents, 25–6, 27, 81
International Congress of Cymmrodorion at World's Fair Eisteddfod, 165–6, 176
International Corresponding Schools, 9
Ireland, 21, 196n, 249, 255
Irish, 11–12, 17, 19, 37, 50, 57, 58, 60 and n, 61, 64, 65, 66, 68, 70, 73, 75, 76, 77, 78, 79, 83, 84, 92–3, 127, 129, 137, 204, 212, 213 and n, 255, 257–9
iron industry
 in Britain, 4
 in Scranton, 3–4, 5, 7, 8, 13–14, 16
 in United States, 3, 4, 14n
 in Wales, 13, 14n
 see also ironworkers
ironworkers, xviii, 13–14, 16, 27
 see also iron industry
Italy, xviiin, 11,
Italians, 11, 19, 82, 83, 86, 233, 255, 257–8
Ivorites
 lodges in Scranton, 69, 95, 114–15, 124, 125, 127, 130, 218
 see also Robert Morris Lodge, Teml Ifor Hael, Thomas Jefferson Lodge

James, Lizzie Parry, 99
James, Thomas L., 153, 162, 168
Jefferson, Thomas, 168
Jenkins, David, 133
Jenny Lind Chorus, 120, 133
Jermyn, 8, 18
Jermyn Coal Co., 33
Job, Samuel, 154, 169
Jones, Revd D. P., 176–7
Jones, Daniel, 67–8
Jones, David M., 24, 26, 68, 74, 79, 116
Jones, Edward, 18, 103
Jones, Emrys, 109, 128
Jones, Revd Erasmus W., 234
Jones, Griffith Rhys ('Caradog'), 123, 161
Jones, Henry D., 21
Jones, Horatio Gates, 102, 103
Jones, J. P., 37
Jones, Revd R. B., 110
Jones, Robert, 98
Jones, Sarah J., 23

Jones, W. B., 200
Jones, W. S., 49, 74
Jones, Walter H., 26
Junger Männerchor, 135

Keystone Bank, 26
Knights of Labor, 76n, 77, 78, 79 and n, 80n

Labor Reform Union of Luzerne County, 74, 75
Lackawanna County, xx, 8, 18, 25, 252
Lackawanna (Pa.), 9
Lackawanna County Druid Society see Scranton Druid Society
Lackawanna County Medical Society, 25
Lackawanna Historical Society, 202
Lackawanna Iron and Coal Co., 5, 64
Lackawanna River, 2, 11, 17
Lackawanna Steel Works, 9
Lackawanna Valley, 4, 5, 6, 7, 8, 14, 15, 18, 34, 98, 110, 138, 145, 146, 211n, 225
Ladies' Night, 119–21, 233 and n
lawyers, Welsh, in Scranton, 2, 25, 27, 81
Leach, Ebeneser, 75
Lehigh (or Middle) anthracite coalfield (north-east Pa.), 5
Levi, John 54
Lewis, Capt. Thomas D., 69
Lewis, John P., 53
Lewis, William T., 25
Liberal Party see Liberalism
Liberalism, 224 and n, 229, 236, 238
Lincoln, Abraham, 232
literature,
 Jewish-American, 234
 Welsh-American, 193n, 234–5
Lithuanians, 85
Liverpool, 113, 152, 154, 165
Lloyd George, David, 198, 222
 visit to United States, 179, 184, 192–3,
 Welsh–American opinions on, 187, 191–6, 199, 225
London, 143, 152, 165, 167
Lusitania, sinking of, 197
Luzerne County, xx, 3, 8, 72, 100, 145, 252

Mabon see Abraham, William, M.P.
Madoc ap Owain Gwynedd, Prince, xvi, 149, 177
Mahanoy City, 213 and n, 214

INDEX

Mankato Free Press, 158
marriage, age of Welsh at, 94n
Matthews, George T., 197
Maxey, George, 25, 243
Mckune, Mayor, 78, 102
Merthyr, 204, 205
Methodists *see* Calvinistic Methodists
migration, Welsh,
   from Wales to England, 245
   from Scranton, 15n, 52–3, 84–5, 245
miners, xviii, xx
   coal, 1, 15, 16, 17, Chapter II, *passim*
Miners and Laborers' Amalgamated Association, 79n
'Miner's Doom, The' (ballad), 44
Miners' Journal (Pottsville), 46, 208
mining *see* anthracite industry;
Minnesota, 9, 250
Modocs, 213 and n, 214
Molly Maguires, 37 and n, 39, 213 and n, 214
Morgan, Abel
   Cyd-Gordiad, 103
Morgan, B. G., 21, 23, 61, 69, 95
Morris, John Courier, 24–5, 89, 90, 115, 136n, 183, 231, 232, 236, 241
Morris, Robert, 124
Morris, T. B. ('Gwyneddfardd'), 88
Mountain Ash, 66, 100, 146n, 190n
Murphy, Thomas, 40, 96, 133
music *see* singing
music-halls, 109, 220–1

National Association of Letter Carriers, 24
National Eisteddfod of Wales, 98n, 143, 150, 151, 152, 153,
   (1884) (Liverpool), 152 and n
   (1887) (London), 152 and n, 161
   (1891) (Swansea), 150
   (1893) (Pontypridd), 150, 158
   (1907) (Swansea), 164
   National Eisteddfod Association of Wales, 150, 160
   see also eisteddfodau
National Life Insurance Co., 25
native-Americans, 13, 59, 60, 62, 63, 86, 100, 105, 202, 246
Neath (Bradford Co., Pa.), 14
New Jersey, 4, 250
New Wales (Pa.), 14
New York and Erie Railroad, 4, 16
New York and Scranton Coal Co., 32
New York City, 4, 6, 7 and n, 8, 131,
   183, 184, 252
New York State, 4, 7, 10, 26, 224, 250
New York Times, 230
New York World, 154, 155
News of the Week, 158
newspapers, Welsh-American *see* press
Nonconformity, 91–95, 106, 107 and n, 111, 224, 229, 236, 238
north Wales, xviii, 142, 165
Northern anthracite coalfield (north-east Pa.) *see* Wyoming–Lackawanna coalfield

Oakland (Cal.), 196,
Ohio, xx, 80, 199, 224, 250
Olyphant, 8, 18, 100, 205, 219
Osborne, Major General Edwin S., 58, 60, 69
Owen, Bob (Croesor), 192
Oxford Iron Furnace (N.J.), 4

Park Coal Co., 17
Parry, Joseph, 98 and n, 221
Patagonia (Argentina), 20
Patagonia (Scranton), 20, 57, 212
paternity suits, 216–17
Pencerdd Gwalia, 160
   'Llewellyn', 167
Penn, William, 168
Pennsylvania, xx, 4, 10, 80, 82, 104, 122, 182, 199, 224, 250
   north-east Pennsylvania xx, 2, 7
   see also anthracite coalfield
Pennsylvania Coal Co., 7, 52
Pennsylvania Mines Inspectorate, 84
Pennsylvania National Guard, 58, 78
Penrhyn, Lord, 116
Penrhyn dispute (1900–3), 222
Penrhyn Male Choir, 160, 161
periodicals, Welsh-American *see* press
Philadelphia, 6, 11, 15, 134, 252
Philadelphia Cambro-American League, 232
Phillips, Ben, 180
Phillips, George, 24, 25
Phillips, Henry D., 32
Phillips, Colonel Reese A., 26, 33, 35n, 40, 103n, 118, 136n, 180
Phillips, Thomas H., 33
Phillips, Revd Thomas J, 96, 103 and n
Pioneer Building and Loan Association, 26
Pittston, 8, 100, 134
Pittsburgh, xx, 11, 133, 178, 180, 184,

INDEX

186, 195, 199, 200, 201, 252
Pittsburgh St David's Society, 178n, 183n
Plymouth (Pa.), 44, 100, 205, 211, 219
Plymouth Welsh Congregational Church (Scranton), 106, 211
Poles, 83, 84, 85, 255, 257–8
police, Welsh in, 24, 27
politics, xv, 24, 27, 59–60, 73–80
  see also Citizen Party, Democratic Party, Greenback-Labor Party, Labor Reform Union, Republican Party
Pontypridd, 150, 158
postal service, Welsh in, 23–4, 27
Pottsville, 34, 252
poverty, 48
Powderly, Terence V., 76 and n, 78, 79
Powell, David C. ('Dewi Cwmtwrch'), 88, 90, 109n, 110, 111, 118n, 121, 128, 140, 205
Powell, John H., 64, 77 and n, 78
Powell, Morgan, 37n
Powell, W. E. ('Gwilym Eryri'), 154, 162
press, Welsh-American, xxi–ii, 88–9
  see also under names
Price, William, and Son's Funeral Parlour and Furniture Warehouse, 22
Prichard, David, 130
Prince of Wales, investiture of (1911), 195, 230, 243
prize-fighting, 217–18
Protheroe, Daniel, 23, 133, 134, 136, 137 and n, 138, 139, 142 and n
Providence (Scranton), 3, 7, 17, 18, 54, 69, 100
Providence Brass Band, 220
Providence Congregationalist Church, 107
Pughe, Lewis, 8n, 75 and n, 76, 116, 202 and n
Puleston, Sir John, M.P., 116
Pullman Iron and Steel Co., 154
Punch, 90, 227–8
Puritan Congregational Church, 107
Pwnsh Cymraeg, Y (Liverpool), 90
Pwnsh Cymraeg, Y (Scranton), 90

Quakers, xxi

railways, 1, 2, 4, 8
  see also under names
Rebecca Riots, 228–9
Rees, Ebeneser, 54 and n

Rees, Revd E. ('Dyfed'), 160, 167, 178
Reese, William M., 21–2
religion *see* Catholicism; churches; Nonconformity
Religious Revivals, 110–12
Republican Party, 24, 57, 59, 60 and n, 61, 63, 73, 74, 75, 76, 78, 79, 89
Reynold's Billiard Rooms, 218
Rhondda, xx, 198, 221
Rhondda Glee Choir, 160, 161
Rhondda Leader, 142
Rhymney, 204, 205
Rhys, Professor John, 160
Richards, Glyndwr, 190n
Richards, Hon. David, 161
Richards, John T., 231, 232
Richards, Revd T. Teifion, 108, 110
Robert Morris Lodge (Ivorites), 114, 115 and n, 127, 218
Roberts, Margaret, 96 and n
Roberts, Samuel, xvi
Roberts, Revd William, 55, 90
Roosevelt, President Theodore, 123
Royal Blue Book: Prize Productions of the Pittsburgh International Eisteddfod, 180, 181, 200
rugby, 219, 220n

saloons, 2, 22, 42, 203, 204–12, 213, 214, 215
Salt Lake City, 195, 252
Schuylkill (or Southern) anthracite coalfield (north-east Pa.), 5, 32, 37, 44, 53, 83, 202n, 212, 213
Schuylkill Co., 39, 252
Scots, 11, 12, 50, 65, 66, 83, 85, 249, 255, 257–8
Scranton family, 4–5, 8, 13, 15, 16
Scranton, George, 4, 5
Scranton, Selden T., 4, 5, 13
Scranton, William, 62, 63, 65, 67, 68, 71, 77
Scranton
  American élite in, 202
  anthracite industry in, 3, 4, 5–6, 7 and n, 8, Chapter II, passim
  early history, 2–3
  immigrant groups in, 9–13, 255, 257–8
  industrial decline, 1, 9–10, 244–5
  industrialization and urban growth, 3–9
  population, 3, 10, 255
  see also Welsh
Scranton Allbright Library, 114

Scranton Board of Trade, 8
Scranton Catholic Choir Association, 127
Scranton Choral Society, 99
Scranton Choral Union, 133, 134, 136–41
Scranton City Guard, 78
Scranton Club, 202
Scranton Druid Society, 103n, 115, 118–24, 183n, 193, 220, 233, 243
  see also Druid; Ladies' Night; Welsh Days
Scranton Glee Club, 133
Scranton Ladies Choir, 133
Scranton National Eisteddfod Association see eisteddfod, Scranton (1902)
Scranton Oratorio Society, 133, 140
Scranton Poor Board, 215–16, 217
Scranton Republican, 27, 33, 36, 52, 55, 57n, 59, 60–2, 67, 69, 70, 71–2, 74–5, 89, 100, 103, 104–5, 130, 135, 137
Scranton St David's Society, 116
Scranton Times, 103, 122n
Scranton Welsh Women's Club see Welsh-American Women's Clubs
Scranton Young Men's Hebrew Association, 245–6
Shamokin, 135, 252
Shanty Hill (Scranton), 17, 18
Shenandoah Herald, 212
singing, 69, 90, 105, 123, 132–45, 163, 173, 221
  soloists, 99, 126, 133, 134, 135
  see also choirs
slate industry, in Wales, 222
slate quarrymen, xviii,
Sloan, Sam, 34, 56, 71, 80n, 102, 131
Slocum Brothers, 3, 4
Slocum Hollow, 3, 15, 92
soccer, 219
south Wales, xviii, xx, 2, 9, 13, 14n, 16, 33, 41, 91, 134 and n, 165, 198, 210, 217, 223, 226, 230, 245, 247
South Wales Choral Union, 123, 133–4, 161
sports, 204, 206
  see also under names
Springbrook (Pa.), 14
St David's Day Banquets, 1, 116–18, 120n, 121, 202
St David's Society see Pittsburgh St David's Society; Scranton St David's Society

St Peter's Cathedral Choir, 127
steel industry, 9
steelworkers, xviii, 16, 27
Stephens, Thomas, 177
Stephens, Tom (Rhondda Glee Choir), 161
Stephens, W. J., 131
Storrs, W. R., 34, 35, 54, 55, 56, 58, 70, 71, 80n
strikes, 9, 20, 21,
  disturbances during, 57–60, 62, 67–8, 77–8, 214
  national railroad (1877), 77
  Scranton, miners' strikes in, 79n; (1869), 53, 54; (1871), 1, 30, 37, 50, 51–73, 85–6, 88, 214, 219, 247; (1877), 76, 77
  south Wales, miners' strikes in, 223, 226n; (1898), lock-out, 227; (1915), 199, 236; attitudes of Welsh-American press towards, 222–9; Cambrian Combine (1910–11), 226, 233
Sunday Schools
  in Scranton, 2, 93, 95, 101, 108
  in Wales, 107n, 166
Survidal, Revd William, 185, 189, 190
Swansea Valley, 14n, 54
Swedes, 85, 257–8

Tarian y Bobl, 89 and n
Taylor, 18, 54
Taylor, Moses, 102
Teml Cambro-America see Good Templars
Teml Gwalia Bellevue see Good Templars
Teml Ifor Hael Lodge, 95
temperance, 96n, 111, 205, 206, 207, 209, 210–11
Tennessee, xvi, xx, 250
textile industry, 8, 9, 46
Thomas, Governor Arthur L., 182, 195
Thomas, E. M., 21
Thomas, Revd Ebenezer Pugh, 179, 185, 186–8, 191, 193
Thomas Jefferson Lodge (Ivorites), 114
Thomas, Morgan, 23, 118
Thomas, Revd R. D. ('Iorthryn Gwynedd'), 91, 206n
  Hanes Cymry America, 91, 206n
Thomas, William M. ('Bully Bill'), 213–14
Thomas Zouaves, 60, 69

INDEX

tin-plate workers, xviii, xix
Tonypandy 'Riots' (1910)
   reactions of Welsh-American press to, 221, 229
Tredegar (Wales), 204
Twain, Mark, 116

unionism, among Welsh miners, 53–4, 76–80
   see also strikes; under names of unions
United Mine Workers of America, 80
United States of America, 10, 26, 34, 45n, 84, 87, 88, 92, 98, 101, 102, 104, 111, 112, 119, 121, 128, 142, 147, 148, 149, 153, 156, 161, 163, 165, 167, 170, 177, 189, 197, 200, 201, 210, 244
   decline of religious observance in, 109
   during Depression, 245
   social change in, 175
University of Wales Act, 166
Utah, xx, 250,
Utica, 109, 128, 142 and n, 155, 156n, 200

Vopalecky, Mrs J. L., 191

wages, xix, 36, 49, 51, 77, 83, 223
Wales, 2, 15, 16, 21, 27, 45n, 53, 61, 84, 88, 98n, 100, 109, 112, 115, 129, 142, 143, 144, 146, 150, 151, 152, 153, 154, 160, 168, 170, 173, 176, 189, 194, 195, 198, 199, 204, 209, 235
   choirs in, 133, 134 and n, 142, 143, 160–1
   eisteddfod in, 98, 129, 162n
   and First World War, 191–2, 197–9
   industrial relations in, 222–9
   Irish in, 65–6
   'national revival' in, 148, 160, 165, 166–7
   public houses in, 208, 210
   religion in, 91, 92, 107, 111–12, 166, 169–70, 229–30
   sports in, 217, 219
   temperance in, 207, 210
   see also north Wales; south Wales; Welsh
Wales, 128, 228
wars
   (1812), 6
   American Civil War, 51, 123, 175
   First World War, 9, 180n, 191–2, 196, 197–8, 199

War of Independence, 3
Washburn Street Cemetery, 1, 45, 69
'Watcyn Wyn', 160
Watkins, John T., 133, 134, 140, 180
Watres, Lt.-Col., L. A., 117
Welsh
   in Scranton, xx, xxii, 1–2, 146, 175, 180, 200, 233, 244–7, 248, 255, 256, 257–8; alternative culture, 203–21; Americanization, 105, 106–45, *passim*, 200, 219–20, 233 247; in anthracite industry, 16, 17, Chapter II, *passim*; cultural life in, Chapter III, *passim*; eisteddfodau, 97–105, 125–32, 142–5; music, 98–100, 132–45; in public life, 24–27; religion, 17–18, 20, 91–5, 106–12; settlement, 15–19; societies, 90, 95–7, 112–25; upward mobility, 81–2, 85; Welsh élite, 202–3, 243, 245–7
   in United States, xv–xxii, 32, 82, 83, 104, 111, 118, 134, 144, Chapter IV, *passim*, 204, 222–42, *passim*, 244–8, 249–253; opinions on David Lloyd George, 191–6, 198–9, 243; on industrial relations in Wales, 222–9; on role of Wales in First World War, 196–9; on Wales and Welshness, 146–91, *passim*, 222–42, 247–8; on writings of Caradoc Evans, 235–42, 243–4
   see also emigration
Welsh Boarding House, 22
Welsh Christian Endeavour Societies in America, 177
Welsh Days, 119, 121, 122–4, 144, 193, 219, 233n, 243
Welsh Hill (Pa.), 14
Welsh language, 17, 35, 63, 69, 87, 90 and n, 95, 96, 99, 104, 111, 121, 152n, 203
   decline in usage, 106–14, 127–9, 175, 245
Welsh Philosophical Society, 35, 41, 77n, 95–7, 98, 99, 101, 103–4, 112, 114, 116, 126, 204 and n, 206n, 207
   Library, 25, 27, 101, 104, 114 and n
Welsh Prize Male Choir, 133
Welsh Review, 158, 160
Welsh Soldier's Relief Societies, 197
Welsh-Amrican see Druid
Welsh-American Women's Clubs, 121n, 185, 191
   Scranton branch, 121n, 243

INDEX

West Side Bank, 19, 26, 90, 202n
West Virginia, xx, 250
Western Mail, 162, 233
wife-beating, 215
Wilkes-Barre, 8, 44, 137, 200, 211, 252
Williams, Ellis R., 71
Williams, Evan, 14
Williams, J. D., and Brothers, 23
Williams, Mrs John P., 21
Williams, John T., 32–3
Williams, Revd John W., 211
Williams, Roger, 168
Williams, Revd Rowland ('Hwfa Môn'), 153, 160, 165
Williams, S. D., 210–11
Williams, Watkin H., 53, 59, 69
Williams, William R., 24, 100
women
  in Cymmrodorion Society, 116–17
  church organizations of, 93
  desertion by husbands, 215–17
  drunkenness among, 204, 206, 209, 214–15
  employment, 29, 30, 46–7
  marriage, age at, 94n
  miners' wives 46–8
  participation in choirs, 134n
  participation in eisteddfodau, 99, 102
  and strikes, 57n, 66
Workingmen's Benevolent Association, 52, 53, 54, 55, 61
World's Columbian Exposition, Chicago, 1893 *see* World's Fair
World's Fair (Chicago, 1893), 138, 139n, 147–9, 151, 155, 174–5, 176, 177–8
World's Fair Eisteddfod (Chicago, 1893), 23, 133, 136, 147–78, 179, 228
  preparations, 149–59
  proceedings, 159–171
  aftermath, 171–8
World's Religious Congress (at Chicago World's Fair), 165
Wurtz brothers, 6
Wurtz, Maurice, 15
Wyoming–Lackawanna (or Northern) anthracite coalfield (north-east Pa.), 5–6, 7, 51, 52, 102, 118
Wyoming Valley, 110, 225

Ymdrechydd, Yr, 177
Ymwelydd, Yr, 89–90
Youngstown, 199, 203n, 252

Zerrahn, Carl, 143n